GERALD W. SWEITZER  DS

W9-BMZ-612

The 50 Best Small Southern Towns

PEACHTREE
ATLANTA

Published by
PEACHTREE PUBLISHERS, LTD.
1700 Chattahoochee Avenue
Atlanta, Georgia 30318-2112

www.peachtree-online.com

Text © 2001, 2007 Gerald W. Sweitzer and Kathy M. Fields
Cover photography © 2007:
    Nancy Kennedy/iStockphoto—magnolia blossoms,
    Mr_Jamsey/iStockphoto—man bass fishing,
    Christine Balderas/iStockphoto—small town American street
    Werner Bokelberg/Image Bank—man and his dog,
    Brad Wieland/iStockphoto—antique shop,
    Stephen Marks/Image Bank—golfer at sunset.

Cover and book design by Loraine M. Joyner
Composition by Melanie McMahon Ives

Manufactured in the United States of America

Second Edition
10 9 8 7 6 5 4 3 2 1

Library of Congress Cataloging-in-Publication Data
Sweitzer, Gerald W.
    The 50 best small southern towns / by Gerald W. Schweitzer and Kathy M. Fields.— 2nd ed.
      p. cm.
    ISBN 13: 978-1-56145-408-2 / ISBN 10: 1-56145-408-7
    1. Retirement, Places of—Southern states—Directories. 2. Cost and standard of living—
Southern states. 3. Cities and towns—Southern states—Statistics. I. Title: Fifty best small
southern towns. II. Fields, Kathy M. III. Title.
    HQ1063 .S94 2001
    646.7'9'0975—dc21
                                         2001003313

TABLE OF CONTENTS

O
ur paths first crossed in 1997 when Jerry signed up for a simple living group Kathy was starting in the Atlanta area. As we moved into our midlife years, we had each raised similar questions, but we brought different perspectives to these inquiries. Jerry had recently lived in a small town and commuted to work in a small city. When he moved back into the Atlanta area, he had concerns about increasing traffic problems, suburban sprawl, rising housing costs, and a significant decline in air quality. He began to research and write about small-town living as an alternative lifestyle. While pursuing an advanced degree, Kathy created and taught lifestyle courses at a local college, including one on simple living. She was wondering if all the working, driving, and hectic lifestyle were what she really wanted to do with the next ten or twenty years of her life. In the group we shared in 1997, we realized that our interests—"simple living" and "living in small towns"—were leading us in the same direction.

We continued to write, conduct internet forums, and teach classes. Jerry started teaching a class on small-town living and Kathy taught her simple living classes. We encountered positive and interested responses from many people we talked to, including clients, co-workers, class participants, friends, and family members. Many were eager to learn ways to find a more relaxed pace of living and a simpler lifestyle; some were looking to make a change in their lives in the near future and they were ready for specific answers to their questions.

From our previous individual research, we already knew there was no one guidebook that provided all the information we were seeking. We decided to gather in one book a body of information for people who, for whatever reasons, were thinking about simplifying their lives by moving to a small town. Over the next several months, we developed an outline and some preliminary criteria for evaluating a small town. We haunted libraries and the internet, combing through census figures and economic data. We pored over maps and travel guides. We read brochures and books on the Southern region. Using the information we had collected, we developed a questionnaire as a tool for searching out towns that would meet our criteria.

With maps and questionnaire responses in hand, we began to tour the South, visiting towns we had seen in the past and exploring lots of new ones. We talked with residents on the streets, in shops, and in restaurants; we interviewed professionals in the chambers of commerce and in real estate offices. As we looked and listened and learned, we drew up the following list of criteria.

▓ The population of the town should be no less than one thousand nor more than twenty-five thousand. (The population of Summerville, South Carolina, went over this number as of the 2000 census, but we decided to leave the town in the book. Because Virginia Tech's student body is included in the population of Blacksburg, Virginia, it also exceeds the criteria.)

▓ The town should be located within seventy-five miles of a small city.

▓ The town should have a stable or growing population, or the potential for growth.

▓ The town should be economically viable and show potential for stability or growth.

▓ Each town should demonstrate an enthusiasm for planned growth and community involvement.

▓ The town should provide a variety of cultural, educational, and recreational facilities and have access to good healthcare facilities.

▓ Local internet access should be available as well as other informational sources, such as local newspapers, radio, and television.

▓ The town should have easy access to highways, interstates, and airports.

We visited more than 150 towns—all the towns in the book as well as many more that were not included—in nine Southern states: Alabama, Florida, Georgia, Kentucky, Mississippi, North Carolina, South Carolina, Tennessee, and Virginia. We chose the five or six towns in each state that best met our criteria. (Several additional towns of interest are listed in the appendix).

We organized the information on each town into the categories described below.

STATISTICAL HIGHLIGHTS

A list of statistics appears on the first page of each town description.

Population: Population figures are based on the 2000 census results, updated to estimates for 2006 by ESRI, the world's leading geographic information system tools provider.

Nearest Cities: Each town selected for this guidebook is located within seventy-five miles of one or more small cities with a population over 25,000.

Cost of Living: Cost-of-living figures are difficult to obtain for small cities and are not usually available for small towns. However, ACCRA (formerly the American Chamber of Commerce Research Association) does collect and report data from various cities with populations over 45,000 that are part of Metropolitan Statistical

Areas. The ACCRA cost-of-living figure is the city's percentage of the national average (100). For each town in the book, we have listed the average of the quarterly cost of living figure for the geographically closest city that reported to ACCRA for the third quarter of 2005 (see appendix). For example, for Apalachicola, Florida, we used 97.7 percent, the figure for Panama City, Florida, the nearest reporting city. The true cost of living for a town, however, is usually lower than the figure for the larger city. To give a more complete picture of the cost of living in each town, we list average costs for both renting an apartment and for purchasing a house. These figures were supplied to us by local real estate agents, local real estate and rental guides, and chambers of commerce. We listed house and rented apartment prices for at least one town in Florida based on whether the location was on the mainland or the beach.

Median Household Income: The data is the estimated figure for 2006, the latest available. This figure was obtained from ESRI.

Taxes: Sales tax is the combined state and local option sales tax, but excludes any special taxes such as hotel/motel or restaurant. Sales tax figures were obtained from local chambers of commerce. Property tax figures were obtained from chambers of commerce, local tax offices, local real estate firms, or town real estate and rental guides.

RECREATION We provide basic information on the town's local recreational and sports opportunities as well as area park and wilderness sites, and coastal and inland waterways.

CULTURAL SCENE We list a sampling of the wide variety of cultural experiences available in each town, including the visual and performance arts, historic sites and museums, unique attractions, and annual festivals.

MAIN STREET Many of the towns included in this book are participants in the National Main Street Program, sponsored by the National Trust for Historic Preservation. The program, designed to improve all aspects of the downtown, has become a powerful local economic development force. (See www.mainstreet.org for a description of this program). We have listed only a few of the many gathering places and happenings in each town.

HOUSING Housing costs, land costs, and apartment rental rates were obtained from chambers of commerce, local real estate firms, or town real estate and rental guides. Since the publication of the first edition, there has been a dramatic increase in real estate prices in towns along the Atlantic and the Gulf coasts. This is particularly true in Florida. As we approach publication of this revised edition, there are signs that these prices are leveling out. Readers should check out local prices to get an accurate picture of current values.

ECONOMICS Information on employers and other data were obtained from local chambers of commerce, economic development offices, and visitors/tourism bureaus.

EDUCATION We provide information on higher education opportunities as well as elementary and secondary facilities.

HEALTHCARE We list the closest hospitals and major medical service providers in the area.

SPIRITUAL LIFE We provide basic information on various forms of worship available to the community.

STAYING CONNECTED We indicate the availability of local newspapers, cable television service, radio stations, and internet service providers. Local high-speed internet service is now available in virtually all of the towns.

GETTING THERE This section provides information about the travel infrastructure: the location of the town, the nearest state highways and interstates, and the local airports and nearest commercial airport.

RESOURCES All towns listed have a chamber of commerce—sometimes part of a larger county organization. We have included information on visitors bureaus and other area websites where available. We have drawn on these and other websites for information about the towns we included in this book.

VITAL STATISTICS

A chart showing detailed statistical data appears at the end of each town's description. While we do not suggest you make a decision to move based on statistics, we have added information that might aid you in your search.

Climate: Elevation figures were obtained from chambers of commerce. All other climate data, including rainfall and snowfall averages, and temperature data was provided by www.weather.com.

Occupations, Adult Education, and Population Data: Population estimates for 2006 and 2011 were obtained from ESRI. Other 2000 census figures are also provided by ESRI.

ACKNOWLEDGMENTS

We wish to give our sincere thanks to the many people who have helped us compile this book. While we cannot name all the individuals in all the many towns, we especially want to thank all the friendly and helpful people in the chambers of commerce, economic development offices, visitors and tourists bureaus, local real estate brokers and sales associates, libraries, shops and restaurants, and city, county, and other governmental offices. Many responded to our personal inquiries, telephone calls, e-mails, and questionnaires. We also thank all the individuals from the classes we taught or who otherwise provided us with inspiration over the years we spent developing the first edition of this book. We acknowledge Lyn Deardorff, editor at Peachtree Publishers, for her valuable contribution and encouragement in editing this publication, as well as all the staff members for their support. We also thank the many readers who e-mailed, called, and even met with Gerald Sweitzer as a result of the website listed in the About The Authors section. Jerry thanks his wife, Beverly, and his family for their patience and support. Kathy expresses her appreciation to Dwight for sharing the journey with loving support. She extends special thanks to all of her family, especially for Jill, Deb, and Tom for their enthusiasm and encouragement.

We also express our appreciation to the following organizations that provided extensive data for this book:

ACCRA. Selected data from "Cost of Living Data." Arlington, VA: ACCRA, 2001. Available at www.coli.org. *Reprinted with permission of the publisher.*

ESRI. Demographic data provided by ESRI, considered the world leader in the geographic information system (GIS) software industry. See www.esri.com. *Reprinted with permission of the publisher.*

The Weather Channel. Selected climatology data. Atlanta, GA: The Weather Channel, 2001. Available at www.weather.com. *Reprinted with permission of the publisher.*

weather.com

THE LURE OF SMALL SOUTHERN TOWNS

Over the past half-century, the South has become a destination for many Americans seeking a good climate, a more relaxed lifestyle, and new vocational and recreational opportunities. The region's relatively low cost of living, diverse geography, and reputation for the finest of southern traditions—warm hospitality, old-fashioned manners, a friendly style, and a slower pace—have attracted people of all ages and income groups. The influx of newcomers is changing the look of the South, spurring not only industrial growth and economic expansion, but also opening up new cultural horizons.

This major trend is continuing into the twenty-first century. Not only are large metropolitan areas in the South still expanding at record rates, but population in small cities and towns is also increasing. The April 2006 U.S. Census Bureau report "Domestic Net Migration in the United States: 2000 to 2004" shows that the South remained the primary destination for migrants within the United States. The South Atlantic division, the most populous of the region's three divisions, saw its net migration increase from an average of 254,000 per year in the 1990s to 313,000 per year in 2000-2004. This is the region where most of our small towns are located. More people live in the South (100 million) than in any other region, according to a report on the 2000 Census published by the Bureau of the Census. As of July 2005, the Southeast (which includes the nine states in this book plus Arkansas and Louisiana) makes up 72.2 million of the 100 million. In an April 2005 report, the Census Bureau estimated that by 2030 nearly four of every ten Americans will live in the South (defined by them as the area from Maryland to Texas), bringing the population of the region to about 143.3 million. An article in the *Atlanta Journal-Constitution*, "Americans are Moving South," reported that large numbers of people ages thirty to sixty-five are migrating to the South, and the median income levels of people moving to the South exceed those of people moving away. The South is not only attracting more people, it is attracting a wide range of better educated, more affluent residents who add to the potential for continued economic expansion. The southward migration of sixty-something retirees and fiftyish baby boomers with their bulging 401Ks and flexible work schedules does not seem to be slowing. Today the South accounts for the highest percentage of senior (over age sixty-five) population growth in the United States. Moreover, according to *America's Demography in the New Century*, published by the Milken Institute in California, the fastest-growing senior population can be found in smaller and medium-size metropolitan areas in the West and South.

In the 1990s, another new trend emerged, and it continues in the 2000s: a significant number of city dwellers moved from large cities to small cities and towns. We reported this trend in our first edition, referring to reports from the Census Bureau such as a press release dated June 30, 1999, which reported, "Smaller cities with populations between 10,000 and 50,000 grew at a faster rate than their larger counterparts... Cities with populations between 10,000 and 50,000 grew faster (8.6 percent) than any other category." On June 21, 2006, *USA Today* referred to the new 2005 city population estimates released by the Census Bureau on the same date and stated "growth is shifting from large central cities to smaller outlying communities in California, Texas, Arizona, and Florida." "Smaller places are grabbing more than half the growth this decade," said William Frey, demographer at the Brookings Institution. On April 20, 2006, the *Associated Press* reported that just about everywhere, people are escaping to the outer suburbs, also know as exurbs. As you will discover in this book, many of the desirable small towns we recommend are in the exurbs.

In our first edition, we referred to Harry Dent Jr.'s book *The Roaring 2000*. According to Dent, technology in the fields of communication, energy, and transportation will prompt major migration from suburbs to small towns and exurbs. Dent predicted that, "We are going to see at least 20 percent of the population of North America, or approximately 70 million people, migrate to exurban areas, small towns and new-growth cities in the next three decades." As the exurbs and towns grow and as demands for services and businesses increase, job opportunities expand. Many of the towns cited in this book offer living proof of this trend. We have found that those new to small town life are choosing smaller cities and towns as the place to live. They can have a larger home than they can afford in or near a city, and are willing to commute for work if they cannot find higher paying jobs in the smaller towns or cities.

The payoffs in small-town living can be extensive: less traffic and congestion, a less complex lifestyle, and cleaner air, to name a few. Also, fewer commuting hours can mean more time for family, children, and friends, and the potential to develop new avocational interests and new business opportunities. Finally, many are attracted to small town living because they are looking for a closer feeling of community along with a stronger sense of personal identity.

The southward migration seems to be driven by several factors. Little data on why people were moving to small towns in the South was available for the first edition of this book, but baby boomers nearing retirement are being actively pursued by smaller communities throughout the South. "Communities are recognizing that retiree migration can be a profitable industry," according to an October 9, 2002, article in *The Charlotte Observer*. An article in *U.S. News and World Report* on June 13, 2005, stated, "smaller communities are starting to recognize the wave of retirees who may come their way." Due to their numbers, baby boomers are going to continue to have a significant impact on the growth of and interest in small towns and small cities in the South. Census Bureau reports released in mid 2006 and interpreted by *USA Today* and *The Associated Press* in several major news stories reveal the desire for cheaper houses and open spaces as the key reason for moves to the exurbs. Additional factors appear to have influenced the decisions of more people to move further out. The first is the lower cost of living, including housing costs. Housing is typically a family's greatest expense; lowering this cost can free up dollars for other areas. It can also make a difference in the number of work hours needed to support a comfortable lifestyle. If costs are lower, you may be able to work fewer hours. Another draw is the South's strong economy, due largely to a significant increase in industry and businesses. Land and office space are generally cheaper and the labor pool is plentiful. The slower pace in small Southern towns can be a welcome contrast to the hurried style of many larger cities. A growing number of people are returning to their hometowns, a reverse of earlier movements from small hometowns to larger urban areas.

FAVORABLE CLIMATE

The moderate climate may be the most appealing aspect of the South. Throughout the nine states covered in this book, you can find a wide range of climates—from the crisp, cool autumns and snowy winters of the Blue Ridge Mountains and the Great Smokies to the warm summers and mild winters of the Golden Isles along Georgia's coast. Although snow accumulation is rare in the southernmost states, in some parts of North Carolina and Tennessee annual snowfalls are sufficient for good skiing and other winter sports. Outside of the mountainous regions, high humidity and temperatures in the nineties are common during the summer months, but air conditioning in most homes, cars, and businesses eases the effect of the heat.

Between these two extremes lie many moderate, four-season locations. Virginia, eastern Kentucky, and northern Georgia and Alabama offer mild temperatures, distinct seasons, occasional light snow, and lower humidity. Winter lasts only two to three months in much of the South, a marked contrast to other parts of the country, where winter begins in October and ends in April. Indian summers often extend the mild weather well into the fall months. Further south, the trade winds along the southeastern coast provide pleasant summer evenings, and tropical breezes bring relief from the high humidity. The hurricanes of 2004 and 2005 have scared some residents away from south Florida, southern Louisiana, and Mississippi. Those who have decided to relocate aren't moving out of the south, but rather are settling in north Florida (inland), Georgia, North and South Carolina, Texas, and other southern states, usually finding the foothills and inland destinations attractive.

LOWER COSTS

The National Association of Realtors reports the national median price for an existing home was $223,000 in the second quarter of 2007. This compares to $139,100 for 2000 when the first edition of this book was released. That's a whopping 60 percent increase in seven years. The same source gives the median home price for the South as $185,000, compared with $128,200 for metropolitan areas in the South in 2000. The increase in the South was 44 percent for the same seven-year period. In an April 1996 article entitled "America's 50 Hottest Little Boomtowns," *Money* magazine compared housing costs for a typical three-bedroom house in each town. Two-thirds of the towns with the lowest housing costs were in southern states.

According to ACCRA's average of the fourth quarter 2006 and first quarter 2007 reports, the housing costs index in cities throughout the United States shows that the overall cost of housing for cities in the South is lower than in the other sections. Some examples are listed below.

While housing prices (whether purchase or rental) are good indicators of the relative cost of living for a community, other factors also come into play. As a rule, small towns in the South have lower land prices and property taxes. A survey prepared by CNNMoney, entitled "How tax-friendly is your state?" and based

COST OF HOUSING INDEX FOR SELECTED U.S. CITIES
(100 is the national average for all participating cities)

SOUTHERN CITIES		NON-SOUTHERN CITIES	
Birmingham, AL	95.4%	Phoenix, AZ	101.7%
Jackson, MS	92.4%	Cleveland, OH	98.1%
Columbia, SC	91.3%	Chicago, IL	111.7%
Nashville, TN	95.1%	Milwaukee, WI	99.5%
Charlotte, NC	88.8%	Portland, OR	121.7%
Louisville, KY	97.6%	Denver, CO	102.3%
Jacksonville, FL	98.0%	Boston, MA	132.8%
Atlanta, GA	95.3%	Los Angeles, CA	145.2%
Richmond, VA	109.9%	Manhattan, NY	213.7%

on a study done by The Tax Foundation for 2005, shows what residents pay in various taxes, including state and local income, property, sales, fuel, and others. For property taxes, three of the best-ranked states were Arkansas, Alabama, and Kentucky (though it is not included in this book, Arkansas is considered by many to be in the South). The ranking by states for overall tax burden showed Tennessee, Alabama, Florida, and Texas were among the ten lowest. For those considering a retirement destination, Retirement Living Information Center (see www.retirementliving.com) has a table showing effective state and local tax burdens by state and rank projected for 2006. All states covered in our book except Kentucky are listed with a tax burden as a percentage of income below the U.S. average. Those moving to small southern towns usually find they also have more modest fees for personal or medical services, and less expensive entertainment and recreation. Groceries, fuel, and household goods, however, can often cost more because of the expense of transporting goods and a lack of intense competition. Utilities will likely cost the same in the small town as the larger city.

Resort areas and small towns located near large cities generally have a higher cost of living than non-resort towns and towns more than seventy miles from a city. Overall, the best value in housing costs and overall living expenses are found in small towns near small cities.

A Gentler Pace

The Hollywood stereotype of life in the South—unhurried and laid back—has a basis in reality. People who move to smaller towns in the South can't help noticing the slower pace—and many like it. Southern residents are perceived as more friendly, more courteous, and less likely to be in a hurry. It's no wonder that so many stressed-out city dwellers from all over the country head south.

Americans' longer working hours and greater responsibilities have led to higher levels of stress, increased health problems, less time for family and friends, and less enjoyment of life. A national shift in priorities, rooted in the movements toward "simple living" and "downsizing," is now building demand for a slower-paced and a more balanced lifestyle.

We usually assume that the natural time to look for simpler, more relaxed living is when you are approaching retirement age. The first edition of this book came out shortly before September 11, 2001. Many people reevaluated their choice of big city life following that day, and chose to relocate to smaller cities away from the large East Coast cities. Beginning in 2002, many readers contacted us via our website about their desire to move their families to southern small cities and towns. People in their twenties feel strongly that the opportunities in small companies and in small towns are preferable to working long hours for large corporations in crowded metropolitan areas. Young families recognize the value of spending more time with each other. People of all ages are choosing a calmer, more rewarding way of life.

Strong Economy

In the 1990s, the South led the nation in housing starts, population growth, and employment gains. Population growth has increased in all the southeastern states. According to *Southern Business and Development* magazine, the south has the world's third-largest economy and is the most preferred region for investment by foreign companies, the region with the lowest utility rates, and the region with the lowest business costs in the United States. It also leads all regions by a wide margin in new incorporations and has the lowest business failure rate. Like the rest of the nation, the recession of 2002 and 2003 led to job losses in the south. Traditional industries like textiles and furniture saw major plant closings and wholesale job losses to Asian manufacturers.

In recent years, the South has been the preferred location for new Japanese, German, and Korean auto manufacturers who have opened assembly plants in Mississippi, Alabama, and Georgia, and expanded existing plants in Kentucky. Nissan Motors recently announced the relocation of its U.S. headquarters from California to Nashville, Tennessee. Boeing Aircraft is assembling part of the new Dreamliner jet in Charleston, South Carolina. Embrear Aircraft (a Brazilian manufacturer of regional jets) is opening a new facility in Nashville and Dell Computers has opened its first assembly plant outside of Texas in Winston-Salem, North Carolina.

Google Inc. is furiously building large data centers in both North and South Carolina. It operates one of its largest data centers outside Atlanta. The south will likely attract more of these centers due to low land cost and the ability to attract qualified technicians and engineers.

Large and midsize companies are attracted to the Southeast because of the lower capital and operation costs. Land is cheaper; buildings cost less to lease, buy, or construct; and overall labor costs are lower. Reduced overhead means greater opportunities for a wider profit margin. More companies moving into the southern region means more jobs for those who live there. While the major cities in the South get a large share of the credit for the strong growth and economic showing, small southern towns have also grown. A ripple of prosperity from the large southern cities has spread to small towns, especially those within a one- or two-hour's drive of large cities.

OUTDOOR RECREATIONAL OPPORTUNITIES

With its diverse geography and mild climate, the South offers a year-round range of outdoor recreation and activities such as gardening, biking, and walking. The extensive coastline and many inland lakes and rivers provide opportunities for boating, swimming, fishing, and related activities. Golf and tennis are popular throughout the South and can be played in most of the southern states for at least nine months of the year. The Appalachian and Blue Ridge Mountains draw a wide range of outdoor enthusiasts for hiking, camping, white-water

rafting, canoeing, kayaking, and fishing. With less time spent commuting to and from work and easier access to recreational facilities, individuals find they have more time to participate in recreational opportunities.

TELECOMMUTING AND E-COMMERCE

As city commuting time captures a larger share of our workday, the dream of telecommuting from or operating a small business in a small town, sparks many to explore this style of living. Working outside a traditional office setting is appealing to employers as well as employees. The development of technology that supports telecommuting enables people to live farther from their employer. Entrepreneurs interested in small town living can build businesses that are not dependent on a specific location.

High-speed internet service providers offer both cable and DSL service in nearly all small towns, giving computer users the same access as the residents of a major city. Alpine Access of Golden, Colorado, the world's leading outsourced call center service, uses home-based customer service agents working from their home PCs. Rural Sourcing Inc. of Durham, North Carolina, provides low-cost, high-quality information technology services to major companies with qualified IT professionals working on their home PCs in small towns all over the country. Web-based meeting software like WebEx and GoToMeeting allow individuals living in small towns to work in collaboration with others anywhere in the world. According to Thomas L. Friedman, author of *The World Is Flat,* the "globalization of the local" is flattening the world, and is strengthening local and regional identities, including the South.

There are many reasons for individuals and families to seek out a new town. In the best of small towns, you can be an individual in a welcoming community, pursue challenging creative and recreational opportunities, realize increased value in the dollars you have to spend, and find greater peace of mind to enjoy life. Whatever the reasons that draw you to exploring the idea, we hope you will find this book the resource you need.

ALABAMA

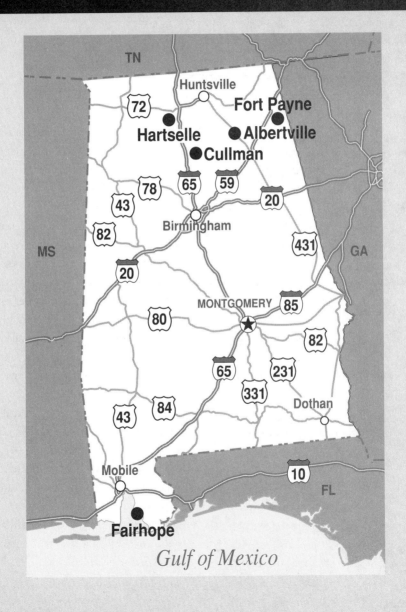

TN

Huntsville

72

Fort Payne

Hartselle

Albertville

Cullman

78 65 59

43 20

82

MS 431 GA

20

MONTGOMERY 85

80

82

65 231

331

Dothan

84

43

Mobile 10

FL

Fairhope

Gulf of Mexico

ALBERTVILLE

2006 POPULATION
18,424

NEAREST CITIES
Gadsden, AL (22 miles)
Huntsville, AL (40 miles)
Birmingham, AL (60 miles)

ESTIMATED 2006
MEDIAN HOUSEHOLD INCOME
$36,704

COST OF LIVING
Average 3-bdrm home—$135,000
Average rent, 2-bdrm apartment—$600
Cost-of-living comparison—88.4%

SALES TAX
8%

PROPERTY TAX
Average 3-bdrm home—$600

The small-town friendliness and forward-looking optimism of Albertville will appeal to young families and retirees. Situated in one of the fastest growing counties, this Alabama town has undertaken renewal of the downtown business district to bring shoppers back to Main Street. Loft condominiums and apartments have been built over downtown commercial space and a new city hall and other public buildings have been constructed. Albertville has a very low crime rate, some of the lowest housing costs in all the South, and very low TVA electricity rates to entice those looking for a solid small town.

Visitors from all over the country marvel at the spectacular natural beauty and colorful panorama of nearby Lake Guntersville, the largest lake in Alabama. To the southeast is Boaz, the first major factory-outlet shopping center in the South. Guntersville (7 miles), a neighboring town in a picturesque lakefront setting, attracts retirees with a variety of programs and services. Residents of Albertville can commute about fifty minutes to Huntsville for high-tech jobs. If you are looking for a wholesome family-oriented community, Albertville is worth consideration.

 RECREATION

Lake Guntersville State Park is home to the crown jewel of Alabama's lakes. This beautiful 69,000-acre lake, with 959 miles of shoreline, is perfect for fishing, swimming, boating, and skiing. The park, featuring 5,500 acres of natural woodlands, is located on the pinnacle of Taylor Mountain, where visitors have a magnificent view of the lake below. Ample accommodations include a rustic resort inn, a lodge, chalets on the ridge tops, lake-view cottages, and a modern campground on the lake below. The park features an eighteen-hole golf course, a beach complex, a fishing center (the finest bass fishing in Alabama), miles of hiking trails, nature programs, and a day-use area. Small to medium-size sailboats and yachts are berthed at several full-service marinas on the lake.

Buck's Pocket State Park, another popular recreation area, is located to the northeast of the main body of Lake Guntersville on an upstream tributary. Set in a natural pocket of the Appalachian Mountain chain, this 2,000-acre park is a nature lover's dream. It features a campground, a playground, and hiking trails, as well as a boat launch and fishing area.

Golfers can enjoy two eighteen-hole golf courses in Guntersville and a private eighteen-hole course in Albertville; there are a total of eight public and private golf courses in the county. Several world-class Robert Trent Jones Trail courses are located in Huntsville. Recreation centers in Albertville offer child and adult team sports and other individual sports for all ages. These facilities include an Olympic-size pool and tennis courts; programs such as softball and basketball for men and women, and soccer for boys and girls are available.

 CULTURAL SCENE

The Mountain Valley Council on the Arts in Guntersville brings workshops and cultural events to the area. The Whole Backstage, a community theater group in Guntersville, performs an annual summer musical. Ryder's Replica Fighter Museum in Guntersville houses the world's largest collection of replica World War I aircraft. The Guntersville Museum and Cultural Center occasionally offers special exhibits in addition to permanent exhibits about the TVA and the damming of the Tennessee River. The museum has dedicated a section to local Native American history in memory of the Cherokee and Creek who were evicted from their homes and forced to travel the Trail of Tears.

Several thousand spectators visit the Taste of Freedom BBQ Cookoff the first weekend in July, which features entertainment and arts and crafts. Guntersville offers Art-on-the-Lake in April, the Gerhart Chamber Music Festival in June, and a Seafood Festival in September. On one evening during the Christmas season, the light-bedecked boats and yachts in the popular Parade of Lights dazzle crowds on the shore.

Residents can easily reach the many major cultural attractions in Huntsville and Birmingham. Huntsville is home to the Huntsville-Madison County Botanical Garden, the world-famous U.S. Space and Rocket Center, the Alabama Constitution Village (a demonstration Southern village), and the Twickenham Historic District (Alabama's largest antebellum district). Birmingham offers the Birmingham Civil Rights Institute, which tells the story of the Civil Rights Movement through audio, video, photography, and artifacts. Birmingham's Alabama Jazz Hall of Fame showcases jazz musicians who have ties to Alabama, such as Nat King Cole and Duke Ellington. The hall is in a historic theater where live jazz performances are held.

Main Street

Albertville Candy Store serves homemade candy and hand-dipped ice cream favorites at an old-fashioned soda fountain. Among the popular local restaurants are Giovanni's (casual, family Italian food); The Red Barn (fresh butter and great smoked chicken); the Food Basket; Jessie's Café; the Yum Yum Tree (good taco salad); Reid's Chicken Stop (fried/rotisserie chicken); and the Albertville Home Bakery (fresh baked cakes). The Lumpkin House caters parties and meetings in a large converted antebellum home.

In Claysville, located between Guntersville and Albertville, Bruce's Restaurant serves an all-you-can-eat buffet of traditional Southern foods. In Guntersville, popular eating places include Wanda's Restaurant and Ice Cream Parlor (hearty breakfasts and sandwiches and burgers); Neena's Lakeside Grill (prime rib); and Craw Moma's Seafood Shoppe (fresh gulf shrimp, crabs, and oysters). Residents of both Albertville and Guntersville enjoy eating in the dining room at the Lodge at Lake Guntersville State Park.

Housing

New home prices are a bargain in Albertville compared to those in urban areas. Many people who work in Huntsville are willing to commute to this area in exchange for greater home value. The new home market is growing and residential subdivisions span a wide price range. Those seeking executive homes in the $300,000 to $400,000 range can find 2,800 to 4,000-square-foot homes on full-size lots convenient to the country club in Spring Lake Cove. Bent Creek has homes for young families, with prices ranging from the low $100,000s to $125,000. Whispering Pines subdivision offers both midrange pricing (the low $100,000s to $130,000) and a great location near Albertville's main highway, US 341. A gated housing community and two assisted-living facilities serve both Albertville and Guntersville.

Economics

Number of employers with fifty or more employees—21

Thanks to the Mueller Company (600 employees), the world's largest manufacturer of fire hydrants, Albertville is known as the "fire hydrant capital of the world." Chicken processors, Tyson Foods (1,200 employees) and Wayne Farms (1,100 employees), are the largest employers; manufacturing and retail are the largest employment sectors. Aerospace Integration Corporation (100 employees), which has recently opened, performs Blackhawk helicopter electronics maintenance.

Nearby Boaz is home to four major factory-outlet shopping centers, with approximately eighty stores. Recently unemployment has been higher than the national average because some plants have closed and moved operations to Latin America and because the Boaz center is losing customers to newer outlet malls opening near Atlanta. For those willing to drive a longer distance, larger employers as well as high-tech employers are located in Gadsden and Huntsville.

 EDUCATION

High schools—1; Middle schools—1; Elementary schools—2; Private school—1

The Marshall Technical School offers vocational training beyond secondary education. Three junior colleges; Snead State College; and the University of Alabama campuses in both Huntsville and Birmingham are within commuting distance. Summer space camps at the U.S. Space and Rocket Center in Huntsville offer unique educational experiences for children and teenagers.

 HEALTHCARE

Marshall Medical Center—150 beds; Physicians—152; Dentists—37

The two facilities at the Marshall Medical Center include 24-hour emergency care, general surgery, obstetrics, cancer care, and other specialties associated with similar-size hospitals. Large regional medical centers are located in Gadsden, Birmingham, and Huntsville.

Spiritual Life

Ten Christian denominations are represented. The nearest synagogue is in Huntsville.

Staying Connected

Daily newspapers from Huntsville, Gadsden, and Birmingham are delivered in Albertville. The local weekly newspaper is the *Sand Mountain Reporter*. Cable television is available, as is local internet service. There are two bookstores in the community.

Getting There

Albertville, located in the north central part of Alabama, is on AL 75 within two miles of US 431, which in turn connects with I-59 in Gadsden. Huntsville International Airport (45 miles) is served by four major carriers, and Birmingham International Airport (60 miles) has ten major and feeder airlines. The Albertville Municipal Airport features a 6,100-foot lighted runway for all-weather service to corporate and private aircraft.

The course of the Tennessee River runs close to Guntersville, permitting boat passage to the Tennessee-Tombigbee Waterway, which links Minneapolis, Minnesota, to the Port of Mobile, Alabama.

Resources

Albertville Chamber of Commerce
316 East Sand Mountain Drive
Albertville, AL 35950
(256) 878-3821
www.cityofalbertville.com

Lake Guntersville Chamber of Commerce
200 Gunter Avenue
Guntersville, AL 35976
(800) 869-LAKE
www.lakeguntersville.org

Marshall County Convention and Visitors Bureau
P.O. Box 711
200 Gunter Avenue
Guntersville, AL 35976
(800) 582-6282
www.marshallcountycvb.com

ALBERTVILLE
VITAL STATISTICS

CLIMATE

Annual average rainfall	47 inches
Snowfall	2.7 inches
Elevation	1,063 feet

Temperatures (in degrees Fahrenheit)

	Jan	Apr	Jul	Oct
High	49	72	89	73
Low	27	46	66	46

OCCUPATIONS

	2006	Projected 2011
Blue collar	37.8%	36.2%
White collar	48.3%	48.7%
Services	13.9%	15.2%

ADULT EDUCATION

	2000
Less than High School	37.8%
High School	27.5%
Some College	15.4%
Associates Degree	6.4%
College Degree	8.5%
Graduate Degree	4.3%

POPULATION

2006	18,424

2000–2006 Population: Annual Compound Growth Rate 1.06%
2006-2011 Population: Annual Compound Growth Rate 1.18%

Population by age group

	2006	Projected 2011
0-4	8.3%	8.1%
5-9	7.7%	7.5%
10-14	7.5%	7.7%
15-19	5.5%	7.0%
20-24	6.1%	5.1%
25-29	8.2%	5.8%
30-34	8.3%	7.7%
35-39	7.3%	7.6%
40-44	6.9%	7.4%
45-49	6.4%	6.9%
50-54	5.3%	6.1%
55-59	5.2%	5.6%
60-64	4.6%	4.7%
65-69	3.6%	3.8%
70-74	3.0%	2.7%
75-79	2.5%	2.4%
80-84	1.9%	1.9%
85+	1.8%	1.9%

Sources for Vital Statistics listed above can be found in the Preface to this book.

CULLMAN

2006 POPULATION
13,938

NEAREST CITIES
Birmingham, AL (45 miles)
Huntsville, AL (45 miles)

ESTIMATED 2006
MEDIAN HOUSEHOLD INCOME
$31,849

COST OF LIVING
Average 3-bdrm home—$135,000
Average rent, 2-bdrm apartment—$550
Cost-of-living comparison—89.1%

SALES TAX
8%

PROPERTY TAX
Average 3-bdrm home—$500

Located in the heartland of Alabama, Cullman defies the stereotypical image of small towns in the Deep South. Cullman was founded in 1873 by Colonel John Cullmann, a German refugee who came to America in 1866. He bought several hundred thousand acres of land between Decatur and Montgomery, Alabama, and brought five German families to Cullman in 1873. The town was laid out in half-acre lots with streets and avenues 100 feet wide. It is estimated that approximately 100,000 Germans moved to Alabama and 20,000 Germans to Cullman over a span of twenty years as a result of Colonel Cullman's actions. The German influence is still present, from stores and bakeries featuring German gifts and baked goods to a popular annual Oktoberfest.

In 1991, Cullman's downtown district was added to the National Register of Historic Places. The downtown area is active; businesspeople have purchased buildings in the area, and the renovation of existing buildings has followed at a rapid pace. Cullman's family-run shops offer an intriguing selection of collectibles, antiques, vintage jewelry, personal gifts, and works of art, as well as a variety of German and other European imports. An area of older warehouses and storefronts has been renovated to house office space, restaurants, and retail shops. A variety of eclectic gift and specialty shops, extra-wide thoroughfares, and ample parking attract shoppers from all over the region to this area. About a dozen Victorian homes add character to one of the downtown residential historic districts. Throughout the town tall steeples reach skyward—over three hundred churches are located in the county.

The Ave Maria Grotto, one of the most popular attractions in Cullman, is on the grounds of St. Bernard Abbey, Alabama's only Benedictine abbey. The Sisters of Sacred Heart Monastery, operated by the Benedictine Sisters, includes a neo-Gothic chapel rising seventy-five feet and featuring stained-glass windows made in Munich, Germany. The Shrine of the Most Blessed Sacrament in nearby Hanceville was built by Mother Angelica, founder of the Eternal World Television Network, and has inlaid Italian marble floors and a hand-carved wood and 24-carat gilded sanctuary with German-crafted stained glass windows.

Farming is a major industry here; Cullman County has more farms than any other in Alabama. It also ranks in the top three counties in the state in attracting new industry. Its proximity to both Birmingham and Huntsville (each 45 miles away) provides easy access to big-city life and shopping. Annual special events, cultural and recreational attractions, and a progressive and diversified economic base are all reasons why young families may consider Cullman.

 RECREATION

The centerpiece of Cullman's fifty parks is Heritage Park, a seventy-acre complex that offers softball and soccer fields, picnic shelters, outdoor basketball courts, a 1.5-mile paved fitness trail, and more. Sportsman Lake Park attracts young visitors with a small-scale train that runs along the shore of the lake. Fishing, biking, miniature golf, pedal boats, camping, and a picnic area with shelters are also available. The Cullman Golf Course, an eighteen-hole historic course, and Chesley Oaks Golf Club, an eighteen-hole championship course, are open to the public. Terri Pines is a private country club and residential community.

Smith Lake has over 500 miles of shoreline and 21,000 acres of clear water for camping, sport fishing, skiing, and boating. Considered the number one lake in Alabama for spotted bass fishing, it is also well known for striped bass. The adjoining Smith Lake Park has a pool, a beach area, picnic facilities, and a large campground. Nearby Hurricane Creek Park features hiking and mountain biking trails traversing a rugged mountainside, a swinging bridge, waterfalls, walking trails, and a picnic area. A new "Field of Miracles," specifically designed for persons with disabilities, is one of the four new ball fields in Ingle Park.

 **CULTURAL SCENE**

Cullman boasts more than the average number of cultural attractions and events for a town this size. The Cullman County Museum, a replica of the home of the city founder, Colonel John Cullmann, houses thousands of items of local historical significance—everything from Native American artifacts to a wall of photographs showing the growth of the town. The nationally known Ave Maria Grotto, located on the three-acre grounds of St. Bernard Abbey, hosts a display built by a Benedictine monk over a period of forty years. It consists of more than 125 miniature reproductions of famous churches, shrines, and buildings. Weiss Cottage, the oldest home in Cullman (1870), is listed on the National Register of Historic Places. The Shrine of the Most Blessed Sacrament was named Alabama's top attraction in 2004.

The Cullman Community Concert Association has been attracting top-notch entertainment to the area for nearly fifty years. Each season the Association offers four major, diverse events, which have in the past included a nationally known dance company, light opera, and a night of traditional jazz. The semiannual Bluegrass Superjam is held the first weekends of April and November. The event is the largest indoor bluegrass festival in Alabama and attracts nearly five thousand people to the Cullman County Agricultural Trade Center, a 36,000-square-foot hall. Cullman's Oktoberfest features an arts and crafts fair, a tour of the downtown historic districts, an Oktoberfest Ball, and, of course, plenty of famous German food in local restaurants. Several thousand visitors from surrounding states attend this event. A parade starts the Cullman County Fair festivities in the fall. Christmas in Cullman Open House attracts residents and visitors to the downtown area in mid-November.

Looney's Amphitheater and Park, located in Double Springs, Alabama (25 miles), hosts an outdoor drama, country music concerts, and a full schedule of theater productions. The outdoor drama tells the story of the people of northwest Alabama and their struggle during the Civil War era.

 MAIN STREET

All Steak Restaurant, located atop a bank building, provides a good view of the town. Open for lunch and dinner, it is known for unusual orange rolls and homemade bread; prime rib is a house specialty. Other popular dining favorites include Lombardo's Restaurant (Italian cuisine, weekday lunches); Duchess Bakery (German-style deserts); Fire Mountain Restaurant; Rumors Deli (a popular lunch destination); The Whole Earth Store and Coffee House; and Moxie Java Café (specialty coffees, delicious sandwiches, and deserts).

 HOUSING

Low property taxes and utility rates contribute to the attractive housing climate. Home prices are slightly higher than in some other Alabama towns. Prices range from $90,000 to $150,000, to $400,000 for larger, luxury homes. More than ten local real-estate firms are ready to assist newcomers in finding a home. Several gated communities are available as well as two retirement housing centers, including Benedictine Manor, operated by the Benedictine Sisters. AngelGate, a gated subdivision where homes are priced from $120,000 to $140,000, offers underground utilities and a four-acre green space with a picnic area and playground equipment. Homes in the subdivision can be selected from a *Southern Living* magazine collection. There are several apartment complexes in Cullman.

 ECONOMICS

Number of employers with fifty or more employees—55

In addition to being located in the top agricultural county in Alabama (first in cattle, eggs, and poultry and second in milk production), Cullman has become a major distribution and manufacturing center, with more than 140 companies producing automotive parts, press release valves, circuit boards, and stainless steel castings. Wal-Mart Distribution Center (over 1,000 employees), is the largest employer in the area. With the addition of REHAU Inc. (German/Swiss), Cash Acme (Australian), Topre America (Japanese), and Concours Mold

Inc. (Canadian), the area has developed an international flavor. Cullman's aggressive economic development effort and its strategic location between Birmingham and Huntsville, in a county crisscrossed with major highways, have led to a prosperous community.

 EDUCATION

High schools—1; Middle schools—2; Elementary schools—3; Private schools—4

Wallace State College is a 7,000-student, two-year community college offering fifty academic programs. Athens State University provides an opportunity for students to complete their college education in Cullman. Major campuses of the University of Alabama in both Birmingham and Huntsville are less than one hour away.

 HEALTHCARE

Cullman Regional Medical Center—115 beds; Woodland Medical Center—100 beds; Physicians—154; Dentists—23

Cullman Regional Medical Center is a full-service, nonprofit facility. The medical center has over one hundred active staff physicians and provides an oncology center, a

24-hour emergency services center, a pediatric and maternity center, a rehab center, and cardiovascular services. Woodland Medical Center, an acute-care, medical/surgical facility, offers a 24-hour emergency department, neurosurgery, a sleep lab, physical therapy, laser surgery, and mental health care. Nursing homes and assisted-living facilities are available in Cullman.

SPIRITUAL LIFE

Fourteen Christian denominations are represented, with the Catholic faith predominating. The nearest synagogues are in Birmingham and Huntsville.

STAYING CONNECTED

The *Cullman Times* is published daily. Newspapers from both Birmingham and Huntsville are delivered to Cullman. There are four local radio stations (one FM), one local cable television station with 24-hour programming, and cable television that broadcasts stations from both Birmingham and Huntsville. Bookstores in the county include Books-a-Million, The Bookstore, and Under the Storytelling Tree, a children's bookstore.

GETTING THERE

Cullman is between Birmingham and Huntsville at the intersection of US 31 and US 278, just four miles from I-65. Birmingham International Airport (45 miles) is a regional airport with ten major and feeder airlines. Four major airlines fly out of Huntsville International Airport (45 miles). Folsom Field, the local airport, offers a 5,500-foot paved and lighted runway.

RESOURCES

Cullman Area
  Chamber of Commerce
301 2nd Avenue SE
Cullman, AL 35055
(800) 313-5114
www.cullmanchamber.org

CULLMAN
VITAL STATISTICS

CLIMATE

Annual average rainfall	54 inches
Snowfall	2 inches
Elevation	800 feet

Temperatures (in degrees Fahrenheit)

	Jan	Apr	Jul	Oct
High	50	74	89	63
Low	28	46	65	46

OCCUPATIONS

	2006	Projected 2011
Blue collar	26.6%	26.0%
White collar	61.3%	60.6%
Services	12.1%	13.3%

ADULT EDUCATION

	2000
Less than High School	25.3%
High School	23.9%
Some College	21.2%
Associates Degree	8.2%
College Degree	13.2%
Graduate Degree	8.3%

POPULATION

2006	13,938
2000-2006 Population: Annual Compound Growth Rate	-0.07%
2006-2011 Population: Annual Compound Growth Rate	0.32%

Population by age group

	2006	Projected 2011
0-4	6.1%	6.1%
5-9	5.9%	5.5%
10-14	5.6%	6.1%
15-19	5.9%	5.8%
20-24	5.7%	5.7%
25-29	6.3%	5.2%
30-34	6.5%	6.0%
35-39	6.1%	6.3%
40-44	6.3%	6.5%
45-49	6.8%	6.4%
50-54	6.4%	7.0%
55-59	6.0%	6.6%
60-64	5.0%	5.7%
65-69	4.9%	4.7%
70-74	4.3%	4.4%
75-79	4.5%	3.9%
80-84	4.0%	4.0%
85+	3.7%	4.3%

Sources for Vital Statistics listed above can be found in the Preface to this book.

FAIRHOPE

2006 POPULATION
  14,219

NEAREST CITIES
  Mobile, AL (15 miles)
  Pensacola, FL (40 miles)

**ESTIMATED 2006
MEDIAN HOUSEHOLD INCOME**
  $47,226

COST OF LIVING
  Average 3-bdrm home—$195,000
  Average rent, 2-bdrm apartment—$700
  Cost-of-living comparison—89.8%

SALES TAX
  4%

PROPERTY TAX
  Average 3-bdrm home—$600

This enchanting town lies on the Eastern Shore, as the fifteen-mile coast along Mobile Bay is called. Fairhope is unique among small Alabama towns. Located in an area whose history spans nearly five hundred years of Spanish, French, and British influence, the town of Fairhope was founded in 1894 by a group who opposed the private ownership of land. They established a colony and named it Fairhope, which stood for a "fair hope of success." Some people referred to the colonists as "Single-Taxes" because of their unusually high proportion of public-use land, such as the public beach and parks that distinguish the town today.

Over the years Fairhope has attracted free-thinking, creative residents, and the town is now known for its large population of artists and writers. Casual coffee shops and European-style restaurants cater to their gatherings, providing comfortable space for creative exchanges. The romantic atmosphere in Fairhope is enhanced by the sweeping views of Mobile Bay. The downtown area is festooned with greenery. Brick walkways accented with small trees and colorful flowers make a delightful setting for cozy cafés, local bookstores, and quaint, unique shops. Well-kept homes, eclectic in style, sit graciously on parklike hilltops overlooking the bay. Scattered tall trees, benches, and an occasional old-fashioned rope swing add magical opportunities for play or for quiet moments watching the bay.

A bluff-side highway hugs the bay shore from Point Clear to Fairhope, offering a spectacular view of Mobile Bay. People frequently use the sculpture-adorned walkways of the mile-long waterfront park for exercise or for casual strolls in a beautiful and friendly setting. Full of activity, the Fairhope Municipal Pier and bayfront park is a popular spot for Fairhope residents and visitors. Fairhope's duck ponds, picnic area, attractive water fountains, and award-winning rose garden are bound to impress newcomers. Living is slow and easy here, but an air of intellectual excitement enlivens this artistic and friendly community.

 RECREATION

As one might expect, the Mobile Bay and the rivers that feed it, as well as the popular Gulf of Mexico just to the south, provide innumerable water-related activities. With its quarter-mile-long pier, Fairhope Municipal Beach is a great place for fishing and walking. Numerous public boat-launching ramps as well as private marinas and yacht clubs are available. Sailing, yachting, and scuba diving are all popular pastimes in the Fairhope area. Gulf Shores and Orange Beach, only twenty miles away, offer the white sand beaches and clear water of the Gulf of Mexico for swimming, deep-sea fishing, and sailing.

Quail Creek Municipal Golf Course in Fairhope and Timber Creek Golf Club in nearby Daphne are public courses. Lake Forest Golf Club in Daphne and the Rock Creek Golf Club in Fairhope are semiprivate; the latter also offer swimming and tennis. Sixteen golf courses in the county beckon golf enthusiasts. The Lakewood Golf Club Dogwood Course at the famous Marriott Grand Hotel in Point Clear (4 miles) has a thirty-six-hole Robert Trent Jones golf course.

Lighted tennis courts in Fairhope and other nearby towns are open to the public.

Horseback riding is available at several stables in the area and the Recreation Sports Association offers activities for all ages. Visitors interested in local fauna and flora can explore the Bon Secour Wildlife Refuge, stroll along Meaher State Park's elevated boardwalk stretching over 1,200 feet through Mobile River Delta, or hike the nature trail that ambles through the Weeks Bay Estuary near Fairhope and is part of the area's wetlands.

The James Nix Center, a large senior center, provides a full calendar of recreation activities and programs for seniors.

 **CULTURAL SCENE**

Fairhope and the adjoining towns on the Eastern Shore have more artists and writers per capita than most other small communities in the country. The Baldwin County Friends of the Opera in Montrose supports a small but active group of opera fans. The Performing Arts Center presents events throughout the year. Another community theater group, Theater 98 Community Theater, active since 1959, offers a regular schedule of plays.

The Eastern Shore Art Center consists of four galleries showing works of local, regional, and national artists. Discussion groups of local writers gather regularly at several restaurants and the library. The unique Museum of Sport Art, part of the United States Sports Academy, celebrates sports with national and international artwork. The American Bicentennial Museum, the Baldwin Heritage Museum, and the Marietta Johnson School of Organic Education Museum offer unique insight into the culture and history of the Eastern Shore area. The Fairhope

Museum, located on the Faulkner State Community College campus, displays photos and memorabilia reflecting the history of Fairhope.

The town hosts many festivals throughout the year, beginning with Fairhope's spectacular Arts and Crafts Festival and Outdoor Art Show in March. Now almost fifty-five years old, the show draws over 200,000 visitors and exhibitors from across the country. May brings Art-in-the-Park to neighboring Foley, and in September, Daphne's big Jubilee Festival occupies the downtown area. A phenomenon in which crabs, fish, shrimp, and other sea life swim to the shallow waters along the eastern shore of Mobile Bay incites local residents to call for a "jubilee." Running to the shore with flashlights or lanterns, the residents quickly collect the live seafood in buckets. By morning, the fish and sea creatures have gone back out to deeper waters. While the exact date is not predictable, it generally occurs two to five times a year between June and October. The Grand Festival of Art takes place in October at the park next to the municipal pier.

Several artists' studios are open to the public, and some offer art classes. Tom Jones Pottery is one of the best-known working enterprises. Bellingrath Gardens, famous for its 250,000 azaleas, is located on the west side of Mobile Bay. The USS *Alabama* Battleship Memorial Park, featuring tours of the famous World War II battleship, is also located on this side of the Bay.

 MAIN STREET

Some popular dining spots are Matters (gourmet); Sandra's Place (chicken salad and other light salads); Old Bay Steamer (steamed seafood specialties); Mary Ann's Deli (good sandwiches, soups, and salads); Fairhope Inn and Restaurant (quaint inn featuring crabcakes and coastal Creole cuisine); and Gambino's Restaurant (Italian and seafood specials). The Grand Dining Room at the famous Marriott Grand Hotel combines first-class dining with a terrific view of Mobile Bay. Music and live entertainment are offered in several of the local restaurants, including the Pub, Old Bay Steamer, and Ravinite.

The downtown area includes a unique collection of shops, far beyond the selection available in more traditional towns of similar size. The sixty businesses vary from shops selling home accessories, gifts and collectibles, toys, children's furniture, and antiques to upscale art galleries. For those seeking entertainment, a fifteen-mile drive to the midsize city of Mobile opens the door to many other Deep South attractions, including nightspots offering jazz and the annual Mardi Gras festival.

HOUSING

Home styles vary widely among the Eastern Shore communities. Waterfront cottages and homes hug the shoreline, some with lawns leading down to private beaches on Mobile Bay. Home prices along the bay are generally in the $300,000 to $600,000 range. Older, historic homes on larger lots are also available. Home prices are lower farther inland and in less well-known towns on the Eastern Shore. Golf course development homes with three bedrooms and two baths (1,750 square feet) can be purchased for $185,000 to $250,000. Condominiums start at about $185,000. Apartments are also plentiful, and several retirement communities are available. As in other coastal towns, home prices are escalating. Word is getting out about these desirable locations and their reasonable cost of living.

ECONOMICS

Number of employers with fifty or more employees—21

Over 750 local businesses employ approximately five thousand people; most employers are small businesses. Major employers include Thomas Hospital (1,100 employees), Marriott's Grand Hotel (590 employees), and Wal-Mart Super Center (500 employees). Other large employers are scattered throughout the county. Tourism (retail and services) is the major industry in Fairhope. Some Eastern Shore residents commute to Mobile for employment.

EDUCATION

High schools—1; Middle schools—2; Elementary schools—3; Private schools—3

Faulkner State Community College and the University of South Alabama each have a campus in Fairhope, and the University of Mobile has plans for classes on the Eastern Shore. Nontraditional higher-education programs are offered by the United States Sports Academy and the Alabama Oriental Studies Institute. Noncredit courses are also offered through the Eastern Shore Institute for Life Long Learning.

 HEALTHCARE

Thomas Hospital—150 beds; Physicians—109; Dentists—25

The Thomas Hospital in Fairhope focuses on acute care and provides a 24-hour emergency department, coronary intensive care, nuclear medical expertise, physical and occupational therapy, maternity and childbirth services, a full-service cancer care center, and an addictive diseases and mental-health facility. Additional medical care is available in nearby Mobile.

 SPIRITUAL LIFE

Twelve Christian denominations are represented. Two synagogues are located in Mobile.

 STAYING CONNECTED

The *Mobile/Baldwin Register* is published daily and the *Fairhope Courier* weekly. Mobile's daily, the *Mobile Register,* is delivered to Fairhope. Nine AM and seventeen FM radio stations, as well as six television stations serve the area. Cable television and several internet service providers are available. There are two bookstores in Fairhope, with more in nearby towns and in Mobile.

 GETTING THERE

Fairhope is located in the southeast corner of Alabama, about twenty miles north of the Gulf of Mexico on Mobile Bay. The town is one mile off US 98, on Alabama Alternate 98, and about eleven miles south of I-10. Mobile is approximately fifteen miles away via I-10 across Mobile Bay. Commercial flights on five major airlines are available at both the Mobile Regional Airport (38 miles) and the Pensacola (Florida) Regional Airport (44 miles). The 6,600-foot runway at the Fairhope Municipal Airport accommodates private aircraft.

The Intracoastal Waterway and the Tensaw and Mobile Rivers, all with access to Fairhope, provide navigable waterways for private boats. Fairhope has a municipal pier and marina for boats on Mobile Bay, and extensive marina facilities are available in Mobile. Amtrak stops in Mobile.

 RESOURCES

Eastern Shore
  Chamber of Commerce
327 Fairhope Avenue
Fairhope, AL 36532
(334) 928-6387
www.eschamber.com

Additional area website:
www.cofairhope.com

FAIRHOPE
VITAL STATISTICS

CLIMATE

Annual average rainfall			64 inches
Snowfall			0 inches
Elevation			5 feet

Temperatures (in degrees Fahrenheit)

	Jan	Apr	Jul	Oct
High	59	77	89	78
Low	38	56	72	56

OCCUPATIONS

	2006	Projected 2011
Blue collar	17.1%	16.4%
White collar	68.3%	68.2%
Services	14.6%	15.4%

ADULT EDUCATION

	2000
Less than High School	10.9%
High School	23.7%
Some College	23.0%
Associates Degree	5.3%
College Degree	21.2%
Graduate Degree	16.0%

POPULATION

2006	14,219
2000-2006 Population: Annual Compound Growth Rate	2.11%
2006-2011 Population: Annual Compound Growth Rate	2.88%

Population by age group

	2006	Projected 2011
0-4	5.4%	5.5%
5-9	5.5%	5.4%
10-14	6.2%	6.1%
15-19	5.6%	5.8%
20-24	4.1%	5.1%
25-29	5.2%	5.6%
30-34	5.9%	4.6%
35-39	5.9%	5.6%
40-44	7.0%	6.7%
45-49	7.9%	7.6%
50-54	7.8%	8.0%
55-59	6.9%	8.2%
60-64	5.8%	6.4%
65-69	4.2%	5.0%
70-74	4.2%	3.5%
75-79	4.2%	3.7%
80-84	4.0%	3.3%
85+	4.1%	4.2%

Sources for Vital Statistics listed above can be found in the Preface to this book.

FORT PAYNE

2006 POPULATION
13,251

NEAREST CITIES
Rome, GA (35 miles)
Gadsden, AL (39 miles)
Chattanooga, TN (55 miles)
Huntsville, AL (68 miles)

ESTIMATED 2006
MEDIAN HOUSEHOLD INCOME
$38,138

COST OF LIVING
Average 3-bdrm home—$125,000
Average rent, 2-bdrm apartment—$550
Cost-of-living comparison—92.7%

SALES TAX
8%

PROPERTY TAX
Average 3-bdrm home—$450

One of the best values in small towns in the United States, Fort Payne has a little of everything that prospective residents might seek. Often referred to as "the Highlands of Alabama," it is located in the mountain lakes region of northeast Alabama, nestled in a scenic valley below Lookout Mountain and Sand Mountain. In addition to the nearby lakes, rivers, waterfalls, and mountain forests, Fort Payne boasts a viable economic base, excellent recreational facilities, good schools, readily available healthcare, an attractive and busy downtown, entertainment and activities for all ages, and reasonable access to major southern metropolitan areas. Some know it as the home of the country singing group Alabama or as the "sock capital of the world."

Fort Payne was founded in 1835 and named for a U.S. Army captain. A stockade was constructed in what is now Fort Payne to hold members of the Cherokee tribe until they began their forced march west on the infamous Trail of Tears. In the 1860s, the town grew as the railroad brought new residents from the North to mine the coal and iron ore discovered in the area. The Fort Payne Opera House, built in 1889, and the Fort Payne Depot, constructed in 1891, served the growing population. By 1890, the iron and coal deposits were almost depleted, and the town settled into a slump in 1893. The first hosiery mills started in the early 1900s. Today there are over 150 sock mills in the county employing over five thousand people.

A large public park furnished with children's playground equipment (made locally by one of the leading manufacturers of recreation equipment) and a beautiful fountain enhance the center of the town. The Depot Museum in the old train depot, an example of Richardson-ian Romanesque architecture, displays collections ranging from Native American relics to political artifacts, and it exhibits unique railroad memorabilia in a train boxcar. Big Mill, one of the old sock mills built in 1889, is on the National Register of Historic Places and has been restored and converted to an antique mall. Directly across the street is another multi-story mill that now contains loft apartments, bringing city-style loft living into this small town.

Seniors receive exceptional treatment in Fort Payne; a very active county council on aging provides a senior center, community services, part-time employment in the hosiery mills, and transportation. Some of the state's most beautiful and unspoiled mountain towns are a short drive from Fort Payne. The small historical community of Mentone, on Lookout Mountain, has several quality bed-and-breakfast inns, historic old hotels, and wedding chapels, as well as craft shops and intimate dining establishments. Visitors to Mentone will also find cool mountain streams, camps, and small resorts. Nearby Little River Canyon National Preserve contains one of the deepest and most extensive networks of canyons and gorges in the East.

RECREATION

Many outdoor recreational activities await visitors to this area; people who have never seen this part of the state are in for a treat. DeSoto State Park offers five thousand acres of spectacular scenery with hiking trails, a picnic area, a swimming pool, fishing, tennis, and camping. DeSoto Falls, located on the Little River, has a 100-foot waterfall, and swimming is permitted in a natural pool above the waterfall. Buck's Pocket State Park, west of Fort Payne in a deep gorge carved into Sand Mountain, covers two thousand acres and offers picnic areas and facilities for camping, hiking, and swimming. Skiing at Cloudmount Ski and Golf Resort in the Mentone area is seasonal, but both a nine-hole golf course and a country dude ranch with horseback riding are in operation there the rest of the year. A private golf course is located near Fort Payne. Serious golfers can play on courses designed by Robert Trent Jones in cities such as Huntsville and Anniston. Other courses in Guntersville and Scottsboro are within an hour's drive of Fort Payne.

Located just minutes from Fort Payne, DeKalb Lake, a 120-acre lake in a 215-acre park, has a fishing pier, rental boats, a boat ramp, picnic grills, and campsites with restrooms. Fort Payne has an excellent twenty-five-acre sports complex offering organized sports for players of all ages. The facility hosts national and state tournaments for softball, baseball, and soccer. Indoor activities include organized volleyball and basketball, as well as racquetball and handball. This new complex also provides a walking track with an aerobic area, meeting rooms, weight rooms, a game room, dressing rooms for adults, and food service. The public Olympic-size pool is home to a youth swim team.

CULTURAL SCENE

The Big Wills Arts Council brings art programs to the community and into the Fort Payne and DeKalb County school systems. In the DeKalb Theater, a renovated movie theater, the council has hosted the Birmingham Children's Theater, the Georgia Mountain Theater, the Montgomery Ballet, the Huntsville Symphony Orchestra, and several other regionally and nationally known performing groups. The council also sponsors concerts in downtown Union Park on several Saturday nights during the summer. The Picture Show, a cooperative art gallery located in a part of DeKalb Theater, exhibits a changing selection of paintings and sculpture. The Depot Museum is housed in the old Fort Payne Depot, a unique structure built in 1891 of Alabama sandstone. The museum features an outstanding collection of Native American pottery, baskets, weapons, and clothing. Items of local history, most from the late 1800s and early 1900s, are also on display.

The museum and fan club for Alabama, the popular country music group, displays memorabilia relating to the band. The restored Fort Payne Opera House, now a cultural center of the community, is on the National Register of Historic Places and the National Register of Nineteenth-Century Theaters in America. The DeKalb-Jackson Writer's Club is an association of writers and those interested in writing. A new museum focused on the history of the sock industry has recently opened. The newly renovated City Hall provides a 300-seat auditorium with all the latest technology and sound equipment.

Numerous fairs and community events in Fort Payne and the surrounding area keep residents and visitors entertained. Well-known members of the local community perform during The Krazy Kudzu Follies to raise money for local nonprofit organizations. The DeKalb County Arts and Crafts Fair, held in November at the fairgrounds, features regional arts, crafts, and entertainment.

The activities continue year-round. Christmas in the Park occurs in downtown Fort Payne in early December. The Rhododendron Festival takes place in beautiful Mentone Brow Park in May. A Fourth of July celebration offers fireworks. Boomdays Music Festival, held the third weekend in September, showcases local and national artists. An Indian Festival in October features dancing, drumming, and other related activities. Fort Payne also participates in the annual World's Largest Yard Sale, 450 miles of bargains held in late August in nearly every town along the Lookout Mountain Parkway. The quaint Mentone community holds a popular fall festival with entertainment, a parade, and booths where local artists and craftspeople display their wares. The nationally known Chattanooga Aquarium in Tennessee is within an hour's drive. Additional cultural attractions, including art museums and the botanical garden, are in Huntsville.

 MAIN STREET

Favorite eating places in the historic district of downtown Fort Payne include The Strand (best hamburgers on earth); Archie's (international cuisine); Banjo's Eatery; and Grill at the Mill. Three Bean Café is a specialty coffee house serving fabulous sandwiches and salads. The Western Sizzlin features a county fair buffet and bakery and an unbelievable breakfast bar. JT's Fish House has pond-raised shrimp and catfish.

If you are willing to drive about ten miles, the Mentone Springs Hotel has an excellent menu by a renowned chef. The Wildflower Café provides musical entertainment on the weekend and brunch on Sundays. Other options are elegant dining atop Lookout Mountain at the romantic, historical Cragsmere Manna. Dessie's Restaurant is known for buttermilk pie and fried catfish.

 HOUSING

Low housing prices and taxes make Fort Payne a terrific value. A wide array of property is available in and around the town, with prices ranging from $115,000 for a small two-bedroom home to over $200,000 for a sprawling mountain retreat. Terrapin Hills, a subdivision built around a private golf course outside of town, overlooks a mountain ridge and lake. The Highlands and Oakdale are $250,000 and up. Pell's Gap is located on the western brow of Sand Mountain. The eastern side of the rim of Little River Canyon has lots for sale. Can you imagine waking every morning to the sight of the deepest gorge east of the Mississippi River? You can live on the brow of beautiful and historic Lookout Mountain and enjoy majestic views, or in a valley home close to Fort Payne or other small towns in the area. Historic homes and small farms are also available. Homes with a little acreage are priced from the low $100,000s.

Many Mentone residents are retired or live in this beautiful community and work in Fort Payne. Although housing costs more in Mentone than Fort Payne, the prices are still very attractive, especially considering the breathtaking views. A limited number of apartments is available, and rental homes are approximately $600 for a three-bedroom, two-bath home. There are two assisted-living facilities for seniors.

 ECONOMICS

Number of employers with fifty or more employees—30

While the sock industry is the leading employer, the diversity and international reach of the other local companies are impressive. The county ranks eighth in Alabama in the number of manufacturing companies. Game Time, the largest manufacturer of park and playground equipment in the world, is headquartered here. Siemens-Westinghouse (380 employees) builds components to

provide electric power, and the Heil Corporation provides dumpster truck bodies. Steadfast Bridges, made in Fort Payne, are found on golf courses from California to Bermuda. Prewett Mills (2,300 employees) and Copper Hosiery (900 employees) are among the larger sock industry employers.

 EDUCATION

High schools—1; Middle schools—1; Elementary schools—2

Northeast Alabama State Community College and Gadsden State Community College both offer two-year programs for transfer to most state four-year colleges, as well as continuing education courses. Four-year colleges within commuting distance include Jacksonville State University and the University of Alabama at Huntsville.

 HEALTHCARE

DeKalb Regional Medical Center—134 beds; Physicians—32; Dentists—8

DeKalb Regional Medical Center provides major services including 24-hour emergency room care, intensive care and surgery, physical therapy, special care nursery and maternity, sports medicine, occupational health services, radiology, a sleep disorders center, and women's services. There are also cancer, dialysis, and several urgent care centers. Rehab facilities are also available, including three orthopedic centers.

 SPIRITUAL LIFE

Twenty Christian denominations are represented. The nearest synagogue is in Huntsville.

 STAYING CONNECTED

The local newspaper is the daily *Fort Payne Times-Journal.* Daily newspapers from Gadsden and Huntsville are delivered locally. Three radio stations serve the area, and cable television pulls in Birmingham and other state stations. Local internet service is available through cable or DSL from the telephone company. The closest bookstore is in Gadsden.

 GETTING THERE

Fort Payne is located in the northeast corner of Alabama on US 11 where it intersects with AL 35, and just one mile off I-59, which links Birmingham to Chattanooga. The nearest major airports are in Chattanooga, Huntsville, and Birmingham. All three have major airline service and are within a seventy-five-minute drive. The local airport, Isbell Field, has a 5,000-foot lighted and paved runway.

 RESOURCES

DeKalb County
 Tourist Association
P.O. Box 681165
Fort Payne, AL 35968
(888) 805-4740
www.tourdekalb.com

Fort Payne
 Chamber of Commerce
300 Gault Avenue
Fort Payne, AL 35967
(256) 845-2741
www.fortpayne.com

FORT PAYNE
VITAL STATISTICS

CLIMATE

Annual average rainfall	55 inches
Snowfall	3 inches
Elevation	934 feet

Temperatures (in degrees Fahrenheit)

	Jan	Apr	Jul	Oct
High	47	70	87	72
Low	24	42	63	42

OCCUPATIONS

	2006	Projected 2011
Blue collar	42.2%	40.6%
White collar	44.2%	44.8%
Services	13.7%	14.7%

ADULT EDUCATION

	2000
Less than High School	33.9%
High School	27.9%
Some College	19.2%
Associates Degree	5.9%
College Degree	8.3%
Graduate Degree	4.8%

POPULATION

2006	13,251
2000–2006 Population: Annual Compound Growth Rate	0.38%
2006-2011 Population: Annual Compound Growth Rate	0.64%

Population by age group

	2006	Projected 2011
0-4	6.9%	6.6%
5-9	6.2%	6.1%
10-14	6.3%	6.3%
15-19	5.5%	5.8%
20-24	6.6%	5.5%
25-29	7.8%	6.3%
30-34	7.4%	7.5%
35-39	7.1%	7.0%
40-44	6.9%	7.4%
45-49	7.8%	7.1%
50-54	6.4%	7.6%
55-59	6.1%	6.7%
60-64	4.2%	5.5%
65-69	3.8%	3.6%
70-74	3.5%	3.4%
75-79	2.8%	2.8%
80-84	2.4%	2.4%
85+	2.1%	2.4%

Sources for Vital Statistics listed above can be found in the Preface to this book.

HARTSELLE

2006 POPULATION
   12,926

NEAREST CITIES
   Decatur, AL (10 miles)
   Huntsville, AL (35 miles)
   Birmingham, AL (70 miles)

ESTIMATED 2006
MEDIAN HOUSEHOLD INCOME
   $46,588

COST OF LIVING
   Average 3-bdrm home—$125,000
   Average rent, 2-bdrm apartment—$550
   Cost-of-living comparison—89.1%

SALES TAX
   8%

PROPERTY TAX
   Average 3-bdrm home—$500

Hartselle embodies the best of small-town living: affordable housing, good schools, southern hospitality, nearby water sports, and proximity to a thriving major city, Huntsville, Alabama. The town is relatively young; it was established in 1870 as a railroad town, and the business district of the early town lay alongside the railroad. Hartselle suffered a major fire that wiped out the business district in 1916. The community's greatest claim to fame occurred in 1926, when the local bank was stripped of all its cash and gold after robbers set off explosives and cut telephone cables to the outside world. The bandits got away and were never captured.

The downtown business district is thriving. About twenty-five antique galleries, cafés, and specialty stores line historic Main Street. An attractive canopy covers most of the downtown sidewalks and protects visitors from sun and rain. The railroad depot was donated to the town after passenger train service was discontinued. Now known as The Station, it has been restored and is the home of the chamber of commerce and the site of evening and weekend community and civic affairs.

 RECREATION

Sparkman Park is a 135-acre recreation complex featuring basketball and racquetball courts, lighted tennis courts and ball fields, a walking trail, carpet golf, an Olympic-size swimming pool, and a twenty-acre wooded area with picnic pavilions, tables, and a playground. There are organized community youth team sport leagues as well as adult softball leagues.

Four eighteen-hole public golf courses are within a twenty-minute drive.

Just fourteen miles north of Hartselle in the city of Decatur is Point Mallard, a 750-acre family park, which includes a popular water park (America's first wave pool), tennis courts, baseball fields, a gymnasium complex,

picnic grounds, and a three-mile-long riverside hiking/biking trail. An eighteen-hole championship golf course, campsites, and a new ice skating rink are also located here, right on the banks of the Tennessee River.

The 67,000-acre Wheeler Reservoir on the Tennessee River, stretching sixty miles west from Decatur, offers excellent sport fishing for small- and largemouth bass, crappie, stripe, and catfish. A dozen ramps for small boats are scattered along the shores of the Tennessee River and Wheeler Reservoir. The Wheeler National Wildlife Refuge is a wintering home for ducks, geese, and other migratory birds. It encompasses 34,500 acres of wetlands, bottomland hardwoods, pine uplands, and agricultural fields on both sides of the Tennessee River from Huntsville to the Elk River. A visitors center provides information on walking trails and the refuge wildlife.

 CULTURAL SCENE

Hartselle, Morgan County, and the nearby cities of Decatur and Huntsville offer residents a rich array of cultural activities. Morgan

County has an adult and children's theater group, a civic chorus, a community band, a concert association, an arts council, and an arts guild. There is a weekly summer concert series from May through September at an environmental park in downtown Hartselle. The historic, beautifully renovated art deco Princess Theater in Decatur serves as the cultural and performing arts center for the county. Decatur has two historic districts, Old Decatur and New Albany, with buildings dating from 1829 to 1939. A brochure describing the walking tour of historic Decatur is available. Cook's Natural Science Museum in Decatur has an extensive collection of beautiful and exotic insects, mountain birds, and animals displayed in a natural setting with informative descriptions, as well as rocks and minerals. Huntsville, just thirty-five miles away, offers a symphony orchestra, a first-rate botanical garden, the world famous U.S. Space and Rocket Center, and an art museum. Tours of homes in both Hartselle and Decatur showcase an assortment of beautiful residences ranging from pre–Civil War to Victorian to contemporary.

The Depot Days Festival, held the last Saturday in September, celebrates Hartselle's railroad heritage. Sixteen thousand people enjoy an arts and crafts show, children's games, musical entertainment, food, and more in the historic downtown. Hartselle is the home of several nationally known artists, some of whom exhibit their work at the Depot Days Art Show. October brings the Halloween Carnival, and in November open houses hosted by local merchants begin the holiday festivities. In December, residents and visitors can attend the Christmas parade and the Hartselle Beautification Association's Christmas Tree Tour of Homes.

Several large festivals take place in Decatur. Among the popular events are the Alabama Jubilee over Memorial Day weekend, featuring hot air balloons, an arts and crafts fair, and an antique/classic auto show, and the Spirit of America Festival at Point Mallard on July 4, which includes a large fireworks display.

 **MAIN STREET**

The banquet room at the Depot is a popular gathering place on the weekends for groups having catered events such as meetings, receptions, or parties. Favorite local restaurants include the Main Street Bistro, a Louisiana-style lunch spot that serves all the spaghetti you can eat on Thursday evening; the popular Las Vias Mexico Grill; and Giovanni's Italian Grill, which is located in an old freight building.

 HOUSING

Home styles range from two-story Elizabethan-style homes to modern suburban ranch houses. Many people who work in Huntsville choose to live in Hartselle because of the reasonable home prices. A small development of single-story cluster homes only a block off Main Street offer small, attractive front lawns and garages on an alley behind each row of homes. The 1,200-square-foot units are available for lease at $675 per month or for sale at $94,000. Hartselle's first planned urban development, Ausley Bend, will feature Craftsman and Victorian style houses of various sizes. Subdivisions in the community range from 1,400 to 6,000 square feet and are priced from $230,000 to $499,000. There are eight gated or retirement communities in the county near Hartselle.

 ECONOMICS

Number of employers with fifty or more employees—12
The largest local employer is Copeland Corporation, a manufacturer of compressors, with 600 employees. Other major employers include Baker Industries (300 employees) and Cerro Wire & Cable (300 employees). Residents also commute to Cullman, Decatur, and Huntsville for employment.

 EDUCATION

High schools—1; Middle schools—1; Elementary schools—3; Private schools—6
The Hartselle city school system ranks in the top ten in Alabama. The Calhoun Community College in Decatur has over eight thousand students and provides many two-year programs. It offers sixty-two associate's degrees and twenty-eight career/certificate programs.

The University of Alabama campus in Huntsville offers a full university curriculum and noncredit adult continuing education courses.

 HEALTHCARE

Hartselle Medical Center—150 beds; Physicians—65; Dentists—10

Hartselle Medical Center is an acute-care facility offering a 24-hour staffed emergency room, cardiac rehabilitation, general surgery, intensive care, physical and respiratory therapy, and complete radiology. More comprehensive medical facilities are located in both Decatur and Huntsville.

 SPIRITUAL LIFE

Fourteen Christian denominations are represented. There is a synagogue in Huntsville.

 STAYING CONNECTED

The local newspaper, the *Hartselle Enquirer*, is published weekly. The *Decatur Daily* also covers Hartselle news. Daily newspapers from Huntsville and Birmingham are delivered to Hartselle. Seven television stations and many AM and FM stations broadcast from Huntsville. Cable television and local and limited national internet access are available. Hartselle has one bookstore. There are several chain bookstores in both Decatur and Huntsville.

 GETTING THERE

Hartselle is in north central Alabama, ten miles south of Decatur at the intersection of US Highway 31 and Alabama 36. I-65 is only a few miles east and connects with I-565 between Decatur and Huntsville, allowing residents easy access to the Huntsville metropolitan area. Several airlines provide connections to Atlanta and other regional hubs from the Huntsville International Jetplex, only twenty-two miles away. The Hartselle Airport has a 3,600-foot paved runway for small aircraft.

 RESOURCES

Hartselle Area
  Chamber of Commerce
110 South Railroad Street
Hartselle, AL 35640
(256) 773-4370
www.hartsellechamber.com

HARTSELLE
VITAL STATISTICS

CLIMATE

Annual average rainfall	57 inches
Snowfall	2.7 inches
Elevation	573 feet

Temperatures (in degrees Fahrenheit)

	Jan	Apr	Jul	Oct
High	49	72	89	73
Low	27	46	66	46

OCCUPATIONS

	2006	Projected 2011
Blue collar	30.4%	29.6%
White collar	54.9%	54.4%
Services	14.7%	16.0%

ADULT EDUCATION

	2000
Less than High School	20.1%
High School	31.6%
Some College	23.6%
Associates Degree	5.6%
College Degree	13.7%
Graduate Degree	5.4%

POPULATION

2006	12,926
2000-2006 Population: Annual Compound Growth Rate	1.17%
2006-2011 Population: Annual Compound Growth Rate	0.59%

Population by age group

	2006	Projected 2011
0-4	6.0%	6.0%
5-9	5.9%	5.8%
10-14	6.5%	6.4%
15-19	6.5%	6.1%
20-24	5.6%	5.1%
25-29	6.1%	5.4%
30-34	6.5%	6.4%
35-39	6.8%	6.6%
40-44	8.2%	7.4%
45-49	8.2%	8.5%
50-54	7.1%	8.0%
55-59	7.0%	7.4%
60-64	5.4%	6.3%
65-69	4.1%	4.4%
70-74	3.6%	3.3%
75-79	3.0%	2.9%
80-84	1.8%	2.3%
85+	1.6%	1.8%

Sources for Vital Statistics listed above can be found in the Preface to this book.

FLORIDA

GA

Atlantic

Ocean

1

75

Jacksonville

TALLAHASSEE

17

27

301

95

98

19

ALT 27

DeLand

Apalachicola

Mount Dora

New Smyrna
Beach

4

Orlando

Gulf of

Tampa

4

441

95

27

Stuart

Mexico

17

98

FLORIDA

75

27

Everglades

75

Pkwy

41

Miami

Key West

1

APALACHICOLA

2006 POPULATION
2,566

NEAREST CITIES
Tallahassee, FL (80 miles)
Panama City, FL (60 miles)

ESTIMATED 2006
MEDIAN HOUSEHOLD INCOME
$28,531

COST OF LIVING
Average 3-bdrm home—$250,000
Average rent, 2-bdrm apartment—$800
Cost-of-living comparison—97.7%

SALES TAX
6%

PROPERTY TAX
Average 3-bdrm home—$2,975

Known to locals and regular visitors as "Apalach," this Franklin County waterfront community lies in the heart of Florida's "Forgotten Coast," so named because it was once overlooked in a Florida tourist article. No longer "forgotten," this oyster and seafood haven is now world-renowned. Apalachicola has been named one of the best fishing spots in Florida and one of the most bio-diverse areas of the United States. Apalachicola is within thirty minutes of three of the most beautiful beaches in the country: the seashores on St. George Island, Cape San Blas, and St. Joseph's Peninsula. In May 2006, *Southern Living* called Apalachicola an "unspoiled town" and "a perfect place to hide away for a few days and blend in with the locals." The April 2006 issue of *Coastal Living* describes Apalachicola as a "fishing village that attracts visitors in search of tranquility."

Sound like paradise? Close to it. The town was established in 1832 and leans heavily on its thriving oyster and seafood industry for jobs and income. The scenery reflects its roots as a historic fishing village, with comfortable old frame houses, rocking chairs on big porches, and locals with suntanned wisdom etched on their faces. Shrimpers and oyster tongers in their rubber boots shuffle about the docks, unloading their catch after a day's work on the bay.

This fun little town has fabulous restaurants, a distinct personality, and lots to do. Market Street reveals a mix of longtime locals and recent urban transplants. The Chestnut Street Cemetery, established in 1831, is a must-see. The markers and cemetery art date back to the Civil War and tell the interesting story of this town's history. When you're ready for a rest, settle into a rocker or storefront bench, sip a Coca-Cola or eat a homemade ice cream cone, and chat with whomever happens to pass by.

RECREATION

Outdoor options are bountiful; most activities center on the Gulf, beaches, rivers, and nature reserves in the area. The City of Apalachicola Recreation Board sponsors a summer children's program; there are two public tennis centers in town and an outdoor basketball court. The nearest golf course is St. James Bay (25 miles), open to the public.

Four barrier islands with miles of pristine beaches and state and national forests with wildlife preserves and refuges are ideal for hiking, nature walks, and photography. The Apalachicola River is the longest in the state and an amazing area for exploring wildlife by canoe, kayak, or riverboat. The Apalachicola Natural Estuarine Research Reserve, one of the largest in the country, incorporates 246,000 acres in the Panhandle. It is also the most important bird habitat in the Southeast, sheltering 315 species of birds.

St. Vincent Island National Wildlife Refuge, a 12,358-acre undeveloped barrier island, is a safe haven for endangered species such as loggerhead sea turtles and bald eagles. Boating, camping, fishing, and hiking are allowed. The St. George Island State Park includes almost 2,000 acres of salt marshes, pine and oak forests, and miles of dunes and undeveloped beaches. Several magazines have rated the park as one of the top ten in the nation and the beach as one of the most beautiful in the country.

The Cape St. George State Reserve is a twenty-eight-mile barrier island that separates Apalachicola Bay from the Gulf of Mexico and offers an outstanding opportunity for wilderness exploration. The Gulf, bays, rivers, inlets, and waterways present varied choices for all types of anglers. The Orvis dealership in Apalachicola caters to every tackle and outdoor outfitting need. If you tire of the water, there is plenty of land to explore, hike, and photograph. The Apalachicola National Forest offers hiking trails, hunting, and fishing on thousands of primitive forest acres.

 **CULTURAL SCENE**

The Dixie Theatre, built in 1912 and located in the downtown historic district, was the center of area entertainment for many years. It was used originally for live performances and later as a motion picture house until 1967. Recent renovation of the theater, resulting in a nostalgic re-creation of the original building, has brought live theater back to the county. The summer season at the Dixie Theatre begins Memorial Day and ends Labor Day. In winter, the facility is used for The Panhandle Players local theater troupe performances, high school band concerts, political forums, once-a-month ballroom dancing, and local or visiting artists and performers. The Ilse Newell Fund for the Performing Arts hosts a concert series throughout the year, bringing a variety of quality musical performances to this historic village.

Several popular festivals entertain visitors and residents throughout the year. The Antique Classic Boatshow is held the fourth Saturday in April. Christmastime brings candlelight sidewalk shopping at the annual Apalachicola Christmas Celebration.

 MAIN STREET

Popular restaurants include Friday night favorite socializing spot Avenue Sea in the Gibson Inn (drinks and oysters); The Owl Café, a re-creation of the 1908 café (homemade delights); The Spoonbill (seafood specials); Boss Oyster (frosty beers and oysters); Magnolia Grill (fancier fare); and Old Time Soda Fountain (Cokes, floats, and cones).

The Grady Market, originally an 1840s cotton warehouse overlooking the Apalachicola River, has been handsomely restored. Once a ship chandlery owned by J. E. Grady, the market later became a retail store selling a variety of goods to lumber mills and transport ships. After the Depression, the store closed. Later it was used by retailers and the military and eventually served as a net factory. Today, The Grady Market features boutiques and open market space for a variety of unusual gifts, clothing, antiques, and local art. The second floor, occupied by the French Consul at the turn of the century, now houses a hotel called The Consulate, offering four luxury suites, reputedly the town's premier accommodations.

Antique lovers will stay busy in this small town with ten antique stores, including The Tin Shed, which specializes in nautical pieces, and Chez Funk, an antique, gift, and everything else kind of shop. Avenue E offers furniture and accessories with a nautical style for any room. Ten galleries showcase local art.

HOUSING

The wide range of real estate prices in Apalachicola are an indication of the growing pains this small town is experiencing. Waterfront property can exceed $1 million. Historic district homes, dating back to 1838, offer old-world charm plus easy access to restaurants, shops, and other local businesses, but they are on the high end of the housing spectrum, ranging from $300,000 to $700,000. Custom-built homes are available on a variety of building sites; prices vary significantly based on size, access to the water and view. Older homes range from $200,000 to $500,000 Beach property, homes on St. George Island, new home subdivisions, and two gated communities in nearby Eastpoint offer other housing options. There is an assisted living home in nearby Mexico Beach (30 miles west) and one in Carabelle (30 miles east).

ECONOMICS

Number of employers with fifty or more employees—4

In the mid-1800s, the local economy centered on the cotton trade, but by 1907, the completion of the railroad created new opportunities for the development of the seafood and timber industries. Today the seafood industry, estimated to be worth $80 million, and tourism are the major contributors to the local economy. The town is known worldwide for its fabulous Apalachicola Bay oysters, and the oyster industry alone employs more than one thousand people in the county. Tourism is growing rapidly, and the influx of visitors contributes significantly to the local economy. The service and trade industries also employ many residents. The largest employer is Franklin County government (200 employees).

 EDUCATION

High schools—1; Middle schools—1; Elementary schools—1; Private schools—3

Gulf Coast Community College serves Bay, Gulf, and Franklin Counties in the Florida Panhandle. The main campus is in Panama City, with one satellite campus in Port St. Joe (20 miles). The college offers primarily business-related classes and programs at this satellite campus.

 HEALTHCARE

Weems Memorial Hospital—29 beds; Physicians—5; Dentist—1

Weems Memorial Hospital is an acute-care facility with a 24-hour full-service emergency room. The hospital also staffs two clinics, one in Apalachicola and the other in Carrabelle. Additional services in the area include ultrasound capabilities, laboratory testing, mammography, CAT scans, and bone density testing. Helicopter transport, based at Tallahassee Memorial Hospital, provides emergency service. Bay Memorial Hospital in Panama City also provides medical services.

 SPIRITUAL LIFE

Eight Christian denominations are represented. The nearest synagogue is in Tallahassee.

 STAYING CONNECTED

Two local newspapers can keep you posted: the weekly *Apalachicola Times* and the biweekly the *Franklin Chronicle*. Newspapers are delivered daily from Panama City and Tallahassee. The Oyster Radio station, WOYS-100.5 FM, offers Buffet tunes and other beach favorites. Cable television and internet access are available. There is one bookstore in the area.

 GETTING THERE

Apalachicola is located in the Florida panhandle on US Highway 98, approximately sixty miles east of Panama City. At Eastpoint (6 miles east) FL 65 links Highway 98 to I-10. The nearest large airport with commercial airline service is in Tallahassee. There are three public airports in Franklin County, including the Apalachicola Municipal Airport, which has a 5,400-foot airstrip for non-commercial aircraft.

 RESOURCES

Apalachicola Bay
  Chamber of Commerce
122 Commerce Street
Apalachicola, FL 32320
(850) 653-9419
www.apalachicolabay.org

Additional area website:
www.forgottencoastline.com

APALACHICOLA
VITAL STATISTICS

CLIMATE

Annual average rainfall	49.99 inches
Snowfall	0 inches
Elevation	16 feet

Temperatures (in degrees Fahrenheit)

	Jan	Apr	Jul	Oct
High	60	75	88	78
Low	43	59	74	61

OCCUPATIONS

	2006	Projected 2011
Blue collar	23.2%	22.0%
White collar	48.1%	50.5%
Services	28.8%	27.5%

ADULT EDUCATION

	2000
Less than High School	30.8%
High School	35.6%
Some College	15.6%
Associates Degree	2.7%
College Degree	11.2%
Graduate Degree	4.1%

POPULATION

2006	2,566
2000-2006 Population: Annual Compound Growth Rate	1.53%
2006-2011 Population: Annual Compound Growth Rate	1.79%

Population by age group

	2006	Projected 2011
0-4	5.1%	4.9%
5-9	4.8%	4.7%
10-14	5.1%	5.1%
15-19	5.7%	4.9%
20-24	6.0%	5.2%
25-29	4.4%	5.6%
30-34	5.2%	4.5%
35-39	4.7%	5.0%
40-44	7.6%	4.9%
45-49	8.0%	8.0%
50-54	7.8%	8.3%
55-59	7.6%	9.0%
60-64	7.4%	8.0%
65-69	6.1%	7.0%
70-74	4.3%	5.0%
75-79	3.8%	3.7%
80-84	2.5%	3.0%
85+	3.7%	3.3%

Sources for Vital Statistics listed above can be found in the Preface to this book.

DeFUNIAK SPRINGS

2006 POPULATION
  5,661
NEAREST CITIES
  Grayton Beach (32 miles)
  Destin (45 miles)
  Fort Walton Beach (48 miles)
  Pensacola (75 miles)
ESTIMATED 2006
MEDIAN HOUSEHOLD INCOME
  $29,574
COST OF LIVING
  Average 3-bdrm home—$220,000
  Average rent, 2-bdrm apartment—$600
  Cost-of-living comparison—98.7%
SALES TAX
  7%
PROPERTY TAX
  Average 3-bdrm home—$2,934

With gracious Victorian homes circling a nearly perfectly round natural lake in a parklike setting, DeFuniak Springs is culturally unique and architecturally nostalgic. Pleasing and peaceful, this serene setting is a reminder of what early-twentieth-century town living must have been like. Surveyors for the L & N Railroad discovered the naturally round, spring fed lake in the late 1800s. "The railroad must come by this beautiful lake," they proclaimed, "and we must make this a splendid winter resort." The town was formally established as a railroad depot and named after a prominent railroad official, Frederick De Funiak.

This charming location was the winter home for the New York Chautauqua, a cultural arts organization whose goal was to provide instruction and courses in art, science, philosophy, and other areas of study. DeFuniak Springs remained a cultural center well into the 1920s. In 1976, local residents revived this tradition by establishing an annual arts calendar of events. Residents are committed to preserving a strong sense of community and a century-old appreciation for the arts. The Chautauqua spirit is still alive, reflecting the town's unique character that originated in the nineteenth century.

Today, this delightful Panhandle hamlet has a quaint Victorian atmosphere and presents an ideal setting for simple living and tranquility with varied cultural and educational opportunities. Charming storefronts that house interesting shops and practical necessities for the locals have revitalized the downtown area. The Hotel DeFuniak, established in 1920 and now tastefully restored, sits proudly at one end of the town as a reminder of a bygone era.

DeFuniak Springs is conveniently located forty minutes from South Walton Beaches, where you can find some of the most beautiful shorelines in the country, including the award-winning Seaside and popular Grayton Beach. The town also allows easy access to the larger metro areas of Pensacola and Mobile. Singular in character and visually nostalgic, DeFuniak Springs is an interesting combination of a simple lifestyle, a dedicated cultural colony, and a quaint Victorian township that appeals to retirees, young families, and beach lovers of all ages.

 RECREATION

Walton County, the home of DeFuniak Springs, is rich in outdoor activities. The Emerald Coast Beaches, only thirty-five miles south of DeFuniak Springs, offer excellent sailing, swimming, fishing, and waterskiing. Vortex Springs has the largest scuba diving facility in Florida. Grayton Beach State Park, a 356-acre park with a lake, is a natural recreation area not far from DeFuniak Springs. Trails wind throughout the pine woods and salt marsh area that provide a home for shorebirds and sea turtles. Deer, alligators, and coyotes can be seen at Point Washington State Park, which has a ten-mile loop for biking and hiking. Sportsfest, one of the largest sporting events along the Emerald Coast, features special events and activities for three weekends in November.

Options for golf are plentiful: DeFuniak Springs Country Club offers a 5,980 yard eighteen-hole course; a public nine-hole golf course and numerous golf clubs are located within forty-five minutes of town. There are four city-owned tennis courts. Biking, abundant freshwater fishing, and public hunting areas round out the recreational activities for this town.

 CULTURAL SCENE

In 1885, the First Annual Session of the Winter Chautauqua was held in DeFuniak Springs, and the Florida legislature approved the establishment of the Florida Chautauqua Association for the purpose of providing courses, lectures, and instruction in the arts, sciences, and other areas of study. The Chautauqua Season is still celebrated here in February, when the Chautauqua Assembly sponsors a three- to four-day seminar series on history, the arts, and industry. The celebration culminates with the Gala Ball, a nationally famous period costume ball with a Victorian theme.

The Florida Chautauqua Theater presents performances by local groups, and the Seaside Music Series provides popular year-round concerts. The Cultural Arts Association, Walton County Art League, and the Porcelain Artists Association sponsor other special events.

ArtsQuest Festival at Eden State Gardens in nearby Point Washington is another popular outdoor event, featuring two days of entertainment and art preceded by ArtsQuest Week. Homemade ornaments, holiday decorations, and Christmas treats are sold at Hometown Christmas, held one Saturday before Christmas. Visitors can view one million lights and decorated yards surrounding the lake during Christmas Reflections, which begins the day after Thanksgiving and ends January 2.

Eden State Gardens, an 1897 mansion surrounded by ten acres of gardens overlooking the Choctawhatchee Bay, is open for tours. The Chautauqua Winery, the largest winery in the state, offers free tours and wine tasting. The town boasts Florida's oldest library, still in its original 1887 building, which contains valuable weaponry dating back to the Crusades. DeFuniak Springs also has an Elderhostel that offers six weeks of programming from January to March.

 MAIN STREET

Interesting eating spots are easy to find. A visit to Murray's Café is like taking a step into Grandma's kitchen. Residents also enjoy Edie's Café (homemade soups and great lunches) and Maime's, a full-service restaurant offering terrific breakfasts, casual lunches, and a dinner menu including everything from seafood dishes to hamburgers. Other options include The Busy Bee; Pig Daddy's; The Honey Hole; and Ed's. In nearby Ponce de Leon, La Loba's Bakery uses natural ingredients to make incredible organic breads and baked goods from scratch.

The Opinion Place, a gazebo in town where locals gather is a must-visit. There are also interesting shops, such as The Porcelain Rose and The Little Big Store, an old-fashioned mercantile store where an apron-clad proprietor sells penny candy.

 HOUSING

While prices have risen since 2001, the property taxes are quite reasonable and there is a $25,000 homestead exemption for those who qualify. Prices start at $150,000. Proximity to popular Gulf Coast beaches and the significant influx of retirees from the North supports the projected figures for population growth and the resulting demand for housing.

In the downtown historic district, elegant Victorian houses in good condition, some dating from the mid-1800s, start at $275,000. Less expensive options include 1960s-era houses selling for approximately $149,000, and homes in new subdivisions, costing approximately $250,000. Rural houses on five acres or more are available for around $205,000. There are no condominiums in DeFuniak Springs, and few rental options.

ECONOMICS

Number of employers with fifty or more employees—12

Tourism, utilities, healthcare, retail trade, and service industries are sources of major employment in DeFuniak Springs. Major employers include Sandestin Golf and Beach Resort (1,200 employees); Hilton Sandestin Beach Resort (560 employees); ResortQuest International/Abbott Resorts (400 employees); Sacred Heart Hospital on the Emerald Coast (320 employees); Wal-Mart (280 employees); Seaside Development Corporation (160 employees); Professional Products, Inc. (170 employees); and CHELCO (108 employees). Wines produced at Chautauqua Vineyard and Refinery have won awards all over the world.

 EDUCATION

High schools —1; Middle schools — 1; Elementary schools —2

Okaloosa-Walton Community College offers opportunities in higher education. The Walton Career Development Center is located in DeFuniak Springs. Adult basic education, vocational training, and liberal arts courses are also available at the Chautauqua Neighborhood Center.

 HEALTHCARE

Healthmark Regional Medical Center—50 beds; Physicians—51; Dentists—3

The hospital, completed in December 2000, is an acute-care facility with fifty-one physicians, twenty-two of whom have full-time active privileges. Specialties include internal and family medicine, pediatrics, geriatrics, radiation and medical oncology, podiatry, nephrology, cardiology, and general and orthopedic surgery. A 24-hour emergency medicine department, a full-service laboratory, respiratory therapy, and radiology are also available. Transfer to a larger facility is possible through Air Ambulance/LifeFlight/Mask. In addition to these services there is a home health agency and a rural health clinic.

 SPIRITUAL LIFE

Fifteen Christian denominations are represented. The closest synagogue is located in Fort Walton Beach.

STAYING CONNECTED

Local newspapers include the daily *Northwest Florida Daily News* and *Pensacola News Journal,* the weekly *DeFuniak Herald Breeze* and the *Walton Sun,* and the biweekly *Destin Log/Walton Log.* Cable television, three local radio stations, and internet access are available. There is one local bookstore.

GETTING THERE

DeFuniak Springs, the seat of Walton County, is located in the northwestern Florida Panhandle along I-10 at the intersection of US Highway 331. It is 125 miles west of Tallahassee and 75 miles east of Pensacola. DeFuniak Springs is served by Okaloosa Regional Airport (40 miles) and Pensacola International Airport. DeFuniak Springs Municipal Airport has a 4,100-foot lighted runway for noncommercial aircraft. The Intracoastal Waterway is accessible in Freeport (15 miles) and has a shallow water barge port.

RESOURCES

Walton County
  Chamber of Commerce
95 Circle Drive
DeFuniak Springs, FL 32435
(850) 892-3191
www.waltoncountychamber.com
www.defuniaksprings.net

Additional area websites:
www.beachesofsouthwalton.com
www.emeraldcoast.com

DEFUNIAK SPRINGS
VITAL STATISTICS

CLIMATE

Annual average rainfall	57.8 inches
Snowfall	0 inches
Elevation	320 feet

Temperatures (in degrees Fahrenheit)

	Jan	Apr	Jul	Oct
High	62	80	92	80
Low	37	52	68	51

OCCUPATIONS

	2006	Projected 2011
Blue collar	26.2%	25.7%
White collar	51.5%	52.1%
Services	22.4%	22.3%

ADULT EDUCATION

	2000
Less than High School	27.9%
High School	29.6%
Some College	24.4%
Associates Degree	4.9%
College Degree	8.6%
Graduate Degree	4.6%

POPULATION

2006	5,661
2000-2006 Population: Annual Compound Growth Rate	1.72%
2006-2011 Population: Annual Compound Growth Rate	4.13%

Population by age group

	2006	Projected 2011
0-4	6.1%	6.1%
5-9	5.8%	5.9%
10-14	6.2%	6.2%
15-19	6.3%	6.2%
20-24	6.5%	5.8%
25-29	6.3%	6.4%
30-34	5.7%	5.9%
35-39	6.0%	5.8%
40-44	7.0%	6.1%
45-49	7.6%	7.0%
50-54	6.6%	7.3%
55-59	5.5%	6.8%
60-64	4.5%	5.4%
65-69	5.1%	4.0%
70-74	4.4%	4.5%
75-79	3.8%	3.8%
80-84	3.1%	3.0%
85+	3.3%	3.7%

Sources for Vital Statistics listed above can be found in the Preface to this book.

DeLAND

2006 POPULATION
22,777
NEAREST CITIES
Daytona Beach, FL (23 miles)
Orlando, FL (30 miles)
ESTIMATED 2006
MEDIAN HOUSEHOLD INCOME
$34,679
COST OF LIVING
Average 3-bdrm home—$218,000
Average rent, 2-bdrm apartment—$750
Cost-of-living comparison—98.4%
SALES TAX
6.5%
PROPERTY TAX
Average 3-bdrm home—$4,700

The home of Stetson University, Florida's oldest private university, DeLand has earned a reputation as a leader among Florida's small towns as a result of its oak-shaded and palm-lined residential neighborhoods, its thriving business districts, and its role as a government center. Tourists delight in the historic downtown area and its long pedestrian shopping district with over one hundred shops offering books, antiques, art, clothing, gifts, and refreshments.

The seat of Volusia County since 1888, DeLand is one of Florida's most beautiful and viable towns. Its stable and diverse economy is based on manufacturing, education, government, and agribusiness. In 1997, the town won first place in the National Main Street Program of the National Trust for Historic

Preservation, and in 2000, it received the Great American Main Street Award for its highly successful downtown restoration. The $2.5 million streetscape project transformed sidewalks and added planters and new grassy areas. New, modern county government buildings housing more than five hundred employees are surrounded by fountains and manicured grounds. The historic county courthouse also has undergone a recent restoration. The streets are lined with 200-year-old oak trees and elegant Victorian two-story homes that have been restored for both professional and residential use.

Stetson University is a few blocks from the heart of the downtown area. With a growing enrollment of over 2,300 students, the university has completed a $10 million expansion and redevelopment of the campus immediately north of downtown. Within a few miles of DeLand, several interesting small towns are situated along the famous St. Johns River. Among the more intriguing is Cassadaga, named after a community in upstate New York. Chartered in 1894, Cassadaga was conceived as a winter home for spiritualists, and many live there year-round today. Visitors will find bookstores, restaurants, and other businesses in this quiet, rural setting.

 RECREATION

The legendary St. Johns River area is a veritable wildlife sanctuary. The eagle population is reported to be the second largest in the nation, with four active nests and eighty roamers. Unusual birds, colorful turtles, and menacing alligators are spied often on this waterway. Boating and fishing are popular pastimes on the St. Johns River and nearby lakes. Houseboat rentals make it possible to spend a peaceful night on the water. Those who prefer tubing and snorkeling may explore the crystal clear waters at Blue Spring in Orange City— seventy-two degrees year-round and a warm water home for the endangered Florida manatee. DeLeon Springs State Recreation Area is a unique park where a freshwater spring gushes nineteen million gallons of water daily, providing a favorite setting for swimming, canoeing, fishing, and paddleboating.

DeLand is also popular with skydivers, who literally "drop in" on the local municipal airport. Skydive DeLand is a world-class drop zone and the "training capital of the world" for skydivers. In the spring, the skies fill with colorful canopies of skydivers as they drift lazily over the airport. Some 350 standardbred trotter horses and pacers train each winter at Spring Garden Ranch in nearby DeLeon Springs. Many of these sessions are open to the public.

Traditional recreation activities are available at seventeen parks, two swimming pools, six tennis courts, and a YMCA complex. Orange City Golf Club, and Victoria Hills Country Club are public golf courses. Three more private courses are in West Volusia County. DeLand is just half an hour from the world-famous Daytona Beach and one hour from the many attractions in Orlando.

 **CULTURAL SCENE**

Because of its cultural, educational, and architectural excellence, DeLand was once known as the "Athens of Florida." The city is home to seven museums and a nonprofit theater group. The Actors Theatre of Central Florida, the Elephant Museum, the Old DeLand Hospital Museum, the African American Museum of the Arts, and the DeLand Naval Air Station Museum offer history and entertainment to visitors and residents.

The DeLand Cultural Arts Center, a $3 million facility near Stetson University, houses art galleries, theater companies, and a performance hall for the DeLand Little Symphony. The Gillespie Museum of Minerals, Duncan Art Gallery, and Stover Theater are associated with Stetson University and are open to the public. The university itself also maintains a full calendar of concerts, theater productions, and exhibitions. The Henry A. DeLand House, home of the West Volusia Historical Society, offers tours. Walking tours of downtown and historic homes are also available.

Work is underway to restore the Athens Theater, a famous landmark in town. From 1921 to the 1950s it served as DeLand's center of social activity, hosting vaudeville shows, first-run movies, talent contests, and minstrel shows. The exterior of the structure has been renovated, and restoration of the interior is underway. Plans for the building include a special events movie house, as well as space for performing arts presentations, conferences, and meetings.

The Pioneer Settlement for the Creative Arts in nearby Barberville is dedicated to preserving the history, crafts, and artifacts from the early 1900s. Historic structures, including a school, a railroad depot, a cabin, and a church, have been moved to the settlement.

Among the many annual events attracting crowds downtown are Tropical Night, featuring live Calypso music in July; a fall craft show in September; Monsters on Main Street in October; and the Fall Festival of Arts. More events take place throughout the year at the local fairgrounds, state parks, the Cultural Arts Center, Stetson University, and in nearby towns. With all the weekly activities in DeLand, the events in nearby towns, and the programs at Stetson University, residents can find interesting activities all year long. Few towns the size of DeLand offer such a rich selection of activities.

 MAIN STREET

A few downtown restaurants draw large lunch crowds as a result of their proximity to the county government offices. Among them are Dublin Station, (Irish); Le Jardin (French Vietnamese); They Call it Macaroni (Italian); and Cecil's (fine dining). Also worth trying are Boston Gourmet Coffeehouse and Elusive Grape, a wine bar. An eclectic mix of cuisines, including Cuban, Southern, seafood, and Italian, is available at Deland's restaurants and outdoor cafés.

 HOUSING

Like other inland Florida towns, DeLand's home prices are lower than the national average. Older frame homes often are reasonably priced. Homebuyers can also find many houses with enclosed pools —a popular feature in Florida. Lakefront homes are more expensive, but even these properties are still affordable for many. Some subdivisions near marinas on the St. John's River have homes priced at $200,000. Apartments are plentiful and very reasonable. Deltona (population 79,500), a well-known planned town built in 1962 that offers tract housing at reasonable prices, is located ten miles southeast of DeLand. Retirement housing is available in DeLand and in several nearby towns. Continuing care centers offer independent living and nursing care. The Florida Lutheran Retirement Center is in DeLand, and the John Know Village of Central Florida is in Orange City.

 ECONOMICS

Number of employers with fifty or more employees—24

Four thousand manufacturing jobs, a $200 million agribusiness industry, and a robust and growing tourism industry contribute to the area's economic vitality. With more than 3,500 workers, Volusia County is the town's largest employer. The largest private sector employers are Tyco-Kendall (770 employees), which makes disposable medical supplies, and Sparton Electronics. Sometimes called the parachute capital of the United States, Deland is home to several companies that make parachutes. Stetson University has more than six hundred people on the payroll.

 EDUCATION

High schools—1; Middle schools—2; Elementary schools—5; Private schools—7

The Daytona Beach Community College has a branch campus in DeLand. There are branches of the University of Central Florida in Deland and Daytona Beach, and Florida Technical College is located in Deland. Stetson University's 165-acre campus, listed on the National Register of Historic Places, is a few blocks from the heart of DeLand. Founded in 1883, the school was named in honor of John Stetson, the nationally known hat manufacturer. It is a nonsectarian university with about 2,300 students and three campuses offering eleven degree programs from music to law. Stetson tied for third place among the top regional universities in the South in the 2000 *U.S. News and World Report* national survey.

 HEALTHCARE

Florida Hospital—156 beds; Florida Hospital (Fish Memorial)—138 beds; Physicians—175; Dentists—18

Florida Hospital, part of a group of four hospitals in Volusia and another county, offers 24-hour emergency service and all major specialties, including open-heart surgery. Florida Hospital is part of the large Adventist Health System and is located in DeLand. These two hospitals merged in 2000.

 SPIRITUAL LIFE

Twenty-five Christian denominations are represented. The Southern Cassadaga Spiritualist Camp is nearby. There is a synagogue in DeLand.

 STAYING CONNECTED

The local newspaper, the *DeLand Beacon,* is published twice weekly, and the *News/Journal/New Volusian,* is published daily in Daytona Beach and covers DeLand happenings. The *Orlando Sentinel,* a major metropolitan daily paper, is also available in DeLand. One local radio station covers the DeLand area, and cable television offers at least sixty-four channels. Internet access is available for both residential and commercial use. There are five local bookstores.

 GETTING THERE

DeLand is twenty-three miles west of Daytona Beach on US 17-92. I-4 passes five miles east of DeLand. The Orlando International Airport is one hour south and is served by all major and many international airlines. Daytona Beach International Airport is twenty minutes east and is served by Continental, Delta, and United Airlines. The DeLand Municipal Airport has a 6,000-foot runway for charter, business, and small plane use. Amtrak has a station in DeLand.

 RESOURCES

DeLand Area
  Chamber of Commerce
336 N. Woodland Boulevard
DeLand, FL 32720
(800) 749-4350
www.delandchamber.org
www.vis-arts.com/E-DeLand

DeLAND
VITAL STATISTICS

CLIMATE

Annual average rainfall	8 inches
Snowfall	0 inches
Elevation	35 feet

Temperatures (in degrees Fahrenheit)

	Jan	Apr	Jul	Oct
High	69	82	91	83
Low	44	55	70	61

OCCUPATIONS

	2006	Projected 2011
Blue collar	24.9%	23.2%
White collar	55.0%	55.9%
Services	20.0%	20.9%

ADULT EDUCATION

	2000
Less than High School	22.0%
High School	30.3%
Some College	23.0%
Associates Degree	6.4%
College Degree	10.3%
Graduate Degree	7.9%

POPULATION

2006	22,777
2000-2006 Population: Annual Compound Growth Rate	1.38%
2006-2011 Population: Annual Compound Growth Rate	1.75%

Population by age group

	2006	Projected 2011
0-4	5.7%	5.8%
5-9	5.2%	5.1%
10-14	8.6%	5.2%
15-19	9.5%	8.3%
20-24	5.9%	9.8%
25-29	5.9%	5.5%
30-34	5.2%	5.3%
35-39	5.1%	4.7%
40-44	6.1%	5.6%
45-49	6.1%	6.2%
50-54	5.5%	6.1%
55-59	5.1%	5.8%
60-64	4.5%	4.8%
65-69	3.7%	4.2%
70-74	3.7%	3.6%
75-79	4.2%	3.8%
80-84	4.5%	4.3%
85+	5.4%	5.8%

Sources for Vital Statistics listed above can be found in the Preface to this book.

MOUNT DORA

2006 POPULATION
10,423

NEAREST CITIES
Leesburg, FL (12 miles)
Orlando, FL (25 miles)
Ocala, FL (35 miles)

ESTIMATED 2006
MEDIAN HOUSEHOLD INCOME
$41,917

COST OF LIVING
Average 3-bdrm home—$251,360
Average rent, 2-bdrm apartment—$1,000
Cost-of-living comparison—97.2%

SALES TAX
7%

PROPERTY TAX
Average 3-bdrm home—$2,500

Rolling hills, Victorian architecture, and stately oak trees have contributed to Mount Dora's reputation as the "New England of the South." Exceptional views of Lake Dora are common, thanks to the many terraces that rise from the lake to a height of 184 feet. Once a winter retreat for many wealthy New Englanders, today Mount Dora offers a peaceful refuge from the theme parks and congestion of Orlando.

Major highways bypass Mount Dora, but thousands still come here to visit the numerous antique shops, stay at one of many charming bed-and-breakfasts, and eat at the unique local restaurants. This is a true old-fashioned American hometown, with free parking and only two traffic lights in the downtown area. Streets are lined with tall sycamores, laurels, and old oaks draped with Spanish moss, and the downtown layout makes it easy to get around whether you're walking, driving, or treating yourself to a horse and carriage ride.

Mount Dora residents have preserved and restored the old homes and buildings that grace this inviting town founded in 1874. The chamber of commerce is located in the former train depot, built in 1915. Twenty-nine buildings date from the late 1800s to the 1920s. The center of attraction is the 1893 Donnelly House, originally owned by the town's first mayor. This yellow Queen Anne–style wedding cake house, with layers of turrets and porches, is listed on the National Register of Historic Places.

The Lakeside Inn, also built in 1893, was the first building constructed in town. Today guests are housed in several low-rise dwellings as well as in the central building. From the rocking chairs on the veranda of the inn's main building, visitors have an ideal view of the Grantham Point lighthouse and the majestic sunsets across Lake Dora. The lighthouse is the only inland freshwater lighthouse in Florida; it was built with donations from local residents in the 1980s.

Mount Dora is known as the "Festival City of Central Florida" because of the many celebrations hosted here. *Money* magazine has listed the town as one of the top ten places to retire. It is also known as the "best antique shopping" town in Florida. Many residents have moved here from south Florida to escape the congestion and are delighted to find a setting that is similar to their New England hometown.

 RECREATION

For a town of its size, Mount Dora has abundant recreational opportunities. The Mount Dora Recreation Department supervises a recreation complex and six parks, providing children's playgrounds; tennis, racquetball, and shuffleboard courts; a nature walk and fitness trails; facilities for croquet and lawn bowling; a heated swimming pool; and a lake for boating, and fishing. The local YMCA offers additional activities. Bicycling is popular here; the town hosts the largest cycling event in the state. There are seven golf courses in the area. Other sporting events include professional golf tournaments, waterskiing championships, triathlons, skydiving and equestrian competitions, and bass-fishing tournaments.

Lake County, home of Mount Dora, lives up to its name, with more than a thousand lakes located within its borders. Mount Dora is on the Ocklawaha Chain of Lakes, which allows boats to travel through the scenic Dora Canal and other lakes leading to the St. Johns River and on to the Atlantic Ocean. The Atlantic and Gulf Coasts are an easy drive. The thrills of Disney World, Universal Studios, and other Orlando attractions are an hour away.

 CULTURAL SCENE

The Mount Dora Road Trolley offers a narrated historic and scenic tour of the town. Departing from Lakeside Inn or Cecile's French Corner, the trolley takes passengers on an hour-long ride along the rim of Lake Dora. Mount Dora has some of the best bed-and-breakfast inns in Florida, perhaps the best in the South.

Many are in historic Victorian homes; at least one is listed on the National Register of Historic Places.

The Mount Dora Center for the Arts is a community-based nonprofit organization that features exhibits, shows, and the popular annual Mount Dora Arts Festival. The Royellou Museum, located in the old city jail and firehouse, contains many local historic items. The Mount Dora Theatre Company, in existence for over fifty years, presents plays and musicals throughout the year in the three hundred-seat Ice House Theatre, originally the site of the town's ice-making and storage business. Plays are staged there nearly every month.

Mount Dora hosts many festivals and events throughout the year, drawing hundreds of thousands into the town. The Bicycle Festival takes place every fall. The Lighting of Mount Dora kicks off the holiday season with a decorated downtown area that twinkles with thousands of miniature lights. Also popular are the Art Festival in February; the Antique Boat Festival in March; the annual

Mount Dora Craft Fair, drawing over three hundred crafters and 150,000 visitors; and several antique fairs during the year.

MAIN STREET

You may be surprised at the excellent dining available in this small town. The Gables Restaurant is a gourmet restaurant with a Victorian garden setting. The owner, who is originally from Scotland, grows his own vegetables and herbs in a garden outside the restaurant. Another well-known eatery is the Goblin Market Restaurant. Housed in a renovated warehouse, it features dining rooms, a tree-shaded courtyard, and a garden patio. There are over a dozen eating establishments in the downtown area. Beauclaire, the restaurant at The Lakeside Inn, is a popular gathering place.

HOUSING

Area home prices are average to slightly above the national average. Lakeside property is somewhat higher. Older, two-story homes, rare in Florida, command a higher price. For those moving from northern urban areas, the local prices will still feel very reasonable, especially after factoring in property taxes.

The Country Club of Mount Dora, which offers golf, tennis, and a nice clubhouse, has homes beginning at approximately $260,000. The Chesterhill Country Estates on the outskirts of Mount Dora has custom homes starting at $400,000. Loch Levan is a popular private gated community with large custom homes, a community dock, a walking park, sidewalks, and more. Homes priced in the upper hundreds are available in other Lake County locations. Many alternative housing options are closer to Orlando. There are condominiums available, but few apartments. Numerous gated adult and retirement communities with golf courses and other amenities are located in nearby towns.

ECONOMICS

Number of employers with fifty or more employees—10

The local economy, based primarily on service and retail industries, is tied to tourism and retirement interests. Major employers include the Waterman Village, a retirement center (300 employees); Florida Waterman Hospital in nearby Tavares (1,600 employees); the mid-Florida Eye Care Center; National Deaf Academy; Super Wal-Mart (500 employees); and Mount Dora Public School System (289 employees). Mount Dora is within commuting distance of both Orlando and Leesburg. With a population of fifteen thousand, Leesburg is the largest town in the county.

EDUCATION

High schools—1; Middle schools—1; Elementary schools—2; Private schools—1

The Lake-Sumter Community College has three campuses; the Leesburg location is the central and largest campus. Continuing education and two-year associate's degrees are offered. The University of Central Florida, part of the University of Florida system, is located in Orlando.

HEALTHCARE

The Florida (Waterman) Hospital—204 beds; Physicians—125; Dentists—25

Florida (Waterman) Hospital, located in Tavares (5 miles), is part of the Adventist Health System. It is ranked very high in several service categorizes within the state. The hospital offers 24-hour emergency care, a cancer unit, and a heart unit, and the staff treats many Medicare patients. The Leesburg Regional Medical Center, twenty miles from Mount Dora, is also ranked as one of the county's top hospitals. Ground and air ambulance service is available to both facilities. Since Orlando is only twenty-five miles away, additional specialized medical services are close by.

SPIRITUAL LIFE

Ten Christian denominations are represented. The nearest synagogue is located in Orlando.

STAYING CONNECTED

The following newspapers are available in Lake County: The *Daily Commercial,* which sponsors two weekly television shows; the weekly *Mount Dora Topic;* and the daily *Orlando/Lake Sentinel,* the Lake County edition of the *Orlando Sentinel.* Seven local television stations are accessible as well as thirty-eight additional stations via cable television. Several radio stations serve the area. Internet service is available. There is one downtown bookstore, as well as several more in other towns in the county and dozens in the Orlando area.

 GETTING THERE

Mount Dora is located in the center of Florida, twenty-four miles northwest of Orlando, on US 441. I-4 is thirty minutes to the east, and the Florida Turnpike is thirty minutes to the west. The Orlando International Airport is about one hour's drive south. Most major U.S. airlines serve the Orlando International Airport, along with Canadian and Caribbean Airlines. There is a local airport for private aircraft. Amtrak has train service into both DeLand (24 miles north) and Winter Park (23 miles, close to Orlando).

 RESOURCES

Mount Dora Area
  Chamber of Commerce
341 Alexander Street
Mount Dora, FL 32757
(352) 383-2165
www.mountdora.com

MOUNT DORA
VITAL STATISTICS

CLIMATE

Annual average rainfall		49 inches
Snowfall		0 inches
Elevation		184 feet

Temperatures (in degrees Fahrenheit)

	Jan	Apr	Jul	Oct
High	68	81	91	83
Low	44	57	71	62

OCCUPATIONS

	2006	Projected 2011
Blue collar	24.9%	23.2%
White collar	55.0%	55.9%
Services	20.0%	20.9%

ADULT EDUCATION

	2000
Less than High School	18.9%
High School	25.0%
Some College	22.0%
Associates Degree	7.1%
College Degree	16.7%
Graduate Degree	10.3%

POPULATION

2006	10,423
2000-2006 Population: Annual Compound Growth Rate	1.64%
2006-2011 Population: Annual Compound Growth Rate	3.90%

Population by age group

	2006	Projected 2011
0-4	5.7%	5.5%
5-9	5.7%	5.2%
10-14	5.7%	6.0%
15-19	5.2%	5.3%
20-24	4.9%	4.6%
25-29	4.8%	4.7%
30-34	4.6%	4.8%
35-39	5.1%	4.4%
40-44	6.1%	5.6%
45-49	6.9%	6.6%
50-54	6.6%	7.0%
55-59	6.4%	6.9%
60-64	5.8%	6.1%
65-69	5.5%	5.5%
70-74	5.1%	5.1%
75-79	5.2%	5.0%
80-84	5.6%	5.4%
85+	5.3%	6.3%

Sources for Vital Statistics listed above can be found in the Preface to this book.

NEW SMYRNA BEACH

2006 POPULATION
  21,592

NEAREST CITIES
  Daytona Beach, FL (15 miles)
  Orlando, FL (60 miles)

ESTIMATED 2006
MEDIAN HOUSEHOLD INCOME
  $42,894

COST OF LIVING
  Average 3-bdrm home (mainland)—
  $250,000
  Average 3-bdrm home (beachside)—
  $450,000
  Average rent, 2-bdrm apartment—$950
  Cost-of-living comparison—98.4%

SALES TAX
  6.5%

PROPERTY TAX
  Average 3-bdrm home—$6,000

New Smyrna Beach sits along the shores of the historic Indian River and the Intracoastal Waterway. In 1513, Ponce de Leon entered the inlet now known as Ponce Inlet to replenish his supply of water and wood. This beach community was also the site of one of the largest British attempts at colonization in America—nearly three times larger than Jamestown, Virginia.

New Smyrna's founding father, a Scottish physician named Dr. Andrew Turnbull, obtained a land grant from the British crown in 1768 and named the settlement after his wife's home in Turkey. Colonists arrived from Greece, Italy, and other countries to transform grassy wetlands and ponds into fertile land for growing indigo and corn. They widened and interconnected existing creeks, creating a complex network of canals. Many were killed by an unknown disease carried by mosquitoes and the colonists subsequently left en masse for St. Augustine in 1777. In 1803, land grants were given to permanent settlers, but it wasn't until after the Civil War that resettlement began in earnest.

Today the beach area offers miles of packed sand starting at the mouth of the Ponce de Leon Inlet, and is ideal for swimming, sunbathing, and barefoot strolls. Moving inland from the beach and crossing the Intracoastal Waterway, you'll find marinas and boat clubs, attractive hotels and condominiums, and bed-and-breakfast inns. The historic downtown is a participant in the Main Street program. Over $4 million has been invested in renovation of downtown Canal Street and the new Riverside Park on the Intracoastal Waterway. Canal Street, the town's main roadway, is lined with graceful palm trees and splendid oaks. Colorful textured sidewalks, remodeled building facades, and pedestrian-scale street lamps add to the beauty of the street. Antique stores, art galleries, boutiques, and sidewalk cafés complement this attractive downtown area.

Take the North Causeway over the wide Intracoastal Waterway and you enter another historic area. Flagler Avenue, located on the beach side of the Waterway, is the main thoroughfare in the town's oldest commercial district. Old oak trees, small shops, and the inviting front porches of old Florida coast–style homes accent the intimate scale of Flagler Avenue. It's a neighborhood business center featuring specialty shops, and casual and formal dining establishments. There is a series of walking and bike trails. This five-block area, which ends at the beach, is one of the most picturesque scenes on Florida's Atlantic coast.

 **RECREATION**

The famous public beaches in the southeast part of Volusia County extend over thirteen miles from north to south, from Ponce de Leon Inlet to the Canaveral National Seashore Park. Parking and driving are allowed on the beach during daylight hours.

Strolling, shell collecting, bird watching, surf fishing, surfing, and swimming are popular for at least ten months of the year. Surfboards and boogie boards are available for rent. This is an angler's heaven, with twenty-two miles of water where you can cast a line from charter boats, from piers, or off the seawalls of the Atlantic, Intracoastal, Indian River, or canals. You can catch many kinds of fish, including grouper, snapper, blue marlin, sailfish, mackerel, tuna, and wahoo. There are also several camps for lake and river fishing. Two public boat launch ramps are close to town on the Intracoastal Waterway.

Three public and two private golf courses serve the area. Five tennis courts and two racquetball facilities are available for public use. The New Smyrna Beach Parks and Recreation Department sponsors programs for children, teens, and adults throughout the year. Residents also enjoy shuffleboard, bridge, senior dances, and square dancing.

Nine miles south of New Smyrna Beach on Highway A1A is the 57,000-acre Canaveral National Seashore, a barrier island famous for bird watching and shell collecting. The salt marshes, mangrove islands, lagoons, and river estuaries on this island are home to more than 700 species of native coastal vegetation and 250 kinds of birds and animals. Additional well-known attractions within an easy drive of New Smyrna Beach include Walt Disney World and Sea World in Orlando, Daytona International Speedway (18 miles), and Greyhound Dog Racing at Daytona Beach.

 CULTURAL SCENE

The arts are well represented in New Smyrna Beach, which was recommended in the book *The 100 Best Small Art Towns in America*. Cultural attractions include a resident playhouse, a world-renowned artists-in-residence facility, an artists' workshop, and several commercial art galleries. The Atlantic Center for the Arts Residency Center was established in 1977 as a nonprofit organization to foster international, interdisciplinary artistic dialogue. The center, located on a sixty-seven-acre ecological preserve, includes a resource library; an amphitheater for concerts, dance performances, and recitals; facilities for dining; and housing in a campus setting. The center provides workspace and technical support to visual artists, composers, playwrights, photographers, choreographers, poets, and sculptors from all over the world. Renowned artists are invited to work with other talented artists for three weeks at a time during each of five yearly residencies. More than two hundred internationally acclaimed master artists have worked at Atlantic Center.

The Harris House of Atlantic Center, located in downtown New Smyrna Beach, is the center's community outreach division. Harris House, which contains a gallery, a gift shop, and class space, also provides children's art programs, adult workshops, and other educational programs for the community. The Artist's Workshop promotes the arts and sponsors monthly demonstrations, workshops, and art classes for adults. There are four other galleries in town. The Little Theater, the local resident playhouse, presents plays year-round. The Indian River Community Concert Association sponsors

concerts January through March.

Special events in town and on the beach include a 10K beach run; Light Up Flagler, an event held in early December that features strolling carolers, a light display, and refreshments on the beach; the annual Christmas parade; an annual arts fiesta in February; frequent jazz festivals on Flagler Avenue; and summer concert festivals in a local park.

 MAIN STREET

Seafood and informality go together here, so most of the restaurants are casual and feature fresh catches. Among those of special interest are Blackbeard's Inn, Chase on the Beach Bar and Restaurant, Guly's Pub 44, Riverfront Brewing Company, Shells Fresh Seafood, and Scott's Bluewater Grill. Norwood's Seafood Restaurant is popular with families, and the Flagler Tavern and Red Rooster Restaurant, located on the beach, feature lives entertainment.

 HOUSING

New Smyrna Beach offers competitive housing prices compared with other Florida coastal areas. Homes start at approximately $250,000 on the mainland and $450,000 on the beachside. Of nine residential communities, three are golf related. There are three manufactured home communities in the area, ranging from deluxe to inexpensive; two are on the Intracoastal Waterway. There are expensive high-rise condominiums on the beach ($675,000) as well as more modest two-story units ($300,000) on the beachside and the Intracoastal. If you travel west from the coast toward I-95, you can find homes priced at around $350,000. Because it is a popular winter destination, the area has a wide selection of apartments and condominiums. Seasonal rates are lower than in other Florida Atlantic Coast cities and towns. A good local bus service provides public transportation to New Smyrna Beach.

 ECONOMICS
Number of employers with fifty or more employees—6
The retail-wholesale trade sector accounts for thirty percent of the work force. Since tourism is a major industry, service employment is responsible for another approximately thirty-three percent. Local large employers include Bert Fish Medical Center (720 employees); Boston Whaler (560 employees); Coronado Paint Company (200 employees); and Publix (280 employees). Other large employers are located in Daytona Beach and nearby cities.

 EDUCATION
High schools—1; Middle schools—1; Elementary schools—7; Private schools—2
The public school system, the tenth largest in Florida, is operated by the county. Adult education courses and degree programs are available at the Daytona Beach Community College (New Smyrna Beach and Daytona Beach campuses) and the University of Central Florida at Daytona Beach. Stetson University, a well-known private institution, is located only thirty miles west in DeLand. Embry Riddle Aeronautical University is located in Daytona Beach.

 HEALTHCARE
Bert Fish Medical Center—112 beds; Physicians—50; Dentists—30

Bert Fish Medical Center offers 24-hour emergency care, cardiac and pulmonary rehabilitation programs, oncology care, and outpatient surgery. Halifax Medical Center, with 525 beds and a physician staff of 500, is the largest hospital in the Daytona Beach area.

 SPIRITUAL LIFE

Twenty-six Christian denominations are represented. A synagogue is located in Daytona Beach. The Cassadaga Spiritualist Camp near DeLand is the home of an active spiritualist community.

 STAYING CONNECTED

There are two local newspapers, the *Observer* (six days per week) and the *News-Journal* (daily), which covers New Smyrna and Daytona Beach. The *Orlando Sentinel* is also delivered. There are two local radio stations and four local affiliate television stations in Daytona Beach. Cable television and internet service are also available. There are three bookstores in New Smyrna Beach and nearby Edgewater.

 GETTING THERE

New Smyrna Beach is located about fifteen miles south of Daytona Beach on the Atlantic coast. Highways A1A and US 1 pass through the town. I-95, running the entire length of the eastern seaboard, is about six miles west of town. The closest major airport is the Daytona Beach International Airport, served by Continental, Delta, and United. The New Smyrna Beach Municipal Airport offers charter and private aircraft services. The Intracoastal Waterway allows pleasure boats to travel from Maine to Miami, Florida, and divides the mainland from the beach. Access to the Atlantic Ocean is available at the Ponce Inlet for fishing boats.

 RESOURCES

Southeast Volusia
  Chamber of Commerce
115 Canal Street
New Smyrna Beach, FL 32168
(877) 460-8410
www.sevchamber.com
www.nsbfla.com

NEW SMYRNA BEACH
VITAL STATISTICS

CLIMATE

Annual average rainfall	48 inches
Snowfall	0 inches
Elevation	9 feet

Temperatures (in degrees Fahrenheit)

	Jan	Apr	Jul	Oct
High	68	80	89	81
Low	46	58	72	65

OCCUPATIONS

	2006	Projected 2011
Blue collar	19.9%	18.4%
White collar	58.0%	59.0%
Services	22.1%	22.5%

ADULT EDUCATION

	2000
Less than High School	15.2%
High School	28.4%
Some College	26.0%
Associates Degree	7.4%
College Degree	14.3%
Graduate Degree	8.7%

POPULATION

2006	21,592
2000-2006 Population: Annual Compound Growth Rate	1.19%
2006-2011 Population: Annual Compound Growth Rate	1.72%

Population by age group

	2006	Projected 2011
0-4	3.2%	3.0%
5-9	3.1%	2.9%
10-14	3.7%	3.1%
15-19	3.9%	3.5%
20-24	3.7%	3.3%
25-29	3.6%	3.7%
30-34	3.7%	3.7%
35-39	4.1%	3.6%
40-44	5.6%	4.7%
45-49	7.1%	6.2%
50-54	7.9%	7.8%
55-59	9.3%	10.2%
60-64	8.0%	11.2%
65-69	7.9%	8.5%
70-74	7.6%	7.3%
75-79	7.1%	6.5%
80-84	5.9%	5.3%
85+	4.7%	5.5%

Sources for Vital Statistics listed above can be found in the Preface to this book.

2006 POPULATION
16,369

NEAREST CITIES
Fort Pierce, FL (18 miles)
West Palm Beach, FL (40 miles)

ESTIMATED 2006
MEDIAN HOUSEHOLD INCOME
$36,276

COST OF LIVING
Average 3-bdrm home—$250,000
Average rent, 2-bdrm apartment—
$1,000
Cost-of-living comparison—102%

SALES TAX
6%

PROPERTY TAX
Average 3-bdrm home—$3,000

Best known as the "sailfish capital of the world," Stuart is an attractive destination for those who want the benefits of excellent beaches, a variety of sports and housing choices, and an area that is less crowded than Florida's southeast coast. Waterways are everywhere, adding ambience as well as mobility.

Stuart presents an upscale, affluent image. A Main Street program participant, Stuart's historic downtown is a compact four-block, pedestrian-friendly shopping and entertainment center with restaurants and numerous retail stores. Buildings cannot be taller than four stories. Victorian-style lampposts dot the landscape. The old Martin County Courthouse has been restored to its original 1937 architectural design and now houses two galleries. The

Mediterranean revival–style Lyric Theater, built in 1925 as a silent movie house, has undergone renovation and has been named to the National Register of Historic Places. The six-hundred-seat theater features excellent acoustics and hosts year-round concerts, plays, and nationally known performing groups for young and old. Several attractive malls are located along US 1, the north-south business thoroughfare. Stuart's one-mile riverwalk along the banks of the St. Lucie River, within easy walking distance of the heart of town, offers beautiful views across the wide waterway.

 RECREATION

The county is a golfer's paradise, with courses for professional and weekend golfers. Several nationally known players live here or maintain homes in the community. In addition to more than twenty private courses, there are four public courses in the county.

Four major public beaches with lifeguards and twelve beach access strips create easy opportunities for ocean-related activities and beachcombing. There is something for every style of fishing enthusiast, from the excitement of offshore fishing for marlin, dolphin, sailfish, or wahoo to the spectacular bass fishing on Lake Okeechobee at the western border of the county. Snorkeling and scuba diving are also popular at both natural and artificial reefs located three to eight miles offshore. Seven county parks offer hiking, camping, canoeing, bicycling, shelling, fishing, and swimming.

 **CULTURAL SCENE**

The Martin County Council for the Arts is an umbrella organization that has restored the old Martin County Courthouse and made it into a community arts center. Here the council hosts galleries and classes in music, art, literature, and history. The council also sponsors an annual ArtsFest, providing an opportunity for residents to exhibit their work. Community theater, several dance companies, a folk music series, and art leagues contribute to the cultural activities. As previously mentioned, the Lyric Theatre also hosts a full schedule of events.

The Elliot Museum houses a collection of Seminole Indian artifacts and American memorabilia dating back to 1865. Many items are displayed, including antique and classic cars, in various turn-of-the century settings such as blacksmith, apothecary, and barber shops. The Gilberts Bar House of Refuge, built in 1875, is the oldest standing structure in the county. This museum, the last remaining U.S. Coast Guard Lifesaving Station on Florida's east coast, houses a collection of marine artifacts, some dating back to the sixteenth century. The Maritime and Yachting Museum preserves the nautical hertiage of the Treasure Coast and Florida. The museum offers extensive educational programs for children.

 MAIN STREET

Florida seafood is always at the top of any menu in Stuart. Some popular dining spots are Gusto's Restaurant in downtown; The Flagler's Grill; Dockside on the waterfront; R. J. Gators, a fun family place; Luna's, a downtown eatery serving Italian cuisine; and Prawnbroker's Grill. Entertainment at the Lyric Theatre draws locals to the historic downtown area for after-theater dining.

 HOUSING

A broad range of housing, from modest to luxurious, should satisfy any taste. There are prime oceanfront and waterfront properties with docks, as well as more modest houses located in quiet, secluded neighborhoods. Housing is also available in communities catering to people interested in golf, tennis, swimming, and boating. Homes range in price from $155,000 to $10 million. Oceanfront and waterfront condos on Hutchinson Island start at about $300,000 and go to several million. Gated golf communities are also popular here, with prices starting at $250,000. Manufactured home communities including clubhouses, boat slips, and pools are available in the area. Rental opportunities are plentiful. A variety of apartments, condos, and homes meet the needs of seasonal residents. Adult-only communities are also available.

ECONOMICS

Number of employers with fifty or more employees—12

The local economy is driven by retail, service, hospitality, construction, and government sectors. Martin County is ranked fifth in the state in citrus and vegetable production. The county also boasts an egg farm producing in excess of 11 million dozen eggs annually; one of the world's best-known aircraft corporations with a manufacturing and testing facility; and the headquarters of the largest transporter of fresh cut flowers in the United States. The area marine industries contribute more than $200 million annually to the local economy. Among the major employers are Martin County Schools (2,100 employees), Martin Memorial Health Systems (1,800 employees), Martin County Government (1,400), Publix Supermarkets (1,000 employees), and the State of Florida (850 employees). Tourism and retirees contribute significantly to the local economy.

EDUCATION

High schools—4; Middle schools—4; Elementary schools—9; Private schools—5

The public school system is county wide. Indian River Community College is the best known among the community colleges that provide comprehensive two-year programs. Florida Atlantic University, based in Boca Raton, offers classes at the Indian River Community College campus. Barry University, a Miami-based private Catholic school, offers upper-level college classes and master's degree programs. Northwood University in West Palm Beach offers associate's and bachelor's degrees.

HEALTHCARE

Martin Memorial Medical Center—236 beds; Martin Memorial Hospital South—100 beds; Physicians—200; Dentists—87

The two hospitals are part of Martin Memorial Health System; the larger is in downtown Stuart and the smaller is on the south side. Services include 24-hour open door emergency care, outpatient care, comprehensive cancer treatment, cardiac catheterization, maternity care, and hyperbaric treatment. The downtown hospital is accessible by water, land, and air. Palm Beach County has a large medical center that specializes in cardiac care, including open-heart surgery, as well as a Veteran's Hospital.

 SPIRITUAL LIFE

Approximately twenty Christian denominations are represented. Stuart has two synagogues.

 STAYING CONNECTED

The local newspaper, *Stuart News,* is published daily. Regional newspapers with local bureaus and coverage include the *Palm Beach Post* and the *Miami Herald.* There's also a weekly business journal, *Business Journal of the Treasure Coast.* Television network affiliates are located in the Palm Beach area, and several cable television systems offer local service. An independent television station, WTCN, is located in the area. Six AM and fourteen FM radio stations are heard in Stuart.

Local internet service is available. There are four bookstores in town. The William Thomas Braille Bookstore ships books worldwide.

 GETTING THERE

Stuart is on the Atlantic coast, forty miles north of West Palm Beach. It is five miles east of I-95 on US 1. US A1A crosses the Indian River (Intracoastal Waterway) from Hutchinson Island to Stuart, where it continues south. The Stuart (Witham Field) Airport offers charter flights and is a general aviation airport. Palm Beach International Airport (45 miles south) is served by most major airlines. Access to the Atlantic Ocean is via the St. Lucie Inlet.

 RESOURCES

Stuart/Martin County
  Chamber of Commerce
1650 South Kanner Highway
Stuart, FL 34994
(772) 287-1088
www.goodnature.org

STUART
VITAL STATISTICS

CLIMATE

Annual average rainfall	56 inches
Snowfall	0 inches
Elevation	12 feet

Temperatures (in degrees Fahrenheit)

	Jan	Apr	Jul	Oct
High	75	82	89	85
Low	54	63	73	68

OCCUPATIONS

	2006	Projected 2011
Blue collar	21.3%	19.7%
White collar	56.9%	58.1%
Services	21.8%	22.2%

ADULT EDUCATION

	2000
Less than High School	18.8%
High School	29.4%
Some College	24.7%
Associates Degree	5.3%
College Degree	13.7%
Graduate Degree	8.2%

POPULATION

2006	16,369
2000-2006 Population: Annual Compound Growth Rate	1.81%
2006-2011 Population: Annual Compound Growth Rate	2.01%

Population by age group

	2006	Projected 2011
0-4	4.0%	3.9%
5-9	3.8%	3.6%
10-14	4.2%	3.9%
15-19	4.4%	4.4%
20-24	5.5%	5.0%
25-29	4.8%	5.2%
30-34	5.1%	4.4%
35-39	5.3%	4.8%
40-44	6.6%	5.7%
45-49	6.6%	6.6%
50-54	6.2%	7.0%
55-59	6.4%	7.4%
60-64	6.7%	7.5%
65-69	5.4%	7.3%
70-74	5.9%	5.3%
75-79	5.8%	5.5%
80-84	5.9%	5.1%
85+	7.4%	7.5%

Sources for Vital Statistics listed above can be found in the Preface to this book.

GEORGIA

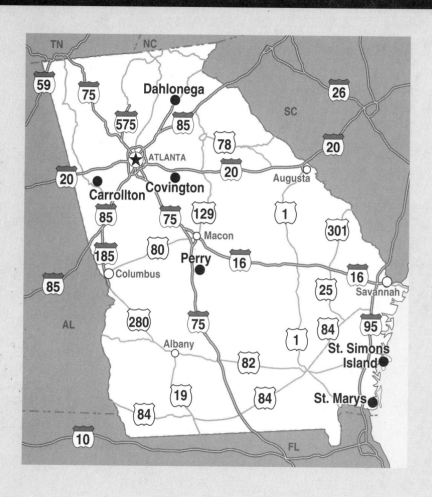

TN   NC

59   75   **Dahlonega**

575   85   SC   26

78   20

20   **ATLANTA**

20   Augusta

Carrollton   **Covington**

85   75   129   1   301

80   Macon

185   **Perry**   16

Columbus   25   16   Savannah

AL   280   75   95

Albany   1   84

82   **St. Simons**
Island

19   84   **St. Marys**

84

10   FL

CARROLLTON

2006 POPULATION
23,314

NEAREST CITIES
Atlanta, GA (50 miles)

ESTIMATED 2006
MEDIAN HOUSEHOLD INCOME
$34,828

COST OF LIVING
Average 3-bdrm home—$145,000
Average rent, 2-bdrm apartment—$750
Cost-of-living comparison—98.4%

SALES TAX
7%

PROPERTY TAX
Average 3-bdrm home—$1,300

Carrollton, named in honor of Charles Carroll, one of the signers of the Declaration of Independence, serves as a retail, commercial, education, manufacturing, and healthcare center for several counties in west Georgia and east Alabama. A designated town in the Main Street program since 1985, Carrollton artfully blends a historic past with a progressive future. Adamson Square and the surrounding sixteen-block Main Street district, with its shops, restaurants, offices, galleries, and old homes, form a close-knit community. Restoration of historic buildings is almost complete on Adamson Square. On one side of the square, a former mercantile building has been restored; there are two new retail shops on the street level and a technology company on the second floor. On another corner, a building repainted in a shade of burgundy frequently used at the turn of the century now houses a restaurant. Redevelopment has spread to the surrounding city blocks. Numerous new businesses have opened, including restaurants, coffee shops, bakeries, art galleries, a clothing boutique, and more. Businesses are moving into downtown office space and newly renovated older homes that surround the square. Dixie Street, a major thoroughfare, is lined with historic old homes and massive oak trees. In the spring, colorful azalea blossoms enhance the street's charm.

Chief William McIntosh was a key figure in the county's early history. A cousin of Georgia governor George Troupe, McIntosh had a Scottish father and a Creek Indian mother. A leader of the Lower Creek Indian tribe, he also achieved the rank of brigadier general in the U.S. Army. McIntosh negotiated the Indian Springs Treaty with the U.S. government in 1825, ceding Creek and Cherokee land holdings within Georgia to the state. Believing that McIntosh received money for the sale while exempting his own property, the infuriated members of the Creek tribe reputedly killed McIntosh and burned his plantation home. The McIntosh plantation site has been preserved as the McIntosh Reserve, a 527-acre recreation area along the Chattahoochee River.

 RECREATION

Carroll County offers an abundance of activities for every member of the family and for every lifestyle. Over 35,000 acres of public and private recreational parks and facilities lie within the county. Picturesque 175-acre Lake Carroll in downtown Carrollton is bordered on one side with homes and a small park. Picnic, concession, and restroom facilities are at the other end of the lake. Twelve parks and recreation facilities offer everything from football, baseball, and soccer fields to walking and fitness trails, swimming pools, and tennis courts. There are six full-time recreation departments in Carroll County, the most of any county in the state. The Carrollton Parks, Recreation, and Cultural Arts Department received the Sports Foundation's first Gold Medal Award in Georgia for a town with a population under twenty thousand. The department offers athletic programs in all major sports; courses such as aerobics and dancing; and therapeutic programs designed for senior citizens or the disabled. A skateboard park is currently under development. Carroll County's program to fund local acquisition of greenspace and recreation facilities is the first program of its kind in the state of Georgia.

John Tanner State Park, located in nearby Mount Zion, is a multiuse outdoor attraction with swimming, boating, picnicking, and camping facilities. Situated on an attractive 136-acre site, the park features the largest sand beach of any state park in Georgia, as well as exercise and nature trails, canoe and pedal boat rentals, miniature golf, lodge accommodations, and tent and trailer campsites. McIntosh Reserve is open for camping, hiking, and picnicking April through October. Outdoor enthusiasts flock to the nearby fields and streams in search of wild game and fish. Serious fishermen can test their skill with some of the world's biggest

bass at nearby West Point Lake.

Golf enthusiasts will find three public courses: a par 3 facility in the nearby town of Bowden, the Oak Mountain Championship Golf Club, and the semi-private Fairfield Plantation Championship Course near Villa Rica. Private courses include Sunset Hills Country Club (an eighteen-hole full-service private facility), The Frog Golf Course at the Georgian Resort, The Lion Club, and Cannongate on Mirror Lake Golf Course. Fairfield Plantation is a private residential resort community offering members access to golf, tennis, swimming, boating, and waterskiing. Callaway Gardens, featuring golf and tennis, is fifty-five miles to the south. Atlanta, home to several professional sports teams, is only an hour away. Six Flags over Georgia, a popular amusement park with roller coasters and other rides, is twenty miles east on Interstate 20.

 **CULTURAL SCENE**

Carrollton offers a wide assortment of events centered on art, dance, and theater. The City of Carrollton operates the $6 million Cultural Arts Center in downtown Carrollton. This facility provides the space for a theater, a gallery, and classrooms. The Carrollton Artists' Guide assists in leading workshops and classes as well as providing works for display in the Cultural Arts Center and private galleries. Two active theater companies use the center, as do the Carroll County Symphony Orchestra, the Youth Orchestra, and the Community Chorus. Programs have included such diverse activities as community theater, chorus, and band; children's theater; art exhibitions; a storytelling festival; violin classes; arts and crafts programs; and special musical performances.

The University of West Georgia is one of the town's most valuable cultural assets. Its Townsend Center for the Performing Arts, a 450-seat venue, presents over three hundred events annually, including music and plays open to the community. The university also hosts art shows, recitals, and concerts throughout the year that are open to the public. The Beth Harmon Williamson Cultural Art Center, located in the West Georgia Regional Library in Carrollton, offers art exhibits, concerts, and special cultural programs. The Atlanta Symphony, Atlanta Ballet, High Museum of Art, Fernbank Museum, and other cultural attractions are approximately one hour away in Atlanta.

The county plays host to many special events throughout the year, including Mayfest, an arts and crafts festival the first Saturday in May with live entertainment by regional bands and entertainers; Arts Gala, a June art auction; a Fourth of July celebration; the Autumn Leaves Arts and Crafts festival at the John Tanner State Park in September; the On the Square Arts and Crafts Show in November; a county fall festival; and a tour of selected private home gardens. A brown bag lunch music performance series is held on Adamson Square every Friday afternoon in June, July, and September.

Several historic attractions are in the area. The Bonner House, a plantation home built in 1843, is the oldest building on the campus of the University of West Georgia. The Buckhorne Tavern, one of the oldest establishments in the country, opened in 1833 as an overnight resting place on an early stage route. The original foundation and framework still stand just east of nearby Temple.

MAIN STREET

The restoration and redevelopment of the downtown area has drawn new restaurants that are doing very well. Among those worth noting are Miller's, a fine-dining restaurant offering excellent cuisine and unique café-style seating on the downtown square; The Highland Deli, serving Scottish cuisine in a casual atmosphere, sometimes accompanied by live bagpipes; and Parelli's Brick Oven Pizza. Other popular restaurants on the square include Pearl's Café (an eclectic menu of burgers, steaks, and crawfish cakes, the house specialty) and an urban 1960s-style coffeehouse called The Corner Café (a variety of coffees and vegetarian sandwiches). The Maple Street Mansion, a twenty-year-old establishment located in a large historic Victorian house (on Maple Street,

of course) about three blocks from the square, features a sports bar, a large meeting room/ballroom, and a railroad car for a unique dining experience. The Rome Street Tavern and Grill, just off the square, boasts the only microbrewery in the downtown area. Gallery Row is a coffee shop specializing in gourmet coffees and teas as well as gelato and deserts. Both of these places host musical entertainment throughout the week (remember, this is a college town), and provide gallery space for local artists to show their works.

Outside of downtown, there are several other popular dining spots. The Lazy Donkey serves Mexican and Caribbean food; their salsa is so popular that it is sold in local grocery stores. The decks at Shuckers Oyster Bar, a seafood restaurant with a casual atmosphere, are perfect for outdoor dining and conversation.

HOUSING

Carrollton offers a broad range of housing options in both style and price. Apartments are abundant because of the university; more than fifty complexes are available.

Graceful old two-story homes are located close to the downtown area. Several new subdivisions offer excellent home values for young families. Elegant horse farms and a private residential resort community are among the choices for upscale living. Mill Pond, a master-planned residential development on one hundred acres, features a recreational complex, a pool, tennis courts, two natural ponds, a children's playground, and nature trails. Homes range from $135,000 to $300,000. Several old mills are being converted into loft apartments. Town homes, some within walking distance of the downtown square, are becoming popular. Oak Mountain Golf Club has a 225-lot subdivision and an eighteen-hole golf course; prices range from $300,000 to over $1 million. The complex is at the highest elevation in Carrollton and has extensive wetlands, a pond, and two lakes. Cottage Lane, a retirement community, features independent living in one- and two-bedroom apartments. Six smaller towns in Carroll County offer additional residential choices. Home and apartment prices are appreciably less than in Atlanta.

 ECONOMICS

Number of employers with fifty or more employees—50

Carroll County has pursued economic growth and capitalized on its access to both Atlanta and Birmingham. More than one hundred manufacturers are located in the county, including seven international firms. The economic base is extremely diversified with a wide variety of manufacturers and services. Products manufactured in the area include wire and cable, automobile parts, dairy products, poultry, baked goods, hosiery, men's suits, metal pipe, wood furniture, textile cord, synthetic turf grass, and irrigation systems. Like other smaller towns, Carrollton has experienced a loss of jobs in many traditional industries as a result of international competition and technology. Carroll County has created a new organization to encourage economic and community development. A new mixed-use small business incubator is opening, and efforts, in which West Georgia University is involved, are underway to unite university research and local companies on the commercialization of nanotechnology. The largest single employer is Southwire (1,500 employees), the world's largest privately owned rod and cable manufacturing company. The county and city school systems (2,400 employees), Tanner Medical Center (1,800 employees), and the University of West Georgia (1,000) employees) are significant service employers. Agriculture continues to play a vital role in the county: the dairy, cattle, and poultry industries are substantial revenue sources. GoldKist Poultry (850 employees) is the area's largest single employer in the industry. Bremen-Bowdon Investments (435 employees) is another major employer.

Founded in 1994, West Georgia Telecommunications Alliance is Georgia's longest existing nonprofit telecommunications advocacy organization. The organization's efforts have led to the opening of a local technology business incubator and development of a broadband network for Carroll County. The Alliance is preparing to provide low-cost, high-speed internet connections to the city and county schools, the technical college, and the university.

EDUCATION
High schools—1; Junior High—1; Middle schools—1; Elementary schools—1; Private schools—4
The broad range of educational offerings is one of Carrollton's strongest attractions. City and county public school systems and private schools offer diversity, quality, and technology seldom found in communities this size. Carrollton City High School has been named one of the best in Georgia and the United States by School-Match (an independent service that helps relocating families and corporations) and *Redbook* magazine. The city school system has been a leader in the use of technology, with internet access for 1,400 computers, graphics arts programs, television programming, and electronic music keyboarding available to all students.

The University of West Georgia offers fifty-eight baccalaureate and fifty graduate degree programs (including a doctorate degree and a new Web MBA program) through four colleges enrolling over 10,000 students. Continuing education programs are also available. Carroll Technical Institute provides technical training. At least a dozen major colleges and universities, including Georgia Tech, Emory, Georgia State University, the Atlanta University Center, and Berry College are within reasonable commuting distance.

The Carroll County Education Foundation demonstrates the dedication of Carroll County residents to quality education. The Foundation is a community- and business-supported nonprofit organization established for the purpose of enhancing the academic, personal, and vocational opportunities and achievements of county citizens. These goals are accomplished by developing community and business resources for use by area schools.

 HEALTHCARE

Tanner Health Systems—202 beds; Physicians—180; Dentists—30
Tanner Health Systems is a Level II acute-care facility that serves local residents and those from surrounding counties as well as some adjoining counties in Alabama. The center offers a 24-hour emergency department, a new state-of-the-art intensive care facility, comprehensive cancer treatment, occupational health and mental health services, maternity care, physical therapy, diabetic care, cardiopulmonary and sleep programs, and outpatient surgery. Because Carrollton is not far from Atlanta, specialized medical services are easily accessible.

 SPIRITUAL LIFE

Twenty Christian denominations are represented. The nearest synagogue is in Atlanta.

 STAYING CONNECTED

Local newspapers include the daily *Times Georgian* and the weekly *The Carroll Star News*. The *Atlanta Journal-Constitution* is also available. Several AM and FM radio stations serve the county. Cable television brings in all major networks and affiliates out of Atlanta. Carrollton is within the metro Atlanta calling area, which includes local access to national internet service providers. There are two local bookstores in Carrollton, and chain bookstores about thirty miles away. Horton's Books and Gifts, located on the square, is one of the oldest bookstores in the country.

 GETTING THERE

Carrollton is fifty miles southwest of Atlanta, close to the Alabama state line. It is fourteen miles south of I–20, at the junction of US 27 and GA 16. West Georgia Regional Airport, Carroll County's public airport, has a 5,000-foot lighted asphalt runway. The nearest commercial air service is at Atlanta Hartsfield International Airport, approximately fifty miles east.

 RESOURCES

Carrollton Area Convention
  and Visitor's Bureau
P. O. Box 532
Carrollton, GA 30117
(800) 292-0871
www.visitcarrollton.com

Additional area website:
www.carrolltongeorgia.com

CARROLLTON
VITAL STATISTICS

CLIMATE

Annual average rainfall	52 inches
Snowfall	2 inches
Elevation	900 feet

Temperatures (in degrees Fahrenheit)

	Jan	Apr	Jul	Oct
High	52	74	88	73
Low	29	46	65	46

OCCUPATIONS

	2006	Projected 2011
Blue collar	8.5%	7.9%
White collar	75.6%	75.0%
Services	15.9%	17.1%

ADULT EDUCATION

	2000
Less than High School	4.5%
High School	13.4%
Some College	23.9%
Associates Degree	6.7%
College Degree	31.2%
Graduate Degree	20.3%

POPULATION

2006	14,140
2000-2006 Population: Annual Compound Growth Rate	0.89%
2006-2011 Population: Annual Compound Growth Rate	0.86%

Population by age group

	2006	Projected 2011
0-4	3.8%	4.0%
5-9	4.3%	3.9%
10-14	5.0%	4.9%
15-19	5.5%	4.8%
20-24	4.3%	4.4%
25-29	3.1%	4.5%
30-34	4.6%	3.5%
35-39	5.5%	5.0%
40-44	6.7%	6.4%
45-49	7.1%	7.6%
50-54	9.5%	7.8%
55-59	9.1%	10.1%
60-64	8.2%	8.7%
65-69	5.4%	7.3%
70-74	5.2%	4.7%
75-79	4.8%	4.4%
80-84	4.0%	4.0%
85+	4.0%	4.3%

Sources for Vital Statistics listed above can be found in the Preface to this book.

COVINGTON

2006 POPULATION
15,962
NEAREST CITIES
Atlanta, GA (36 miles)
Athens, GA (46 miles)
ESTIMATED 2006
MEDIAN HOUSEHOLD INCOME
$44,105
COST OF LIVING
Average 3-bdrm home—$145,000
Average rent, 2-bdrm apartment—$700
Cost-of-living comparison—97.1%
SALES TAX
7%
PROPERTY TAX
Average 3-bdrm home—$1,600

Located just outside the Atlanta metropolitan area, the charming town of Covington boasts a reputation as one of the most picturesque and historic towns in Georgia. Founded in 1822, Covington has preserved a number of appealing homes with white columns and wide verandas, as well as brick two-stories graced by floor-to-ceiling windows with handblown glass panes. Legend has it that General Sherman found the houses so beautiful that he spared the town from burning during his march to the sea.

Sometimes referred to as "Hollywood South," Covington has become a popular shooting location for many feature films and television series, including *In the Heat of the Night*, which was filmed here for eight seasons. A self-guided tour of the shooting locations is available;

most are no more than four blocks from the square. Other productions shot in Covington include *I'll Fly Away, My Cousin Vinny,* and *The Dukes of Hazzard.*

In 1988, Covington was awarded the Georgia Main Street town designation, due in part to the community's dedication to the preservation of its nineteenth-century structures. Both the Main Street and the National Register of Historic Places districts are home to carefully restored antebellum and Victorian-era houses, stately old churches, and neatly manicured parks. The inviting downtown square is an ideal setting for festive social events such as outdoor luncheon concerts. The buildings, shops, and restaurants feature Victorian and turn-of-the-century brickwork; they are sparkling clean and frequently are painted white or are embellished with white accents. The Newton County Courthouse, a restored Victorian gem built in 1884, anchors one corner of the square and is used for cultural activities, exhibits, and meeting space.

The visitors center is a convenient starting place to learn about Covington. Visitors can take a number of self-guided tours of magnificent homes and buildings in the historic district. Many of the thirty-five homes on the tours were built between 1830 and 1860. Some of them, with their Doric and fluted Ionic columns and hanging balconies, are excellent examples of Greek Revival and English Regency architecture. But the main attractions are the lovely, stark-white antebellum two-story houses situated on large, well-tended lots framed in spring by pink azaleas and blooming dogwood trees. In her novel *Gone with the Wind,* Margaret Mitchell modeled Twelve Oaks plantation on the Whitehall Home, built in 1830. This house and several others are open to the public for tours. Many are furnished with period antiques and contain graceful curving staircases. The Annual Christmas Tour of Homes is popular with Atlantans as well as local residents.

In 2000, Covington's Georgia Main Street program was one of twenty-two that received recognition from the National Trust for

Historic Preservation's National Main Street Program for excellence in the field of downtown revitalization. Town leaders have focused on "smart growth" for several years. The local government and residents are interested in continuing to accommodate growth while preserving the town's historic character. The opening of a Montessori school in a close-in neighborhood is just one example of the ongoing revitalization.

 RECREATION

Covington has eighteen parks; twenty-six recreation areas totaling over 4,300 acres; six tennis facilities; and a large YMCA Community Center with summer day camp, soccer, and swimming. The county recreation commission offers adult basketball and softball and a full range of sports for youth. There are two premier eighteen-hole public golf courses. Covington Plantation was designed by Desmond Muirhead. In 1993, *Golf Digest* nomiated the Oaks as one of the top fifty new public courses in the United States. Atlanta's numerous sports attractions are within an hour's drive of Covington.

The Charlie Elliott Wildlife Center, which offers outreach programs for children, covers 6,000 acres and features twenty-two lakes for fishing and areas for hunting and camping. Swimming, fishing, and camping are available at Hard Labor Creek State Park, while Jackson Lake has facilities for swimming, fishing, camping, waterskiing, and motorboating. Nearby Lake Oconee has excellent fishing, boating, and a private golf course. The International Equestrian Center, which was the venue for the 1996 Olympics equestrian competition, is located in nearby Conyers.

 CULTURAL SCENE

Local art and cultural activities abound in Covington. The Concert Association of Newton County sponsors a minimum of eight concerts a year at Porter Memorial Auditorium. The series has featured such internationally renowned performers as Ballet National De Mexico, the piano virtuoso Mac Frampton, the Polish Chamber Orchestra

Philharmonic, the Canadian Brass, the Ink Spots, and the Atlanta Symphony. The Newton County Library offers puppet shows, storytellers, and craft programs for children. Its adult programming includes art exhibits and programs from Atlanta's High Museum of Art. The Choral Guild, a group of about fifty community members, presents fall and spring performances and is often accompanied by members of the Atlanta Symphony. Nearby Oxford College, the birthplace of Emory University (the main campus is now located in Atlanta), opens its lecture and cultural series to the public.

Each Thursday at noon in May and September, residents bring lunches and blankets to the square to enjoy free concerts sponsored by the Concert Association of Newton County. Past performances have included bluegrass, jazz, blues, gospel, and country music, as well as Native American and ethnic folk music. Main Street Covington offers a summer series of concerts on the second and fourth Friday evenings from June through September. Local citizens can take an easy drive to the Cultural Center in nearby Madison (another small town with beautiful antebellum homes), see the attractions at the University of Georgia in Athens, or take in the numerous museums and performances in Atlanta.

 MAIN STREET

On the square you will find an interesting array of dining and shopping choices. Chef R. L., who owns and operates R.L.'s Off the Square, trained under Chef Paul Prudhomme. At Town Center Breads, Charles Skrobot offers a changing selection of artisan breads baked fresh daily. The local dining scene also includes Jim Stalvey's Restaurant (steaks, seafood, and native Georgia chicken).

The Blue Willow Inn, a nationally acclaimed restaurant and a regional favorite, is a short drive away in the quaint town of Social Circle, Georgia. This restaurant has been voted the "Best Small Town Restaurant in the South" by *Southern Living* magazine for five consecutive years. Housed in a turn-of-the-century Greek Revival mansion, the restaurant's interior walls are adorned with fine art and selections from the owner's Blue Willow dish collection, which gives the restaurant its name. (Yes, the tables are also set with Blue Willow china.) "To die for" Southern fried chicken and nationally acclaimed fried green tomatoes are a must. Gaither's Plantation, a restored historic farm about ten miles outside Covington, is also popular. School groups come here on educational field trips, and the outdoor pavilion is frequently used for weddings and other catered events.

Several unique shops on the square complement the basic businesses, including a hardware store (which has a gift department), flower shops, clothing stores, an art gallery (which acts as a cooperative for many local artists), a spa, a youth hair salon, and an ice-cream shop. Patrick's is an old-fashioned general store selling pecans, home-style jams and preserves, cross-stitch and quilting supplies, and western wear.

 HOUSING

There is an excellent selection of homes in new subdivisions around Covington with prices from the mid $100,000s to $170,000s. Compared to similar housing in Atlanta, resale prices are very reasonable. An elegant, large (4 bedroom/3 bath) home on a one-acre lot in a prestigious subdivision will cost $250,000 to $300,000. Historic homes close to the square are very expensive (over $1.5 million) and they seldom go on the market. Senior housing is available and apartments are in good supply.

The small community of Oxford, located adjacent to Covington, has some older homes near the Oxford College campus, but historic houses usually cost more than $300,000. Newer homes in Oxford are $150,000 and up. Rural farmland suitable for home building is available at $8,000 to $10,000 per acre. The second largest lake in Georgia, Lake Oconee, located about thirty-five miles east of Covington, is surrounded by a rapidly growing, upscale housing market. Six gated golf communities with championship golf courses are available. Homes range from $250,000 to $1 million on the lake and golf courses.

ECONOMICS

Number of employers with fifty or more employees—21

Eight Fortune 500 companies have facilities based in the county. The largest county employers are Newton County School System (over 2,500 employees), Pactiv (700 employees), C. R. Bard, Inc. (600 employees), Newton General Hospital (550 employees), Dan River, Inc. (430 employees), Guardian Automotive (330 employees), and Fiberr Vision (330 employees). Some of the international companies that call Covington home are General Mills (330 employees), Bridgestone, Komatsu, and SKC, which made the largest capital investment of a Korean industry in the southeastern United States. Because of excellent cooperation between local government and business leaders, Covington looks forward to a bright future; the town continues to attract sound investment and provide a high quality of life for residents. Its pursuit of a smart growth plan is well ahead of other towns near metro Atlanta.

 EDUCATION

High schools—3; Middle schools—4; Elementary schools—12; Private school—1

Three schools are Georgia Schools of Excellence and one high school is a National School of Excellence. Six hundred students are enrolled in Oxford College, a two-year college associated with Emory University. It is located on a small campus about one mile from Covington in the community of Oxford. The fifteen major buildings (some date back to the 1850s) surround a wooded quadrangle. Students who graduate from Oxford College are eligible to continue their studies on Emory's Atlanta campus. Troy State University and Dekalb Technical College have campuses in Covington. Within a reasonable commuting distance are the major colleges and universities of Atlanta, including Agnes Scott College, the Atlanta University Center, Emory University, Georgia Tech, and Georgia State University. The University of Georgia in Athens is also within one hour's drive.

HEALTHCARE

Newton General Hospital—90 beds; Physicians—190; Dentists—19

Newton General is an acute-care facility featuring a 24-hour emergency department; critical care unit; surgery, maternity, pain relief, and women's diagnostic centers; and a fitness forum. Newton General is an affiliate member of the Emory University System of Health Care.

 SPIRITUAL LIFE

Twenty-one Christian denominations are represented. The closest synagogue is in Atlanta.

 STAYING CONNECTED

The *Covington News* is published three days a week. The *Newton Citizen* is a daily newspaper published in adjoining Rockdale County. The *Atlanta Journal-Constitution* is delivered to Covington. Cable television and high-speed internet access are available through Covington CableNet. National internet service is available locally. There are two local bookstores.

 GETTING THERE

Covington is located thirty-six miles east of Atlanta on US 278. I-20, linking Atlanta with Augusta, passes the edge of town. The Covington-Newton County Airport has a 4,200-foot paved and lighted runway for private aircraft. Atlanta's Hartsfield International Airport is within one hour's drive of Covington.

 RESOURCES

Covington Visitors Bureau
and Welcome Center
Newton County Chamber
of Commerce
P.O. Box 168
Covington, GA 30015
(800) 616-8626
www.newtonchamber.com

COVINGTON
VITAL STATISTICS

CLIMATE

Annual average rainfall	49 inches
Snowfall	2 inches
Elevation	1,000 feet

Temperatures (in degrees Fahrenheit)

	Jan	Apr	Jul	Oct
High	51	73	88	72
Low	30	48	67	49

OCCUPATIONS

	2006	Projected 2011
Blue collar	32.8%	30.4%
White collar	48.6%	49.8%
Services	18.6%	19.8%

ADULT EDUCATION

	2000
Less than High School	37.7%
High School	32.3%
Some College	14.5%
Associates Degree	2.8%
College Degree	8.3%
Graduate Degree	4.4%

POPULATION

2006	15,962
2000-2006 Population: Annual Compound Growth Rate	5.32%
2006-2011 Population: Annual Compound Growth Rate	6.69%

Population by age group

	2006	Projected 2011
0-4	7.4%	7.6%
5-9	6.9%	6.8%
10-14	7.6%	6.9%
15-19	8.7%	7.8%
20-24	7.0%	8.0%
25-29	6.1%	6.1%
30-34	6.7%	5.9%
35-39	7.1%	6.3%
40-44	7.5%	7.2%
45-49	7.0%	7.3%
50-54	5.9%	6.8%
55-59	5.3%	5.8%
60-64	4.1%	4.8%
65-69	3.4%	3.5%
70-74	2.9%	2.8%
75-79	2.4%	2.4%
80-84	1.9%	2.0%
85+	2.0%	1.9%

Sources for Vital Statistics listed above can be found in the Preface to this book.

DAHLONEGA

2006 POPULATION
4,703

NEAREST CITIES
Gainesville, GA (18 miles)
Atlanta, GA (70 miles)

**ESTIMATED 2006
MEDIAN HOUSEHOLD INCOME**
$34,906

COST OF LIVING
Average 3-bdrm home—$190,000
Average rent, 2-bdrm apartment—$600
Cost-of-living comparison—97.1%

SALES TAX
7%

PROPERTY TAX
Average 3-bdrm home—$1,500

In 1828 the Cherokee Indians occupied over four million acres in north Georgia. The Cherokee named the region *Ta-lo-ne-ga,* their word for yellow. Dahlonega was the early settlers' version of the Cherokee word. The first major U.S. gold rush occurred in Dahlonega. From 1828 to 1848, Dahlonega and its surrounding area produced more than $36 million in gold. In 1849, the California Gold Rush drew most of the local miners west, and by 1906 the last large Dahlonega mining company closed. There is still plenty of gold left in the area, but the cost of modern mining operations exceeds the value of the refined gold.

Today this Southern mountain mining town is listed on the National Register of Historic Places. In the center of the town square is the oldest public building in north Georgia, the splendid courthouse built in 1836. The building now houses the Dahlonega Gold Museum, whose exhibits reflect the rich history of the Cherokee Indians and the influence of the gold rush on this mountain town. This Federal-style building has twenty-two-inch-thick walls, handblown glass windows, and a Greek Revival–style portico. Flecks of gold are enmeshed in the clay of the remaining original floor bricks.

Dahlonega's historic downtown area is authentic nineteenth-century Georgia. The historic courthouse is surrounded by lawns and old trees, brick walls, and colorful flower gardens. Many of the buildings are part of the Dahlonega Historic Commercial District and now house antique and gift stores; specialty shops selling Appalachian crafts, candy, and other products; and sandwich shops. The Hawkins Street neighborhood, also listed on the National Register of Historic Places, is located two blocks northwest of the public square. This historic commercial district includes fifteen buildings, most dating back to the 1880s. Tours of the Consolidated Gold Mine include a guided walk through a massive tunnel network complete with the original track system. The Crisson Gold Mine also offers tours, and visitors have the opportunity to pan for gold.

Today, Dahlonega is a weekend getaway destination for many Atlanta residents. Visitors enjoy strolling along the sidewalks of the town square, browsing interesting shops, and viewing spectacular mountain scenery. Bed-and-breakfast inns can be found in town and scattered throughout the surrounding mountain areas. Several are in the historic district in large, restored Victorian homes, with expansive porches offering mountain views. Luxury cabin resorts with hot tubs, fireplaces, and spectacular mountain views are also popular. The community is growing rapidly, attracting new residents from both Florida and metro Atlanta seeking second and retirement homes. The town's appeal is enhanced by the growth of the arts and entertainment industry and the opening of several wineries. The presence of the North Georgia College and State University provides a youthful influence in this thriving town. Though Atlanta is growing and moving north, Dahlonega should continue to maintain its identity as a picturesque and remarkable mountain town. *U.S. News and World Report* ranked Dahlonega as the third most economical retirement location in their June 3, 2007, issue.

RECREATION

One-third of Lumpkin County, home of Dahlonega, is in the Chattahoochee National Forest, where you can find a variety of wildlife as well as trails for hiking, mountain biking, horseback riding, and four-wheel touring. The Chestatee and Etowah Rivers wind through the county, providing opportunities for fishing, canoeing, rafting, and tubing. The ruggedly beautiful 2,100-mile Appalachian Trail starts just outside Dahlonega at Springer Mountain and follows the northern border of the county, reaching elevations of over 4,000 feet. You can hike a section of the trail as a day trip or backpack up Blood Mountain and spend the night in the rustic stone cabin on the trail. The less adventuresome can drive to Woody Gap and take spectacular photos from the scenic overlook, then spend the night in one of the many rental cabins or cozy bed-and-breakfast inns in the area. Beautiful camping areas are located at Dockery Lake, Lake Winfield Scott, Amicalola State Park, and Waters Creek Recreation Area. Some of these areas have lakes for swimming and fishing and spectacular waterfalls. The Ford Tour De Georgia in April is North America's premier professional cycling event. Dahlonega is the finish point for the stage four segment; according to Lance Armstrong, the Dahlonega segment is "The Toughest Day of Racing in North America." The county maintains a boat ramp on nearby Lake Lanier. A number of RV campgrounds and resorts are available in the area for the growing number of people who choose the traveling lifestyle.

The city and county offer a variety of recreational activities and sports for all ages. Facilities include a county swimming pool, tennis courts, soccer fields, and a modern community recreation building with a kitchen and gym. The newest addition to Dahlonega's recreational offerings is the Nicklaus Golf Club at Birch River, a potentially world-class 1,100-acre, eighteen-hole golf and residential community. The first golf course in the county, it was designed by Jack Nicklaus and includes five hundred homesites in a village atmosphere. Other excellent mountain golf and residential centers are Big Canoe, Gold Creek, and Chestatee, located in adjoining counties.

 CULTURAL SCENE

Annual festivals, an integral part of the rich heritage of Dahlonega, feature mountain music, folk art, gold panning, and other unique mountain customs. When a mountain black bear wandered into the town square several years ago, the town decided to mark the occasion; an annual Bear on the Square Festival now takes place every April. This festival includes mountain crafts, bluegrass music, clogging, children's events, and a "Taste of the Mountains" food court. Dahlonega has had a reputation for attracting great bluegrass and old-time mountain music. It began hosting famous fiddling conventions in the early 1990s. You can hear live performances on the historic Public Square. The World Gold Panning Championships also occur in April. In May, Dahlonega comes into bloom with the Mountain Flower Festival of the Arts. This juried fine arts show provides an opportunity for artists from around the Southeast to show and sell their works of art.

Other popular events include the annual Fourth of July Family Day, the largest Independence Day celebration in north Georgia; and the Autumn Fest in September, sponsored by the local merchants association. Thousands of people attend Gold Rush Days in October to see spectacular fall colors and more than three hundred arts and crafts exhibitors showing their work on the square. During the Old Fashioned Christmas Celebration in December, the square is magically lit by thousands of tiny lights. Shoppers are entertained with caroling, hospitality tables, a parade, and the arrival of Old St. Nick "gold-rush style" in a horse-drawn wagon. In September, the Six Gap Century and Three Gap Fifty bike rides take place on mountain highways. The Six Gap Century ride covers one hundred miles and climbs over 10,700 feet. An average of seventeen major events take place here each year. The Buisson Art Center, located in the 1890s-era First Baptist Church, houses studios, art organizations, a gallery, and a dinner theater. The Music Hall is in the remodeled church sanctuary, and is now the premier performance venue in the North Georgia mountains.

The local Holly Theatre has been restored and hosts current movies and nine annual local community theater productions. It's listed as a national historic site. The Theater Company is one of the top ten performing theater centers in the state. The North Georgia College and State University schedules a series of free, public cultural events, including faculty and student recitals and vocal and instrumental music performances. The campus planetarium show on Friday nights is open to the public. Three local art galleries are located in the historic district.

 **MAIN STREET**

No visit to Dahlonega would be complete without a meal at the famous Smith House, one block off the square. Dinner is served family style, with platters piled high with fried chicken, sweet baked ham, roast beef, and homemade rolls, as well as bowls full of dumplings, fried okra, candied yams, and steamed vegetables. Atlanta residents drive up for Sunday dinner, waiting patiently in the front yard until there's space available at the long tables and benches in the dining room. The restaurant often serves two thousand meals to visitors on Sunday. The Smith House was converted into an inn for travelers in 1922 and still offers comfortable lodging in fifty rooms furnished with antiques.

Other fine restaurants in Dahlonega include the McGuire House, located off the square in a converted historic home; Caruso's Italian (reasonably priced Italian fare); a popular lunchtime eatery called El Maguey Mexican Restaurant; Rick's, located in the Crimson Moon Café; The Corkscrew Café (located in the former City Hall);

Dominique's Bartina, a French restaurant and pub; Pueblos (Central American); and Wylie's, where you can enjoy a full lunch or dinner, great cheesecake and coffee, and live entertainment on the weekends. Tourists are unlikely to see some of the restaurants favored by locals. Community leaders and business people like to meet for lunch at the Robyn's Nest, a great deli in the Wal-Mart shopping center. The Wagon Wheel, located on the outskirts of town, is popular with workers who want large-portioned, home-cooked lunches. Several resorts in the area offer public fine dining, including the Mountain Hideaway Resorts and the Jack Nicklaus Golf Club and Restaurant.

Dahlonega's unique shops, studios, galleries, and eateries offer an excellent example of what small towns can offer city dwellers who are tired of crowded malls. Among the more interesting shops are the Dahlonega General Store, where you can purchase marbles, classic metal signs, relishes and jellies, and coffee for a nickel a cup; Hummingbird Lane, offering nature-oriented gifts and an art gallery;

and Mountain Christmas, selling everything to enhance the holiday season. Golden Classics of Dahlonega attracts men off the "husband benches" on the sidewalks and into the store to buy gifts related to golf, hunting, and fishing. The town maintains an excellent welcome center on the square; staff can direct visitors to area accommodations and attractions. Outside the historic district, three local wineries are gearing up to turn Lumpkin County into Georgia's version of Napa Valley. The best known is the 184-acre Three Sisters Vineyards, which produced its first harvest in 2000.

 HOUSING

Drawn to Dahlonega by the mountains, new residents from metro Atlanta are changing the housing scene. Older, historic homes in town are expensive and in high demand. Moderately priced houses (30 percent lower than in town) are available outside town in the county, but there are few subdivisions and zoning restrictions. As in other rural areas, mobile homes and manufactured homes are common in the county. New apartments have been built, and there is a selection of cabins for short stays or weekend enjoyment.

There is a surprisingly good selection of large, more expensive homes ($250,000 plus) in exclusive and restricted subdivisions and in newer golf communities. The Birch River Golf Club, a gated community on the outskirts of Dahlonega, features a Jack Nicklaus golf course. Homes range from $300,000 to $750,000; space is reserved for future condos, golf villas, and townhouses. Several new active adult communities are opening around Dahlonega.

 ECONOMICS

Number of employers with fifty or more employees—10

As the tourism industry grows, the local economy is shifting from a reliance on manufacturing to a service economy. Among the larger employers are North Georgia College and University (420 employees), Mohawk Industries (350 employees), Super Wal-Mart (325 employees), Torrington Company (250 employees), and the Chestatee

Regional Hospital (250 employees). Poultry farms are scattered around the county. Residents can commute to work in north metro Atlanta or Gainesville.

 EDUCATION

High schools—1; Middle schools—1; Elementary schools—2; Private schools—1

In addition to the excellent public schools, Dahlonega is home to a private boarding and day high school that specializes in helping students in grades 7–12 with low self-esteem. North Georgia College and State University has 5,000 students and also offers continuing education classes in everything from computers to art. More than fifty majors, several master's degree programs, and one PhD program are available. The coeducational college is one of only six institutions in the United States designated as a military college by the Department of the Army. The school is listed in the current edition of *The Student Guide to America's 100 Best College Buys.*

Gainesville College, a two-year University of Georgia system college, is located in Gainesville, as is Lanier Technical College. North Georgia Technical Institute in Clarksville, another good technical college with an excellent computer program, is about forty-five miles away. The major universities of metro Atlanta, including Georgia State, Emory, Georgia Tech, and the Atlanta University Center, are within a one- to two-hour drive.

 HEALTHCARE

Chestatee Regional Hospital—52 beds; Northeast Georgia Medical Center (Gainesville)—294 beds; Physicians—25; Dentists—5

Chestatee Regional Hospital provides a full range of diagnostic and therapeutic services; facilities include a 24-hour emergency room, an intensive care unit, and a birthing center. Rehabilitation outreach programs as well as cardiopulmonary, lab, radiology, nutrition, pain management, and corporate care services are also available to the community. Northeast Georgia Health Systems operates a Neighborhood Healthcare Center in Dahlonega that is open on weekdays. Many residents choose the large Northeast

Georgia Medical Center in Gainesville, a regional referral hospital with all the services available at most urban hospitals. Open-heart surgery has recently been added to the list of services offered there.

 SPIRITUAL LIFE

Ten Christian denominations are represented. There is one synagogue.

 STAYING CONNECTED

The local *Dahlonega Nugget* is published weekly. The daily *Gainesville Times* and *Atlanta Journal-Constitution* are delivered in the county.

Dahlonega's historic square is wi-fi accessible, which is rare for a town of its size. The community is served by a local AM and FM radio station and a North Georgia College and State University FM station that is a member of the Peach State Public Radio network. Alltel provides cable television and dial-up internet service. Because of the mountain terrain, satellite television is also popular. Quigley's Rare Books and Antiques sells books. Chain bookstores can be found in nearby Gainesville.

GETTING THERE

Dahlonega is located in the north Georgia mountains, seventy miles north of Atlanta. It is on GA 60 and US 19, and is seven miles from GA 400, a major divided highway going north from Atlanta. GA 60 links Dahlonega with Gainesville. There is a small (3,000-foot runway) county airport near Dahlonega. Atlanta Hartsfield International Airport, the busiest airport in the United States, is a 90-minute drive south. Amtrak train service is available in Gainesville.

RESOURCES

Dahlonega-Lumpkin County
  Chamber of Commerce
13 South Park Street
Dahlonega, GA 30533
(800) 231-5543
www.dahlonega.org

DAHLONEGA
VITAL STATISTICS

CLIMATE

Annual average rainfall	50 inches
Snowfall	6 inches
Elevation	1,454 feet

Temperatures (in degrees Fahrenheit)

	Jan	Apr	Jul	Oct
High	48	70	86	69
Low	27	44	64	46

OCCUPATIONS

	2006	Projected 2011
Blue collar	21.1%	19.7%
White collar	58.0%	58.1%
Services	20.8%	22.2%

ADULT EDUCATION

	2000
Less than High School	23.8%
High School	21.7%
Some College	17.4%
Associates Degree	4.6%
College Degree	16.1%
Graduate Degree	16.3%

POPULATION

2006	4,703

2000-2006 Population: Annual
Compound Growth Rate   4.19%

2006-2011 Population: Annual
Compound Growth Rate   3.67%

Population by age group

	2006	Projected 2011
0-4	4.9%	5.0%
5-9	4.3%	4.2%
10-14	4.7%	4.6%
15-19	12.0%	10.9%
20-24	17.3%	16.8%
25-29	6.7%	6.2%
30-34	5.7%	5.6%
35-39	5.1%	5.2%
40-44	5.8%	5.3%
45-49	6.5%	6.7%
50-54	4.7%	5.3%
55-59	5.0%	5.4%
60-64	4.3%	5.2%
65-69	3.3%	3.6%
70-74	2.5%	2.5%
75-79	2.3%	2.3%
80-84	2.1%	2.2%
85+	2.8%	2.9%

Sources for Vital Statistics listed above can be found in the Preface to this book.

PERRY

2006 POPULATION
10,083

NEAREST CITIES
Warner Robins, GA (6 miles)
Macon, GA (26 miles)

**ESTIMATED 2006
MEDIAN HOUSEHOLD INCOME**
$39,102

COST OF LIVING
Average 3-bdrm home—$135,000
Average rent, 2-bdrm apartment—$550
Cost-of-living comparison—92.4%

SALES TAX
7%

PROPERTY TAX
Average 3-bdrm home—$1,250

Perry is often referred to as the "Crossroads of Georgia" because three major highways intersect there. An excellent quality of life and a progressive image lure new residents and businesses to this central Georgia town. Incorporated in 1824, the town was named for Commodore Oliver Perry, a famous leader in the War of 1812. The local citizens are also proud of their native son, retired United States Senator Sam Nunn Jr.

Much of Perry's recent success is attributed to the Georgia National Fairgrounds and Agricenter. The state-owned multipurpose 1,100-acre rental complex is open year-round. It is specially designed for meetings and conferences, livestock and horse shows, concerts, rodeos, RV rallies, trade shows, and sporting events. Since opening in 1990, the facility has attracted 12 million people and had an estimated direct impact of almost $700 million dollars. The beautifully landscaped site hosts many events every week, many of which are free and open to the public. The award- winning Georgia National Fair, the largest in the Southeast, draws over 350,000 people and is held at the Center over a span of ten days in early October.

Perry is also located on Georgia's Antique Trail and has become a highly respected antique center. Over 1,500 motel and hotel rooms are available, many more than other towns of this size.

 RECREATION

The Perry Recreation Department offers competitive league play for all ages. Numerous instructional classes such as gymnastics, modeling, clogging, dog obedience, dance and aerobics are also available. Perry's four city parks contain ballparks, basketball and tennis courts, one swimming facility, and two stocked fishing ponds with nature trails and picnic areas. A 28,000-square-foot community center serves both the Perry Recreation Department and local seniors. The facility provides a community room, complete with a stage and a kitchen; a gym including shower and locker facilities; and an arts and crafts room. Golf buffs will be challenged by the eighteen-hole championship courses at Houston Lake Country Club and Perry Country Club, Perry's two semiprivate country clubs. A new golf course, Southern Hills, recently opened near Hawkinsville, about fifteen miles away.

Boating and fishing are available on the Ocmulgee River in Hawkinsville and at Lake Tobesofkee Recreation Area in Macon, thirty-five miles north. Fishing and nonmotorized boating is permitted in Houston Lake, formerly part of Houston Lake Country Club. Hunting on large public and private tracts near Perry is also popular. In 1998, a successful German electronics entrepreneur opened Henderson Village, an 8,500-acre development made up of nineteenth-century homes and cottages; some buildings are original to the property and others were moved here. Guests can hunt for quail, dove, turkey, deer, and hog. Located eight miles from Perry, Henderson Village also offers guided horseback trail rides in both English and Western style.

 **CULTURAL SCENE**

Art connoisseurs and museum lovers will find that Perry offers a number of cultural attractions. A walking/driving tour covers a twelve-block route. The tour begins with the historic New Perry Hotel and includes fifty structures including historic homes, churches, and commercial buildings, some dating back to the mid-1800s and others to the early 1900s. The tour also stops at the boyhood home of former Senator Sam Nunn Jr. and a museum in the board of education building honoring his many achievements. The Perry Players acquired an old automobile showroom in the downtown district and turned it into a 168-seat community theater, where they present three to four Broadway-style performances each year. The nonprofit Perry Arts Center provides opportunities for visual arts appreciation and awareness through educational programs.

Perry offers many local festivals throughout the year. The Dogwood Festival, held in April, includes a road race, concerts, a home and garden show, and an arts and crafts show. The Mossy Creek Barnyard Festival, occurring in April and October at the Georgia National Fairgrounds, features work by national artists and craftspeople as well as music, entertainment, and food. Perry also hosts a Christmas celebration with a townwide lights display.

Perry is a convenient base for other interesting side trips. The Massee Lane Gardens, home of the American Camellia Society, is located twelve miles west of town. Beautiful walkways through gardens of camellias, azaleas, roses, dogwoods, and other perennials are situated on nine acres covered in towering pines. The Museum of Aviation at Robins Air Force Base in nearby Warner Robins is the second largest museum of the United States Air Force. Their collection of more than one hundred aircraft and missiles housed in hangars and on display outdoors spans a century of flight. The Andersonville National Cemetery and the Confederate prison site and museum chronicle American wars from the Revolution to Vietnam. Plains, Georgia, the home of former president Jimmy Carter, is an easy drive from Perry.

 MAIN STREET

Tourists and residents alike visit the famous New Perry Hotel in the heart of the town for lunch or dinner. The original Perry Hotel was erected in 1870 to accommodate the stagecoach line and the extension of the railroad into Perry. The current structure was built in 1925 on the site of the old building. The hotel stands in a flower garden designed to bloom year-round. The restaurant and tavern at the New Perry Hotel is a middle Georgia institution. More than eighty percent of the diners have eaten at the hotel before, including many tourists who plan their trips to or from Florida to arrive in Perry at mealtime. The hotel makes its own rolls and pies, cuts its own meat, cooks whole turkeys, and always serves cream of turkey soup on Sundays.

On the outskirts of Perry is Angelina's Italian Garden Café, a local favorite offering Italian food, a lounge, and music and dancing on the weekend. At the Langston House Restaurant, located in Henderson Village, diners can enjoy meals that are "the absolute best dining experience" in the state according to Ed Lightsey, critic and restaurant reviewer for *Georgia Trend* magazine.

A quaint collection of shops graces the renovated Williamsburg-style downtown area. Sidewalks are lined with majestic dogwood trees, benches, and beds of colorful flowers. Large malls are located in Macon, and Atlanta is 100 miles away.

 HOUSING

Housing in Perry is an excellent value. Overall, the housing cost in the county is about 65 percent of the national average. Renovated colonial and Victorian homes enhance the beauty of the downtown district. Mammoth pecan trees canopy highways and roads, producing a seductive and welcome shade. Rambling acreage around houses and farms is very much a part of the landscape, and property with land is often affordable in rural parts of the county.

There are homes on large lots with underground utilities in numerous subdivision. Many of these houses cost less than $135,000. The Houston Lake Country Club has homes from $250,000 to over $500,000, but these same homes would be priced considerably higher in Atlanta, Charlotte, or other large Southern cities. Rural acreage in the county ranges from $5,000 to $7,000 per acre. Apartments are plentiful and rent prices are very modest. There are gated, conventional, and manu-factured home communities in the county, as well as several assisted-living facilities. Houston Springs is a new master-planned 500-acre golf community. It's a gated com-munity for active adults 55 and over, offering an 18-hole golf course, tennis, swimming, a fitness center, social activities, and more. Prices start in the mid $100,000s.

 ECONOMICS

Number of employers with fifty or more employees—12

Ideally located along Interstate 75, Perry has made tourism its num-ber one industry. More than eigh-teen hundred residents are employed in hospitality-related businesses. Many Perry residents work at Robins Air Force Base in neighboring Warner Robins. The Robins Base, which has a total workforce of 25,000, including 4,500 military personnel, is unlikely to face any serious work-force reduction. Other large employers include Graphic Pack-aging International, a beverage packaging facility; Perdue Farms, with approximately 1,850 employ-ees; and Frito Lay Corporation, with approximately 1,000 employ-ees. Row crops, livestock, and forestry also play a major role in the economy. Perry is near the heart of the peanut and peach pro-duction and processing industry.

 EDUCATION

High schools—1; Middle schools—1; Elementary schools—5; Private schools—1

Four schools in the county have won National Blue Ribbon School of Excellence Awards from the U.S. Department of Education. Stu-dents routinely achieve scores above the national norms on the

Scholastic Aptitude Test and the Iowa Test of Basic Skills. Pupils attend one facility for kindergarten and first grade and a second one for the remaining elementary grades. Between 2003 and 2005 four schools opened, and five more are to open by the fall of 2009.

Eight colleges are located within a fifty-mile radius of Perry. Macon, is home to three colleges: Macon State College, a division of the University System of Georgia; Mercer University, a private four-year college with a liberal arts program and schools of law, medicine, and engineering; and Wesleyan College, a private four-year women's college. Fort Valley State University, a four-year liberal arts college that is part of the University System of Georgia, is thirteen miles from Perry. Other nearby institutions include Georgia College and State University in Milledgeville, Middle Georgia College in Cochran, and Georgia Southwestern College in Americus. Middle Georgia Technical College in Warner Robins offers technical programs. Adult non-credit continuing education is offered at most of these schools.

 HEALTHCARE

Perry Hospital—45 beds; Houston Medical Center (Warner Robins)— 186 beds; Physicians—38; Dentists—7

Perry Hospital offers 24-hour emergency services, intensive care, surgery, radiology, and more. Houston Medical Center is fifteen miles north of Perry Hospital and provides 24-hour emergency services, surgery, obstetrics and maternity services, pediatrics, neonatal intensive care, behavioral health and psychiatric treatment, pain treatment, and full radiology services. Both hospitals are part of Houston Healthcare, the nonprofit county healthcare system that also operates the Houston Heart Institute for cardiac-related diagnostic and rehabilitation services.

 SPIRITUAL LIFE

Ten Christian denominations are represented. A variety of places of worship are available in both Warner Robins and Macon. The closest synagogue is in Atlanta.

STAYING CONNECTED

The local newspaper, the *Houston Home Journal,* is published daily. Other daily newspapers available include the *Macon Telegraph* and the *Atlanta Journal-Constitution.* Cable television broadcasts stations based in Macon. A Perry radio station offers both AM and FM formats. National internet service is available. There are three bookstores in the area; Perry Bookstore is in the historic downtown.

 GETTING THERE

Situated on US 41, US 341, and I-75, the major interstate highway between Atlanta and central Florida, Perry is in the geographic center of Georgia. The Golden Isles Parkway, a main route to coastal Georgia, begins in Perry at I-75. The Perry–Houston County Airport, with a 5,000-foot runway, serves local general aviation needs, and the Macon–Lewis Wilson Airport in Macon is the closest commercial airport.

 RESOURCES

Perry Area
  Chamber of Commerce
101 Courtney Hodges Boulevard
Perry, GA 31069
(912) 987-1234
www.perry-georgia.com

PERRY
VITAL STATISTICS

CLIMATE

Annual average rainfall	47 inches
Snowfall	0 inches
Elevation	900 feet

Temperatures (in degrees Fahrenheit)

	Jan	Apr	Jul	Oct
High	57	79	91	78
Low	34	51	69	52

OCCUPATIONS

	2006	Projected 2011
Blue collar	23.7%	22.2%
White collar	52.6%	53.2%
Services	23.7%	24.6%

ADULT EDUCATION

	2000
Less than High School	24.8%
High School	34.4%
Some College	18.3%
Associates Degree	4.8%
College Degree	11.8%
Graduate Degree	5.9%

POPULATION

2006	10,083
2000-2006 Population: Annual Compound Growth Rate	0.79%
2006-2011 Population: Annual Compound Growth Rate	2.03%

Population by age group

	2006	Projected 2011
0-4	7.0%	6.9%
5-9	6.0%	6.0%
10-14	6.6%	6.1%
15-19	6.4%	6.0%
20-24	7.9%	6.7%
25-29	6.9%	7.8%
30-34	6.3%	6.3%
35-39	5.7%	6.2%
40-44	7.7%	5.8%
45-49	8.5%	7.9%
50-54	6.5%	7.9%
55-59	6.2%	6.5%
60-64	4.6%	5.8%
65-69	3.1%	3.6%
70-74	3.3%	2.7%
75-79	2.5%	2.8%
80-84	2.4%	2.2%
85+	2.3%	2.7%

Sources for Vital Statistics listed above can be found in the Preface to this book.

ST. MARYS

2006 POPULATION
16,458

NEAREST CITIES
Jacksonville, FL (40 miles)
Brunswick, GA (30 miles)

ESTIMATED 2006 MEDIAN HOUSEHOLD INCOME
$53,625

COST OF LIVING
Average 3-bdrm home—$195,000
Average rent, 2-bdrm apartment—$700
Cost-of-living comparison—93%

SALES TAX
7%

PROPERTY TAX
Average 3-bdrm home—$1,500

St. Marys was settled in the 1500s and is one of the oldest cities in the United States. The English formally established the town in 1787. In the 1990s, thanks to the opening of the ten-thousand-staff Kings Bay Submarine Base, it became a boomtown. In 1996, *Money* magazine rated St. Marys as the number one small town in Amerca.

The quiet beauty of the historic area results from a unique blend of graceful old homes and charming churches, wide welcoming avenues, and gentle ocean breezes. Osborne Street, lined with white picket fences, swaying palm trees, and ancient live oaks, runs through the center of St. Marys. A four-block promenade to the waterfront is lined with historic buildings, interesting shops, bed-and-breakfast inns, and restaurants. You can stroll through the Oak Grove Cemetery, established in 1780, or walk the quiet, idyllic historic district and marvel at the original and restored architecture dating back as early as 1801.

Further inland, the newer part of St. Marys consists of the usual assortment of modern stores, restaurants, and suburban conveniences on US 40 and other major roads. The separation between the historic district and the rest of the town is so pronounced that it is almost as if two towns adjoin each other.

Cumberland Island, one of the country's richest eco-tourism destinations, is visible from the waterfront. Herds of wild horses, white-tailed deer, wild turkeys, and other wildlife inhabit the island, and loggerhead turtles nest on the seventeen miles of secluded and spacious white sand beaches. The island achieved worldwide fame when John F. Kennedy Jr. was married there in 1996. The largest wilderness island and the southernmost barrier island in the United States, Cumberland Island National Seashore can be reached in forty-five minutes by a daily

pedestrian ferry from St. Marys.

There is much beauty and grace to experience in this waterfront town. This modern and expanding community, deeply committed to retaining its charm as a historic coastal village, offers residents the best of both worlds.

 **RECREATION**

The Cumberland Island National Seashore is a major recreational attraction for this small coastal town. On Cumberland Island, you can explore the beach, the maritime forest, and the marshes, or watch for wild horses and other wildlife roaming freely on the island. Swimming, fishing, and camping are also popular. The elegant Greyfield Inn, opened in 1901 by the Carnegie family, is now a nationally known bed-and-breakfast inn. Today it is still operated by the family and is the only overnight accommodation on the island besides camping. The passenger ferry (no cars allowed on the island) operates seven days a week, March 1 through November 30, and makes two trips per day.

Laurel Island Links Golf Course is open to the public. The eighteen-hole private Osprey Cove golf course has received a four-and-a-half-star rating from *Golf Digest* and has been ranked in the top one hundred modern courses in the United States by *GolfWeek*. You can enjoy world-class golf on magnificently groomed grounds set among tidal inlets and pristine marshes. Two modern marinas on St. Marys River can accommodate everything from large luxury yachts to small fishing boats. Kayak instruction and tours are available. Crooked River State Park provides cottages and facilities for swimming, fishing, camping, waterskiing, and boating. The county recreation department offers both indoor and outdoor programs for youth.

 **CULTURAL SCENE**

Several celebrations and festivals are held in St. Marys throughout the year. One of the best is the huge fireworks show on the Fourth of July. The annual Rock Shrimp Festival takes place in early October, and the traditional historic Christmas Tour is held the second Saturday in December. Other attractions include a local theater group; the Orange Hall Museum; the Submarine Museum; St Marys Aquatic Center; the amphitheater in Waterfront Park on St. Marys River; and the Cumberland Island National Seashore Museum in downtown St. Marys, which includes memorabilia from the Gilded Age and the War of 1812 and exhibits of the flora and fauna of Cumberland Island. Big city cultural attractions can be found in Jacksonville, Florida, about 45 minutes south.

 **MAIN STREET**

Check out these eateries on the riverfront that feature the area's abundant seafood: Lang's Marina Restaurant; Riverside Cafe, located in the historic Riverview Hotel; Pauly's Café; Sterling's Southern Cafe; Lang's Seafood Restaurant; Sorrell Creek Landing; and St. Marys Seafood and Steakhouse. For those seeking a romantic place for an overnight stay, the famous Greyfield Inn on Cumberland Island serves an elegant candlelight dinner to inn guests.

Those who rely on nearby urban services will appreciate the proximity to shopping, cultural events, and other attractions in Jacksonville, Florida.

 HOUSING

Housing choices in St. Marys are plentiful and varied. Older, restored homes for sale in the historic section are limited and somewhat expensive. There are many modestly priced subdivisions outside the historic section, where homes sell for $140,000 to $200,000. Osprey Cove, a popular gated golf community, has one of the best golf courses in Georgia. The homes range from $300,000 to over $1 million in this 1,200-acre community with one thousand homesites. Building lots start under $100,000. The 2004 HGTV Dream Home was located in Cumberland Harbor, a waterfront community. Home sites start at $200,000 and go up to $2 million.

 ECONOMICS

Number of employers with fifty or more employees—9

When the Kings Bay Naval Submarine Base opened in 1982, the local economy took off as St. Marys and the surrounding area expanded to provide housing and services for the ten thousand military personnel and civilians working on the base. Major employers are Camden County Schools (1,200 employees), V. T. Griffin (650 employees), Express Scripts (550 employees), Lockheed Missiles & Space (495 employees), and Camden County Government (300 employees).

 EDUCATION

High schools—1; Middle schools— 1; Elementary schools—5; Private schools—1

The county school system serving St. Marys has an excellent reputation. Higher education institutions include Coastal Georgia Community College at Brunswick; a branch of the University of North Florida at Jacksonville, Florida; and Valdosta State University at Valdosta (95 miles away).

HEALTHCARE

Camden Campus, Southeast Georgia Regional Medical Center—40 beds; Southeast Georgia Regional Medical Center (Brunswick)—340 beds; Physicians—50; Dentists—15

Since St. Marys is growing rapidly, the number of local medical professionals and facilities is expanding. The Camden Campus of the Southeast Georgia Regional Medical Center has 24-hour emergency room service. Southeast Georgia Regional Medical Center in Brunswick offers a 24-hour emergency department, maternity and cardiac care, MRI and CAT scan capability, oncology, psychiatry, and many other services. For major medical services, residents may also choose from several hospitals in Jacksonville. Among them are St. Vincent's Medical Center, a 528-bed full-service tertiary care medical center; Shands Jacksonville, a 760-bed affiliate of the University of Florida Medical School; and Orange Park Medical Center. The world-famous Mayo Clinic of Rochester, Minnesota, has a branch in Jacksonville.

 SPIRITUAL LIFE

Ten major Christian denominations are represented. Synagogues and many other places of worship are available in Jacksonville.

 STAYING CONNECTED

The main local daily paper is the *Georgian Times-Union*, published by the *Jacksonville Times-Union*. The *Camden Tribune & The Georgian* is published twice a week. Newspapers from Brunswick and Jacksonville are also delivered. Cable television offers major network stations. Local internet service is also available. Once Upon a Bookseller, located in the historic district, is one of two local bookstores.

 GETTING THERE

St. Marys is located at the end of US 40, nine miles east of I-95, in the southeast corner of Georgia. The town is on the St. Marys River, which empties into the Intracoastal Waterway and the Atlantic Ocean. The Intracoastal Waterway provides safe passage up the coast of Georgia for small to medium-large-size craft. St. Marys has a local airport with a 5,000-foot lighted runway for private aircraft. Commercial airline service with more than twelve major and commuter airlines is available in Jacksonville.

 RESOURCES

St. Marys Convention
& Visitors Bureau
406 Osborne Street
St. Marys, GA 31558
(800) 868-8687
www.stmaryswelcome.com
www.gacoast.com

ST. MARY'S
VITAL STATISTICS

CLIMATE

Annual average rainfall	51 inches
Snowfall	0 inches
Elevation	13 feet

Temperatures (in degrees Fahrenheit)

	Jan	Apr	Jul	Oct
High	62	77	89	78
Low	42	57	72	62

OCCUPATIONS

	2006	Projected 2011
Blue collar	21.7%	20.1%
White collar	56.1%	56.3%
Services	22.1%	23.6%

ADULT EDUCATION

	2000
Less than High School	12.9%
High School	31.3%
Some College	26.3%
Associates Degree	7.9%
College Degree	13.8%
Graduate Degree	7.8%

POPULATION

2006	16,458
2000-2006 Population: Annual Compound Growth Rate	2.90%
2006-2011 Population: Annual Compound Growth Rate	2.10%

Population by age group

	2006	Projected 2011
0-4	9.3%	9.7%
5-9	7.7%	7.9%
10-14	7.9%	7.1%
15-19	8.1%	6.4%
20-24	7.0%	7.4%
25-29	10.8%	8.2%
30-34	8.9%	11.7%
35-39	8.3%	8.1%
40-44	8.2%	7.6%
45-49	6.8%	7.2%
50-54	5.0%	5.7%
55-59	4.1%	4.4%
60-64	2.6%	3.2%
65-69	1.9%	1.9%
70-74	1.4%	1.3%
75-79	1.1%	1.0%
80-84	0.5%	0.7%
85+	0.5%	0.5%

Sources for Vital Statistics listed above can be found in the Preface to this book.

2006 POPULATION
14,140

NEAREST CITIES
Brunswick, GA (5 miles)
Jacksonville, FL (65 miles)
Savannah, GA (75 miles)

ESTIMATED 2006 MEDIAN HOUSEHOLD INCOME
$73,529

COST OF LIVING
Average 3-bdrm home—$300,000
Average rent, 2-bdrm apartment—$1,000
Cost-of-living comparison—93%

SALES TAX
6%

PROPERTY TAX
Average 3-bdrm home—$3,000

About the size of Manhattan, St. Simons Island is the largest of the barrier islands that lie off Georgia's Atlantic coast. The semitropical climate, abundance of sunshine, and gentle Atlantic breezes make it both a popular resort and a sought-after permanent residence. Stands of swaying, moss-laden oaks, acres of lush marshland, and a range of historic sites evoke the island's rich and colorful past.

Gold-seeking Spanish explorers landed here in the 1500s. The English built Fort Frederica on St. Simons in 1736 to protect themselves from the Spanish. John and Charles Wesley, the founders of Methodism, began their American mission here in 1737. Christ Church is the third-oldest Episcopal church in the country. The mast of the famous

American sailing ship, *Old Ironsides*, was cut from the beloved live oak trees native to this area.

Today the island provides residents with outstanding boating, golf, tennis, miles of bike trails, an active art and theater life, fine dining and nightlife, excellent shopping, and a relaxed, playful lifestyle. Shopping areas and office complexes must follow architectural guidelines, including four-story height limitations, to blend with the historic and natural landscape. A gleaming white lighthouse still guides ships into the St. Simons Sound and stands guard over the village center and fishing pier. Vacationers come to visit for a week and find themselves hunting for permanent residences here. Often compared favorably to Hilton Head, South Carolina, St. Simons is one of the most sought-after coastal communities for early retirees. St. Simons Island is unincorporated, with all municipal services provided by the county government.

 **RECREATION**

Golf is a year-round preoccupation here. There are more golf courses in the area—216 holes—than any place in Georgia outside of Atlanta. Seven of the courses are public or semiprivate.

Boating opportunities in the Atlantic, the Intracoastal Waterway, and nearby rivers are plentiful. Charter fishing boats are available for offshore fishing. Surf fishing from the beach or off the St. Simons village pier is a favorite pastime. Dolphin tours are popular, and some of the best kayak tours in the country explore the marsh creeks and the pristine coastal islands.

You can easily find instruction in popular sports, including sailing, parasailing, scuba diving, kayaking, tennis, golfing, and horseback riding. Residents and visitors alike enjoy biking on the twenty miles of paved bike and jogging paths here and on nearby Jekyll Island. Tennis players can choose from thirteen clay tennis courts and seventeen hard courts. There are three public swimming pools, with one large pool on the beach by the lighthouse and pier. A total of thirty-two parks offer beach and picnic areas, athletic fields, tennis courts, playgrounds, boat ramps, and community buildings.

Jekyll Island is one of the few places on the Georgia coast that offers horseback riding on the beach. Jekyll Island's ten miles of wide, sandy beaches are perfect for a relaxing stroll, collecting sea-shells, or sunbathing. A private campground is located on the island. Young visitors to the Summer Waves Water Park on Jekyll Island can enjoy giant water slides, a huge wave pool, and a variety of water-park activities.

The breathtakingly beautiful seven-mile beach at Little St. Simons Island is awash in shells. Loggerhead sea turtles come ashore at night during nesting season to lay their eggs. Visitors can reach the island by boat and they can stay at a private lodge. Blythe Island Regional Campground, near Brunswick, offers camping facilities and forty recreational vehicle campsites near five hundred acres of wooded area fronting two salt-water rivers and a marsh.

 CULTURAL SCENE

The community composed of St. Simons Island, Jekyll Island, Sea Island, and the small city of Brunswick is one of the most culturally rich in the South. The historic Ritz Theatre (built in 1898) in downtown Brunswick plays host to nearly one hundred events each year, including the Preservation Hall Jazz Band, the local civic ballet company, and the symphony orchestra. More than twenty-five organizations in the county are dedicated to the arts and humanities. There are over twenty art galleries in the area. Several well-known artists have lived here, including the late Eugenia Price, author of many books set in the area.

The calendar of events will keep visitors and residents busy from spring through fall. The Georgia Sea Island Singers perform each year at the Georgia Sea Island Heritage Festival. The Beach Music Festival on Jekyll Island delivers a fun-filled weekend. Reflections Along the Shore, an art show, takes place in August at the Left Bank Art Gallery in St. Simons. At the end of August, residents and visitors bring blankets and picnic dinners to Jazz in the Park and enjoy an outdoor concert by the water. In mid-September, the Artist Attic Sale is held at the Coastal Center for the Arts. Sapelo Cultural Day celebrates the local Gullah/Geechee culture with dance, music, storytelling, and folklore of native Sapelo Island residents. Since St. Simons is so attuned to writers and artists, there are opportunities to attend local shows and events at the many galleries and bookstores. Local and regional bands play at several of the restaurants, cafés, and bars on weekend nights.

Historic sites draw residents and visitors to learn more about the cultural significance of the Golden Isles. The 104-foot-tall St. Simons Island lighthouse, a short walk from the pier and central business district, is the most visited and recognizable lighthouse in Georgia. The original structure was built in 1808; the current lighthouse was built in 1872, about twenty-five feet from the first site, and continues to guide ships into the St. Simons Sound. Visitors can tour the Museum of Coastal History in the keeper's cottage at the base of the lighthouse, and climb to the top for a breathtaking panoramic view. Christ Church, the third oldest Episcopal Church in the country, is still in use today.

The National Park Service maintains the ruins of Fort Frederica and its once-thriving river community, affording visitors a glimpse of coastal life in prerevolutionary Georgia.

Jekyll Island was the home of many early twentieth-century millionaires, including the Rockefellers, Pulitzers, Goulds, Morgans, and Astors, who flocked to the island and built private vacation "cottages"—mansions by today's standards—and a clubhouse. With the onset of the Great Depression, their retreat fell on hard times. The State of Georgia purchased the island, and in 1978, the 240-acre district of former millionaires' homes was designated a National Historic Landmark. Visitors can tour several of the restored homes, and a visitors center and museum depicts the grand lifestyle of the famous part-time residents.

More historic attractions are located in Brunswick, including the beautiful Glynn County Courthouse (1907) and the Hofwyl-Broadfield Plantation.

 **MAIN STREET**

The Golden Isles resort area supports a multitude of restaurants and entertainment options to meet the tastes of summer visitors, young and old. Located near the pier and lighthouse, the village of St. Simons is filled with interesting shops, good restaurants, and nighttime entertainment. Most of the stores and restaurants in the village are on Mallory Street, which runs right down to the pier. Eight more cozy shopping villages with restaurants and inviting stores populate the center of the island.

To sample the local ambience in a more formal setting, visit Chelsea's Restaurant (prime rib, great pasta dishes); or Spankys Seafood Company, two locations, one on the large waterfront with great views and two huge outdoor decks (fresh Southern-style seafood). If you prefer a casual atmosphere and porch dining, you can eat at Mullet Bay Seafood Restaurant (outstanding seafood, salads, and burgers); for dining in a rustic atmosphere, try the Crab Trap (excellent fresh seafood, crab soup, hush puppies,

and coleslaw). Other local favorites are Barbara Jean's (delicious crab cakes); and Brogen's North (good crab sandwiches).

Brunswick has two restaurants of special note, the Cargo Portside Grill downtown (creative menu in a hip, friendly space) and Jinright's Seafood House (all-you-can-eat shrimp plates with hush puppies and coleslaw). The Cloister, a five-star resort on Sea Island (linked by a short bridge to St. Simons), opened in 1928 and has been visited by nearly every United States president since. The Cloister offers hotel rooms, beach cottages, a spa, stables, a golf course, tennis courts, miles of private beach, and a formal restaurant. The Jekyll Island Club Hotel, once a millionaire's club, is now a four-star resort serving gourmet cuisine.

 HOUSING

Housing choices are plentiful on St. Simons Island and in Brunswick. Spanish moss–draped live oak trees frame lushly landscaped coastal-style homes. Bike paths are common throughout St. Simons, Sea, and Jekyll Islands, making short trips to the beach easy.

Prices are high on St. Simons Island, Sea Island, and Jekyll Island, but are comparable to other island resort towns. Houses on St. Simons Island range from $200,000 to over $1 million; the average price is between $300,000 and $350,000. St. Simons Island boasts several gated communities, some offering golf or waterfront amenities. Condominiums are popular, and many are part of seasonal rental programs. Luxury apartment homes have been built in recent years. The average home price on Sea Island is $4 million. A modest, three-bedroom, two-bath home on Jekyll is $450,000 and up. Condominiums, often purchased for investment-rental potential, average $250,000 to $300,000 for a modest two-bedroom, two-bath unit. Brunswick houses are considerably less than properties on the islands. Housing styles in the area include Victorian-Edwardian homes near historic downtown, single-story town homes and cottage communities, and gated golf communities on the coastal marshes. Retirement communities are available, along with several assisted-living facilities.

 ECONOMICS

Number of employers with fifty or more employees—30

Tourism is the number one employer in the area, with retail sales as the main component. Brunswick, a major seaport, is an increasingly important East Coast import-export center for automobiless and grain. Additional industries in Brunswick include paper and food processing, chemical manufacturing, metal fabrication, and beverage distribution. Major employers include the Federal Law Enforcement Training Center (3,047 employees); Sea Island Company (2,100 employees); Glynn County Board of Education (1,900 employees); Southeast Georgia Health Systems, Brunswick Campus (1,682 employees); Koch Cellulose Georgia Pacific (790 employees); Rich-Seapak (600 employees); King & Prince Seafood (570 employees); and Super Wal-Mart (550 employees).

 EDUCATION

High schools—2 (Brunswick); Middle schools—2 (Brunswick); Elementary schools—9 (St. Simons Island and Brunswick); Private schools—5

The county school system has three National Schools of Excellence and seven Georgia public Schools of Excellence. Coastal Georgia Community College in Brunswick offers two-year associate's degrees, and credits from the college transfer to four-year colleges in the University of Georgia system. Georgia Southern University, located in nearby Statesboro, has a branch at Coastal Georgia Community Campus Brunswick. Residents can take continuing education classes in a variety of fields at the same campus.

 HEALTHCARE

Southeast Georgia Regional Medical Center (Brunswick)—316 beds; Physicians—140; Dentists—35

An urgent-care facility operated by Southeast Georgia Regional Medical Center is located on St. Simons Island. The main branch in Brunswick offers a wide variety of services, including a 24-hour emergency department, full surgery services, maternity care, cardiac rehabilitation, and oncology.

 SPIRITUAL LIFE

There are twenty-five Christian denominations represented in Brunswick and the three islands. There is a synagogue in Brunswick.

 **STAYING CONNECTED**

The *Brunswick News* is published daily and covers the Golden Isles. The *Georgia Times-Union* is a supplement of the daily *Jacksonville Times-Union*. The *Atlanta Journal-Constitution* is available to local subscribers. Other local newspapers are two biweeklies, *Glynco Observer* and *Jekyll's Golden Islander;* the weekly *Harbor Sound;* and the weekly the *Islander*. Tourist-oriented guides to island life are distributed seasonally in shops and restaurants and through the Chamber of Commerce. Cable television offers programming from five stations in Jacksonville and three stations in Savannah, plus all other major cable networks. There are fourteen radio stations in the county. Approximately a dozen providers offer local internet service. Two well-known bookstores, G. J. Ford

Bookshop and the BookMark, offer frequent book signings. Another bookstore is located in Brunswick.

 GETTING THERE

Located on the southeastern coast of Georgia, St. Simons Island is five miles east of Brunswick at US 17. A causeway connects the island to the mainland. I-95, the major interstate along the eastern seaboard, is approximately twelve miles west. On the island, Malcolm McKinnon Airport has a lighted, 5,800-foot runway. The airport offers private jet maintenance, charter and rental service. During the summer, airplane tours of the island are available at reasonable rates. Brunswick Golden Isles Airport, six miles north of Brunswick, has an 8,000-foot runway and daily nonstop commuter jet flights to Atlanta on ASA Delta Connection, a Delta Airline partner. Jacksonville International Airport, with over a dozen national airlines, provides air service to major cities throughout the United States.

Brunswick is the nation's westernmost port on the Atlantic coast; its channel width and draft accommodate large car and grain ships and break-bulk and other ocean freighters. The Intracoastal Waterway has many full-service marinas in the area for docking. Small cruise ships stop at St. Simons Island to allow passengers the opportunity to tour the area and shop.

 RESOURCES

Brunswick-Golden Isles
  Chamber of Commerce
4 Glynn Avenue
Brunswick, GA 31520
(912) 265-0620
www.bgiccc.com

Additional area websites:
www.coastalgeorgia.com
www.stsimonswebsite.com
www.stsimonsexperience.com
www.bgicoc.com

ST. SIMONS ISLAND
VITAL STATISTICS

CLIMATE

Annual average rainfall	51 inches
Snowfall	0 inches
Elevation	Sea Level

Temperatures (in degrees Fahrenheit)

	Jan	Apr	Jul	Oct
High	61	77	91	79
Low	39	56	72	59

OCCUPATIONS

	2006	Projected 2011
Blue collar	8.5%	7.9%
White collar	75.6%	75.0%
Services	15.9%	17.1%

ADULT EDUCATION

	2000
Less than High School	4.5%
High School	13.4%
Some College	23.9%
Associates Degree	6.7%
College Degree	31.2%
Graduate Degree	20.3%

POPULATION

2006	14,140
2000-2006 Population: Annual Compound Growth Rate	0.89%
2006-2011 Population: Annual Compound Growth Rate	0.86%

Population by age group

	2006	Projected 2011
0-4	3.8%	4.0%
5-9	4.3%	3.9%
10-14	5.0%	4.9%
15-19	5.5%	4.8%
20-24	4.3%	4.4%
25-29	3.1%	4.5%
30-34	4.6%	3.5%
35-39	5.5%	5.0%
40-44	6.7%	6.4%
45-49	7.1%	7.6%
50-54	9.5%	7.8%
55-59	9.1%	10.1%
60-64	8.2%	8.7%
65-69	5.4%	7.3%
70-74	5.2%	4.7%
75-79	4.8%	4.4%
80-84	4.0%	4.0%
85+	4.0%	4.3%

Sources for Vital Statistics listed above can be found in the Preface to this book.

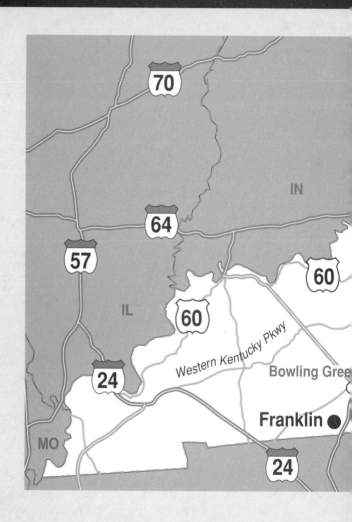

KENTUCKY

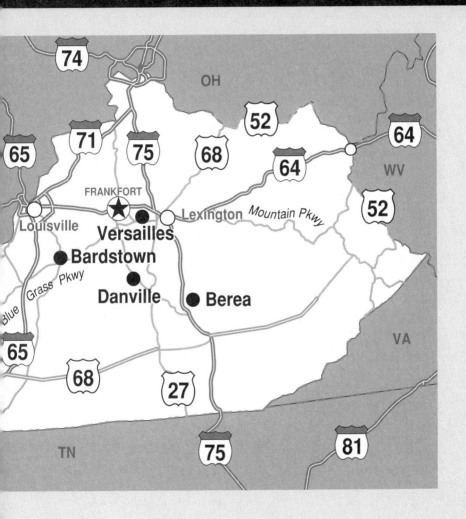

OH

74

52

64

71

65

75

68

64

WV

52

FRANKFORT

Louisville

Lexington   *Mountain Pkwy*

Versailles

Bardstown

Blue Grass Pkwy

Danville

Berea

VA

65

68

27

TN

75

81

BARDSTOWN

2006 POPULATION
11,326

NEAREST CITIES
Louisville, KY (34 miles)
Lexington, KY (58 miles)

ESTIMATED 2006
MEDIAN HOUSEHOLD INCOME
$43,280

COST OF LIVING
Average 3-bdrm home—$85,000
Average rent, 2-bdrm apartment—$500
Cost-of-living comparison—94.7%

SALES TAX
6%

PROPERTY TAX
Average 3-bdrm home—$785

Considered a bedroom community by some because of its proximity to Louisville, Bardstown offers a beautiful countryside setting, an impressively restored downtown historic district, a growth-minded business community that is guided by efficient planning, and a friendly and diverse community. Situated in Nelson County, Bardstown is home to skilled workers, farmers, educators, and government workers, as well as business owners, musicians and artists, and retirees.

Known as Historic Bardstown, this Kentucky village was first settled in 1780 by families from Virginia, Maryland, and Pennsylvania, and is the second oldest town in the state. The city was named after William Baird, who received one thousand acres under a land grant from the Virginia General Assembly. In 1785, a group of Maryland Catholics came to the region, and in 1812, the church sent Bishop Benedict Joseph Flaget to oversee this early diocese. A seminary was created and Saint Mary's College was established. By the late 1800s, Catholics made up the largest religious group in the county. In 1841, the bishop moved the diocese headquarters to Louisville, but the Catholic heritage is alive today in Bardstown.

In spite of its supposed neutrality, Kentucky was divided during the Civil War. General Braxton Bragg and his twenty-six thousand Confederate soldiers camped around Bardstown before moving on to Perryville, where the tragic Battle of Perryville took the lives of seventy-five hundred soldiers. Bardstown faced another challenge with the onset of Prohibition in the 1920s. Bourbon making had been a booming Bardstown business since the late 1700s; by the late 1800s there were twenty-six distilleries in the county. When Prohibition began, the distilleries were forced to close, leaving many workers without jobs. The county was unable to develop a substitute industry, and workers struggled to develop new trades. Out of these hard times came a willingness to explore, change, and adapt—qualities that are still evident. Town leaders have forged a balance between progressiveness and historic preservation. Home to four distilleries, Bardstown is now known as "The Bourbon Capital of the World."

Today, Bardstown is a friendly and close-knit community where shopkeepers know residents by name and people feel safe walking at night. The town has not only kept a feeling of intimacy, it has also retained its historical integrity: three hundred structures in the Bardstown historic district and surrounding area, many of them beautifully restored, are listed on the National Register of Historic Places. Bards-town visitors will notice the town's dedication to preserving its historic tradition as well as its simple elegance and authentic sense of community.

 **RECREATION**

Nelson County's forests, three rivers, and numerous springs

present opportunities for a wide variety of recreational activities. My Old Kentucky Home State Park is the site of Federal Hill, the inspiration for Stephen Foster's nostalgic song. The park has an eighteen-hole regulation golf course, campgrounds, and picnic areas. Each summer, thousands come to the park to see the long-running outdoor play, *Stephen Foster—The Musical.*

Bernheim Arboretum and Research Forest (15 miles) encompasses acres of exquisite gardens and calm lakes, as well as a nature center, a research forest, and thirty miles of hiking trails. I. W. Bernheim, a German immigrant who developed his fortune through the whiskey business, donated fourteen thousand acres in 1929 to the people of Kentucky. The arboretum on the grounds contains 240 acres with almost two thousand varieties of trees—including 185 varieties of hollies—and is home to over 250 species of birds. There is a Visitors Center, and a Nature Center Museum, offering educational programs and serving as a display center for nature art. The

Arboretum Center is surrounded by vibrant-colored perennial gardens and a water-lily pool. Bernheim's love of art inspired him to include numerous bronze, metal, and stone sculptures throughout the garden. Picnicking and fishing are permitted on the grounds.

There are several state parks within about thirty miles of Bardstown. Bardstown boasts three community parks. There are walking trails just north of town in Nazareth and south at the Abbey of Gethsemani, where world-famous author Thomas Merton lived and is buried. Taylorsville State Park, which surrounds a 3,050-acre lake, covers 1,600 acres; visitors can explore the fabulous landscape on horseback or by foot on the sixteen-mile trail system. E. P. "Tom" Sawyer State Park, located just outside Louisville, honors one of the city's leaders (also the father of Diane Sawyer, host of *Good Morning America);* it features an activity center with a gymnasium, a pool and bathhouse, and hiking trails on 369 acres. Lincoln Homestead Park celebrates the heritage of Abraham Lincoln's parents, Thomas Lincoln and Nancy Hanks. This park includes the Berry House, childhood home of Nancy Hanks, and a replica of Thomas Lincoln's cabin. Visitors can also enjoy the eighteen-hole golf course and the picnic areas. Sympson Lake, a local reservoir, is located on the outskirts of town and provides opportunities for boating and fishing.

One nine-hole golf course and four eighteen-hole courses are in the area, including the May Wood Golf Course, an eighteen-hole championship course with tennis courts galore. The Bardstown-Nelson County Recreation Department offers an abundance of youth and adult sports teams and leagues, a swimming pool, and tennis courts. The new county seventeen-acre park is home to nine soccer and football fields.

My Old Kentucky Dinner Train offers a thirty-five-mile excursion in a 1940 dining car that winds through the picturesque countryside of Rolling Fork River Valley. Locals recommend the impressive five-course dinner that is served during the trip. The Bluegrass

Speedway just outside of town hosts dirt track racing from mid-April to mid-October. College basketball cannot go unmentioned. Avid Bardstown fans are more than willing to drive to the games at the University of Kentucky (Lexington) and the University of Louisville.

 CULTURAL SCENE

Bardstown offers a wide variety of cultural opportunities to residents and visitors. Federal Hill was home to the Rowan family, cousins of Stephen Foster. The mansion was the inspiration for Foster's ballad, "My Old Kentucky Home." Stephen Foster's music and life are celebrated in the outdoor production, *Stephen Foster— The Musical,* which has played for over 48 years. Old Bardstown Village, in the heart of town, includes nine log cabins dating from 1776 to 1820 and portrays the life and work of Bardstonians in the pioneer era. Museums in town include the Bardstown Historical Museum; the Wildlife and Natural History Museum; the Women in the Civil War Museum, presenting rare and inspiring information on women's roles as spies, nurses, plantation and factory workers, and soldiers during the war; and the Civil War Museum, an impressive 7000-square-foot facility with a unique collection of weapons, uniforms, flags, and maps from the Union and Confederate troops. The Kentucky Railway Museum (12 miles) celebrates the historic and significant railroad era in a 5,000-square-foot re-creation of the original L & N depot. This museum is home to Kentucky's official steam engine, L & N 152, which first hit the rails in 1905. It reportedly pulled the re-election campaign train of President Theodore Roosevelt and transported Al Capone to jail.

The bourbon industry has played a significant role in Bardstown since its founding in the late 1700s. Heaven Hill Distillery is the largest family-owned distillery in the country and ages twenty-five million gallons of bourbon at a time. Bardstown is the start of Kentucky's Bourbon Trail, which includes the Oscar Getz Museum of Whiskey History, the Heaven Hills Distilleries Bourbon Heritage Center, Jim Beam American Outpost, and Maker's Mark Distillery—all within minutes of downtown Bardstown. On the third weekend of September, the distilleries all come together for the Kentucky Bourbon Festival.

Visitors can enjoy an intimate carriage ride through the Historic District or get a more in-depth tour on the trolley. Several significant landmarks reflect Bardstown's diverse history. The Talbott Tavern, now a restaurant and bed-and-breakfast inn, dates back to 1779 and was a former stagecoach stop reputed to have been visited by Jesse James, Abraham Lincoln, and George Rogers Clark (of Lewis and Clark fame). The Old County Jail, built in 1874, was in operation until 1987. Visitors can see the poetic and artistic graffiti left by former inmates and perhaps even catch a glimpse of the resident ghost. Other interesting tours and landmarks include a tour of Wickland, the 1817 Home of Three Governors; and the Abbey of Gethsemani in nearby Trappist. This monastery is run by monks who spend their days in prayer, study, and the work of maintaining the abbey; they also make cheese, fruitcakes, and bourbon fudge as a source of income. The Saint Joseph Proto-Cathedral, built in 1819, was the first cathedral west of the Allegheny Mountains.

In addition to *Stephen Foster—The Musical,* The Dan Talbott Amphitheater in My Old Kentucky Home State Park offers other productions by the Stephen Foster Drama Association, as well as performances by groups like The Dixie Chicks, The Four Tops, The Temptations, and the Louisville Orchestra. More than thirty annual festivals draw people from around the globe. The Nelson County Civic Center in Bardstown hosts the Bardstown Community Theater, which presents several annual productions. The Fine Arts Bardstown Society offers art workshops for all ages and provides support to local artists by sponsoring concerts and art events.

Several art galleries in Bardstown display the work of local artists, and festivals showcase the area's many talented musicians.

The Kentucky Folk Festival is a summer event held on the grounds of Wickland Estate. The Kentucky Standard Band, from Nelson County, performs traditional Kentucky music locally and nationally and is a popular draw for local events. The Bluegrass Music Festival in June features three days of bluegrass music and arts and crafts. The Arts, Crafts, and Antiques Fair is held in the fall.

Thanksgiving weekend brings the beginning of the month-long Christmas 'Round Bardstown celebration with an annual parade, street carolers, and music programs in the downtown historic district. The Christmas Music Program involves the entire community by bringing together several choral groups. Eight to ten Bardstown homes are open during the Candlelight Tour of Homes. My Old Kentucky Home State Park's Federal Hill mansion is also open that weekend, and Makers Mark Distillery hosts their own candlelight tours. The Kentucky Bourbon Festival, the biggest event of the year, is a celebration of the art of making fine bourbon. Held on the lawn of historic Spalding Hall in September, the festival offers arts and crafts booths, live bands, special activities for children, and the Bourbon Festival Gala, an elegant black-tie event.

 MAIN STREET

Old Talbott Tavern, a historic tavern and stagecoach stop established around 1779, serves interesting specials like cornmeal catfish and Kentucky bourbon ribeye. Xavier's, located in the basement of historic Spalding Hall, provides fine dining in the evening and during the day serves lunch under the name The Lovin' Oven. Other popular hangouts include The Hurst Drugstore; The Java Joint, for specialty coffees, breakfast, and lunch; Kurtz Restaurant, a sixty-year-old family-run business with great Southern country cooking; and Dagwood's, an uptown casual spot for business lunches and bourbon-seasoned steaks; and Kreso's Restaurant, a remodeled movie theater.

Downtown Bardstown is home to specialty shops, boutiques, bed-and-breakfast inns, and dining and entertainment venues. The downtown area has over three hundred buildings listed on the National Register of Historic Places. The Old Courthouse, located in the middle of the town at the crossroads of three major highways, is now the Community's Welcome Center.

 HOUSING

The historic district has lovely one-hundred-year-old homes, but few are available for purchase; they tend to be larger and more expensive than other options. Other historic houses start at $100,000, but are more typically priced around $250,000. Many of the historic in-town buildings have residential space above businesses, but these are not yet considered premium rentals.

Several older, established neighborhoods offer midrange options from $80,000 to $180,000; some are on two-acre lots. Many newcomers opt for newly built homes, which are plentiful. Small three-bedroom, one-bath homes start at $85,000. Executive homes located in three golf course developments range from $250,000 to

$400,000. All city amenities (gas, water, and internet service) are included in these developments. Condominiums, garden homes, and duplexes are available in town and in golf course communities. A new 2,000-square-foot condominium with four bedrooms and three baths sells for $250,000 in one of the golf communities. Most neighborhoods are extremely well maintained, and builders have done a good job retaining many trees in most new subdivisions.

 ECONOMICS

Number of employers with fifty or more employees—13

There are many manufacturing operations in Bardstown. Primary industries include manufacturing (concrete, vinyl siding, car parts, and greeting cards), distilleries (bourbon), agriculture, bottling and distribution, plastics, and retail trade. Some of the leading employers in Bardstown include American Greetings (500 employees); Jideco of Bardstown, Inc. (375 employees); Tower Automotive (500 employees); Heaven Hill Distilleries (475 employees); and American Fuji Seal, Inc. (400

employees). Bardstown is attractive to manufacturers because of its proximity to major cities associated with the automobile industry. Diversity, location, and good planning all contribute to a positive outlook for the local economy.

 EDUCATION

High schools—3; Middle schools—3; Elementary schools—3; Private Schools—3

There are two public school systems in Bardstown: the Nelson County School System and the Bardstown Independent School System. A parochial school system and several Christian schools are also available. Higher education needs are met through Kentucky Tech in Bardstown; Saint Catherine College, a four-year college in Springfield, Kentucky (17 miles); and Elizabethtown Community College in Elizabethtown, Kentucky, (25 miles). The University of Louisville, Spalding University, Bellarmine College, and Jefferson Community College are all located in Louisville. There are two universities in Lexington—the University of Kentucky and

Transylvania University—as well as Lexington Community College.

HEALTHCARE

Flaget Memorial Hospital—52 beds; Physicians—101; Dentists—5

Flaget Memorial Hospital, serving Bardstown and Nelson County, opened a new state-of-the-art facility in 2005, with an active staff of thirty-five physicians and a host of consulting physicians. Hospital services include cardiology, dermatology, emergency care, general surgery, gynecology, nuclear medicine, cardiac rehabilitation, intensive care, oncology, orthopedics, pain management, hospice, and radiology. Flaget also operates an immediate care facility in Bardstown. Many hospitals in the Louisville area provide additional healthcare and specialty services.

SPIRITUAL LIFE

Thirteen Christian denominations are represented. The nearest synagogue is in Louisville.

STAYING CONNECTED

The *Kentucky Standard,* a local paper, is published three times a week and is available online. The *Courier Journal* is delivered daily from Louisville. Local high-speed internet service, cable television, and two local radio stations are available. There is one bookstore and many wireless internet hot spots.

GETTING THERE

Bardstown is located in the central part of the Kentucky Bluegrass region and is served by US Highways 31-E, 150, and 62, and Kentucky Highways 49 and 245. The Kentucky Bluegrass Parkway offers a direct route to Lexington and I-65. Air transportation is provided through the Louisville International Airport, served by fourteen major and feeder airlines, and the Blue Grass Airport in Lexington, with access to most major airlines. The Bardstown–Nelson County Airport (Honaker Aviation) is six miles from town and has a 5,000-foot runway that provides general aviation service, private charter service, and aviation lessons.

RESOURCES

Bardstown–Nelson County
  Chamber of Commerce
One Court Square
Bardstown, KY 40004
(502) 348-9545
www.bardstownchamber.com

Bardstown–Nelson County Tourist
  and Convention Commission
One Court Square
Bardstown, KY 40004
(800) 638-4877
www.visitbardstown.com

Nelson County Economic
  Development Agency
One Court Square
Bardstown, KY 40004
(502) 348-6402
www.nceda.net

BARDSTOWN VITAL STATISTICS

CLIMATE

Annual average rainfall	44.4 inches
Snowfall	17.5 inches
Elevation	800 feet

Temperatures (in degrees Fahrenheit)

	Jan	Apr	Jul	Oct
High	41	68	88	70
Low	22	44	64	44

OCCUPATIONS

	2006	Projected 2011
Blue collar	32.5%	31.9%
White collar	50.8%	51.0%
Services	16.7%	17.1%

ADULT EDUCATION

	2000
Less than High School	20.1%
High School	37.5%
Some College	18.5%
Associates Degree	7.4%
College Degree	9.7%
Graduate Degree	6.8%

POPULATION

2006	11,326
2000-2006 Population: Annual Compound Growth Rate	1.41%
2006-2011 Population: Annual Compound Growth Rate	1.79%

Population by age group

	2006	Projected 2011
0-4	8.2%	8.4%
5-9	7.1%	6.8%
10-14	6.7%	6.4%
15-19	7.0%	6.3%
20-24	8.0%	8.3%
25-29	7.8%	8.3%
30-34	6.1%	6.8%
35-39	6.4%	5.3%
40-44	7.4%	6.2%
45-49	7.4%	7.2%
50-54	6.2%	6.7%
55-59	5.9%	6.0%
60-64	4.1%	5.2%
65-69	3.2%	3.5%
70-74	2.7%	2.6%
75-79	2.4%	2.2%
80-84	1.9%	1.9%
85+	1.7%	1.8%

Sources for Vital Statistics listed above can be found in the Preface to this book.

BEREA

2006 POPULATION
10,671

NEAREST CITIES
Richmond, KY (12 miles)
Lexington, KY (39 miles)

ESTIMATED 2006
MEDIAN HOUSEHOLD INCOME
$38,021

COST OF LIVING
Average 3-bdrm home—$127,500
Average rent, 2-bdrm apartment—$450
Cost-of-living comparison—95.6%

SALES TAX
6%

PROPERTY TAX
Average 3-bdrm home—$1,050

Situated in the foothills of the Cumberland Mountains is a remarkable Southern village busy producing handcrafted Shaker furniture, fused-glass jewelry set with semiprecious stones, handmade bead baskets, and Appalachian Mountain dulcimers. Berea is known as the Folk Arts and Crafts Capital of Kentucky. This attractive Kentucky town is home to over fifty artists and craftspeople, many of whom have working studios open to the public. Berea College, a tuition-free liberal arts institution, has become a focal point for activity in this town. Berea provides a special program for southern Appalachian and Kentucky residents, offering them opportunities to enhance their artistic skills and a place to market their work. As a result, numerous art and craft stores in Berea sell work created by local college students and area artisans.

Originally known as the Glade, Berea dates back to 1850. Once little more than a sparsely populated farm community with a racetrack, this area soon became known for its spirited support for emancipation. A decade before the outbreak of the Civil War, Cassius Marcellus Clay, a prominent landowner and avid abolitionist, gave a free tract of land to his friend the Reverend John G. Fee to entice him to join his political efforts in the Glade. Fee took the ten-acre tract on the ridge and established a small village with a church and a school. Basing his settlement upon the utopian philosophy that all races should live harmoniously in an integrated community, Fee named it Berea after the Biblical town. It became a center for support of abolitionists and missionaries. In 1866, the Berea Literary Institute opened its doors and in 1889, there were 450 students enrolled in primary grades through college level. The college recruited black students, and sold parcels of land with the stipulation that families live next to people of a different race.

In 1890, Berea was incorporated, separating the town from the college for the first time. In an effort to raise funds to support the college, President William Frost took student-made bed covers, donated in exchange for tuition, on his trips to the North. They were received with such enthusiasm that Frost was inspired to establish the Berea College Fireside Industries for marketing homemade crafts on a national level. Artisans and crafters were lured to the area when a loom house was built for weavers and the Student Craft Industries was established. The institution allowed mountain people to earn an income while retaining their traditional lifestyle. At the turn of the century, Berea became one of the centers of the American Crafts Revival. Churchill Weavers, the town's first independent industry, was founded in 1922; it attracted many artisans and crafters who set up businesses in the town. Today Berea has evolved into an impressive cultural center for the region.

Nestled in the foothills of the Appalachians not far from bluegrass country, Berea is a picturesque town. The buildings of Berea College are clustered around a central square on the attractive tree-lined campus. Across the street, a cranberry-colored awning extends the length of Main Street, outlining the storefronts along College Square. On the corner sits the white-columned Boone Tavern Hotel (built in 1909), one of the Historic Hotels of America. Bustling Main Street, home to several art galleries, a bookstore, and a coffeehouse, offers options for latte lovers, browsers, and art seekers.

RECREATION

Located at the edge of the Cumberland Mountain foothills, Berea offers easy access to activities such as hiking, biking, swimming, rafting, and camping. Outdoor enthusiasts can hike the eight-mile trail in the 7,000-acre Berea College Forest in the Indian Fort Mountain area. Owsley Fork Reservoir, five miles east of Berea, is a wonderful lake for nonmotorized boating and fishing; this area also has hiking trails. The John B. Stephenson Memorial Forest State Nature Preserve, approximately ten miles from Berea, includes a 124-acre wooded gorge with two waterfalls.

Battlefield Park is the site of the Battle of Richmond, the second largest Civil War battle in Kentucky, which was fought in August 1862. The Battle of Richmond Association works to preserve Herndon House, which served as a hospital during the war; acquire additional land; create interpretive trails; and continue the development of the park.

The Daniel Boone National Forest, about forty miles east of Berea, consists of almost 700,000 acres of land, including two wilderness areas. Most of it is rugged, with steep ridges, narrow valleys, and 3,400 miles of cliff line. Ideal for mountain biking, horseback riding, backpacking, rock climbing, hunting, and hiking, it draws over five million visitors a year. There are two large lakes in the forest for fishing, boating, and relaxing: Cave Run Lake in the northern part and Laurel River Lake in the southern part. Both are within fifty miles of

Berea. Sheltowee Trace National Recreation Trail extends the length of the forest for 268 miles, running north to south. The wildlife is abundant, the scenery is magnificent, and the recreational opportunities are plentiful.

Less than two hours' drive away, the Cumberland Gap National Historic Park is located in the southeastern part of Kentucky, where the state meets Tennessee and Virginia. The park, which covers over 20,000 acres, offers ranger-guided activities, historical sites, and the Wilderness Road. The nearby Cumberland Gap, carved eons ago by wind and water, provided a natural path across the Appalachian Mountains for early settlers who were on their way to Kentucky and beyond.

The Berea city park system offers a variety of sports activities for local youth. There is a nine-hole golf course at the Berea Country Club and Golf Course, and twelve miles north of Berea is the eighteen-hole championship Gibson Bay Golf Course. Battlefield Golf Course and Country Club is a semi-private 18-hole course open to the public; historic

markers throughout the course describe local Civil War History. The Kentucky Horse Park, located in nearby Lexington, includes a state-run park; a museum; and facilities for horseback riding, polo, and other special events related to horses. Horse races are held at Keenland Race Course (50 miles) during the spring and fall.

 **CULTURAL SCENE**

In Old Town Berea, a thriving arts and crafts community, visitors can view more than fifty artisans at work in their studios. On display are a variety of craftworks, such as hand-thrown earthenware, original oil paintings and watercolors, handmade quilts, functional and decorative pottery, handcrafted chairs and rockers, traditional weavings, handmade brooms, porcelain pottery, and musical instruments.

The Berea College Museum houses a collection of historical artifacts and an engaging photography collection depicting the history of the college. Gallery-V at Berea College, a virtual museum operated by the school, is home to an innovative and educational collection of artifacts and images about the Appalachian region and Berea College. The college also supports an active performing arts program: including theatrical performances and a number of folk dancing events. The music department presents recitals, concerts, and ensembles throughout the year. Convocations sponsored by the college include weekly guest speakers and musical performances. Monthly forums feature presentations by historians, authors, and musicians. Bereans have been educated by Desmond Tutu, His Holiness the Dalai Lama, and Bobby Seale, and entertained by Caribbean bands and Japanese Taiko drummers.

Many festivals are held in this active art community. The Kentucky Guild of Artists and Craftsmen Fairs, held in May and October, are among the most popular. Held at Memorial Park, the Fairs present exquisite works by over one hundred regional artists and crafters and include live music, dancing, and artisan demonstrations. In July, more than 125 artists and craftspeople from across the country exhibit and sell their unique works at the Berea Craft Festival at the Indian Fort Theater. The Southeast Tourism Society voted this one of the region's top twenty events. Every year more than twenty special events bring art, music, and dance to Berea. Renfro Valley (14 miles), Kentucky's Country Music Capital, attracts crowds from March through December with shows featuring music headliners such as Loretta Lynn, George Jones, Lynn Anderson, the Oak Ridge Boys, and the Statler Brothers.

Participants in Berea College's Elderhostel Program lodge at the Boone Tavern Hotel and attend the Berea Forum. Free to retired residents from the area, this program offers educational presentations on Appalachian art, history, and culture.

 MAIN STREET

For excellent regional Southern fare, try Boone Tavern Hotel Dining Room (spoon bread and chicken flakes in a bird basket); the new Cracker Barrel; and Cedar Village Restaurant. For delicious brews and warm chocolate chip cookies, visit Berea Coffee and Tea

Company. The Dinner Bell Restaurant serves a good blue-plate special, old-fashioned hamburgers, and fabulous fruit cobblers, while Papaleno's Restaurant is a favorite spot for pizza.

Shopping is a treat in Berea. The three main shopping areas are Old Town, Chestnut Street, and College Square. Old Town is home to Berea's Welcome Center, located in the 1917 L & N Railroad Depot and listed on the National Register of Historic Places. This area includes such interesting shops as Honeysuckle Vine and Honeysuckle Vine II, where you can buy corn shuck dolls, musical instruments, pottery, glass beads, and white oak baskets, and Top Drawer Gallery, where you'll find regional crafts. The Chestnut Street area has twelve antique shops and several craft studios and antique malls. The Contemporary Artifacts Gallery on Chestnut Street offers a wonderful collection of porcelain pottery, bead baskets, and forged iron and steel sculptures. At College Square you will find the Appalachian Fireside Gallery, which showcases handmade quilts, woven rugs, and natural wreaths. Near the square is Churchill Weavers, situated in a lovely rose garden. This well-known studio displays impressive handwoven items made with quality yarns. The Log House Craft Gallery offers Berea College student crafts including woodcraft, weaving, broom craft, ceramics, wrought iron, and furniture. The Wallace Nutting Museum, on the second floor of this gallery, sells seventeenth- and eighteenth-century antiques.

The Kentucky Artisan Center, a 25,000-square-foot facility, showcases the quality work of Kentucky artisans immediately off Interstate 75. In addition to providing educational programs and demonstrations, interactive artistic opportunities, and a computer kiosk for helping travelers identify and find specific artists, the Center has a restaurant and 4,000 square feet of retail and exhibit space filled with crafts, art, music, and specialty food.

Housing

Housing choices are varied. A wide selection of thirty- to fifty-year-old homes in well-kept, attractive neighborhoods range from $89,000 to $150,000. A few older, historic homes in town—some dating as far back as 1885—are priced from $150,000 to $250,000. Some homes in the many new subdivisions surrounding Berea are priced under $125,000, but most are in the $150,000 to $200,000 range. The few really high-priced homes in the area are primarily custom-built, some on five- to six-acre tracts. There are no condominiums or town houses in Berea, but a number of apartments are available. The strong job market tends to keep the apartments full.

 Economics

Number of employers with fifty or more employees—13

The primary local employers are Berea College (553 employees), and the manufacturing and tourism industries. Some of the largest employers include NACCO Materials Handling (1,200 employees); Tokico (USA) Inc. (900 employees); Guildhouse (300 employees); KI USA Corporation (300 employees); and Berea College Industries (200 employees).

 Education

High schools—1; Middle schools—1; Elementary schools—1

The Berea Community School is an independent school district within the city, covering grades K–12 in one school. Madison County has nine elementary schools, three middle schools, and two high schools, as well as a variety of district-wide programs. Berea College, ranked as one of the best liberal arts colleges in the South by *U.S. News and World Report,* is the heartbeat of the town. The school only admits low-income students, and every student receives a full scholarship. All students are required to work ten to fifteen hours per week in a college job and carry a full academic load. Although the majority of the students come from southern Appalachia and Kentucky, Berea's student body represents more than sixty countries. Within an easy commute are Eastern Kentucky

University in Richmond (12 miles), and University of Kentucky and Transylvania College in Lexington (39 miles). The University of Kentucky includes eleven colleges, five professional schools, and a graduate school. Almost thirty-one thousand students are enrolled in the various programs.

 HEALTHCARE

St. Joseph Berea Hospital—25 beds; Physicians—30; Dentists—4

St. Joseph Berea Hospital, a part of St. Joseph Healthcare in Lexington, is a primary healthcare facility serving Berea, southern Madison County, and the rural areas of five additional counties. On staff are thirty-four active physicians and dentists, twenty-five consulting physicians, and nine courtesy physicians specializing in family practice, gynecology, pediatrics, orthopedics, general surgery, internal medicine, urology, neurology, cardiology, oncology, and other fields. A twelve-physician ER group also serves Berea. The hospital also offers a regional cancer center. The Berea Healthcare Center is a skilled nursing facility. Central Kentucky

Radiology, with fifteen physicians, serves Berea and Lexington.

 SPIRITUAL LIFE

Sixteen Christian denominations are represented. The closest synagogue is in Lexington.

 STAYING CONNECTED

The *Berea Citizen* is the local weekly newspaper. Daily papers from Richmond and Lexington are also available. Internet service and cable television are available. Berea has two bookstores, the Berea College Bookstore and Robie and Robie, for new and used books. Books are also sold in certain galleries and gift shops.

 GETTING THERE

Berea is located in the central part of Kentucky on I-75, south of Lexington. US 25 and KY 21 also access Berea. The Bluegrass Airport in Lexington hosts several major airlines and feeder airlines that serve major cities.

RESOURCES

Berea Chamber of Commerce
926 West Jefferson Street, Suite 1
Berea, KY 40403
(859) 986-9760
www.bereachamber.com

Berea Convention and
 Visitors Bureau
210 North Broadway
Berea, KY 40403
(800) 598-5263
www.berea.com

BEREA
VITAL STATISTICS

CLIMATE

Annual average rainfall	45 inches
Snowfall	17.1 inches
Elevation	900 feet

Temperatures (in degrees Fahrenheit)

	Jan	Apr	Jul	Oct
High	43	69	86	69
Low	24	45	65	47

OCCUPATIONS

	2006	Projected 2011
Blue collar	23.8%	22.3%
White collar	60.7%	61.8%
Services	15.2%	15.9%

ADULT EDUCATION

	2000
Less than High School	25.6%
High School	27.5%
Some College	18.9%
Associates Degree	4.7%
College Degree	14.2%
Graduate Degree	9.2%

POPULATION

2006	10,671
2000-2006 Population: Annual Compound Growth Rate	1.29%
2006-2011 Population: Annual Compound Growth Rate	1.55%

Population by age group

	2006	Projected 2011
0-4	6.9%	6.8%
5-9	6.2%	6.1%
10-14	5.5%	6.2%
15-19	9.7%	9.4%
20-24	10.4%	10.0%
25-29	9.1%	5.9%
30-34	7.0%	8.4%
35-39	6.1%	6.4%
40-44	6.3%	6.2%
45-49	5.5%	6.3%
50-54	5.8%	5.3%
55-59	5.5%	5.8%
60-64	3.9%	4.9%
65-69	3.5%	3.3%
70-74	2.4%	3.0%
75-79	2.5%	2.0%
80-84	2.0%	2.0%
85+	1.8%	2.0%

Sources for Vital Statistics listed above can be found in the Preface to this book.

2006 POPULATION
15,780

NEAREST CITIES
Lexington, KY (35 miles)
Louisville, KY (85 miles)

ESTIMATED 2006
MEDIAN HOUSEHOLD INCOME
$41,947

COST OF LIVING
Average 3-bdrm home—$114,000
Average rent, 2-bdrm apartment—
$450
Cost-of-living comparison—
95.6%

SALES TAX
6%

PROPERTY TAX
Average 3-bdrm home—$1,178

Often referred to as the "Birthplace of the Bluegrass," Danville is also known as the "City of Firsts" because of its pioneering work in education, law, government, and medicine. In 1785 the first Kentucky courthouse was built in Danville, and in 1792 the first state constitution was written and signed here. Danville also hosted a series of constitutional conventions at Constitution Square beginning in December 1784. The first college west of the Allegheny Mountains was established in Danville in 1783 and the first law school in 1799.

The Cumberland Mountains along the eastern edge of Kentucky provided a natural barrier between the eastern and western United States for many centuries. Kentucky was a part of Virginia until pioneers forged their way through the mountains by cutting a path called the Wilderness Road. Led by Daniel Boone, these trailblazers opened a door for thousands of settlers to explore the new frontier. Danville's prime location on the Wilderness Road led to its early development as a town and a political center and established it as a popular crossroads for early settlers. In 1790, Kentucky separated from Virginia, and in 1792, it became the fifteenth state in the union.

Boyle County, home of Danville, captured national attention during the Civil War as a result of the Battle of Perryville, the culmination of a Confederate attempt to reclaim Kentucky. This 1862 battle was one of the bloodiest of the war, with over seventy-five hundred casualties. Sixteen thousand Confederate soldiers and twenty-five thousand Union troops fought two miles north of Perryville. The town was hit by cannonball fire and became a place of medical convalescence for the many wounded soldiers. Both sides withdrew from the battle, with

the Union ultimately retaining control of Kentucky. In the historic village of Perryville, named a National Historic Landmark area in 1961, many streets bear the names of the leaders of that battle. Union officers are honored on the west side of the river and Confederates on the east side.

Danville was listed on the National Register of Historic Places in 1973. Today this appealing Kentucky hamlet, not only historically significant but also incredibly beautiful, attracts many tourists each year. Danville residents are rightly proud of their rolling hills of bluegrass, gracious Southern horse farms, and elegant historic homes graced by white dogwoods, towering maples, sturdy oaks, and pink cherry blossoms. Danville is now a Main Street Program participant with a vital downtown district and several historic areas, boasting over 120 historic homes. The National Trust for Historic Preservation recognized Danville citizens for their efforts in downtown revitalization through historic preservation and named their town one of five winners of the

2001 Great American Main Street Award. Danville was the first Kentucky town to win this award.

This dedicated community also promotes the arts and music, values education, and supports economic growth and diversity. In the downtown area, the streets are wide and the storefronts tastefully restored. The lifestyle here is easy: there are few traffic problems, and the nearby lake and wooded areas offer opportunities for play and relaxation. The energetic tone of this town is evident in the variety of activities, events, and performances taking place here. Centre College has drawn national attention as a premier liberal arts college offering high-quality education for a reasonable cost. Its lovely wooded campus adds visual charm to Danville, and its cultural and educational programs complement the town's efforts to provide artistic and intellectually stimulating events for its citizens.

 RECREATION

Danville is strategically located in central Kentucky near a number of recreational sites, including lakes, state parks, a national forest, and wildlife refuges. Herrington Lake, within three miles of Danville, is home to several marinas and a beautiful eighteen-hole golf course overlooking a 3,500-acre lake that is well stocked with bass, perch, rockfish, bluegill, and catfish. Gwinn Island Resort and Marina, on Herrington Lake, offers cabin and boat rentals and a full-service marina.

The 500-acre Central Kentucky Wildlife Refuge, located thirteen miles from Danville, borders a stretch of the North Rolling Fork in Parksville known as knobland. The knobs are a ring of hills that surround the rolling plateau area of the bluegrass region on the western, southern, and eastern sides. This preserve protects birds, animals, plants, and other forms of wildlife in their natural habitat and offers five main hiking trails, including cliff-side, waterfall gorge, and hollow walks. Cardinals, purple finches, and Carolina chickadees feed at the bird blind. Ferns, mosses, bird's foot violets, bluebells, and lady slippers grace the grounds of the reserve, adding lush touches of color to a peaceful retreat.

The town provides tennis and youth sports through the City Parks Department and two local recreation centers. The Parks and Recreation Complex includes lighted tennis courts, playground areas at two parks, a public pool, a disc golf course, and a sport and fitness center with racquetball courts, fitness equipment, and classes. There is a public eighteen-hole golf course at Old Bridge Golf Club and a private golf course at the Danville Country Club. The McDowell Wellness Center offers classes and exercise equipment for locals. The Senior Citizens Center, equipped to serve up to seven hundred people a week, includes an activity room, an exercise room, and a dining room.

 CULTURAL SCENE

The Danville and Boyle County walking and driving tour takes visitors past nineteenth-century log homes and churches, stately Greek Revival architecture, and Federal-style brick structures. Most of the fifty-nine historic structures in the downtown area are within walking distance; two other historic areas are on the edge of town. The McDowell House (1802) and Apothecary Shop (1797) were the home and office of Dr. Ephraim McDowell, the physician who performed the world's first successful abdominal surgery in 1809. Constitution Square State Historic Site is the formal birthplace of Kentucky. Today this historic site includes several original homes, the oldest post office building west of the Alleghenies, a schoolhouse, and a tavern, as well as replicas of the original log courthouse, a meetinghouse, a jail, a church, and a bronze statue depicting the state seal.

The Shaker Village of Pleasant Hill gives visitors an opportunity to experience the Shaker culture, to tour the thirty-three buildings built in the 1800s, and to learn about the Shaker lifestyle, which was based on community property ownership, celibacy, racial and sexual equality, conservation of resources, religion, a strong work ethic, and simplicity. The Civil War Museum in Perryville has an interesting collection of battle artifacts.

Harrodsburg, established in

1774, is Kentucky's oldest English settlement. Located ten miles north of Danville, this town is home to Old Fort Harrod State Park, where visitors can view a full-scale replica of the fort, the Lincoln Marriage Temple (where Abraham Lincoln's parents were married), the George Rogers Clark Memorial, and the Mansion Museum, which exhibits Native American artifacts, Civil War relics, and other historical items.

The outdoor Pioneer Playhouse, Kentucky's oldest outdoor theater, offers summertime theater as well as training for young actors. This two-hundred-acre complex was designed like an eighteenth-century pioneer village. Campgrounds, picnic areas, and biking trails are also available. Centre College's Norton Center for the Arts presents world-class performances in ballet and dance, Broadway shows, opera, concerts, and lectures. The center was host to the only vice presidential debate in the 2000 campaign. Other special events have included performances by Mikhail Baryshnikov, Twyla Tharp, the Boston Pops, the Bolshoi Orchestra, and the Chamber Music of Lincoln Center.

The Arts Commission of Danville/Boyle County is a non-profit group formed to link artists with the community by promoting the works of artists and art organizations. The commission sponsors monthly Gathering Artists Exhibits at three locations. The West T. Hill Community Theater also presents local performances. The new Community Arts Center, located in a restored Federal Building, hosts changing monthly art displays.

Art and music festivals are scheduled throughout the year. One of the local favorites, the Great American Brass Band Festival, draws forty thousand visitors annually. Held in June, this festival features continuous live music of more than two dozen brass bands, a Saturday evening picnic with a decorative table contest, and a parade. The Boyle County Fair and Horse Show is a summer event with traditional exhibits, rides, and old-fashioned county fair fun. The Historic Constitution Square Festival in mid-September offers historic reenactments, a juried arts and crafts festival, and live entertainment. The Old Fashioned Hometown Christmas hosts an annual holiday parade, a downtown celebration, and special Christmas activities for the entire family.

The surrounding areas also have special annual events, including the Forkland Festival and Heritage Revue, a genuine Kentucky folk festival with folk art, living history demonstrations, live music, an old country theater, and a bean and corn bread supper. The Battle of Perryville Commemoration offers live demonstrations, the Civil War battle reenactment, and educational sessions. In summer, the World's Longest Outdoor Sale stretches along the US 127 corridor that runs 450 miles from Covington, Kentucky, to Gadsden, Alabama.

 Main Street

The Corner Cafe, located in an old church now used as an antique mall, serves buffet lunches, coffee, tea, and desserts. Freddie's has a great Italian menu. Other favorite hangouts include Reno's Roadhouse and The Hub Coffee Shop & Cafe, where patrons enjoy specialty coffee drinks and live music on the weekends. The Beaumont Inn (1845) has been run by the same family since its opening and is known for its fine food and charming Southern atmosphere.

Danville's many artists and craftspeople display their handcrafted works in the town's shops and galleries. Stained glass, bronze sculptures, thrown pottery, glass ornaments and bowls, and original paintings and crafts by many talented artists can be found in the galleries and studios in the downtown historic district.

 Housing

Homes and neighborhoods in Danville are well maintained, a reflection of uniform community pride. The cost of housing is reasonable, and several historic districts offer home buyers a variety of architectural choices, from Federal and Greek Revival to Queen Anne and historic bungalows. Homes in the historical districts range from $175,000 to $450,000. Houses in the older, established neighborhoods cost from $60,000 to $250,000; the midrange price is $150,000 for a 2,000-square-foot home. Several older subdivisions have homes on two-acre lots. Options are abundant in new subdivisions: prices start around $100,000 and reach $450,000. Custom building sites are plentiful. Condominiums, town houses, and patio homes vary from $90,000 to $350,000, and there is a good supply of apartments in the area, with more on the way.

 ECONOMICS

Number of employers with fifty or more employees—30

A reliance on area natural resources and agriculture has given Danville a solid base for steady growth. Today economic diversity—manufacturing, business services, and agriculture all play major roles—and planned growth helps this progressive community continue to thrive. The historic nature of the town enhances the growth potential for the tourism industry. Leading employers in the Danville area include Ephraim McDowell Health (1,500 employees); R. R. Donnelley (950 employees); American Greetings (700 employees); Victor Products Division, Dana Corporation (350 employees); Centre College (350 employees); Danville Public Schools (300 employees); Panasonic Home Appliances Co. of America (300 employees); and FKI Logistex, Mathews Conveyors (300 employees). The Danville-Boyle County Economic Development Partnership, comprised of the Boyle County Industrial Foundation, The Danville-Boyle County Chamber of Commerce, the Heart of Danville, City of Danville, and the Boyle County Fiscal Court, works to provide a positive, inviting atmosphere that will attract new businesses.

 EDUCATION

High schools—2; Middle schools—2; Elementary schools—3; Private schools—2

Higher education is available through Centre College, the National College of Business and Technology, the Bluegrass Community and Technical College, and the Eastern Kentucky University branch campus in Danville. Centre College, with 1,050 students, has been listed among the top fifty national liberal arts colleges by *U.S. News and World Report,* the *New York Times,* and *Money* magazine. Twenty-five majors are offered, and the student-faculty ratio is ten to one. Residents of Danville are only thirty-five miles from the University of Kentucky (21,000 students) and Transylvania (1,000 students) in Lexington. The Kentucky School for the Deaf, located on a 175-acre residential campus in Danville, offers education to hearing-impaired students ages five to twenty-one.

The Danville–Boyle County Community Education Program—the result of an impressive collaboration among the Danville Independent Schools, the Boyle County Schools, and the Kentucky School for the Deaf—offers classes on computer skills, business, language, personal growth, and general interest topics. The Success Through Arts and Recreation and School (STARS) summer program was awarded a first place Multicultural Leadership and Involvement Award by the National Community Education Association in 2001.

 HEALTHCARE

Ephraim McDowell Regional Medical Center—177 beds; Physicians—66; Dentists—22

The Ephraim McDowell Regional Medical Center offers state-of-the-art technology with twenty-five medical specialties. Services include 24-hour emergency care, surgery, adult day health, pain management, women's healthcare, a cardiac catheterization laboratory, inpatient/outpatient behavioral healthcare, cancer care, critical care, and long-term nursing.

 SPIRITUAL LIFE

Twenty-one Christian denominations are represented. The closest synagogue is in Lexington.

 STAYING CONNECTED

There is one local newspaper, The *Advocate Messenger,* published daily except on Saturday. The Danville metro-area daily newspaper, the *Lexington-Herald Leader,* is also available. Local internet service and cable television are available. Two local AM radio stations and three FM stations serve the area. Danville has an impressive library with more than 72,000 volumes. There are five bookstores in Danville, including the student bookstore for Centre College.

 GETTING THERE

Danville is located in the heart of the Bluegrass Region in the central part of Kentucky. It is served by US Highways 150 and 127. Interstates 75 and 64 are thirty-five miles northeast of Danville. Air transportation is provided through Bluegrass Airport in Lexington, Louisville International Airport (80 miles), and Greater Cincinnati Airport in Erlanger, Kentucky (115 miles). The Danville/Boyle County Airport is four miles from Danville and has a 5,000-foot runway for general aviation.

 RESOURCES

Danville–Boyle County
  Chamber of Commerce
304 South 4th Street
Danville, KY 40422
(859) 236-2361
www.danvilleboylechamber.com

Danville–Boyle County
  Convention and Visitors Bureau
304 South 4th Street
Danville, KY 40422
(800) 755-0076
www.danville-ky.com

DANVILLE
VITAL STATISTICS

CLIMATE

Annual average rainfall	43.9 inches
Snowfall	17.3 inches
Elevation	1,030 feet

Temperatures (in degrees Fahrenheit)

	Jan	Apr	Jul	Oct
High	40	66	86	68
Low	21	42	64	44

OCCUPATIONS

	2006	Projected 2011
Blue collar	22.4%	22.5%
White collar	62.2%	62.4%
Services	15.3%	15.1%

ADULT EDUCATION

	2000
Less than High School	21.8%
High School	31.8%
Some College	19.4%
Associates Degree	4.4%
College Degree	12.7%
Graduate Degree	10.0%

POPULATION

2006	15,780
2000-2006 Population: Annual Compound Growth Rate	0.31%
2006-2011 Population: Annual Compound Growth Rate	0.37%

Population by age group

	2006	Projected 2011
0-4	5.2%	5.2%
5-9	5.1%	4.9%
10-14	6.2%	5.4%
15-19	8.2%	8.0%
20-24	9.6%	9.9%
25-29	6.0%	6.0%
30-34	5.4%	5.6%
35-39	6.2%	5.3%
40-44	6.4%	6.4%
45-49	7.0%	6.6%
50-54	6.9%	6.8%
55-59	6.5%	7.1%
60-64	5.1%	6.0%
65-69	4.1%	4.5%
70-74	3.7%	3.5%
75-79	3.2%	3.2%
80-84	2.6%	2.6%
85+	2.6%	2.9%

Sources for Vital Statistics listed above can be found in the Preface to this book.

FRANKLIN

2006 POPULATION
8,155

NEAREST CITIES
Bowling Green, KY (19 miles)
Nashville, TN (45 miles)

ESTIMATED 2006
MEDIAN HOUSEHOLD INCOME
$40,575

COST OF LIVING
Average 3-bdrm home—$94,000
Average rent, 2-bdrm apartment—$425
Cost-of-living comparison—93.9%

SALES TAX
6%

PROPERTY TAX
Average 3-bdrm home—$750

In the spring, blossoming cherry trees grace the lawn of Franklin's 1882 courthouse, adding a whisper of color to the stately brick structure. The picturesque town square frames this historic building that has been the gathering place for locals for many decades. In summertime, the residents attend the Summer Night Concert series, listening to live blues, classical guitar, or Southern rock music performed on the square. Antiques are a big attraction; numerous shops and antique malls sit on or near the town square.

Franklin was established in 1820 and serves as the justice center for Simpson County. The land was originally purchased from William Hudspeth, who hauled water by hand all night to fill an empty water well—clean water being a necessary resource—to ensure the selection of his land as the town site. Simpson County has been the home of a number of well-known Americans. James Bowie, the frontiersman and Bowie knife namesake, and one of the heroes of the Alamo, was born here in 1796. Alexander Majorca, one of the founders of the Pony Express, was born here in 1814. Although no major battles were fought here, the town is rich in Civil War history.

Some of the architecture in the area dates back to pre–Civil War times. The Octagon House, an unusual eight-sided antebellum home, was owned by Jackson Caldwell, a Confederate sympathizer. He allowed Confederate troops to use the cupola on the house to watch for Federal troops. This home was later reputed to be part of the underground railroad. All of the churches around the square were established in the early 1800s, and each has its own story. The Old Jail, built in 1879, was actively used until 1986. Civil War graffiti has been found in the Jailer's Quarters. The Jail Museum exhibits a collection of Civil War uniforms and artifacts.

Other events have marked Franklin's history. The Beauchamp-Sharp tragedy involved several prominent figures who were entangled in an 1819 romance that ended in a social and political scandal, murder, suicide, and a hanging. Mystery still surrounds the 1948 controversial plane crash that killed Captain Thomas Mantell Jr.—some claimed a UFO caused the accident.

A family-focused lifestyle is at the heart of this attractive Kentucky town. There is a strong sense of community, a noticeable appreciation for history, a dedication to friendship, and a high regard for nature. Extensive cultural opportunities, recreational sites, and college town perks in nearby Nashville and Bowling Green make Franklin a delightful place to live.

 RECREATION

Many area lakes and state parks provide opportunities for hiking, biking, and other outdoor recreation. Barren River State Park has an attractive lodge overlooking a

10,000-acre lake, as well as boat rentals, camping, hiking, and horseback riding. The scenic lake is surrounded by wooded rolling hills and is not far from Kentucky's famous cave system.

Lost River Cave Valley, located near Bowling Green, has one of the largest cave openings in the East. Used as shelter by Native Americans thousands of years ago, as a hideout for the Jesse James Gang in the mid-1800s, and as an underground nightclub in the nineteenth century, the cave is now the site for fascinating and educational programs on geology, folklore, and history. Mammoth Cave National Park (48 miles) protects 336 miles of caves, the longest recorded cave system in the world, and the scenic river valleys of the Nolin and Green Rivers. The park offers nature trails, thirteen tours, and scenic boat rides. Nolin Lake State Park, situated along the northern edge of Mammoth Cave National Park, has a 5,795-acre lake for boating, fishing, and swimming. At the southern end of cave country is Green River Lake State Park. This 8,200-acre facility offers

camping, boating, swimming, fishing, and a twenty-mile hiking trail. Other lakes in the area are Lake Malone, Old Hickory Lake, and Dale Hollow Lake.

Recreational options in town include tennis, swimming, and golf. Franklin has one public eighteen-hole course and one private course at Country Creek Golf Course. PGA touring pro Kenny Perry, a Simpson County native, designed the course at Country Creek. Franklin boasts an excellent community park system with eight tennis courts, one racquetball court, and three public parks with picnic areas and playground equipment. Youth programs are offered for several sports. Other recreational events in the Franklin area include live thoroughbred horse racing in September, year-round simulcast racing at Kentucky Downs Race Course, and stock car racing at Beech Bend Raceway in Bowling Green and Highland Rim Racetrack in Tennessee.

CULTURAL SCENE

Attractive, architecturally significant buildings in the downtown historic district include the African-American Heritage Center, the Historical Society Museum, and the Library Museum.

The Franklin-Simpson Arts Council presents monthly displays of local, regional, and state artists' works at the Gallery on the Square. The council also offers a major musical production in the summer, a high school play, and children's art outreach programs at the local elementary and middle schools. The council, along with other local sponsors, presents a concert series at the Goodnight Auditorium. The series has brought such big-name artists as Ricky Scaggs, Kathy Mattea, The Lettermen, and Riders in the Sky to entertain Franklin residents. The Auditorium, an 800-seat facility, also hosts visiting orchestras, musical events, and theatrical productions.

The July Jam, held the weekend before Independence Day, is a celebration that includes the Firecracker 100 Kiddie Parade (for ages six and under), several live bands, dancing, and games for the kids. The Franklin Festival is a fun-filled, two-day event with local and regional bluegrass bands and other entertainment at the Community Park. During the first weekend in November, the area Vietnam War Veterans sponsor an event that honors vets with special activities for children, music, and a memorial service. Holiday season brings Franklin's annual Christmas parade and traditional Small Town Christmas celebration, which includes old-fashioned carriage rides and pictures with Santa.

Bowling Green is home to the Capitol Arts Center, featuring two art galleries and an 840-seat auditorium. Also located in Bowling Green are the Barren River Imaginative Museum of Science and the start of the Civil War Heritage Trail (a statewide driving tour of Civil War historic sites). The Duncan Hines Scenic Byway, an eighty-two-mile route, leads north from Bowling Green and loops back around to town.

Other area historic sites include the Jefferson Davis Monument State Historic Site (9 miles east of Hopkinsville), Hermitage, the home of Andrew Jackson (12 miles east of Nashville), and the home of James K. Polk in Columbia, Tennessee. The Shaker Museum in South Union (15 minutes from Franklin) commemorates a community that was established in 1807 and closed in 1922. This religious organization emphasized honesty, humility, simplicity, and communal ownership of property.

A very different type of experience can be found in Nashville. With the Grand Ole Opry, more than thirty music clubs, and 125 restaurants, downtown Nashville offers plenty of entertainment. The Frist Center for the Visual Arts, a community arts exhibition center, recently opened. Vanderbilt University provides many additional cultural opportunities such as art, dance, music, and lectures.

 MAIN STREET

Several restaurants draw visitors and locals to downtown Franklin. The Gas Light Café, an establishment with a warm atmosphere right on the square in the heart of the historic district, serves sandwiches, soups, salads, and desserts.

The Old Tyme Sub Shop, housed in the fountain area of the Moore Drug Company, serves fresh fruit plates, delicious chicken salad, and ice cream cones. The Brickyard Café on West Cedar Street serves lunch and dinner in a beautifully renovated building with a wonderful view of the courthouse lawn. North of the city on 31-W is the Hot Plate, which serves a plate lunch of meat and three vegetables. South of town is the Mexican restaurant Sol Azteca, a very popular spot with locals. Directly across the street is the Sassie Lassie, specializing in hot and cold coffees and teas along with homemade breads, soups, and sandwiches. There are many more dining options in nearby Bowling Green and Nashville.

Antiques are big in Franklin. Over three hundred antique booths and four antique shops are within a six-mile radius of town. Special antiques shows are held in May, July, October, and November. In September, the Southern Kentucky Region AACA Antique Auto Show and Swap Meet, in conjunction with the Festival on the Square, draws thousands of visitors. Over two hundred cars are exhibited at this popular annual event where residents and visitors enjoy the many craft booths, the sidewalk chalk drawing contest, live music, and other entertainment.

 HOUSING

A variety of housing, from new subdivisions to historic homes, is offered in Franklin. While no residential areas have been designated as historic districts, a number of historic homes dating back over one hundred years are interspersed with other homes in the area surrounding the square. Prices range from $50,000 for a small frame home to $250,000 for a large, restored Revival-style brick home. Twenty- to forty-year-old homes in established neighborhoods can cost $90,000 to $150,000, depending on age and size. There is more variety in new home subdivisions: starter homes sell for around $80,000, and new, larger homes run from $140,000 to $250,000. Exclusive home subdivisions are available for around $300,000. Two country-club golf communities offer attractive lots and golf-course views for $200,000 to $300,000.

Acreage is available for new construction or mini-farms.

 ECONOMICS

Number of employers with fifty or more employees—30

The industry base in Franklin is diverse, and the focus is on manufacturing, education services, and farming. Some leading local employers include Covalence Specialty Adhesives (975 employees); Quebecor World (540 employees); Franklin Precision Industry, Inc. (345 employees); and Simpson County Schools (430 employees). The town has the twenty-third highest per capita industrial wage income in the nation. An influx of foreign companies adds an international flavor to the business community. There are one thousand acres of industrial land available.

The Franklin-Simpson Renaissance is part of the Kentucky Main Street Program, designed to promote business in the downtown Franklin area. The program provides facade grants for local businesses and sponsors many local festivals and events. In 2000, they built a bandstand on the courthouse lawn and put in new streetlights around the square.

Tourism is a growing industry, and Franklin is equipped to handle the business, with over four hundred motel rooms and many attractive bed-and-breakfast inns.

 EDUCATION

High schools—1; Middle schools—1; Elementary schools—3; Private schools—2

Higher education needs are met through Western Kentucky University (14,700 students) and Draughons Junior College in Bowling Green and Vanderbilt University and eight other colleges in Nashville. Western Kentucky University is located on a two hundred-acre campus and offers undergraduate and graduate degrees. Senior citizens can take classes for free. Vanderbilt University, with 10,194 students, has undergraduate programs in the liberal arts and sciences, engineering, music, education, and human development, and a full range of graduate and professional degrees.

 HEALTHCARE

Medical Center at Franklin—44 beds; Physicians—7; Dentists—10

The Medical Center at Franklin is an acute-care hospital with a 24-hour emergency room. There are seven active physicians on staff and many visiting staff representing several areas of specialization. Additional services offered by the hospital include radiology and diagnostic services as well as cardiac and pulmonary rehabilitation. They also offer physical, occupational, and speech therapies along with community wellness programs. Also on the medical campus are ambulance service and a lighted heliport for air access to hospitals in Nashville. Extensive healthcare is available in Nashville. Baptist Hospital is Nashville's largest not-for-profit medical center, Saint Thomas Hospital is recognized for its heart and cancer units, and Vanderbilt University Medical Center is known for orthopedic, heart, psychiatric, and cancer units as well as the Vanderbilt Children's Hospital.

SPIRITUAL LIFE

Fourteen Christian denominations are represented. The closest synagogue is in Nashville.

 STAYING CONNECTED

The *Franklin Favorite* is the local weekly newspaper. Metro-area daily newspapers are available from Nashville (the *Tennessean*), Bowling Green *(Bowling Green Daily News)*, and Louisville *(the Courier Journal)*. Internet service, cable television, and one local radio station are available. There are bookstores in Bowling Green and Nashville.

 GETTING THERE

Franklin is located in the southwestern part of Kentucky, very close to the Tennessee border. It is served by US-31W, which is two miles west of I-65 and approximately forty miles north of Nashville. Interstates 40 and 24 are located forty-five miles south of Franklin. Commercial air service is provided through the Nashville International Airport, where sixteen major and feeder airlines offer flights to more than eighty cities. The Bowling Green Regional Airport provides charter service.

 RESOURCES

Franklin-Simpson County
  Chamber of Commerce
201 South Main Street
Franklin, KY 42134
(270) 586-7609
www.f-schamber.com

Simpson County
  Tourism Commission
81 Steele Road
Franklin, KY 42135-0737
(866) 531-2040
www.franklinky.com

FRANKLIN VITAL STATISTICS

CLIMATE

Annual average rainfall	47.3 inches
Snowfall	10.1 inches
Elevation	928 feet

Temperatures (in degrees Fahrenheit)

	Jan	Apr	Jul	Oct
High	42	68	87	70
Low	22	45	65	44

OCCUPATIONS

	2006	Projected 2011
Blue collar	41.2%	39.2%
White collar	45.0%	46.2%
Services	13.8%	14.6%

ADULT EDUCATION

	2000
Less than High School	31.7%
High School	40.3%
Some College	12.2%
Associates Degree	4.9%
College Degree	5.2%
Graduate Degree	5.8%

POPULATION

2006	8,155
2000-2006 Population: Annual Compound Growth Rate	0.32%
2006-2011 Population: Annual Compound Growth Rate	0.19%

Population by age group

	2006	Projected 2011
0-4	7.8%	7.6%
5-9	7.5%	7.0%
10-14	6.2%	7.2%
15-19	5.8%	5.8%
20-24	5.9%	5.9%
25-29	7.5%	5.7%
30-34	7.1%	7.3%
35-39	6.9%	6.5%
40-44	7.2%	7.0%
45-49	6.8%	7.0%
50-54	6.5%	6.6%
55-59	5.9%	6.5%
60-64	4.9%	5.6%
65-69	3.9%	4.3%
70-74	2.9%	3.0%
75-79	2.5%	2.5%
80-84	2.3%	2.0%
85+	2.5%	2.6%

Sources for Vital Statistics listed above can be found in the Preface to this book.

VERSAILLES

2006 POPULATION
7,997

NEAREST CITIES
Frankfort, KY (12 miles)
Lexington, KY (13 miles)
Louisville, KY (63 miles)

ESTIMATED 2006 MEDIAN HOUSEHOLD INCOME
$54,216

COST OF LIVING
Average 3-bdrm home—$165,000
Average rent, 2-bdrm apartment—$675
Cost-of-living comparison—95.6%

SALES TAX
6%

PROPERTY TAX
Average 3-bdrm home—$1,379

Versailles's natural beauty remains much the same as it did one hundred years ago. Breathtaking back-country roads are graced with canopies of arching trees, providing welcoming summer shade. Handmade stone walls and historic churches adorn the roadsides that lead into this irresistible town. Known as the "Horse Capital of the World," Versailles is surrounded by rolling rural terrain. Magnificent farms with eye-catching barns provide a luxurious home for top-quality horses. Two unusual industries, thoroughbreds and bourbon whiskey, are the foundation of the town's economy.

Founded in 1792, the town was named by General Marquis Calmes after the French city of Versailles, out of gratitude for

French assistance during the Revolutionary War. Fertile farmland led to the growth of the agricultural industry and helped make Versailles an important agricultural trading center by the early 1800s. During the Civil War, the town was occupied by soldiers from both the Confederate and the Union armies, but dominated by Federal troops. By the 1880s, Versailles was once again a prospering and growing agricultural community. Manufacturing changed the economic outlook for the area in the twentieth century. Today it is a prime contributor to the local economy.

Versailles' vibrant energy is evident in the interesting activities going on all around town. The public library is a hub of activity in the center of town, and local shops' bulletin boards alert visitors and residents of poetry readings, dance performances, and other events. Easygoing, comfortable, and filled with community spirit, the town has authentic appeal for small-town seekers who prefer being very close to a large metro area. Located only thirteen miles from Lexington and twelve miles from Frankfort, Versailles is in the enviable position of offering the best of both worlds.

 RECREATION

The Clyde E. Buckley Wildlife Sanctuary, a 374-acre site located near Millville (12 miles) has small ponds and fields that offer serene spots for nature walks and bird watching. Operated by the National Audubon Society, this is a favorite location for hiking and interpretive talks as well as educational programs. Water lovers can reach 3,500-acre Herrington Lake in about forty-five minutes. It has several marinas, camping, swimming, fishing, boating, skiing, and golfing on an eighteen-hole course overlooking the lake. The lake has 325 miles of shoreline and is well stocked with white and black bass, crappie, bluegill, and catfish.

Elkhorn Creek is close by for canoeing, and Camp Nelson Heritage Park on the Kentucky River (20 miles) has a lovely park and historic veterans' cemetery that dates back to the Civil War. Old Fort Harrod State Park (30 miles) and Taylorsville Lake State Park (52 miles) offer water activities, camping, picnicking, and hiking. Several nature preserves are near Versailles. The Jim Beam Nature Preserve and the Sally Brown Nature Preserve, which protect the Palisades portion of the Kentucky River, are open for hiking, bird watching, and nature study. The Tom Dorman State Nature Preserve features a splendid spring wildflower display on wooded slopes and spectacular views across the Kentucky River from 300-foot cliffs.

The scenic byways, horse farm tours, and the Bluegrass Scenic Railroad six-mile round trip through bluegrass and Kentucky River country offer appealing alternatives for those seeking less rigorous activities. The Pisgah Pike travels several miles through the Pisgah Rural Historic District, one of the largest in the country. It passes by fields of wildflowers, rolling green pastures lined with stone or plank fencing, old cemeteries, stone spring houses, and historic dwellings and churches, including the 1784 Pisgah Church, the burial site of five Revolutionary War soldiers. Old Frankfort Pike is a fifteen-mile route that

begins northeast of Lexington; known as "Shady Lane," it passes under a long canopy of trees. This scenic road leads through horse farm country.

The local recreation department offers a variety of sports, programs, and classes for all ages. There are nine county parks, indoor and outdoor swimming pools, seven playgrounds, twelve tennis courts, and an eighteen-hole public golf course for a variety of outdoor activities. Many additional golf courses are in the area, including some in Lexington and Frankfort. Five miles from Versailles is the Keeneland Race Course, a popular attraction for horse racing and betting. The Red Mile Track features harness racing. Professional minor league baseball and arena football are both within thirteen miles. Fans from Versailles can easily reach home games played by the nationally recognized football and basketball teams at the University of Kentucky.

 **CULTURAL SCENE**

The Woodford County Historical Society Museum collects material on the area and shares it with the community through a newsletter and exhibits. The museum serves as the county's Genealogical Research Center. Housed in the L & N Railroad Passenger Station (1911), the Nostalgia Station Toy and Train Museum exhibits toys and toy trains dating back to 1900. The Bluegrass Scenic Railroad offers a six-mile round trip ride in a vintage railroad car, and the associated museum has exhibits of passenger trains and railroad memorabilia.

Many historical sites are open for viewing. The Captain John "Jack" Jouett House, built by a Revolutionary War hero in 1797, was home to the man who rode all night to warn Virginia legislators—among them Thomas Jefferson and Patrick Henry—about a British plot. Several other interesting historic buildings grace this part of the Bluegrass Region: the log home of John Crittenden, chief justice of the Supreme Court; Welsenberger Mill, the oldest commercial water-powered mill in the state; and the Old Taylor Distillery. Woodford Reserve Distillery (1812), situated between two lavish horse farms just outside

of Versailles, is the oldest operating distillery in Kentucky. Visitors can tour the facilities and see bourbon being made the traditional way, using pot stills. At the Shaker Village of Pleasant Hill (24 miles away), visitors can experience an historic Shaker habitat.

Seven miles from Versailles is the charming town of Midway, a railroad town built by the Lexington and Ohio Railroad in 1832. It is home to Midway College (founded in 1847), whose lovely tree-covered campus sits atop a hill overlooking this quaint town. Main Street is divided by an active train line and lined with Victorian antique stores, boutiques, restaurants, and innovative gift shops. Midway, a Kentucky gem, boasts 176 buildings listed on the National Register of Historic Places.

Versailles hosts a number of festivals and special events throughout the year. In June, the old-fashioned Woodford County Fair is held at the county park with a rodeo, various exhibits, a talent show, pageants, horse shows, and 4-H competitions. The Magical Musical 4th of July celebration is held at Woodford County Park. The Lexington Philharmonic plays every year while "Uncle Sam" roams the grounds, greeting festival goers. The climax of the celebration is a spectacular fireworks display. The two-day Midway Fall Festival offers arts-and-crafts exhibits, live music, and entertainment. The Annual Holiday Parade and Festival is the main December event in downtown Versailles.

Every year the Woodford Theatrical Arts Association produces four major performances as well as children's shows. The organization also sponsors theater workshops, free lectures, and coaching, and provides information to local schools and groups. The Woodford Educational Endowment Foundation sponsors concerts, ballet performances, and other special events. The cultural calendars in nearby Lexington and Frankfort are filled with concerts, performances, art exhibits, and lectures.

 **MAIN STREET**

Several popular downtown restaurants are housed in historic buildings: Kessler's 1891 Eatery features fine home-style cooking in a relaxed environment, and Railheads at the Depot is known for a varied menu ranging from great burgers and beer to succulent filets and fine wine. The Woodford Inn Restaurant and Tavern offers premium dining and overnight accommodations. There are several good restaurants in Midway, including Bistro LaBelle, where patrons can enjoy casual gourmet dining in a lovely historic setting, and Holly Hill Inn, which consistently draws national rave reviews. The Black Tulip offers gourmet fare that can be enjoyed in an outdoor English pub setting. Locals also frequent the many restaurants in nearby historic Lexington.

Antique shops draw visitors to Versailles and the surrounding area. Main Street is home to the Olde Town Antique Mall, with over thirty dealers. Irish Acres Gallery of Antiques, a 32,000-square-foot antique center, is located in the rural countryside outside of Versailles in a town called Nonesuch, founded in 1870; downstairs, The Glitz restaurant serves a gourmet lunch.

Housing

Housing options include historic homes dating from the 1700s and 1800s and newer homes within the town's limits. Some small historic houses are found on a few streets in Versailles. They are rarely on the market, but prices range from $175,000 to $650,000 when they do come up for sale. Lovely homes in older, established neighborhoods cost from $125,000 to $450,000. A few speculatively built new houses and resales in subdivisions range from $150,000 to $600,000. Custom building on acreage is another option, and existing rural properties and horse farms of all sizes are often for sale, for prices ranging from $250,000 to $5 million.

Economics

Number of employers with fifty or more employees—6

Woodford County consistently has one of the lowest unemployment rates in the state. The industries with the greatest number of employees include manufacturing, wholesale and retail trade, services, and state and local government. Some of the leading manufactur-

ers in the county are Quebecor World (1,500 employees); Osram Sylvania, Inc. (990 employees); and YH America, Inc. (300 employees).

Education

High schools—1; Middle schools—1; Elementary schools—4; Private schools—3

Higher education opportunities are available at Midway College, Lexington Community College, Transylvania University, and the University of Kentucky in Lexington. The latter institution offers ninety-eight certified programs for bachelor's degrees, ninety-six fields for master's degrees, and sixty-two programs for doctoral degrees. Other institutions of higher education in the area include Chandler Medical Center and Lexington Community College in Lexington, Kentucky State University in Frankfort, Asbury College in Wilmore (17 miles), and Georgetown College in Georgetown (18 miles). The Woodford County Community Education Program offers classes on computer skills, business, foreign language, art, wellness, and other subjects.

HEALTHCARE

Bluegrass Community Hospital—25 beds; Physicians—21; Dentists—10
Versailles is served by the Bluegrass Community Hospital, a critical-access facility offering a broad range of acute care, surgical, emergency, and diagnostic services. Over seventy healthcare professionals are on staff and are affiliated with more than thirty area physicians. Additional medical care is available through Lexington and Frankfort hospitals. Lexington offers ten hospitals, including the University of Kentucky Hospital, a 473-bed patient care, education, and research facility with more than five hundred faculty physicians. The UK Hospital is a part of the University of Kentucky Chandler Medical Center, which also includes the Children's Hospital and three clinics. The Frankfort Regional Medical Center serves the Frankfort area.

 SPIRITUAL LIFE

Sixteen Christian denominations are represented. The closest synagogue is in Lexington.

 STAYING CONNECTED

The local county newspaper, the *Woodford Sun*, is published weekly. Metro-area daily newspapers from Lexington and Frankfort are delivered locally. Internet service, cable television, and two local radio stations are available. There is one bookstore in historic downtown Versailles, and Midway has a college bookstore on the campus. Other major bookstores are available in Lexington and Frankfort.

 GETTING THERE

Versailles is located in the Bluegrass Region of central Kentucky between Lexington and Frankfort, the state capital. It is served by US Highways 60 and 62. The Blue Grass Parkway is three miles from Versailles via KY 33. I-64 and I-75 intersect approximately four miles north of Lexington. Air transportation is available through the Blue Grass Airport in Lexington, five miles east of Versailles. Five major airlines and three feeders provide service to major cities such as Atlanta, Saint Louis, Chicago, and Pittsburgh. The

Kentucky River, five miles west of Versailles, maintains a six-foot navigation channel from Frankfort to the Ohio River.

 RESOURCES

Woodford County
  Chamber of Commerce
141 N. Main Street
Versailles, KY 40383
(859) 873-5122
www.woodfordchamber-ky.com

Additional area website:
www.versaillesky.com

VERSAILLES
VITAL STATISTICS

CLIMATE

Annual average rainfall		46.5 inches
Snowfall		5.8 inches
Elevation		900 feet

Temperatures (in degrees Fahrenheit)

	Jan	Apr	Jul	Oct
High	39	65	85	67
Low	22	44	65	46

OCCUPATIONS

	2006	Projected 2011
Blue collar	25.4%	25.3%
White collar	61.2%	61.3%
Services	13.4%	13.4%

ADULT EDUCATION

	2000
Less than High School	26.2%
High School	36.2%
Some College	15.6%
Associates Degree	4.2%
College Degree	11.3%
Graduate Degree	6.5%

POPULATION

2006	7,997
2000-2006 Population: Annual Compound Growth Rate	1.01%
2006-2011 Population: Annual Compound Growth Rate	0.88%

Population by age group

	2006	Projected 2011
0-4	6.5%	6.4%
5-9	6.2%	6.1%
10-14	6.5%	6.6%
15-19	6.9%	6.1%
20-24	6.2%	6.1%
25-29	6.5%	6.2%
30-34	6.9%	6.8%
35-39	6.7%	6.8%
40-44	8.0%	7.2%
45-49	8.5%	8.0%
50-54	7.6%	8.1%
55-59	7.0%	7.5%
60-64	4.4%	6.0%
65-69	3.5%	3.5%
70-74	2.6%	2.8%
75-79	2.3%	2.0%
80-84	1.9%	1.8%
85+	1.7%	2.0%

Sources for Vital Statistics listed above can be found in the Preface to this book.

MISSISSIPPI

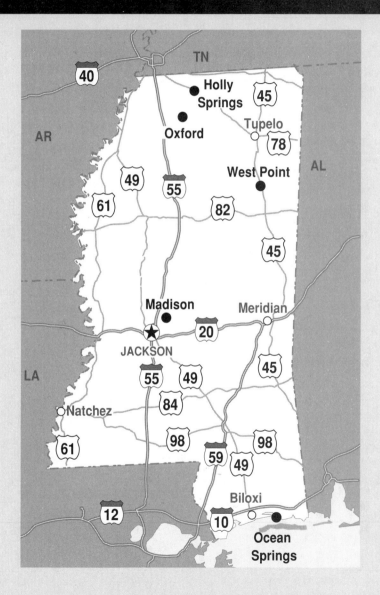

HOLLY SPRINGS

2006 POPULATION
8,140

NEAREST CITIES
Memphis, TN (35 miles)
Oxford, MS (37 miles)

ESTIMATED 2006
MEDIAN HOUSEHOLD INCOME
$26,190

COST OF LIVING
Average 3-bdrm home—$85,000
Average rent, 2-bdrm apartment—$550
Cost-of-living comparison—91.5%

SALES TAX
7%

PROPERTY TAX
Average 3-bdrm home—$1,030

Nestled in the rolling green hills and wooded countryside of northern Mississippi lies the "City of Flowers," a pleasing Southern town with a distinctive personality and a colorful history. Holly Springs, the seat of Marshall County, prides itself on the numerous antebellum homes that were spared during the Civil War. Ancient cedar-lined walkways lead to white-columned Greek Revival homes graced with grand circular stairways, medallioned ceilings, hand-cut Bohemian glass windows, and carefully tended, elegant gardens. The classic town square is built around a historic courthouse with two gazebos that serve as gathering spots for lively local discussions.

Members of the Chickasaw tribe first inhabited this region; in 1835, Carolina and Virginia settlers established a town there and named it for its abundant native holly and numerous cold water springs. Many of the settlers took up cotton farming, and they were so successful that Marshall County became the world's top producer per capita prior to the Civil War.

Ten Confederate generals were from Holly Springs, and the town saw a lot of action during the course of the war. Because of its strategic location on the railroad line leading south, Northern troops used the town as a storage center for military supplies. For much of the war, General Ulysses S. Grant occupied the town. A surprise raid, led by General Van Dorn of the Confederate Army, resulted in the destruction of all of the Union's military supplies. Mrs. Grant pleaded with the general to spare her family from harm and asked him not to burn General Grant's papers. General Van Dorn honored these requests, and in response to this kind gesture, General Grant later decided not to burn Holly Springs. Occupied by Union troops for ten years after the war, Holly Springs suffered more than most other Southern towns during Reconstruction. In 1878 the town experienced further devastation when it lost many of its citizens to a yellow fever epidemic.

Today Holly Springs has evolved into an engaging and proud community. Blending a laid-back style and comfortable sophistication, this community is proud of its history, yet open to new ideas and fresh faces. A mild year-round climate, a cost of living well below the national average, charming cottages and elegant antebellum homes, and a location within commuting distance of Memphis make Holly Springs an attractive small-town option.

 RECREATION

Holly Springs boasts a mild climate appropriate for year-round outdoor activities. There are five ball fields, two swimming pools, and eight tennis courts in town. The Kirkwood National Golf Club, a full PGA facility and member of the state Golf Association, is rated as one of the top five new public courses in the country. Holly Springs Country Club offers golf, swimming, tennis, and a clubhouse with dining facilities. Dunn's Shooting Grounds hosts seasonal quail hunts and sporting clays; fishing and meeting facilities are available year-round. Horse and cattle shows and sales, as well as rodeos, are held at the Agricultural Center Complex. Mississippi riverboat casinos, sixty miles away near Tunica, attract crowds of visitors throughout the year.

Wall Doxey State Park is located seven miles from Holly Springs. The sixty-acre spring lake is a popular spot for swimming, boating, and fishing. The park also features hiking trails and a disc golf course. Sardis Lake, approximately thirty miles away from town, has a 58,500-acre reservoir with twenty recreation sites, six beaches, and many boating ramps for lake activities.

The Holly Springs National Forest covers 154,654 acres, and is home to more than forty lakes for boating, sailing, canoeing, tubing, swimming, and fishing. Chewalla Lake Recreation Area, only five miles from Holly Springs, features a 260-acre lake for swimming, boating, and fishing. A primitive and somewhat difficult nearly

five-mile hiking trail circles the lake. Ninety-six-acre Puskus Lake, forty miles from Holly Springs, has a fishing pier, campgrounds, and an interpretive hiking trail.

 CULTURAL SCENE

Holly Springs is the state headquarters for the National Audubon Society. The Society owns both Finley Place, a historic home, and Strawberry Plains, a 35,000-acre estate that includes a Greek Revival house that was burned during the Civil War, but restored in the 1920s. Today Strawberry Plains serves as a refuge for native birds and wildlife. The Hummingbird Festival, which celebrates the September migration of the ruby-throated hummingbird to Central America, is held at Strawberry Plains. Montrose, an historic estate, is the site of the Montrose Arboretum and an antebellum Greek Revival mansion that is now the home of the Holly Springs Garden Club. The arboretum, a beautiful setting for fifty different native trees, is open by appointment.

Hillcrest Cemetery is the resting place of Hirum Revels, the first African-American U.S. Senator; Confederate war heroes; and many who died during the yellow fever epidemic of 1878. The Marshall County Historical Museum offers diverse exhibits including Chickasaw and Civil War artifacts and vintage clothing. The Yellow Fever Martyrs' Church, built in 1841, has been restored as a tribute to the thirteen Sisters of Charity and the parish priest who cared for victims of the 1878 outbreak. It now houses a museum.

The Kate Freeman Clark Art Gallery is the exclusive exhibitor of this talented portrait and landscape artist who refused to sell any of her work. The Ida B. Wells Museum is named after the journalist, teacher, civil rights pioneer, anti-lynching activist, and women's rights advocate. The gallery exhibits the works of African and African-American artists. Rust College hosts numerous cultural events. The famous Rust College A Cappella Choir tours every spring and performs locally for the college and the community. On a different note, Graceland, Too, owned by Paul McLeod, is a tribute to the King.

Open to visitors 24 hours a day, it is a unique experience for diehard Presley fans.

Several local festivals draw visitors to the region. Boasting over three hundred buildings listed on the National Register of Historic Places, Holly Springs hosts several home tours. Every April during the Annual Holly Springs Pilgrimage Tour of Homes, sponsored by the Holly Springs Garden Club, visitors can tour a sampling of the antebellum homes. The event also includes carriage rides and a seated luncheon. The Kudzu Festival takes place in June and includes a carnival, a rodeo, a 5K run, gospel, and other entertainment. Harvest Fest on the Square, featuring arts and crafts, food, and fun, is held on the last Saturday in October. December brings the Christmas Tour of Homes to benefit the Historical Museum, High Tea at the Art Gallery, the Christmas tree lighting, and the annual parade.

Proximity to Memphis and convenient access to nearby colleges and universities, such as the University of Mississippi in Oxford, make it easy for residents to find additional opportunities for culture and entertainment. Memphis, less than one hour's drive away, is home to museums, galleries, theaters, opera, and concerts, as well as Graceland and the blues of Beale Street.

 MAIN STREET

Granny Walnut's, on the town square, offers southern chicken salad, delicious desserts, and a daily plate lunch. Other favorite local hangouts include Phillips Grocery, where patrons sit at old wooden school desks and enjoy world-famous burgers; Cousin's Shell (a local gas station), where Holly Springs residents meet for morning coffee and town gossip; and Annie's Restaurant, renowned for their down country buffet at lunch. Junior Kimbrough's juke joint, featured in the film *Cookie's Fortune,* was a famous landmark for incredible Saturday night delta blues and ice-cold beer. Sadly, it was destroyed in a fire, but plans are underway to rebuild this hot Mississippi blues bar.

 HOUSING

If you are interested in owning a historic home but want to stay within a moderate budget, you will find this small town a good choice. Spacious historic homes in Holly Springs are priced much lower than comparable housing in larger cities. The town boasts many old homes, including antebellum mansions, 1800s cottages, and Victorian-style houses. Historic houses vary greatly in size, and they range in price from $100,000 to $300,000 for a 2,000-square-foot home. Larger properties are priced at $400,000 to $600,000.

New home subdivisions offer houses averaging $80,000. Prices at the housing development at Kirkwood National Golf Course range from $135,000 to $165,000, depending on lot size. Land for custom building costs approximately $10,000 to $20,000 for a two-acre lot, and building costs, approximately $70 per square foot, are exceptionally low.

Property taxes are also very low compared to the national average. Holly Springs offers a state income tax exemption for retirement plan benefits and a $7,500 property tax exemption, based on assessed value, for those over the age of sixty-five.

 ECONOMICS

Number of employers with fifty or more employees—30

Originally a major center for cotton farming, today Holly Springs specializes in light manufacturing and distribution. The largest employers in the county include Thomas and Betts (403 employees); Farr Company (270 employees); and Marshall County Correctional Facility (240 employees). A plan has been approved to build Chickasaw Trails, a 4,000-acre industrial park in the northern part of Marshall County, near the state line.

 EDUCATION

High schools—1; Middle schools—1; Elementary schools—1; Private schools—3

Rust College was established in 1866 by the Freedman's Aid Society of the Methodist Episcopal Church. It is the oldest of eleven historically black colleges and universities related to the United Methodist Church. This accredited four-year, coeducational liberal arts college offers degrees in sixteen areas of study. Other institutions for higher education in the area are the University of Mississippi in Oxford; Northwest Community College in Senatobia (30 miles); and Blue Mountain College, a Baptist women's college (40 miles).

 HEALTHCARE

Alliance HealthCare—40 beds; Physicians—12; Dentists—3

Alliance HealthCare is an acute-care facility with seven active physicians and nine emergency room physicians on rotating shifts. There are also over fourteen consulting physicians on staff. Special services include primary care, radiology, mammography, CAT scan, ultrasound, general surgery, cardiology, and ophthalmology. Dr. Kenneth Williams, who envisioned a community-oriented hospital that would meet the needs of all residents, purchased the local hospital in November 1999. Focused on preventive healthcare, the hospital is operated and staffed by members of Dr. Williams's family. Dr. Williams has even been known to make house calls. The hospital also operates a separate clinic in Holly Springs that is staffed with three physicians (one pediatrician and two internal medicine physicians) and four nurse practitioners. Additional medical services and hospitals are in nearby Memphis.

 SPIRITUAL LIFE

Sixteen Christian denominations are represented. The closest synagogue is in Memphis.

 STAYING CONNECTED

The *South Reporter* is the weekly local newspaper. The Memphis daily newspaper, the *Commercial Appeal*, is also available. There is one local radio station (WKRA) plus Rust College's campus-based radio station, and a television station offering satellite and closed-circuit programs for the college and community. Local internet service and cable television are available. There is one Christian bookstore and Rust College operates a campus bookstore. Many additional bookstores are available in Memphis, and the famous Square Bookstore is in nearby Oxford.

 GETTING THERE

Holly Springs is located in the northeastern section of Mississippi with easy access to Memphis and Oxford. It is two miles off US 78 on MS 7. Four other state highways feed into Holly Springs. Six major carriers and seven feeder airlines provide service through the Memphis International Airport (33 miles). Small aircraft are serviced through the Marshall County Airport in Holly Springs, which has a 3,201-foot runway.

 RESOURCES

Holly Springs
  Chamber of Commerce
148 East College Avenue
Holly Springs, MS 38635
(662) 252-2943
www.hollyspringsmschamber.com

Additional area websites
www.visithollysprings.org
www.hollyspringsms.us

HOLLY SPRINGS
VITAL STATISTICS

CLIMATE

Annual average rainfall	55 inches
Snowfall	4 inches
Elevation	580 feet

Temperatures (in degrees Fahrenheit)

	Jan	Apr	Jul	Oct
High	48	72	90	74
Low	29	49	68	47

OCCUPATIONS

	2006	Projected 2011
Blue collar	29.9%	29.9%
White collar	50.8%	50.3%
Services	19.2%	19.8%

ADULT EDUCATION

	2000
Less than High School	38.0%
High School	26.1%
Some College	16.1%
Associates Degree	1.6%
College Degree	11.7%
Graduate Degree	6.4%

POPULATION

2006	8,140
2000-2006 Population: Annual Compound Growth Rate	0.36%
2006-2011 Population: Annual Compound Growth Rate	0.48%

Population by age group

	2006	Projected 2011
0-4	7.0%	7.0%
5-9	6.3%	6.6%
10-14	6.6%	6.2%
15-19	8.8%	8.7%
20-24	13.7%	13.1%
25-29	8.6%	7.9%
30-34	6.8%	7.5%
35-39	5.6%	5.9%
40-44	6.5%	5.5%
45-49	6.4%	6.4%
50-54	5.3%	5.8%
55-59	4.3%	5.0%
60-64	3.3%	3.9%
65-69	3.1%	2.8%
70-74	2.7%	2.6%
75-79	1.8%	1.9%
80-84	1.6%	1.4%
85+	1.6%	1.8%

Sources for Vital Statistics listed above can be found in the Preface to this book.

MADISON

2006 POPULATION
17,369

NEAREST CITIES
Jackson, MS (15 miles)
Vicksburg, MS (55 miles)

ESTIMATED 2006
MEDIAN HOUSEHOLD INCOME
$85,408

COST OF LIVING
Average 3-bdrm home—$184,912
Average rent, 2-bdrm apartment—
No apartments
Cost-of-living comparison—
87.2%

SALES TAX
7%

PROPERTY TAX
Average 3-bdrm home—$1,860

The rolling hill country in this part of east-central Mississippi was originally a part of the Choctaw Nation. By 1828, when Madison County was established and named for James Madison, the fourth president of the United States, the hamlet of Madison had evolved into a small farming community. In 1856, the Illinois Central Railroad opened its Madison Station, bringing an influx of people and businesses attracted by the prospects of growth and prosperity. Madison was severely damaged during the Civil War following the 1861 attack on Jackson.

To encourage growth after the war, the Madison Land Company, located in Chicago on the Illinois Central Railroad line, put prime Madison land on sale for a few dollars an acre. The railroad continued to play a significant role in the town's growth. Madison eventually emerged as a major shipping center for cotton and strawberries from the 1870s until the 1930s. Today agriculture is still an active industry in the region, and manufacturing and retail/wholesale businesses have broadened the commercial base for this area.

Madison is an appealing small town located in the suburbs of Jackson, the capital of Mississippi. Antebellum and Victorian architectural treasures still grace the streets of Madison, and several buildings are on the National Register of Historic Places. When Jackson began to grow north toward Madison in the 1980s, city officials took action. Envisioning the impact of this growth on Madison, they made a commitment to preserve a high quality of life in the area. The town received a grant from the National Endowment of the Arts to develop and implement a plan to protect the area from unrestricted development. New buildings are welcome in Madison, but structures must be architect designed and approved by the city. Strict zoning

and landscape development regulations and a detailed sign ordinance further protect Madison's traditions.

Madison is the fastest growing and most affluent city in the state. Crime rates are very low. The cost of living is lower than the national average, and there is no state income tax on retirement income.

 RECREATION

Because of the mild climate, year-round outdoor activities are a way of life in Madison. Extended summers provide extra time for boating, fishing, sailing, and skiing at the Ross Barnett Reservoir, a 33,000-acre hot spot for water lovers, just a few miles from Madison. Referred to as "the Rez," it extends for forty-five miles and runs along the edge of the Natchez Trace Parkway for almost ten miles. The lake is full of bass, catfish, and perch, and anglers can choose to fish from the shore or from a boat on the lake, the spillway, or up the Pearl River. Visitors often spot white-tailed deer darting through the woods and blue herons standing quietly in marsh water. There are twenty public boat ramps, six parks and picnic areas, four camper/recreational vehicle sites, and four marinas located around the reservoir. More than ten thousand people live around the reservoir in single-family homes, apartments, or condominiums.

The Natchez Trace Parkway is ideal for hiking, walking, and driving. Maintained by the National Park Service, the Parkway offers historic sites, many breathtaking overlooks, and nature trails for hiking and off-road biking.

Once a part of a strawberry farm, Strawberry Patch Park is a delightful seven-acre park with playgrounds, walking paths, and exercise stations. Nearby is the Simmons Arboretum, a ten-acre home to a variety of trees, shrubs, flowers, and other plants. Walking trails afford a closer look at some of Mississippi's native plant life.

Liberty Park has five baseball and five soccer fields, batting cages, two volleyball courts, a walking track, and a playground. Youth sports are available for ages four and up, and summer camp programs are also offered. Golf can be played year-round on courses at five private country clubs with professionally designed eighteen-hole courses. Additional activities, including college football and professional baseball, are available in nearby Jackson.

 CULTURAL SCENE

The Madison Square Center for the Arts, a 1910 building on the National Register of Historic Buildings, presents dance, theater, and music programs throughout the year. The center is home to the Mississippi Metropolitan Ballet Company, the Center Players, and the Merchants and Farmers Bank Family Arts Series. The Center Players, a community theater group, presents several plays a year, such as *Lend Me a Tenor* and *Crimes of the Heart.* The Merchants and Farmers Bank Family Art Series brings music, theater, dance, and Broadway productions like *A Closer Walk with Patsy Cline* to Madison. A variety of classes related to art, dance, and music are also offered in this historic building in the center of town. The Mississippi Symphony Orchestra performs at the nearby

Ross Barnett Reservoir and the Strawberry Patch Park.

There are numerous festivals and special events in the area. In early May, the Swedish Festival celebrates Madison's relationship with Solleftea, her Swedish sister city. Since 1997, many Madison delegates have traveled to Sweden, and several educational and cultural exchanges have taken place. Swing into Summer, a month-long picnic occurring every Thursday evening in May, attracts locals to the Madison Cultural Center for outdoor eats, music, and a competition for the best-decorated picnic basket. The Family Fourth Celebration includes fabulous fireworks, fresh watermelon, cold lemonade, and live entertainment.

A Day in the Country, a popular fall festival, takes place at the historic Chapel of the Cross, an antebellum chapel and churchyard, home of the legendary ghost known as the Bride of Annandale. Freedom Fest, another fall event, takes place in Liberty Park and offers live music, free food, and family fun.

The Scarecrow Festival, a citywide contest and celebration, draws entries from students, area businesses, and residents. The City of Madison Annual Christmas Parade is a big event with celebrity grand marshals, decorated floats, and marching bands. Other special events include Trustmark Pre 4th of July Spectacular, Germanfest, Cajun Fest, and Christmas in the Park.

Scores of cultural opportunities, including those provided by the Mississippi Museum of Art and the Mississippi Opera, are available in nearby Jackson. The International Ballet Competition takes place in Jackson every four years, and the New Stage Theater, a professional theater company, presents five performances a year. Jackson area colleges and universities offer cultural events as well as lectures and symposiums.

 MAIN STREET

Dining choices in Madison have expanded, and today there are many options to choose from, including Chinese, Mexican, and American fare. Haute Pig, an old gas station that was miraculously turned into an elegant restaurant, is known for its warm ambience and top-quality entrées. Strawberry Café, a hot lunch spot with a casual atmosphere, serves gourmet meals. Other favorites include Bonefish Grille, where diners are greeted with white tablecloths and great fish entrees; Vasilios, a good place to get reasonably priced Greek dishes and spectacular baklava; and Hamils, a casual eatery famous for their barbecue. Residents can find many other dining options in Jackson.

Once the center of the railroad district, the Old Madison Station District is now the town's central shopping section. Housed in an old church that dates back to pre–Civil War days, Pickenpaugh Pottery is a longtime business that has sold Mississippi mud pottery for twenty-seven years. The Inside Story is located in a Victorian house and sells a little bit of everything, from unique gifts and accessories to candles and ornaments. Antique shops, art galleries, and boutiques line the nearby streets.

HOUSING

Madison is a well-planned community with over seventy subdivisions offering a wide variety of living opportunities. A few historic homes remain in the area, but most of them have been converted to commercial properties. Local committees and officials carefully oversee design, zoning, and construction and enforce the strict ordinances.

Prices vary depending on the size and description of the house. Homes in the golf course community of Annandale start at $200,000 and go as high as $1 million. The general cost per square foot for a home in a newer subdivision, including the cost of land, is approximately $100 per square foot. The cost for houses in subdivisions eight to ten years old is closer to $90 to $95 per square foot. Many of the subdivisions have recreational facilities such as pools, tennis courts, clubhouses, and lakes. Most homes in Madison are custom built on half-acre lots. A few homes are constructed on larger lots, typically one to two acres in size. Local restrictions encourage tree preservation and efforts to retain the natural beauty of the area. There are no apartments in Madison, but some condominiums can be found around the Ross Barnett Reservoir.

Madison is one of Mississippi's 21 Certified Retirement Cities, as designated by the state program, Hometown Mississippi Retirement. Positive attributes required for inclusion in the program include affordable cost of living, quality healthcare, low taxes, low crime rate, a variety of recreation activities, cultural events, education programs, and friendliness. There is a property tax exemption of $7,500 of the assessed value of a residential property for those over sixty-five. The Caboose Society is a local organization dedicated to providing educational opportunities, social activities, and community service options for senior citizens.

 ECONOMICS

Number of employers with fifty or more employees—27
Business is booming under the careful guidance of local officials. Expansion is encouraged and there are many opportunities here for future economic development. The current leading industries include manufacturing, services, local government, and retail/wholesale. Some of Madison County's leading employers are the Madison County School System (986 employees); Johnson Controls (630 employees); Peco Foods of Mississippi (526 employees); L-3 Vertex Aerospace (500 employees); Raytheon Aerospace (450 employees); Madison County Medical Center (415 employees); M-Tek Mississippi, (400 employees); State Rehabilitation Corporation (400 employees); Netcom (370 employees); Levi Strauss and Company (322 employees); The Falcon Companies (300 employees); Parker Hannifin Corporation (168 employees); and Sourcelink (145 employees). In 1997, a satellite link was established between public officials and businesspeople in Madison and Solleftea, Sweden, to encourage international business opportunities as well as cultural and educational exchanges. Haglof, Inc., a forestry products company headquartered in Solleftea, established a branch in Madison in 1997.

EDUCATION

High schools—1; Middle schools—1; Elementary schools—2; Private Schools—2

Madison's education system is one of the best in the state. There are five four-year colleges and universities in the area, including Belhaven College (1,167 students), Jackson State University (5,955 students), Milsaps College (1,300 students), Mississippi College (2,904 students), and Tougaloo College (898 students). Two-year programs are available at Hinds Community College Jackson Raymond campus (10,057 students), and Holmes Community College in Goodman (2,485 students). Retirees are allowed to audit courses or attend classes at reduced fees. The Institute for Creative Learning in Retirement on the Hinds Community College campus in nearby Raymond offers retirees expanded opportunities for learning.

HEALTHCARE

Physicians—8; Dentists—12

While there are no hospitals in Madison, there are seven major hospitals in the Jackson area, including St. Dominic-Jackson Memorial Hospital, a 571-bed acute-care facility with 450 physicians, which houses the Mississippi Heart Institute; the University of Mississippi Medical Center, which includes five hospitals and is known for transplant technology; the Baptist Health System, offering 564 beds in two hospitals; the River Oaks Health System, a 221-bed, two-campus hospital with 400 physicians; and the Methodist Rehabilitation Center, a 124-bed facility. There are three medical clinics in Madison.

SPIRITUAL LIFE

Fifteen Christian denominations are represented. The closest synagogue is in Jackson.

STAYING CONNECTED

Madison is served by two local weekly newspapers, the *Madison County Herald* and the *Madison County Journal*. The *Clarion-Ledger* is Jackson's daily newspaper and the weekly *Northside Sun* also covers the Jackson metro area, including Madison. Internet service and cable television are

available. There are many bookstores in the Jackson metropolitan
area.

 GETTING THERE

Madison is located in the central
part of Mississippi, one mile east
of I-55 on MS 463, and ten miles
north of the capital city of Jackson. The Natchez Trace Parkway
passes through Madison and goes
to the northeastern border of Mississippi and Alabama. The Jackson
International Airport, twenty
minutes from Madison, provides
air transportation on major carriers to destinations throughout the
world. Bruce Campbell Field Airport in Madison has a 4,444-foot
runway for small aircraft.

 RESOURCES

Madison TriCity Chamber of
Commerce
2168 Main Street, P.O. Box 544
Madison, MS 39130-0544
(601) 856-7060
www.madisonthecitychamber.com

Additional area website:
www.ci.madison.ms.us

MADISON
VITAL STATISTICS

CLIMATE

Annual average rainfall	52 inches
Snowfall	1 inch
Elevation	320 feet

Temperatures (in degrees Fahrenheit)

	Jan	Apr	Jul	Oct
High	55	77	92	79
Low	32	51	70	50

OCCUPATIONS

	2006	Projected 2011
Blue collar	7.7%	7.7%
White collar	86.0%	85.5%
Services	6.2%	6.8%

ADULT EDUCATION

	2000
Less than High School	2.8%
High School	11.8%
Some College	22.8%
Associates Degree	7.6%
College Degree	39.6%
Graduate Degree	15.5%

POPULATION

2006	17,369
2000-2006 Population: Annual Compound Growth Rate	2.71%
2006-2011 Population: Annual Compound Growth Rate	2.55%

Population by age group

	2006	Projected 2011
0-4	8.2%	7.9%
5-9	9.2%	8.2%
10-14	8.9%	9.7%
15-19	7.4%	7.1%
20-24	4.4%	4.2%
25-29	2.7%	5.1%
30-34	6.2%	4.1%
35-39	8.5%	7.2%
40-44	11.2%	9.2%
45-49	10.0%	10.4%
50-54	8.0%	8.7%
55-59	5.5%	7.0%
60-64	2.9%	4.3%
65-69	2.1%	2.2%
70-74	1.7%	1.5%
75-79	1.5%	1.2%
80-84	0.9%	1.1%
85+	0.8%	0.9%

Sources for Vital Statistics listed above can be found in the Preface to this book.

OCEAN SPRINGS

2006 POPULATION
17,982

NEAREST CITIES
Biloxi, MS (8 miles)
Gulfport, MS (15 miles)
Mobile, AL (57 miles)

ESTIMATED 2006
MEDIAN HOUSEHOLD INCOME
$50,627

COST OF LIVING
Average 3-bdrm home—$190,000
Average rent, 2-bdrm apartment—$820
Cost-of-living comparison—93.5%

SALES TAX
7%

PROPERTY TAX
Average 3-bdrm home—$2470

In August 2005, Hurricane Katrina attacked the shores of the Gulf Coast, wreaking havoc on cities and towns that had once graced the waterfront. Ocean Springs was one of the towns affected by this hurricane. The scenic drive along the coast and many of the grand homes overlooking the Gulf were significantly damaged and some houses were completely destroyed. The "City of Discovery" has become the "City of Recovery." Most of the town itself, however, was spared. We've tried to present an accurate description of Ocean Springs, but it is in a state of continual change and reconstruction. We recommend you contact the Ocean Springs Chamber of Commerce for current information. In spite of the damage incurred, the dedicated residents, businesses, organizations, local government, and the Ocean Springs Chamber of Commerce are working together to rebuild and repair.

Protected by the waters of Biloxi Bay, the Inner Harbor juts inland to create an ideal spot for the town. Situated on the bay that opens to the Gulf of Mexico and the Intracoastal Waterway, Ocean Springs was separated from Biloxi by a one-mile bridge to the west. This bridge was destroyed by Hurricane Katrina in 2005, but hopefully the new bridge will be completed by 2008. The town is bordered on the east by the Gulf Islands National Seashore Park and Davis Bayou Park. Live oaks line the streets of the historic district and flowers are planted in front of shops and restaurants. Charming Victorian homes blend nicely with beachside bungalows and ivy-covered cottages.

Settled in 1699 by Pierre LeMoyne d'Iberville, Ocean Springs was the first French settlement in America. After the introduction of paddle-wheel steamboats in the early 1800s, the coastal village became a place to stop for fresh water and lodging on the route

between New Orleans and Mobile. In 1854, Dr. George W. Austin of New Orleans established a sanitarium in the town, where patients could benefit from the healing freshwater springs, and changed the town's name from Lynchburg Springs to Ocean Springs. The town was incorporated that same year. Compared to the experience of many other Southern towns, the impact of the Civil War on Ocean Springs was minimal, but steamboat traffic did diminish. By 1880, the Louisville & Nashville Railroad provided a means for transporting local products like oysters and pecans to the rest of the country.

A walking tour of the historic district reveals mid-nineteenth-century houses and churches and a quaint downtown area, where ancient live oaks shade the sidewalks and shops. The Old L & N Train Depot, built in 1907, was the focal point of the town for several decades. Rail service was terminated in 1965, and today the depot is the home for the Ocean Springs Chamber of Commerce.

Sailboats dot the bay and bayou, and gulls, pelicans, and

terns circle overhead. The flat terrain is ideal for biking—either through the town, along the shore, or on the bike path. The local art community adds appeal to this charming waterfront village, attracting visitors and retirees.

RECREATION

The Ocean Springs community appreciates nature and is dedicated to its preservation. The local beaches are great spots for bird watching, walking, jogging, swimming, and picnicking. Front Beach and East Beach are divided by the Inner Harbor. Sailing, boating, fishing, and many other water sports are available. The Live Oaks Bicycle Route begins at the train depot in the downtown district and extends through the town and along the coastline for about fifteen miles.

The Mississippi Sandhill Crane National Wildlife Refuge and visitors center was established near the town of Gautier (10 miles) in 1975 to protect the endangered sandhill crane. Shepard State Park, a 396-acre park located near Gautier, offers biking, hiking, camping, and picnicking.

The Gulf Islands National Seashore was developed to protect and preserve the natural assets of five barrier islands lying off the coast of Mississippi and Davis Bayou, a salt marsh area on the mainland. This national seashore stretches for 150 miles from West Ship Island to Santa Rosa Island, Florida. The barrier islands buffer the mainland from storm impact. They are approximately ten miles offshore and can be reached only by boat. White sand beaches, dunes, coastal marshland, and maritime forest provide an efficient ecosystem for native plant and animal life, such as egrets, alligators, herons, and fiddler crabs. Excursion trips are available from Gulfport to West Ship Island for tours of Fort Massachusetts, where swimming and picnicking are allowed. Davis Bayou offers campsites, a self-guided nature trail, and a boat launch. A visitors center provides educational programs, exhibits, and a bookstore. Boat charters are available to explore these wilderness areas.

There are fifteen wonderful parks in Ocean Springs. Public and private golf courses can be found at the St. Andrews Golf Club and Gulf Hills Golf Club. Tennis is available at the Treasure Oak Tennis and Country Club and the Gulf Hills Racquet Club as well as several public parks in the area. The local recreation department offers organized sports, including youth basketball, soccer, T-ball, tackle and flag football, softball, and baseball. Swimming, fencing, and other classes are available through the YMCA.

 **CULTURAL SCENE**

This waterfront town is focused on art. Artists with sketchbooks, watercolors, and oils are common in the parks, at the beach, and on the bayou.

The Walter Anderson Museum, opened in 1991 in the historic district, pays tribute to the work of the famous twentieth-century American painter. The museum hosts lectures, concerts, films, and educational programs as well as a permanent collection of Anderson's watercolors, oils, and other works. Anderson suffered from mental illness and spent most of the last two decades of his life in relative isolation, seeking a closeness with nature and painting many animals, birds, and vegetation on the island. Peter Anderson, Walter's brother, established Shearwater Pottery in 1928 to display his own pottery as well as some of his brother's work. Today the family-owned pottery business exhibits original dinnerware, vases, and sculpted pieces.

The Art House is a newer gallery that features painted rugs, weavings, paintings, and outdoor sculpture gardens. A cooperative representing thirty working artists is run by the Ocean Springs Art Association.

The Walter Anderson Players, a community theater group, has staged live theater in the town for over twenty years. Ocean Springs also hosts dance studio productions and school programs.

Other special events include Art Walk, sponsored by downtown businesses on Labor Day weekend; the Herb and Garden Fest in March; the Christmas tree lighting; and a holiday open house. A three-day celebration commemorating the landing of d'Iberville includes a reenactment, a pageant, a parade, an arts and crafts fair, and a festive Saturday night ball. The Peter Anderson Memorial Arts and Crafts Festival in November features the work of artists from all over the South. A crowd of over 120,000 descends on Ocean Springs for this two-day event. During Art Walk, chefs, painters, musicians, potters, and sculptors demonstrate their skills at businesses and galleries throughout town.

The Mississippi Vietnam Veterans Memorial honors the state's 668 casualties. NASA-Stennis Space Center near Bay St. Louis is accessible to visitors by shuttle bus. On a more playful note, Biloxi is just down the coast from Ocean Springs, but a world away in terms of activity.

 MAIN STREET

The main fare at Ocean Springs's thirty-plus restaurants is fresh seafood. Incredible shrimp, crab, oysters, and fresh fish are widely available in this waterfront town.

Phoenicia Gourmet, Al Fresco's, and the Manhattan Grill, as well as several bars, keep the town alive at night. Ocean Springs is also home to four sushi restaurants and five coffee shops, each with their own unique ambience. Tato-Nut Shop, owned and operated by residents since 1960, is a popular meeting place for breakfast (gourmet coffee and great homemade donuts) and for lunch. Patrons at Aunt Jenny's Catfish Restaurant, known for its country atmosphere and magnificent old oak trees, enjoy their meals (good shrimp and chicken) and great views of the Bayou. Martha's Tea Room, a lovely Victorian home in the historic district (homemade soups, quiches, fabulous bread, and good coffee drinks) is also popular.

The historic districts are absolutely charming, with ancient oak trees, handsomely restored 1800s and early 1900s homes and buildings, and colorful flowers planted everywhere. Shopping here is unusually fun because nearly one hundred working artists live and sell their work in the area. There are seven lovely bed-and-breakfast inns offering charming surroundings and warm ambience.

Housing

The impact of Hurricane Katrina on the housing market in this small art town has been significant. Many properties on the beachfront areas of Front Beach, East Beach, and Belefontian Beach were completely destroyed or declared "unlivable." However, because of the high, natural elevation of Ocean Springs, homes just one block from the waterfront were not damaged. The real estate market is currently very active and local real estate agents report a continued demand for housing.

The charming historic cottages and grand homes of the mid-1800s and early 1900s found in the historic districts in the downtown area are popular with homebuyers. Prices can be high; a 3,000-square-foot home may be as much as $500,000. Houses in this area rarely come on the market and usually sell by word of mouth.

Newer homes in attractively landscaped subdivisions are more readily available for between $150,000 and $349,000. Custom-built homes are also an option. Houses in older established neighborhoods are priced at approximately $330,000 for a 1,600-square foot, three bedroom, two bath home. Ocean Springs is in demand, in part because of the excellent school system. Property is still affordable here, but the market is rising rapidly and waterfront property is becoming difficult to find. There are a few condominiums and no townhouses. Some apartments are available.

Economics

Number of employers with fifty or more employees—13

The leading industries include healthcare, the school system, apparel manufacturing, retail, and academic research. Some of the leading employers in Ocean Springs are the Ocean Springs Hospital (680 employees); Ocean Springs Schools (563 employees); Wal-Mart (186 employees); Gulf Coast Research Lab (184 employees); and Litton Data Systems (122 employees). The local art community enhances the retail businesses in this area, and tourism is a growing industry. Ocean Springs participates in the Main Street Program, which encourages business growth and development and has attracted new businesses to the area.

 EDUCATION

High schools—1; Middle schools—2; Elementary schools—4; Private Schools—2

Ocean Springs School District has received the highest level of accreditation given by the state. Opportunities for higher education are available through Mississippi Gulf Coast Community College (3,053 students) in Gautier, the University of Southern Mississippi (1,720 students) in Long Beach, and the University of Southern Alabama (12,000 students) in Mobile. The community is also served by the E. H. Keyes Vo-Tech Center and the Gulf Coast Research Laboratory, a marine biological station affiliated with the University of Southern Mississippi.

 HEALTHCARE

Ocean Springs Hospital—136 beds; Physicians—200; Dentists—14

The Ocean Springs Hospital, offering only private rooms, is a part of Singing River Hospital System, and has an active medical staff of over five hundred physicians covering every major specialty. The facility includes a new state-of-the-art 24-hour emergency department, a twenty-four-bed intensive care unit, a new cardiac catheterization lab, a s64 slice CT scanner, and MRI technology. The Ocean Springs Wellness Center is across from the hospital. There is also a ten-bed labor, delivery, recovery, and post partum department (LDRP).

 SPIRITUAL LIFE

Eleven Christian denominations are represented. The closest synagogue is in Mobile.

 STAYING CONNECTED

There are two daily newspapers, the *Sun Herald* and the *Mississippi Press Register*. The *Ocean Springs Record* and the *Bay Press* are published weekly. Cable television, one local radio station, and local internet service are available. The closest bookstores are in Gautier and Gulfport.

 **GETTING THERE**

Ocean Springs is located in the Gulf Coast region of Mississippi on MS 90, about three miles east of Biloxi. MS 609 runs north from Ocean Springs and connects to I-10 (3 miles north). Air transportation is provided through the Gulfport-Biloxi Regional Airport (20 miles west), where five major carriers as well as feeder airlines provide service to large cities like Atlanta, Fort Lauderdale, Houston, Memphis, and Nashville. The Ocean Springs Airport has a 3,500-foot runway for small aircraft.

 RESOURCES

Ocean Springs
  Chamber of Commerce
1000 Washington Avenue
Ocean Springs, MS 39564
(228) 875-4424
www.oceanspringschamber.com

OCEAN SPRINGS VITAL STATISTICS

CLIMATE

Annual average rainfall	63.2 inches
Snowfall	0 inches
Elevation	Sea Level

Temperatures (in degrees Fahrenheit)

	Jan	Apr	Jul	Oct
High	59	76	90	79
Low	42	59	74	59

OCCUPATIONS

	2006	Projected 2011
Blue collar	18.6%	19.4%
White collar	60.5%	59.3%
Services	21.0%	21.3%

ADULT EDUCATION

	2000
Less than High School	11.4%
High School	24.3%
Some College	23.9%
Associates Degree	9.9%
College Degree	19.2%
Graduate Degree	11.3%

POPULATION

2006	17,982
2000-2006 Population: Annual Compound Growth Rate	0.69%
2006-2011 Population: Annual Compound Growth Rate	0.68%

Population by age group

	2006	Projected 2011
0-4	6.0%	6.1%
5-9	5.8%	5.7%
10-14	6.8%	6.2%
15-19	7.1%	5.9%
20-24	6.2%	5.8%
25-29	5.8%	6.8%
30-34	5.7%	6.6%
35-39	6.2%	5.6%
40-44	8.7%	6.5%
45-49	8.2%	8.5%
50-54	7.8%	7.8%
55-59	6.6%	7.7%
60-64	4.8%	5.9%
65-69	4.3%	4.1%
70-74	3.3%	3.6%
75-79	2.8%	2.8%
80-84	2.0%	2.3%
85+	1.7%	2.0%

Sources for Vital Statistics listed above can be found in the Preface to this book.

OXFORD

2006 POPULATION
12,862

NEAREST CITIES
Tupelo, MS (55 miles)
Memphis, TN (75 miles)

ESTIMATED 2006
MEDIAN HOUSEHOLD INCOME
$23,627

COST OF LIVING
Average 3-bdrm home—$181,000
Average rent 2-bdrm apartment—$800
Cost-of-living comparison—86.6%

SALES TAX
7%

PROPERTY TAX
Average 3-bdrm home—$1,300

This northern Mississippi town has much to offer, and its captivating charm begins right in the center of town. There you'll find the square, which brings to mind a scene from a William Faulkner novel. The Nobel Prize–winning author lived in the Oxford house now known as Rowan Oak from 1930 to 1962. His novels reflect the charismatic settings, history, and Southern spirit of Oxford and its residents.

The Chickasaws were the area's original inhabitants. By 1829, the tribes were placed under state law, and ownership of their land was transferred to early settlers. The town of Oxford began when a general store and a log cabin were built on a hilltop. Today that plot of land is "the square." T. D. Isom, who ran the store, suggested that the town be named "Oxford" after the English town and university. In 1848, Isom established a university with an enrollment of eighty students. That school is now the University of Mississippi.

Oxford saw difficult times during the Civil War. Because the town did not have a strong military presence, it was particularly vulnerable; in 1864, both businesses and the cherished courthouse were brutally obliterated at the command of Yankee General A. J. Smith. Reconstruction took years, but Oxford continued to be the commercial and cultural center for the area during this time. The courthouse was rebuilt in 1873 and is now a popular gathering spot for locals.

Today the square is still the center of commerce and culture, offering interesting shops, attractive galleries, good restaurants, and late night blues. The extensive activities available through the University of Mississippi, better known as "Ole Miss," complement the cultural, literary, musical, and recreational opportunities in this quaint yet cosmopolitan community.

National publications have listed Oxford as a top retirement community for years; the town is now designated by the state as a Mississippi Retirement City. The college town atmosphere, varied activities, thriving cultural center, profusion of regional artists, and excellent healthcare facilities continue to support Oxford's high ranking as an appealing place to live in the South.

RECREATION

Oxford is flanked on one side by the massive Holly Springs National Forest, which offers exceptional opportunities for hiking, camping, and nature walks. One of Mississippi's six national forests, Holly Springs begins within a few miles of Oxford and extends north and east, covering about 147,000 acres. The forest holds over forty lakes, including Puskus Lake Recreation Area, only about ten miles from Oxford. Puskus is a ninety-six-acre lake perfect for boating, fishing, hiking, and camping. Nearby Sardis Lake (11 miles) is a 58,500-acre reservoir with twenty recreation sites, six swimming beaches, twenty-seven boat ramps, and over five hundred campsites. Sardis Lake Reservoir offers cabins to rent, an indoor sports gym, a restaurant, a marina, and an amphitheater. The John W. Kyle State Park adjoins part of the reservoir and has a swimming pool, tennis courts, cabins, camping, a nature trail, and Mallard Pointe, an eighteen-hole public golf course. If that doesn't offer enough variety, there are four other state parks with reservoirs within forty miles of Oxford.

In Oxford, there are two eighteen-hole golf courses, thirty-seven outdoor tennis courts, a fifty-meter public pool, and three public parks. The year-round mild temperatures are ideal for golfing, tennis, and biking (an easy and practical way to get around the town of Oxford). Local sports are popular; Avent Park has a lighted field where many teams play. The University of Mississippi draws avid supporters of football, basketball, baseball, tennis, track, and golf. Many of the Ole Miss teams are nationally ranked, and fall brings crowds of diehard Rebel football fans to the stadium.

 **CULTURAL SCENE**

Oxford is renowned as a mecca for writers, Mississippi blues musicians, and alternative artists. Two annual writers' conferences are held in Oxford: the Oxford Conference for the Book and the Faulkner Conference. Both attract writers from around the world for lectures, panel discussions, dramatic readings, and teaching sessions. Rowan Oak, home to Faulkner for over thirty years, is a significant part of the Oxford cultural tradition. The white-columned 1840s home sits on thirty-two acres and is surrounded by dignified oaks and towering cedar trees. In 1972, the author's daughter, Jill Faulkner, sold it to the University of Mississippi. A tour of the home allows visitors to see Faulkner's office; his portable typewriter and a bottle of ink still stand on the table as they did at the time of his death.

Performances, lectures, workshops, and special presentations are available through Ole Miss. The University Artist Series offers several performances in music, dance, and theater. The Center for the Study of Southern Culture, a teaching and research center, explores all aspects of Southern culture, from politics to food. The university library houses the personal album collection of B. B. King in the Blues Archive and the works of William Faulkner, Eudora Welty, and John Grisham in the Mississippi Collection. The Kate Skipwith Teaching Museum exhibits Southern folk art, Greek and Roman artifacts, nineteenth-century scientific instruments, and other collections. The Department of Theater Arts at Ole Miss presents performances throughout the year. The Ford Center for the Performing Arts is a modern facility for the University and the community, as well as a venue for Broadway shows, concerts, and theatrical productions.

The Yoknapatawpha Arts Council (YAC), housed in the newly renovated Powerhouse Community Arts Center, helps to promote the arts in Oxford and Lafayette County. It sponsors summer art camps, including dance, drama, and music classes; cosponsors an art exhibition for local schools in conjunction with Southside Gallery; assists with the Oxford Double Decker Arts Festival; and sponsors other programs that help

develop art in the community. The Southside Gallery on the square exhibits the work of local and national artists. A weekly community radio show called *Thacker Mountain Radio* is recorded live at Off Square Books and highlights musical and literary talent.

There are many annual festivals in the Oxford area. The Oxford Double Decker Arts Festival, held the last Saturday in April, is the event of the year and one of the South's largest free festivals. It regularly draws crowds of over 40,000 people to the square. One hundred artists, including painters, sculptors, photographers, potters, and metal workers, exhibit their work. The festival features an exciting lineup of Southern rock, zydeco and Cajun, pop, country, and rock and roll musicians. In May, The JazzFest features live music, big-band dances, and many jam sessions. The Oxford July 4th Celebration features fireworks and a street dance. Restaurants offer samplers of their finest cuisine at The Taste of Oxford. Local merchants sponsor a sidewalk sale and a special all-day children's festival.

The festival also includes a 10K Spring Run, a 5K Walk, and a one-mile Fun Run sponsored by the Chamber of Commerce.

 MAIN STREET

When your stomach starts growling in Oxford, you'll have a wide choice of menus—a casual meal of burgers, fried catfish, or eggs and grits, or an elegant candlelight dinner overlooking the famous downtown square. The Bottletree Bakery serves up mouth-watering pastries and homemade breads, special coffee drinks, and deli-style lunches. Go to Pearl Street Pasta for the great atmosphere, the savory dishes, and their good selection of wine and beer; if you're hungry for pizza, try the "John Wayne" special at the Old Venice Pizza Company. City Grocery, an eatery in an old livery stable with brick walls adorned with local art and a balcony bar that overlooks the square, features specialties like Virginia veal and shrimp and grits. Other options include the Downtown Grill (gussied-up traditional Southern fare like fried green tomatoes topped with crawfish);

Uptown Coffee (good espresso and scrumptious desserts); Proud Larry's (where the menu is casual and the blues bands are hot); and a comfortable neighborhood bar called Murff's (fabulous Philly cheesesteaks and good beer).

Square Books is one of the most popular hangouts in Oxford. This independent bookstore, which opened in 1979, focuses on the literature of Mississippi and the South. Over the years it has hosted many famous writers, such as William Styron, Barry Hannah, Allen Ginsburg, Alice Walker, Alex Haley, and John Grisham. The employees are friendly and knowledgeable, and the coffee shop upstairs has a cozy, at-home feeling. Just down the street, Off Square Books handles the overflow from the primary establishment, selling bargain books and used and collectible books. Square Books Jr., also located on the town square, is a children's bookstore.

 HOUSING

Oxford offers many housing options for a town its size. Many buyers want to live on the square, where historic homes range from charming cottages to elegant antebellum houses. These homes vary in size, and prices run from $180,000 to $1.2 million; the average price for an 1,800-square-foot home in good condition is approximately $260,000.

Prices for established subdivision houses begin at approximately $150,000 and go to $350,000. Larger homes in newer subdivisions cost from $320,000 to $500,000. There is one Jim Fazio golf-course community covering 500 acres. Other options include small farms and new houses on acreage. Prices for the new condominiums start at $150,000. Others range from $225,000 to 425,000—the closer to the university or the square the higher the price. There are also some new town houses that average $130,000.

 ECONOMICS

Number of employers with fifty or more employees—12
The outlook for industry and service for this small town is excellent. The primary industries in Oxford are manufacturing, education, and healthcare. Some of the leading

employers are The University of Mississippi (2,500 employees); North Mississippi Regional Center (1,100 employees); Baptist Memorial Hospital (1,000 employees); and Whirlpool Corporation Kitchenaid Appliance Group (900 employees).

 EDUCATION

High schools—2; Middle schools—2; Elementary schools—2; Private Schools—2
The University of Mississippi, founded in 1848, has grown from the original eighty students to a current student population of approximately 13,500 on the Oxford campus. This institution steeped in Southern tradition is one of the most respected universities in the South and the oldest one in the state. It was also one of the first in the country to establish an engineering program (1854) and to admit women (1882). Over one hundred programs are available, and residents aged sixty-five and older may take up to four hours in credited classes free of charge. Northwest Mississippi Community College offers continuing education classes.

HEALTHCARE

Baptist Memorial Hospital-North Mississippi—217 beds; Physicians—90; Dentists—11

Baptist Memorial Hospital-North Mississippi is a regional, acute-care facility that serves an eight-county area. The hospital has approximately ninety physicians on staff with over thirty specializations represented. Some of the services include comprehensive heart care, 24-hour emergency service, family medicine, internal medicine, neurology, obstetrics and gynecology, oncology and hematology, orthopedic surgery, pediatrics, plastic and reconstructive surgery, sleep disorder clinic, and a women's pavilion. Home healthcare is also available through area agencies.

 SPIRITUAL LIFE

Seventeen Christian denominations and several nondenominational groups are represented. There is one mosque. The closest synagogue is in Memphis.

 STAYING CONNECTED

Oxford is served by one daily local newspaper, the *Oxford Eagle,* and a University of Mississippi newspaper, the *Daily Mississippian.* There are three local radio stations, including the university station U92 (92.1 FM), which plays alternative music. Cable television and local and high-speed internet service are available. There are several local bookstores, including two student bookstores, and one on the university campus.

 GETTING THERE

Oxford is located in the north central part of Mississippi and is situated southeast of Memphis on MS 6, which connects to I-55 to the west (21 miles). MS 7 runs north to south through Oxford. Air transportation is available at Memphis International Airport, where major carriers and feeder airlines fly to principal cities. The Oxford Airport has a 5,600-foot paved runway for small aircraft.

 RESOURCES

Oxford–Lafayette County
  Economic Development
  Foundation and Chamber
  of Commerce
299 West Jackson
P.O. Box 108

Oxford, MS 38655
(800) 880-6967
www.oxfordms.com

Oxford Convention & Visitors
Bureau
102 Ed Perry Blvd.
Oxford, MS 38655
(800) 758-9177
www.oxfordcvb.com

Additional area website:
www.retire.oxfordms.com

OXFORD
VITAL STATISTICS

CLIMATE

Annual average rainfall	52.1 inches
Snowfall	1 inch
Elevation	380 feet

Temperatures (in degrees Fahrenheit)

	Jan	Apr	Jul	Oct
High	48	72	90	73
Low	26	48	68	47

OCCUPATIONS

	2006	Projected 2011
Blue collar	12.9%	13.2%
White collar	69.8%	69.0%
Services	17.3%	17.8%

ADULT EDUCATION

	2000
Less than High School	19.8%
High School	14.0%
Some College	17.0%
Associates Degree	3.2%
College Degree	23.3%
Graduate Degree	22.7%

POPULATION

2006	12,862
2000-2006 Population: Annual Compound Growth Rate	1.45%
2006-2011 Population: Annual Compound Growth Rate	1.78%

Population by age group

	2006	Projected 2011
0-4	4.9%	5.1%
5-9	4.3%	4.3%
10-14	3.6%	3.8%
15-19	8.2%	7.7%
20-24	23.5%	22.5%
25-29	11.5%	8.5%
30-34	6.3%	8.2%
35-39	4.6%	5.2%
40-44	5.2%	4.8%
45-49	4.8%	4.9%
50-54	4.4%	4.7%
55-59	4.1%	4.9%
60-64	2.8%	3.5%
65-69	2.9%	2.7%
70-74	2.3%	2.3%
75-79	2.4%	2.5%
80-84	1.9%	2.0%
85+	2.3%	2.5%

Sources for Vital Statistics listed above can be found in the Preface to this book.

WEST POINT

2006 POPULATION
11,704
NEAREST CITIES
Starkville (19 miles)
Columbus (22 miles)
Tupelo (50 miles)
ESTIMATED 2006
MEDIAN HOUSEHOLD INCOME
$28,969
COST OF LIVING
Average 3-bdrm home—$150,000
Average rent, 2-bdrm apartment—
$400
Cost-of-living comparison—
86.6%
SALES TAX
7%
PROPERTY TAX
Average 3-bdrm home—$1560

This community-minded town was one of the original Main Street Program towns in the state. Impeccably clean and attractively old-fashioned with stunning public parks placed throughout the town, West Point presents an inviting and congenial atmosphere.

The Chickasaw tribe occupied the West Point area as early as the 1500s. Their heritage is proudly remembered today in the names of surrounding towns, counties, and state parks like Oktibbeha, Noxubee, and Neshob. In 1541, famed explorer Hernando DeSoto camped near what is now West Point. By the 1690s, French and English traders had settled in the area. Soon after the settlers arrived, the French and Indian War began in the area around Tibbee Creek and the Tombigbee River. With the assistance of the Chickasaws, the British were victorious over the French. The arrival of the Mobile and Ohio Railroad in the mid-1800s led to a town charter in 1858, and expanded opportunities for trade. The Battle of West Point took place in the town in 1864, during the Civil War.

This central Mississippi plains town offers much for its residents: a serene setting, a spirited community, a revitalized downtown area, beautiful parks, easy access to the Tennessee Tombigbee Waterway for recreation, and nearby colleges and universities.

 RECREATION

The 234-mile-long Tennessee Tombigbee Waterway includes 44,000 acres of lakes and 13,000 acres of land designated as recreation areas; an additional 88,000 acres are part of an expansion plan for wildlife refuges and hunting areas. Environmental preservation and protection have taken precedence since the opening of the waterway in 1985. The "Tenn-Tom" Waterway is easy to navigate and provides opportunities for

excursions to interesting towns like Aberdeen and Columbus. Hunting is popular in the Tenn-Tom region. Deer, waterfowl, turkey, and small game are abundant. West Point is home to Mossy Oak, the number one camouflage company in the United States. A national hunting show "Hunting the Country" is produced in downtown West Point. The Town Creek Recreation Area sits on the banks of the old Tombigbee River and has over one hundred campsites, a sand beach, boat docks, and launching ramps. Kennedy Lake, located on a hilltop overlooking the waterway, is encircled by an enchanting hiking path with a series of wooden footbridges. There are scenic biking trails and multi-use play courts for basketball, volleyball, and badminton. The Waverly Recreation Area offers similar amenities as well as a trail that passes by the Waverly Slave Cemetery historic site.

Two state parks are within forty minutes of West Point. Lake Lowndes State Park has a 150-acre lake and 529-acre recreational complex with indoor and outdoor tennis courts, indoor basketball and volleyball courts, campsites, soft-ball fields, and a self-guided nature trail. The Legion State Park is within the 40,000-acre Tombigbee National Forest and has a 25-acre lake and a 420-acre park with cab-ins for rent, two fishing lakes, camping, and a nature trail. The 100-acre Choctaw Lake, part of the Tombigbee National Forest, has recreational facilities for lake sports, hiking, and camping. The Noxubee National Wildlife Refuge is a 47,000-acre haven for migra-tory birds such as the endangered red-cockaded woodpecker. Both the Tombigbee National Forest and the Noxubee National Wildlife Refuge are within thirty-five miles of West Point.

Town Creek Park is a new addition. This one-hundred-pad campground and primitive camp-ing area, located on approximately sixty acres at the river, is run by the Corps of Engineers. Waverly Waters is a unique fishing camp and skeet-shooting lodge in a beautiful setting overlooking a lake.

Residents of West Point joined together to donate and collect funds to relocate the railroad

tracks that used to run through the town. The tracks were trans-formed into a Rails to Trails Park-way, now known as the Kitty Bryan Dill Memorial Parkway. It extends for three miles through the town, linking a total of five local parks for community enjoy-ment. Each park includes lighted walkways, open areas, beautifully landscaped grounds with attrac-tive plantings, native hardwood trees, picnic areas, and a variety of structures such as gazebos, arbors, and a windmill. The Sally Kate Winters Park is situated next to the downtown commercial area. It features fountains, an old-fashioned bandstand, an elaborate playground, a romantic gazebo, and an "Arbor of Memories" made with bricks purchased in memory of loved ones.

There are two golf clubs. The Old Waverly Country Club has a 350-acre, eighteen-hole golf course designed by Jerry Pate and Bob Cupp, as well as an attractive residential community with waterfront homesites. The U.S. Women's Open Championship Golf Tournament was held at the Old Waverly Country Club in

1999. In October 2006, the Old Waverly Club held the US Women's Mid-Amateur Championship. West Point also has eight public tennis courts, ten ballparks, and an active recreation center.

 CULTURAL SCENE

West Point's downtown district is listed on the National Register of Historic Places. Located fifteen minutes from West Point is Waverly Mansion, an elegant antebellum Greek Revival mansion built in 1852. This impressive 8,000-square-foot structure has a self-supporting stairway and an octagonal sixty-five-foot opening that rises to a domed observatory. At one time the property covered 50,000 acres and was completely self-sustaining with a tannery, lumber mill, livestock, gardens, orchards, cotton gin, brick kiln, and swimming pool. After fifty years of neglect and vandalism, the home was bought in 1962 and lovingly restored over thirty-three years. Today it is open daily for tours.

The Clay County Historical Arts Museum is housed in the Friday House, one of the oldest surviving structures in the Court Street Historic District. The West Point Transportation Museum, located in the renovated train depot, exhibits a wide range of transportation history along with an extensive model train display.

The Clay County Arts Council actively promotes the arts in this Mississippi community. The Follies, featuring song and dance performed by West Pointers, is held biannually. Visiting groups have included the Mississippi Symphony, the Mississippi Ballet, Ballet Magnificat, the National Shakespeare Company, art and pottery exhibitors, madrigal singers, and barber shop quartets. The council also sponsors educational art programs. Many programs are held at Center Stage, a 450-seat performing arts facility housed in a charming 1928 historic building. Funds were raised to renovate Center Stage, and the auditorium now boasts an orchestra pit, elevated house seats, and state-of-the-art projection, sound, and lighting equipment. The Robert Harrell Amphitheater, behind Center Stage, seats 300.

The music scene in West Point

has been driven by the music of hometown artist and farmer Chester Arthur Bennett, better known as Howlin' Wolf. His music rivaled that of Muddy Waters, and he performed with some all-time great musicians like the Rolling Stones, Eric Clapton, and Ringo Starr. The Howlin' Wolf Memorial Blues Festival is an annual tribute to this musician who got his start playing juke joints in West Point. The festival is held on Friday of Labor Day weekend and hosts over fifty musicians, including blues greats like Clarence "Bluesman" Davis, the Kenny Brown Blues Band, and R. L. Burnside. The new Howlin' Wolf Museum, located one block from the Howlin' Wolf monument in the center of town, is filled with memorabilia.

The Prairie Arts Festival draws over 40,000 people each year. Held the Saturday of Labor Day weekend in downtown West Point, the event features a fine arts competitive exhibition, a huge flea market, antiques, music, food, four stages for entertainment, and a Saturday night street dance. This festival, recognized as one of the top ten events in the South for over ten years, makes for a memorable weekend in West Point. West Point is only nineteen miles from Starkville, home of Mississippi State University, which offers numerous cultural and performing arts opportunities as well as lecture series and other special events.

 MAIN STREET

Locals often gather at The Point in the historic Henry Clay Hotel for breakfast, lunch, or coffee with friends. Anthony's Restaurant, a regional landmark housed in an old grocery store, serves up Cajun-influenced lunches and dinners. Zeke-Marie's offers Southern home cooking with vegetables, fried cornbread, sweet tea, and desserts—all homemade. Staffords has the best milkshake in town, terrific burgers, barbeque, and fried eggplant. Other popular spots are Dave's Bar-b-que, Tin Lizzie (breakfast 24 hours a day); and Tank's Bar-b-que.

The Bryan Reading Park at the Bryan Public Library was built using donations to the West Point Community Foundation. This outdoor reading area features sculptures of Southern writers, a fountain, and benches. The downtown area includes practical stores as well as gift shops, antique stores, and a variety of outdoor and recreational merchandise stores.

HOUSING

Housing prices in West Point range from $30,000 to over $1 million. A few historic residences still stand near the downtown area; two neighborhoods are listed on the National Register of Historic Places. These homes are priced around $200,000. Newer houses on wooded lots, custom homes, and renovated historic buildings provide a variety of housing opportunities. Prices for updated houses in older established neighborhoods range from $125,000 to $200,000. Few new homes are built on a speculative basis, but custom building is an option. Country-club living is available at Old Waverly Golf Club, a gated community, where condominiums are priced at $225,000 and single-family homes range from $295,000 to over $1 million. Newcomers can also choose from garden homes,

estate homes, and apartments. The Henry Clay Hotel in downtown West Point, built in the 1930s and now impressively restored, offers unique residential options for active retirees. The hotel has a restaurant, meeting rooms, a parlor, and 24-hour security.

West Point's property taxes are low. For those over sixty-five there is a property tax exemption, substantially reducing the already low fees. West Point is designated as a Certified Retirement Community by the Mississippi Department of Economic and Community Development and provides various additional tax incentives. West Point is one of the first "Excel by Five" sites in the nation. This process certifies the town as a great place to raise children because it offers a balance of healthcare, community support, good education, and parental involvement.

ECONOMICS

Number of employers with fifty or more employees—15

An official Main Street Program is managed by the Clay County

Economic Development Corporation. In addition to demonstrating the town's interest in increasing business development, the program's revitalization of the downtown area has improved aesthetics and expanded available community services. Manufacturing is the leading industry, and a combination of local, regional, and national companies employ many residents. Agriculture, business, and retail trade also play a significant role in West Point's economy. Some of the leading employers include Bryan Foods, Inc. (2,500 employees); Babcock & Wilcox Company (594 employees); the West Point Schools (400 employees); Griffin Armor (400 employees); District Artex International, Inc. (317 employees); Flexible Flyer (200 employees;) and Ellis Steel.

The West Point Community Foundation, Inc. is a publicly supported organization that provides donors with a philanthropic vehicle, makes grants to nonprofit organizations, and initiates improvements to the quality of life for the community. There are only five hundred such foundations in the country, and West Point is proud to be among the smaller communities able to offer this resource.

 EDUCATION

High schools—1; Middle schools— 1; Elementary schools—4; Private Schools—2

There are five major colleges and universities in the area. Mississippi State University in Starkville has over twelve thousand students and a 4,200-acre campus. It offers degree programs at the bachelor's, master's, professional, and doctoral levels. Mississippi University for Women in Columbus was established in 1884 as the first public college for women in America. It is now a coeducational liberal arts college with over two thousand students enrolled in undergraduate and graduate degree programs. Mary Holmes College in West Point is a two-year, coeducational institution affiliated with the Presbyterian Church. East Mississippi Community College Golden Triangle Campus (10 miles) and West Point Area Vo-Tech Center are both located in town. The University of Mississippi in Oxford (82 miles) and University of Alabama in Tuscaloosa (80 miles) are additional options for West Point residents.

 HEALTHCARE

Clay County Medical Center—60 beds; Physicians—25; Dentists—4

The Clay County Medical Center is a modern primary-care facility located on a fifty-acre campus; it includes the 14,000-square-foot Clay County Wellness Center, featuring the newest exercise programs. Other services offered by the hospital include neurosurgery, oncology, radiology, intensive care, and newborn care. The center also provides seven outpatient clinics to meet community health needs. The Clay County Medical Center, part of the North Mississippi Medical Services, is located in Tupelo and offers excellent medical facilities at the largest center in the state.

 SPIRITUAL LIFE

Nineteen Christian denominations are represented. The nearest synagogue is in Columbus.

 STAYING CONNECTED

There is one daily local newspaper, the *Daily Times Leader*. Three major newspapers are delivered from Columbus, Starkville, and Memphis. Local internet service, DSL, two radio stations, and cable television are available. Local gift shops also sell books.

 GETTING THERE

West Point is located in the eastern part of the state on MS 50 and US Alternate Route 45, nine miles north of US 82. It is part of the Golden Triangle formed by West Point, Starkville, and Columbus, a fast-growing economic area. The Tennessee-Tombigbee (Tenn-Tom) Waterway is an important inland waterway linking Clay County to over 16,000 miles of inland waterway systems and the Gulf of Mexico. West Point is served by the Golden Triangle Regional Airport (11 miles), with daily connections to Atlanta, Memphis, Birmingham, and Nashville. The local McCharen Airport, within two miles of the downtown area, is available for small aircraft.

RESOURCES

West Point
  Chamber of Commerce
Clay County Economic
  Development Corporation
510 Broad Street
P.O. Box 177
West Point, MS 39773.
(662) 494-5121
www.wpnet.org

WEST POINT
VITAL STATISTICS

CLIMATE

Annual average rainfall	55.9 inches
Snowfall	2.9 inches
Elevation	250 feet

Temperatures (in degrees Fahrenheit)

	Jan	Apr	Jul	Oct
High	51	74	91	75
Low	30	51	70	51

OCCUPATIONS

	2006	Projected 2011
Blue collar	35.5%	37.1%
White collar	48.2%	46.2%
Services	16.2%	16.8%

ADULT EDUCATION

	2000
Less than High School	29.8%
High School	30.2%
Some College	19.5%
Associates Degree	3.6%
College Degree	13.0%
Graduate Degree	4.0%

POPULATION

2006	11,704
2000-2006 Population: Annual Compound Growth Rate	-0.59%
2006-2011 Population: Annual Compound Growth Rate	-0.70%

Population by age group

	2006	Projected 2011
0-4	8.0%	7.9%
5-9	7.5%	7.7%
10-14	8.1%	7.6%
15-19	7.0%	7.5%
20-24	7.6%	6.7%
25-29	7.1%	6.8%
30-34	6.6%	6.6%
35-39	5.4%	6.1%
40-44	6.1%	5.5%
45-49	7.4%	6.3%
50-54	6.6%	7.1%
55-59	5.7%	6.5%
60-64	3.9%	5.4%
65-69	3.2%	3.2%
70-74	2.9%	2.5%
75-79	2.4%	2.4%
80-84	2.1%	1.9%
85+	2.2%	2.3%

Sources for Vital Statistics listed above can be found in the Preface to this book.

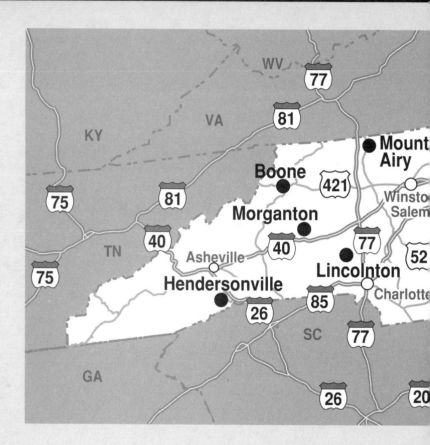

NORTH CAROLINA

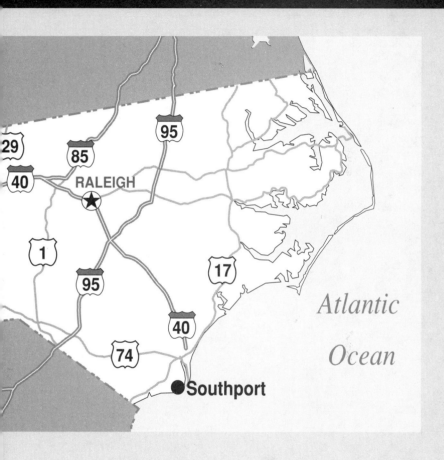

29

85

95

40

RALEIGH

1

95

17

40

74

Southport

Atlantic

Ocean

BOONE

2006 POPULATION
13,518

NEAREST CITIES
Johnson City, TN (45 miles)
Hickory, NC (50 miles)
Winston-Salem, NC (85 miles)

ESTIMATED 2006
MEDIAN HOUSEHOLD INCOME
$27,374

COST OF LIVING
Average 3-bdrm home—$240,000
Average rent, 2-bdrm apartment—
$750
Cost-of-living comparison—89.9%

SALES TAX
6%

PROPERTY TAX
Average 3-bdrm home—$1680

Boone is nestled in a breathtaking valley amidst some of the oldest, most beautiful mountains in the country. The area is dotted with wildflowers and wildlife, cascading waterfalls, and a variety of trees found only at the highest elevations of the Blue Ridge Mountains. Just one mile off the scenic Blue Ridge Parkway, Boone is a dynamic mountain town, home to a state university and an attractive resort community. There are trails to hike, mountains to climb, country roads to explore, and white-water runs to challenge the adventurous. A four-wheel-drive vehicle is the preferred transportation for off-road adventures. As a result of Boone's 3,333-foot elevation, summer temperatures typically average 78 degrees; an average of 36 inches of snow falls during the winters. Four of the best snow skiing resorts in the Southeast—and the highest skiing resort east of the Mississippi River—are in the Boone vicinity.

The Cherokee, who frequented the area to hunt and gather food, named the area Watauga, which means "whispering waters." The area was discovered by Moravians, a religious reform group from Czechoslovakia, seeking a place to live. Later, Daniel Boone —the town's namesake—explored the region and lived in a log cabin on what is now the campus of Appalachian State University.

Boone has been called the Boulder, Colorado, of the Southeast. The mountainous area, with its rugged, natural beauty, is an artist's haven; more than four hundred artists live and work here, many of them drawing inspiration from the beauty of the landscape. And Appalachian State University adds youthful vitality and culture to the town. Dozens of cafés and chic shops in the business district, only two blocks from the heart of the campus, appeal not only to the college crowd, but also to residents.

Boone was listed in *The 100 Best Small Towns in America,* and in 1998 was voted a Platinum winner of Best Mountain Town by *Blue Ridge Mountain* magazine. It was rated the best retirement bargain in the June 3, 2007 issue of *U.S. News and World Report.*

 RECREATION

Skiers flock to Appalachian Ski Mountain in Boone and the two ski resorts in the Banner Elk area, about twenty minutes from Boone. At a peak elevation of 5,500 feet, Beech Mountain is the highest ski area in eastern North America and offers fifteen slopes with a lift capacity of 8,600 skiers per hour and complete slope coverage by snowmaking equipment. Snowboarding, tubing, and ice skating are available, and an alpine village contains shops and eating establishments. Sugar Mountain, a favorite of experienced skiers, has a 5,300-foot peak, twenty slopes, and a vertical drop of 1,200 feet. Both resorts are surrounded by hundreds of private homes and condominiums, many available for rent.

The New River, one of four rivers that originate in the area, has been designated a Wild and

Scenic River and an American Heritage River. It is a challenging course for white-water rafters. Several mountain guide services, outfitters, and rafting services are located around Boone. The vast forests and high mountains of the surrounding wilderness areas are popular hunting grounds for big and small game. Streams and lakes are full of trout, bass, blue gill, and other native varieties of fish. Hikers and campers can choose from many outstanding mountain settings, including the famous Linville Falls and Linville Gorge Wilderness Area, home of an Outward Bound camp. Horseback riding is also offered at several local stables.

There are five golf courses in the county, two of which are open to the public. Most of the courses, many of which are known for their beautiful mountain vistas, are open for six months of the year, weather permitting. Boone Golf Club is a popular eighteen-hole public course; Hounds Ears Club and Grandfather Golf and Country Club are two of the local private courses.

The Watauga County Parks and Recreation Department has year-round programs for children and adults, including baseball, softball, tennis, skiing, football, soccer, basketball, volleyball, and swimming. The county's main recreation complex has an indoor pool, lighted tennis courts, and ballparks. The Deer Valley Sports and Fitness Center is a private club and fitness center with indoor tennis courts, racquetball courts, indoor and outdoor pools, a gymnasium, and a weight and cardiovascular room; resident and nonresident memberships are available. Several county parks offer scenic overlooks, and the Boone Greenway Pedestrian/ Biking Trail is a 3.5-mile path for walking, jogging, biking, and cross-country skiing.

 **CULTURAL SCENE**

More than four hundred artists live and work in the region, and at least fourteen galleries and numerous shops and showrooms display fine arts and crafts native to the area. The local arts agency, the Watauga County Arts Council, supports visual and performing arts and maintains the Jones

House, a historic home in the heart of Boone; three art galleries are located in the house. The Turchin Center for the Visual Arts on King Street and on the Appalachian State University campus, features rotating art and sculpture exhibits. The Alta Vista Gallery and Bed and Breakfast in the town of Valle Crucis has a collection of mountain landscape paintings and other works by over two hundred world-renowned and locally recognized artists.

The Appalachian Heritage Museum focuses on the culture and history of the Blue Ridge Mountains and their people. Authentically costumed interpreters at Hickory Ridge Homestead demonstrate eighteenth-century mountain life. The *Horn in the West,* part of the Homestead, is the third-oldest outdoor drama in the United States. The late eighteenth-century saga depicts the life of Daniel Boone and the other rugged mountain settlers who struggled against the British militia and the Cherokee. The Daniel Boone Native Gardens, also part of the complex, displays an impressive array of the native flora of the Appalachian region.

The Blowing Rock Stage Company, a professional theater offering drama, music, and comedy, performs during the summer at the Blowing Rock Arts Center. Boone also is home to the Blue Ridge Community Theatre. Appalachian State University, through its Office of Cultural Affairs, presents an excellent schedule of performing arts, lectures, and visual arts throughout the year, including an Irish dance company, the North Carolina Symphony, chamber ensembles, jazz groups, organ concerts, ballet performances, and a summer music festival. The Appalachian Summer Festival, a showcase of music, dance, theater, and visual arts, is held at various locations on the Appalachian State University campus.

Numerous other festivals occur in and around Boone. Merlefest is an annual celebration commemorating the life and music of Merle Watson, son of Doc Watson, who made this region's bluegrass and folk music world famous. The gospel music of "Singing on the

Mountain" marks the start of summer at Grandfather Mountain in Linville, North Carolina's top scenic attraction. On the second weekend in July, the call of the bagpipes on Grandfather Mountain heralds the Highland Games and Gathering of the Scottish Clans at MacRae Meadows. This popular event draws visitors from adjoining states and is one of the largest Scottish festivals in the country. Other events include an Easter Eggstravaganza, a Fourth of July parade, the downtown Halloween "BOO," the Annual Kraut Creek Festival in late September, and the Boone Christmas parade.

 MAIN STREET

Local bands entertain on weekends at the Caribbean Café (authentic Caribbean cuisine); the Daniel Boone Inn Restaurant, housed in a historic inn, serves family-style lunches and suppers. Other local favorites are Black Cat Burrito; Our Daily Bread (breakfast and sandwiches, as well as vegetarian specialties); Bandana's Bar-B-Que and Grill (pit-smoked Southern-style barbecue); and Red Onion Café (soups, salads, gourmet pizza, and burgers). More than seventy other restaurants in Boone offer a variety of fare, from international cuisine to country cooking. Additional dining choices are plentiful in nearby towns such as Blowing Rock.

The Mast General Store is a popular attraction for young and old. At this 1913 downtown Boone landmark, scented with the aromas of freshly ground coffee and well-oiled floors, you can buy goods ranging from casual clothing to old-timey housewares, or you can visit the outfitters department or the Mast Candy Barrel. The Wilcox Emporium Warehouse is a historic downtown warehouse, home to more than 240 vendors (antiques to souvenirs), and Café 161, serving lunch and dinner.

 HOUSING

Housing in the mountains often revolves around golfing, skiing, and resort living, and prices are slightly higher than in other small towns. The expense of transporting materials to mountain building sites adds to the cost of construction. Prospective home-buyers can find several gated private developments—including Chota, Jefferson Landing, Yonahlossee, Chetola, Hound Ears, Grandfather Golf and Country Club, and the Elk River Club—within twenty miles of Boone. Prices are generally over $300,000. There are no traditional subdivisions in the area. A typical condominium with two bedrooms sells from around $150,000. Inexpensive apartments and condos in Boone attract students; university faculty and staff own some of the larger homes. Both apartments and seasonal homes are available for rent.

 ECONOMICS

Number of employers with fifty or more employees—27
Appalachian State University (2,300 employees), is the single largest employer. Other major employers include Watauga County Board of Education (900 employees); the Appalachian Regional Medical Center (925 employees); IRC Corporation (300 employees); Charleston Forge (250 employees); Samaritan's Purse International Relief;

ECR Software; and Hospitality Mints. Tourism is the dominant industry in the county; the housing market, primarily second home and resort communities, is also a significant source of economic activity. A small-business incubator and technology development center associated with the university encourages small-business growth.

 EDUCATION

High schools—1; Elementary/Middle schools—8; Private schools—2
Three local schools participate in a distance learning project, a nontraditional nonclassroom approach to education. Appalachian State University has 15,000 students and offers more than 170 undergraduate majors and approximately 130 graduate majors in the arts and sciences, business, fine and applied arts, education, and music. Senior citizens can take special classes at the Institute for Senior Scholars and can audit one course per term without charge. Caldwell Community College and Technical Institute campus in Boone offers two-year programs and technical training.

HEALTHCARE

Watauga Medical Center—117 beds; Physicians—125; Dentists—17
Watauga Medical Center is a regional primary and secondary hospital offering a 24-hour emergency department, a pain clinic, maternity services, and other traditional medical services. The Seby B. Jones Regional Cancer Center on the hospital campus administers radiation and chemotherapy treatment.

 SPIRITUAL LIFE

Twenty-two Christian denominations are represented. There is one Unitarian Universalist Congregation and a synagogue.

 STAYING CONNECTED

The *Watauga Democrat* newspaper is published three times per week and the *Mountain Times* and the *High Country News* are published weekly. Six radio stations serve the area. Cable television is available, and satellite television is popular in the rural areas. Several internet service providers are available. There are five bookstores in the area.

 GETTING THERE

Located in the northwestern mountains of North Carolina, Boone is at the intersection of US 321, 421, and 221. Interstates 77, 81, and 40 are all within one hour. The Blue Ridge Parkway passes near the city limits. The Boone Airport features a 2,650-foot runway for general aviation. Commercial airline flights are available from the Tri-City Regional Airport in Johnson City, Tennessee; the Douglas International Airport in Charlotte, North Carolina; and the Piedmont Triad Airport in Greensboro, North Carolina.

 RESOURCES

Boone Chamber of Commerce
208 Howard Street
Boone, NC 28607
(828) 264-2225
www.boonechamber.com

Boone Convention and
Visitors Bureau
208 Howard Street
Boone, NC 28607.
(800) 852-9506
www.VisitBooneNC.com

BOONE
VITAL STATISTICS

CLIMATE

Annual average rainfall	50 inches
Snowfall	36 inches
Elevation	3,333 feet

Temperatures (in degrees Fahrenheit)

	Jan	Apr	Jul	Oct
High	38	58	75	59
Low	20	38	58	41

OCCUPATIONS

	2006	Projected 2011
Blue collar	9.7%	9.6%
White collar	62.8%	62.0%
Services	27.5%	28.4%

ADULT EDUCATION

	2000
Less than High School	13.7%
High School	17.7%
Some College	15.2%
Associates Degree	7.0%
College Degree	23.2%
Graduate Degree	23.3%

POPULATION

2006	13,518
2000-2006 Population: Annual Compound Growth Rate	0.05%
2006-2011 Population: Annual Compound Growth Rate	0.50%

Population by age group

	2006	Projected 2011
0-4	3.0%	2.9%
5-9	2.7%	2.6%
10-14	3.0%	2.9%
15-19	16.0%	15.6%
20-24	29.6%	30.6%
25-29	6.3%	5.6%
30-34	4.3%	4.0%
35-39	4.4%	4.2%
40-44	4.6%	4.4%
45-49	4.4%	4.4%
50-54	4.5%	4.7%
55-59	4.2%	4.5%
60-64	3.2%	3.6%
65-69	2.5%	2.7%
70-74	2.0%	2.0%
75-79	2.0%	1.9%
80-84	1.6%	1.6%
85+	1.7%	1.8%

Sources for Vital Statistics listed above can be found in the Preface to this book.

2006 POPULATION
    10,809

NEAREST CITIES
    Asheville, NC (22 miles)
    Greenville, SC (30 miles)

ESTIMATED 2006
MEDIAN HOUSEHOLD INCOME
    $39,158

COST OF LIVING
    Average 3-bdrm home—$245,000
    Average rent, 2-bdrm apartment—$750
    Cost-of-living comparison—100%

SALES TAX
    6%

PROPERTY TAX
    Average 3-bdrm home—$1,600

Perched atop a 2,200-foot scenic mountain plateau, Hendersonville is a beautiful, clean town and a popular retirement community with abundant cultural and recreational opportunities. Thanks to higher mountain ranges to the north and west that block arctic blasts, this four-season area enjoys moderate summers and mild winters. Some compare Hendersonville to Aspen, Colorado, because of the spectacular mountain views and upscale attractions.

Hendersonville's picturesque and thriving historic downtown district covers eight blocks. Main Street, the key thoroughfare through the historic district, was transformed into a serpentine drive and landscaped with raised brick flowerbeds surrounding midsize trees. Sidewalk benches under the shade trees on Main Street invite people to sit down and relax. The Claddagh and Waverly Inns, both registered historic buildings, are located on the north end of Main Street. The old train depot is painted in crisp yellow and white. Visitors can pick up a brochure and take a self-guided walking tour of the town's significant landmarks.

RECREATION

The beautiful Great Smoky Mountain National Park and the Pisgah National Forest, a short drive or day trip from Hendersonville, offer white-water rafting, fishing, hiking, canoeing and boating, horseback riding, and more. The North Carolina Arboretum, located in the Pisgah National Forest, is an unusual public garden where workshops and seminars are offered; visitors can stroll through the grounds on the handicapped-accessible marked trails and walkways. The French Broad River and Mills River, a short distance north of town, provide ideal spots for fishing, boating, kayaking, and canoeing.

North Carolina is well known as a golfer's paradise, and the selection of public and private courses in the Hendersonville area rivals the selection expected in a large city. The moderate climate permits nearly year-round play. The six public courses range from several championship eighteen-hole courses to two nine-hole executive courses. The five private and semiprivate courses include Champion Hills, designed by renowned course designer and Hendersonville resident, Tom Fazio.

There are plenty of city and county parks offering tennis courts, fields for soccer and baseball, walking trails, pools, and picnic facilities. The YMCA operates a large complex, which has a heated indoor pool complete with a special lift for those with limited mobility, as well as a gym, indoor tennis courts, a weight training center, a childcare center, and a youth center.

CULTURAL SCENE

The sheer number and variety of arts available in the community will amaze visitors, even those from a large city. Renowned art exhibits, nationally recognized theater productions, a seventy-piece symphony orchestra, and a one hundred-voice chorale quickly impress newcomers.

The Arts Center includes a gallery with a community reception and meeting area, classrooms, and rental studio space. The Arts Council of Henderson County sponsors the annual Sidewalk Art Show along historic Main Street and monthly one-artist shows at a local gallery. Galleries include Wickware Fine Art/Folk Art, a gallery space for artists and artisans, and Touchstone, specializing in contemporary art and fine American craft. Also noteworthy are Hand in Hand, a charming gallery in nearby Flat Rock; Singleton Center, a collection of artist galleries and studios, art schools, and businesses; A Show of Hands; McCarter Gallery; and Silver Fox Gallery.

There are also many options for performing arts, including the Carolina Chamber Singers, who present classical, religious, and secular music concerts; the one-hundred member Hendersonville Chorale; the Hendersonville Symphony Orchestra, whose seventy musicians give five concerts a year; the Hendersonville Community Concert Band; and the Hendersonville Swing Band, which plays the music of the '30s, '40s, and '50s. Several groups, including the Belfry Players and Hendersonville Little Theater, offer a variety of theatrical productions.

The Hendersonville Film Society specializes in high-quality foreign, private, and alternative films. The Skyland Arts Cinema Center, a theater where patrons can order food, wine, beer, and coffee in an intimate film-viewing atmosphere, is housed in the Skyland Hotel, a 1920s Hendersonville landmark. The hotel is also home to an arts center.

Interesting events include Garden Party Jubilee downtown in late May; an antique show in June; Music on Main, held downtown every Friday night from June through August; Monday Night Street Dances from July until Labor Day at the Visiter Center on Main Street; the Fabulous 4th Celebration; the Sidewalk Art Show and Sale in August, where over one hundred artists exhibit frameable art; the North Carolina Apple Festival on Labor Day Weekend, which attracts 250,000 people; the Christmas parade through downtown; Holiday Tour, featuring several historic Hendersonville and Flat Rock homes; and the Olde Fashioned Hendersonville Christmas in downtown, the first Friday night in December.

Flat Rock, the home of the Carl Sandburg Historic Site, is just three miles from Hendersonville. The nationally known Flat Rock Playhouse, the home of the State Theater of North Carolina, stages ten professional productions between May and October, featuring performers who hail from Broadway and the West Coast. About twenty-five miles southwest of Hendersonville is the lovely town of Brevard, home

of the Brevard Music Center. Each summer, 370 of the world's most promising young musicians and sixty of the nation's most respected music teachers come together for a seven-week music camp. On several weekends, students and faculty perform. Hendersonville residents can also drive to the city of Asheville and take in the large art and mountain craft galleries and shops, entertainment, and events held at the University of North Carolina.

 MAIN STREET

Café Calabria is a quaint Italian restaurant. Cypress Cellar offers authentic Cajun cuisine for lunch and dinner. Hannah Flanagan's Pub and Eatery serves delectable Irish dishes and selections from their extensive beer and draft selection. Other popular restaurants are Expressions, an upscale restaurant that has an extensive wine list; The Pampered Palate, offering sandwiches, vegetable dishes, and quiches; and Three Chopt Sandwich Shop. Several local inns have small dining rooms open to the public and some places provide entertainment on weekends.

There are over 150 businesses in Hendersonville, representing a mix of specialty shops, banks, antique stores, galleries, restaurants, and services. One of the four famous Mast General Stores opened in downtown Hendersonville in 1904 (see Boone, North Carolina). The store features old-timey mercantile products such as cast-iron cookware, folk toys, oil lamps, and rockers, along with traditional clothing, mountain outfitting gear, and rugged and casual footwear. The Curb Market, opened in 1924, is a genuine farmer's market where about one hundred Henderson residents sell fresh vegetables, homemade foods, and other specialty items.

 HOUSING

Much of the housing selection in Hendersonville is upscale. There are more than 350 housing developments in the county and dozens of gated, golf, retirement, and manufactured home communities. Prices start at $87,000 for lots in

Glenroy Heights at Kenmure, a gated community with a country club, located in Flat Rock. Mountaintop homes with views are in the $200s and $300s. Highland Lake, a 100-acre resort with a golf course, has single-family homes from the high $200s to the $400s. A large selection of condominium communities and apartments is also available.

Retirement housing is diverse. Individual homes in a retirement community are priced in the $100s. There are several continuing-care centers, though they currently are fully occupied. The senior services and amenities associated with senior housing are far above average in Hendersonville and the surrounding area.

 ECONOMICS

Number of employers with fifty or more employees—66

The economic base is a well-balanced mix of industries, including manufacturing, agriculture, tourism, and retirement. Henderson is the seventh largest apple-growing region in the country, producing 85 percent of the state's crop. The area is also the second in ornamental plant production in North Carolina. The largest employer is the Henderson County School system with over 1,600 employees. Among the remaining major employers are Pardee Hospital (1360 employees); Park Ridge Hospital (760 employees); Wilsonart International (800 employees); General Electric Lighting Systems (725 employees); and Arvin Meritor Automotive (700 employees). There are twenty stock brokerage firms located in Henderson County, possibly because of the number of retirees.

EDUCATION

High schools—4; Middle schools—4; Elementary schools—2; Charter schools—1; Private schools—7
The consolidated county school system, with over 12,000 students, serves both the City of Hendersonville and Henderson County. Blue Ridge Community College, with 1,500 students, offers programs leading to an associates degree. For those over age fifty-five, the Center for Lifelong Learning at Blue Ridge offers courses of varying lengths, workshops, seminars, and lectures. Brevard College, in nearby Brevard, offers a two-year certificate. The University of North Carolina at Asheville has a broad range of liberal arts degree programs. It is also the site of the North Carolina Center for Creative Retirement, a program that has received national recognition for its education programs and projects for retirement-age people.

HEALTHCARE

Pardee Hospital—262 beds; Park Ridge Hospital—100 beds; Physicians—140; Dentists—35
Pardee Hospital is a county-owned, nonprofit hospital that provides surgical, orthopedic, comprehensive cancer, maternal, pediatric, intensive, and coronary care as well as mental health services. It has a large 24-hour emergency department, a cancer care unit, and a 110-bed skilled nursing unit. Park Ridge Hospital, located in the town of Fletcher and operated by the Seventh-Day Adventist Church, is a full-service general, acute, and surgical-care

hospital with psychiatric services. It also has a 24-hour emergency care center and a maternity unit.

 SPIRITUAL LIFE

Forty-two Christian and non-Christian denominations or religious organizations are represented. There is one synagogue.

 STAYING CONNECTED

The *Times-News,* affiliated with the *New York Times,* is published daily. The *Asheville Citizen-Times* is published daily and delivered to the Hendersonville community. Other publications include the *Mountain Express,* a weekly covering local entertainment, and *Bold Life,* a monthly featuring art, music, and cultural events. Cable television is available, with stations in Asheville, North Carolina, and Greenville and Spartanburg, South Carolina. There is also a good selection of radio stations, including an NPR affiliate in Asheville. Local and national internet service is available. There are two local bookstores in Hendersonville and one in Flat Rock.

 GETTING THERE

Hendersonville is southeast of Asheville, between the Blue Ridge and Great Smoky Mountains. US Highways 64, 25, and 176 go through the town, and I-26 passes the edge of town. Hendersonville Airport has a 3,300-foot paved and lighted runway. The Asheville Regional Airport (10 miles) offers daily flights to Houston, Minneapolis, and Newark, and other cities via Delta, US Airways, Delta connector airline ASA, Continental, and Northwest. At the Greenville-Spartanburg Jetport, thirty miles to the south, American, Continental, Delta, United, and US Airways provide daily connections to several major cities.

 RESOURCES

Hendersonville County
  Chamber of Commerce
330 North King Street
Hendersonville, NC 28792
(882) 592-1413
www.hendersonvillechamber.org

Hendersonville County
 Travel and Tourism
201 South Main Street
Hendersonville, NC 28792
(800) 828-4244
www.historichendersonville.org

Additional area website:
www.wncguide.com

HENDERSONVILLE
VITAL STATISTICS

CLIMATE

Annual average rainfall	58 inches
Snowfall	12 inches
Elevation	2,200 feet

Temperatures (in degrees Fahrenheit)

	Jan	Apr	Jul	Oct
High	47	69	84	68
Low	25	42	62	43

OCCUPATIONS

	2006	Projected 2011
Blue collar	27.6%	27.1%
White collar	55.3%	54.9%
Services	17.1%	18.0%

ADULT EDUCATION

	2000
Less than High School	19.3%
High School	22.2%
Some College	23.2%
Associates Degree	4.9%
College Degree	18.8%
Graduate Degree	11.7%

POPULATION

2006	10,809
2000-2006 Population: Annual Compound Growth Rate	0.59%
2006-2011 Population: Annual Compound Growth Rate	1.46%

Population by age group

	2006	Projected 2011
0-4	5.2%	5.3%
5-9	4.9%	4.7%
10-14	5.5%	5.2%
15-19	5.1%	5.1%
20-24	6.0%	5.8%
25-29	5.2%	5.6%
30-34	5.4%	5.1%
35-39	5.5%	5.1%
40-44	6.0%	6.0%
45-49	6.5%	6.0%
50-54	6.5%	6.7%
55-59	6.2%	6.8%
60-64	5.4%	6.6%
65-69	4.3%	5.1%
70-74	4.7%	4.3%
75-79	5.5%	4.4%
80-84	5.8%	5.2%
85+	6.1%	7.0%

Sources for Vital Statistics listed above can be found in the Preface to this book.

2006 POPULATION
10,422

NEAREST CITIES
Hickory, NC (20 miles)
Charlotte, NC (35 miles)

ESTIMATED 2006
MEDIAN HOUSEHOLD INCOME
$38,875

COST OF LIVING
Average 3-bdrm home—
$125,000
Average rent, 2-bdrm apartment—$550
Cost-of-living comparison—
92.8%

SALES TAX
6%

PROPERTY TAX
Average 3-bdrm home—
$1200

Lincolnton provides not only a family-oriented atmosphere and a low cost of living but also an expansive slate of cultural offerings. Over fifty civic clubs and organizations sponsor a multitude of programs. The spirit of volunteerism, civic pride, and responsibility run deep in this small town. Religion plays a significant role in the town's history; Lincoln County is the only North Carolina county to have six churches listed on the National Register of Historic Places.

The county, formed in 1779, was named for Major General Benjamin Lincoln, the man selected by General George Washington to accept the official sword of the British surrender at Yorktown. Lincolnton and the surrounding area was the site of both Revolutionary and Civil War battles and events.

The town has prospered partly because of economic diversification, spurred by the business community's encouragement of industrial expansion and relocation. The stores in the downtown district are traditional small-town establishments, and few spots are vacant. Attractive "Downtown Lincolnton" banners are attached to period street lamps. The stately Greek Revival county courthouse, whose entrance is flanked by massive columns, sits in the center of the downtown area; the main business district thoroughfares radiate from it in four directions. Because of Lincolnton's convenience to metropolitan Charlotte, residents are able to take advantage of larger cultural and sports events and other big city amenities while enjoying the benefits of living in a thriving small town.

 RECREATION

The eastern border of Lincoln County follows the shoreline of Lake Norman, the region's largest lake, which has 520 miles of shoreline. Water sports such as waterskiing, swimming, fishing, sailing, and jet skiing are popular.

Queens Landing, a family entertainment center on the lake, provides two eighteen-hole miniature golf courses, a large bumper boat pool, two tennis courts, and a paddlewheel riverboat for lake cruising.

Betty Ross Park is home to a public swimming pool, tennis courts, softball fields, a gymnasium, racquetball courts, playgrounds, and a picnic area. There are three golf courses in the county; two are public and one private. A unified city/county recreation department offers organized sports. The Lincoln County Family YMCA contains an indoor heated pool, a fitness center, a full gym, and an indoor jogging and walking track. There is a Senior Center at Gaston College.

Professional spectator sports are available in nearby Charlotte and include football, basketball, and hockey. NASCAR racing can be enjoyed at Lowe's Charlotte-Motor Speedway.

 **CULTURE SCENE**

At several different venues the Lincoln Arts Council sponsors a wide assortment of performing and visual arts events, such as art exhibits, recitals, opera, and ballet. The Lincoln Cultural Center provides space for the Lincoln County Museum of History, a performance hall, art galleries, an art studio, a resource library, a gift shop, and a reception/exhibition hall. The Lincoln Choral Guild produces a Christmas program and offers classes for children and adults. The Lincoln Theater Guild, which involves many local volunteers, brings several productions to the community and sponsors an annual drama camp. The North Carolina Symphony makes an annual visit to Lincolnton and presents a free concert to county school students. The Lincoln Community Concert Association hosts at least three nationally known performing artists annually. Performances by a local choral guild and a local group of the North Carolina Symphony are held at the twelve-hundred-seat Citizen's Center.

The major outdoor community events are the annual Lincoln County Apple Festival in September, which attracts over forty thousand visitors; the Tree Lighting Ceremony at the courthouse on the square in late November; and the Christmas parade in mid-December.

 ## MAIN STREET

Some of the locals' favorite restaurants include the Lincoln House (upscale dining); City Lunch (good Southern cooking); Home Place Restaurant; Aunt Bessie's (home-style cooking); Ramseur's (sandwiches); Sagebrush Steakhouse; and Melamoose Ice Cream Shop. Fausto Coffee/Ride-A-Bike Bicycle Shop is a unique espresso coffee bar combined with a bicycle shop.

 ## HOUSING

Many of the old Federal-style homes in the historic district have been restored or preserved. Few of these houses are available for sale, but when they do come on the market, they are cheaper than comparable houses in metropolitan areas. Families will find a good assortment of large homes within subdivisions near schools and shopping. The elegant houses adjacent to golf courses and the houses and condominiums flanking Lake Norman are also popular.

A luxury, custom-built house with 2,200 square feet recently sold for $250,000. Parcels of land with or without houses are also available. Outside the city limits, three-bedroom, two-bath homes with 1,500 square feet or more of living space sell for $115,000 to $150,000. Condominiums are available. A good assortment of apartments is available in Lincolnton, as well as retirement-oriented condominium communities around Lake Norman.

 ECONOMICS

Number of employers with fifty or more employees—36

No one company dominates the local economy. The community has done an excellent job attracting such well-known national and international companies as Robert Bosch Tools to invest in plants in the area. Some of the major employers are Cochrane Furniture (400 employees); R'Anell Custom Homes (425 employees); Julius Blum, Inc. (350 employees); La-Z-Boy Chair Co. (400 employees); Mohi-can Mills (350 employees); The Timken Company (790 employees); and Robert Bosch Tools (500 employees). Proximity to Charlotte and the excellent highway connections should assure Lincolnton's continued economic growth.

 EDUCATION

High schools—5; Middle schools—4; Elementary schools—11; Private schools—2

Gaston College has two campuses, the main campus in Dallas and one in Lincolnton. Catawba Valley Community College is another local college. Eight additional colleges and universities are within forty-five miles of the county. Among the well-known colleges in the area are the University of North Carolina at Charlotte, Lenoir-Rhyne College, Winthrop University, Appalachian State University, Gardner-Webb University, Belmont Abbey College, and Davidson College.

 HEALTHCARE

Lincoln Medical Center—101 beds; Physicians—75; Dentists—20

The hospital provides 24-hour emergency care, a 24-hour critical-care unit, and programs including maternity, surgery, and diagnostic services. Lincoln Medical Center has recently been awarded "Accreditation with Commendation" by the Joint Commission on Accreditation of Healthcare Organizations (JCAHO), a level of excellence achieved by only 10 percent of all accredited hospitals in the United States. More extensive medical services are within an hour's drive in Charlotte.

 SPIRITUAL LIFE

Sixteen Christian denominations are represented. The closest synagogue is in Charlotte.

 STAYING CONNECTED

The *Lincoln Times-News* is published three times per week. The *Charlotte Observer,* published daily, is delivered locally. Charlotte's network affiliate television stations and public radio extend to Lincolnton, and cable television and local internet service are available. There is one local bookstore.

 GETTING THERE

Lincolnton is northwest of Charlotte and only twenty minutes from Interstates 85, 40, and 77. US 321 runs through town. Lincolnton is two hours from the North Carolina mountains and four hours from the Carolina beaches. The local airport has a 5,500-foot paved, lighted runway. The closest commercial airport is Charlotte Douglas International Airport, forty-five minutes southeast, where several major airlines offer over five hundred flights daily, including nonstop service to Europe.

 RESOURCES

Lincolnton/Lincoln County
Chamber of Commerce
P.O. Box 1617
Lincolnton, NC 28093
(704) 735-3096
www.lincolnchamber.org

LINCOLNTON VITAL STATISTICS

CLIMATE

Annual average rainfall	47 inches
Snowfall	10 inches
Elevation	860 feet

Temperatures (in degrees Fahrenheit)

	Jan	Apr	Jul	Oct
High	49	72	87	72
Low	28	46	66	47

OCCUPATIONS

	2006	Projected 2011
Blue collar	38.1%	38.6%
White collar	51.2%	50.3%
Services	10.8%	11.1%

ADULT EDUCATION

	2000
Less than High School	32.9%
High School	25.9%
Some College	18.3%
Associates Degree	5.3%
College Degree	12.6%
Graduate Degree	5.0%

POPULATION

2006	10,422
2000-2006 Population: Annual Compound Growth Rate	0.72%
2006-2011 Population: Annual Compound Growth Rate	1.33%

Population by age group

	2006	Projected 2011
0-4	6.1%	6.2%
5-9	5.8%	5.5%
10-14	5.8%	6.0%
15-19	6.1%	5.6%
20-24	5.9%	6.2%
25-29	7.0%	5.8%
30-34	6.9%	6.8%
35-39	7.2%	6.6%
40-44	7.0%	7.4%
45-49	6.6%	7.1%
50-54	6.9%	6.4%
55-59	5.7%	7.2%
60-64	5.3%	5.3%
65-69	3.7%	4.7%
70-74	3.8%	3.1%
75-79	3.6%	3.5%
80-84	3.4%	3.1%
85+	3.3%	3.7%

Sources for Vital Statistics listed above can be found in the Preface to this book.

MORGANTON

2006 POPULATION
17,310

NEAREST CITIES
Hickory, N.C. (25 miles east)
Asheville, N.C. (54 miles west)

**ESTIMATED 2006
MEDIAN HOUSEHOLD INCOME**
$42, 564

COST OF LIVING
Average 3-bdrm home—
$125,000
Average rent, 2-bdrm apartment—$475
Cost-of-living comparison—80%

SALES TAX
6%

PROPERTY TAX
Average 3-bdrm home—$950

Tucked in among the foothills of the Blue Ridge Mountains lies the appealing mountain town of Morganton. In 1997, *Reader's Digest* rated Morganton as one of the "Top 10 Cities in the U.S. for raising a family." Morganton was named a finalist for an All-America City Award in 2001. Morganton appeals both to families and to retirees because of its high quality of life and its keen emphasis on the arts, leisure activities, and entertainment. The area has affordable housing, plenty of recreation opportunities, and excellent senior services.

The Catawba and Cherokee originally inhabited the area. Established in 1784, the town was later named for Revolutionary War General Daniel Morgan. Other war heroes and famous adventurers like Daniel Boone and Andrew Jackson also lived in the area. Morganton has long served the region as a judicial center. The courthouse was built in 1837 and has been put to good use ever since; it now houses the Visitor Information Center, the Historic Burke Foundation, and the Heritage Museum. Morganton is a Main Street Program town, qualifying under the guidelines set by the National Trust for Historic Preservation.

There is an ongoing effort to attract high-quality apparel shops, specialty retail stores, fine dining establishments, and entertainment to the downtown area. Currently seventy-five quaint shops and boutiques are intermingled with stores selling more practical goods. The downtown area has an inviting feel to it—clean, colorful, and charming. The town plants thousands of red and yellow tulips every year. Proprietors place pots of pink and red geraniums in front of their stores. Classical music plays through strategically placed speakers throughout the town. Ongoing lighting and sidewalk improvements make this attractive mountain town even more pedestrian-friendly.

 RECREATION

Burke County's natural forests, state parks, rivers, and lakes make it a paradise for nature lovers and outdoor enthusiasts. The elevation climbs from 1,000 to over 4,300 feet within the county. The 12,000-acre Linville Gorge Wilderness Area of the Pisgah National Forest is thirty miles northwest of Morganton. About thirty miles west of Morganton is the famous Blue Ridge Parkway, known as "America's most scenic drive."

Plenty of boating and fishing takes place on several large lakes, including Lake James, which has 6,500 acres and 154 miles of shoreline. Two marinas on Lake James rent boats, sell gas and fishing supplies, and provide boat ramps and parking spaces. Both Lake James and South Mountain State Parks are good places for hiking, camping, and picnicking.

The Catawba River Greenway Park, paralleling the Catawba River, offers a well-maintained, paved 1.5-mile handicapped-accessible walking trail and picnic facilities, a fishing pier, public restrooms, a canoe launch, and exercise trails. A four-hour Catawba River canoe trip with escort and equipment is also an option. Bikes can be rented in Morganton for excursions into two nearby state parks with miles of trails for adventurous explorers. Cross country and downhill snow skiing is less than an hour away. There is a new 3,000-acre state park on Lake James.

Three eighteen-hole golf courses are open to the public: Quaker Meadows and the courses at the Silver Creek Plantation and Pine Mountain Golf Course, both gated residential communities. Nearby Hickory is home to a minor league baseball team.

CULTURAL SCENE

The 1,058-seat Morganton Municipal Auditorium has hosted performances of such plays as *The Phantom of The Opera* and *Showboat* as well as appearances by groups like The Oak Ridge Boys. The outdoor drama *From this Day Forward* tells the story of the pre-Reformation persecution, relocation, and subsequent hardships of the Waldensian people, an ancient branch of Christians who fled northern Italy and settled in this area in 1893. This play is performed from mid-July to mid-August annually. The Western Piedmont Symphony, plays regularly in Hickory and at least annually in Morganton.

The Burke Arts Council, located on the old Courthouse Square, maintains an art gallery featuring work created by local and national artists. Art classes, special performances, and cultural activities are coordinated through the Council. The October Oyster Outing draws thousands to the square for a fundraiser for the Burke Arts Council that includes music and fine food. Two Friday night concert series take place in Morganton and Valdese during the summer. These free programs attract hundreds of music lovers who enjoy everything from bluegrass to symphonies.

The Historic Morganton Festival, held on the first weekend after Labor Day, draws nearly 80,000 visitors over two days. The festival offers more than four hundred booths displaying artwork, crafts, and food; a children's play area; and family entertainment. Live music and nationally known acts are featured on Friday and Saturday nights. Local merchants sponsor an annual Halloween program. A Memorial Tree Lighting Ceremony is held at the Old Burke County Courthouse on November 25, and a popular Christmas parade through downtown takes place in early December.

 **MAIN STREET**

Some local hot spots are Legends (wings and special sandwiches); Mythos, a restaurant and bar (Greek dishes and pasta); and the lounge at the Holiday Inn (weekend entertainment). Members gather frequently at the Elks and Moose Lodges. The Community House, located in downtown, provides a site for meetings, receptions, and banquets for up to 450 people.

 HOUSING

Housing prices vary from the low $100s for new, single-story townhouses to several hundred thousand for large homes. Older historic homes found in the central part of town tend to stay in families. Home and real estate prices decrease as you look farther out into rural areas. There are several fine golf- and lake-oriented gated communities, including Silver Creek Plantation. Housing costs at nearby Lake James range from $300,000 to over $1 million. Grace Ridge, a continuing-care retirement community that is situated on a wooded fifty-two-acre parklike area in Morganton, provides cottages and apartments for independent living, assisted living, and skilled nursing care. Like other CCRC facilities, Grace Ridge charges an entrance fee and a monthly service fee. Attractive town homes and apartments are being built within walking distance of the Morganton Central Business District.

 ECONOMICS

Number of employers with fifty or more employees—79

Morganton has experienced the loss of furniture manufacturing, and is now positioning itself as a retirement destination. The community is mobilizing its resources to develop and market amenities and services that are of interest to aging baby-boomers. Local government, the North Carolina School for the Deaf, the J. Iverson Riddle Developmental Center (a facility serving mentally retarded citizens of thirty-five counties), and local hospitals make up 19 percent of area employers. Major employers include the Burke County Schools, (2,000 employees); Blue Ridge Health Care (1,800 employees); Broughton Hospital (1,300 employees); J. Iverson Riddle Developmental Center (1,025 employees); and Leviton Southern Devices, (700 employees).

EDUCATION

High schools—2; Middle schools—2; Elementary schools—7; Private schools—2

New public high, middle, and elementary schools have recently been constructed. The town is the home of the North Carolina School for the Deaf and J. Iverson Riddle Developmental Center. Western Piedmont Community College is a two-year college for occupational education and transferable college level programs.

Additional programs are offered at Lenoir-Rhyne College in Hickory, the University of North Carolina at Asheville, and Appalachian State University (part of the University of North Carolina system) in Boone. The Catawba Science Center for children is located in Hickory.

HEALTHCARE

Blue Ridge HealthCare System—335 beds; Physicians—177; Dentists—25

The Blue Ridge HealthCare System operates two hospitals in Burke County with a total of 335 beds: Grace Hospital in Morganton, and Valdese Hospital in Valdese. The system is in the midst of a $100 million expansion program. Grace Hospital offers 24-hour emergency care, a cancer center, cardiac care and rehabilitation services, occupational health and therapy services, physical and speech therapy, pediatrics, behavioral health services, and many more specialties.

SPIRITUAL LIFE

Twenty-four Christian denominations are represented. The nearest synagogue is in Asheville.

STAYING CONNECTED

Local newspapers include the *News Herald,* published six days per week, and the daily *Hickory Daily Record.* Several major North Carolina newspapers are delivered locally, including those from Charlotte and Asheville. Cable television brings in all major network and cable stations. Four national and seven local internet companies provide service. Muses is a popular local bookstore, and there are national chain bookstores in Hickory.

 GETTING THERE

Morganton is located in the foothills of the Blue Ridge Mountains on I-40, NC 181, NC 64, and NC 18. It is fifty-four miles east of Asheville, twenty-five miles west of Hickory, and sixty-eight miles northwest of Charlotte. Commercial air service via several airlines, including US Airways and Delta, is available from both Asheville and Charlotte.

 RESOURCES

Burke County
 Visitor Information Center
102 East Union Street
Courthouse Square
Morganton, NC 28655
(888) 462-2921
www.burkecountytourism.com

Burke County Chamber
 of Commerce
110 East Meeting Streeet
Morganton, NC 28655
(828) 437-3021
www.burkecounty.org

MORGANTON
VITAL STATISTICS

CLIMATE

Annual average rainfall	50 inches
Snowfall	13 inches
Elevation	1,182 feet

Temperatures (in degrees Fahrenheit)

	Jan	Apr	Jul	Oct
High	51	71	88	73
Low	31	46	66	48

OCCUPATIONS

	2006	Projected 2011
Blue collar	28.8%	29.0%
White collar	54.1%	53.1%
Services	17.2%	17.9%

ADULT EDUCATION

	2000
Less than High School	30.2%
High School	24.5%
Some College	17.6%
Associates Degree	6.9%
College Degree	13.5%
Graduate Degree	7.3%

POPULATION

2006	17,246
2000-2006 Population: Annual Compound Growth Rate	-0.06%
2006-2011 Population: Annual Compound Growth Rate	0.28%

Population by age group

	2006	Projected 2011
0-4	5.9%	5.9%
5-9	5.7%	5.2%
10-14	5.8%	5.9%
15-19	6.0%	5.9%
20-24	5.7%	6.2%
25-29	6.8%	5.3%
30-34	7.1%	6.6%
35-39	6.9%	6.9%
40-44	7.3%	7.2%
45-49	7.1%	7.4%
50-54	6.9%	7.1%
55-59	6.5%	6.8%
60-64	4.8%	6.1%
65-69	4.3%	4.4%
70-74	3.9%	3.6%
75-79	3.5%	3.5%
80-84	3.0%	2.9%
85+	3.0%	3.2%

Sources for Vital Statistics listed above can be found in the Preface to this book.

MOUNT AIRY

2006 POPULATION
8,043

NEAREST CITIES
Winston-Salem, NC (40 miles)
Greensboro, NC (62 miles)

ESTIMATED 2006
MEDIAN HOUSEHOLD INCOME
$33,299

COST OF LIVING
Average 3-bdrm home—$135,000
Average rent, 2-bdrm apartment—$450
Cost-of-living comparison—90.1%

SALES TAX
6%

PROPERTY TAX
Average 3-bdrm home—$1,250

Mount Airy is one of the best-known and friendliest small towns in America. Filled with the charm and character of Mayberry, Mount Airy is the hometown of actor Andy Griffith and was the inspiration for his long-running television series. You can step back in time and visit the famous landmarks mentioned on the show, order a pork chop sandwich from Snappy Lunch on North Main, or stop by Floyd's Barbershop next door to get a haircut and catch the latest local news.

Nestled at the foot of the beautiful Blue Ridge Mountains, Mount Airy was originally settled by a mixture of English, Scottish, Irish, and German farmers in the late eighteenth and early nineteenth centuries. The rolling foothills along the eastern slopes of the mountains offer mild weather, ideal growing conditions, and ample natural resources.

In 1996, Mount Airy was listed in *The 100 Best Small Towns in America,* and was named an All-American City by the National League of Cities. The historic downtown may be well connected to the Andy Griffith era, but the town's leaders have found ways to combine progress with its nostalgic atmosphere.

 RECREATION

The Blue Ridge Parkway, only fifteen miles to the west, offers hiking, camping, and picnic areas. Pilot Mountain is located south of Mount Airy along US 52. Formed from molten rock and rising 1,500 feet above the surrounding valley, the mountain is now the site of a state park. Mount Airy has two public parks. The county is now home to five annual cycling events. Mount Airy has been designated as one of only eight "Fit Cities" by the state of North Carolina. Snow skiing at the ski resorts in the Boone area is only an hour and a half away. The New River Trail State Park in Virginia, within an hour's

drive, offers a trail for hikers, mountain bikers, and horse riders.

The Reeves Community Center in Mount Airy has a wide range of recreational facilities, including an indoor pool, a gymnasium, racquetball courts, and a weight room, and offers classes for youth and adults. There are two eighteen-hole public golf courses in the county. You can see NASCAR racing in Martinsville, Virginia, and Charlotte, North Carolina, and college and professional basketball, football, and hockey in Greensboro, Winston-Salem, and Charlotte.

 CULTURAL SCENE

The influence of Andy Griffith is still felt in Mount Airy. The Andy Griffith Playhouse is a theater and arts center located in the renovated public school that Griffith attended. The playhouse hosts children's and community theater, lectures, and musical concerts ranging from bluegrass to classical. The largest collection of Andy Griffith memorabilia in the country is located in Mount Airy. The Robert Smith Memorial Park is the setting for the Summer Music Series in the Park.

Bluegrass music is part of the area's heritage and two nationally recognized fiddlers' conventions are held in June (in Mount Airy) and August (in nearby Galax). Musicians from all over the region gather every Thursday evening at the Andy Griffith Playhouse for a jam session. The Surry Chorale, a group of nearly sixty of the county's finest voices, performs several times throughout the year. The Blackman Amphitheater, located across from the Playhouse, is the newest entertainment venue.

The Mount Airy Museum of Regional History houses exhibits about the local open-face granite quarry, the largest in the world; the Saura Indians; Eng and Chang Bunker, the original Siamese twins; the railroad; the Yadkin River natural history; and more.

The historic Downtown Cinema is an old 450-seat movie house that closed in the 1980s, but was renovated and reopened by a combination of volunteers and a downtown business group. It now hosts movies, bingo, bluegrass music jam sessions on Saturdays, and a live weekly radio broadcast.

The Gertrude Smith House,

built in 1903 by the Jefferson Davis Smith Family, is on the National Register of Historic Homes. The large Victorian home contains unique period furnishings collected by Gertrude Smith, one of the family's daughters who was an interior designer in New York City. She returned to Mount Airy and lived in this home until her death in 1981. The house remains as it was when Gertrude lived there and is open at various times throughout the year for tours, special exhibits, and musical programs. Trinity Episcopal Church, built in 1896, is the oldest church in Mount Airy.

The Mayberry Days festival spans three days in late September and includes music at the Andy Griffith Playhouse, a parade down Main Street, a barbecue cook-off, dinners and shows at the Downtown Cinema, a pie- and pork chop-eating contest, and appearances by celebrity impersonators and stars of *The Andy Griffith Show*. The Annual Autumn Leaf Festival attracts over 250,000 visitors to downtown Mount Airy in October. A Christmas parade in early December kicks off holiday activities, including a tour of historic homes.

The Horne Creek Living Historical Farm is located south of Pilot Mountain on US 52. The farm re-creates the farming life of the early 1900s; it is open for tours and also hosts activities such as corn shucking in the fall. Winston-Salem is home to a symphony orchestra; events at Wake Forest University; performances of music, dance, and drama at the North Carolina School of the Arts; and seasonal celebrations at Old Salem, a historic Moravian village.

MAIN STREET

Snappy Lunch, the oldest restaurant in Mount Airy, gained fame on *The Andy Griffith Show;* the eatery is known for its pork chop sandwich. Other favorite restaurants are Goober's; Harvest Grill; Pandowdy's (American fare with a German flair); Sagebrush (a chain steakhouse); and Derby's (good basic country cooking).

Downtown, an empty building was converted into a 30,000-square-foot emporium where two hundred vendors sell everything from pottery to pastries. Colorful canopies sheltering storefront windows on Main Street add a nostalgic touch. There are now six wineries in the county; Black Wolf Vineyards also has a fine restaurant.

HOUSING

Mount Airy offers a variety of housing options, including homes in the historic district, in-town apartments and condominiums, and houses in subdivisions and in less developed areas outside the town limits but within the city's school district. Older historic homes in the downtown area cost from $200,000 to $350,000. Stately, two-story older homes on North Main Street are within easy walking distance of the downtown business district; a city dweller seeking a unique, older home might find a bargain here. A factory conversion to condominiums sold out quickly at $95,000 to $120,000. Popular subdivisions in Mount Airy include Country Manor Estates and Saddle Brook. Rivermont, a new subdivision within the city limits, is priced from $130,000 to $150,000. Laurel Creek subdivision has larger homes priced from $250,000 to $300,000. New condominium developments, including Greystone Condominiums and the Hazel Nut Plantation, are under construction or available on the outskirts of Mount Airy. Farms and acreage are also available, along with a retirement community featuring both individual apartments and assisted living facilities. Manufactured housing, common in the rural areas outside town, offers another viable housing alternative.

 ECONOMICS

Number of employers with fifty or more employees—42

More than 6,500 people work at Floyd S. Pike Electrical Contractors. Kentucky Derby Hosier (1,000 employees) produces hosiery. Established in 1889, North Carolina Granite Corporation is the world's largest open-face granite quarry; it employs more than 125 workers. Insteel Industries (manufacture of wire products), Southdata (forms printer), and Gerard's Bakery are other local employers. Textiles and agriculture (tobacco, strawberries, poultry, grapes, and animal feed) are also major industries.

 EDUCATION

High schools—1; Middle schools—1; Elementary schools—2; Private schools—1

Surry Community College (12,000 students) offers two-year and vocational programs and adult education classes. The Community College has a cooperative agreement with Gardner-Webb College. Wake Forest University, Winston-Salem State University, and Salem College (women only) in Winston-Salem all have full undergraduate and some graduate programs.

 HEALTHCARE

Northern Hospital of Surry County—137 beds; Physicians—57; Dentists—23

The Northern Hospital of Surry County provides a comprehensive array of services: orthopedics, internal medicine, neurology, cardiology, obstetrics, pediatrics, surgery, urology, and oncology, as well as 24-hour emergency care. For patients who require more extensive medical treatment, the

North Carolina Baptist Hospital and Bowman Gray School of Medicine in Winston-Salem are within an hour's drive.

 SPIRITUAL LIFE

Fifteen Christian denominations are represented in the community. The nearest synagogue is in Greensboro.

 STAYING CONNECTED

The *Mount Airy News* is published seven days a week. Daily newspapers are delivered locally from Winston-Salem and Greensboro. Local cable television and internet services are available. Local coffee shops offer wi-fi hotspots. There are several chain bookstores in Winston-Salem.

 GETTING THERE

Mount Airy is in the northwest part of North Carolina, almost at the Virginia state line. It is located on US 52(Bypass) and the I-74 Connector (Hwy. 89). I-77 is eight miles to the west and provides access to Charlotte, North Carolina (90 miles south). The Mount Airy-Surry County Airport has a 4,300-foot lighted runway for general aviation. Piedmont Triad International Airport, between Winston-Salem and Greensboro, is the closest major airport. Several major airlines provide daily flights to large Southern and East Coast cities.

 RESOURCES

Greater Mount Airy
  Chamber of Commerce
P.O. Box 913
Mount Airy, NC 27030
(336) 786-6116
www.mtairyncchamber.org

Additional area website:
www.visitmayberry.com

MOUNT AIRY
VITAL STATISTICS

CLIMATE

Annual average rainfall	42 inches
Snowfall	24 inches
Elevation	1,100 feet

Temperatures (in degrees Fahrenheit)

	Jan	**Apr**	**Jul**	**Oct**
High	47	71	87	71
Low	25	42	63	44

OCCUPATIONS

	2006	**Projected 2011**
Blue collar	32.0%	32.9%
White collar	53.6%	52.1%
Services	14.3%	14.9%

ADULT EDUCATION

	2000
Less than High School	34.2%
High School	22.8%
Some College	17.7%
Associates Degree	5.1%
College Degree	15.1%
Graduate Degree	5.1%

POPULATION

2006	8,043
2000-2006 Population: Annual Compound Growth Rate	-0.85%
2006-2011 Population: Annual Compound Growth Rate	-0.09%

Population by age group

	2006	**Projected 2011**
0-4	5.7%	5.8%
5-9	5.3%	4.9%
10-14	6.1%	5.3%
15-19	6.3%	5.9%
20-24	5.6%	6.8%
25-29	5.0%	5.5%
30-34	5.8%	4.6%
35-39	6.0%	5.4%
40-44	6.5%	6.3%
45-49	7.2%	6.8%
50-54	6.6%	7.1%
55-59	6.1%	6.8%
60-64	5.1%	5.9%
65-69	4.9%	4.7%
70-74	4.6%	4.5%
75-79	5.2%	4.2%
80-84	4.1%	4.7%
85+	4.1%	4.6%

Sources for Vital Statistics listed above can be found in the Preface to this book.

2006 POPULATION
2,635

NEAREST CITIES
Wilmington, NC (28 miles)
Myrtle Beach, SC (80 miles)

ESTIMATED 2006

MEDIAN HOUSEHOLD INCOME
$45,244

COST OF LIVING
Average 3-bdrm home—$250,000
Average rent, 2-bdrm apartment—$650
Cost-of-living comparison—96.1%

SALES TAX
6%

PROPERTY TAX
Average 3-bdrm home—$1,500

Reminiscent of an old New England fishing village, the historic waterfront town of Southport overlooks the Cape Fear River where it merges into the Atlantic Ocean. Oak trees draped with Spanish moss line the streets of enticing neighborhoods marked by a Victorian influence. The town is a virtual treasure chest of seacoast life, antiques, and photogenic scenery.

Southport was established in 1792. Its history is rich with stories of pirates and Confederate blockade runners. The town is home to two significant lighthouses: Old Baldy, erected in 1817, the oldest in North Carolina; and Oak Island, the brightest light in the United States. You can see both lighthouses from Waterfront Park, where you can also watch large ocean-going ships as they head up the Cape Fear River toward Wilmington.

The town of Oak Island lies across the Intracoastal Waterway, on one of the five barrier islands known as the Brunswick Islands. The most populated town in the county, Oak Island is located on the sixteen-mile-long island of the same name. Southport's quiet hospitality is likely to be most appreciated by those looking for a town with a friendly and down-to-earth atmosphere and a diverse community of artists, historians, and retirees. This relatively undiscovered seaport, an appealing coastal retirement destination, is near the equally attractive coastal city of Wilmington, North Carolina.

 RECREATION

Saltwater fishing is a major recreational activity in Southport and the nearby islands. Anglers enjoy fishing from piers on the ocean and inlets and from charter boats in the Gulf Stream (approximately fifty miles out), as well as surf fishing. Ocean swimming, sailing, boating, and walking on the nearly white beaches are also popular.

With over thirty courses in the county and nearly year-round golf weather, the area deserves its nickname "North Carolina's Golf Coast." There are courses designed by Fazio, Maples, and Jones, and many offer views of untamed coastal marshes, the broad Cape Fear River, stretches of the Intracoastal Waterway, and the Atlantic Ocean. Some of the better-known eighteen-hole courses include Bald Head Island Golf Course, Brick Landing Plantation Golf and Country Club, Brierwood Golf Club, and Oak Island Golf and Country Club.

The Southport Parks and Recreation Department operates programs for almost everyone and sponsors a very active 55 and Over Club with its own clubhouse. There are seven public city parks, youth team sports programs, and a county park in Southport.

 CULTURAL SCENE

The one-mile walking tour of this charming and historic town takes you by twenty-five historic sites, including parks, homes, churches, inns, forts, and public buildings. There are several noteworthy museums, including the Museum of Coastal Carolina, which contains exhibits of coastal waterfowl, swamps, forests, and mounted birds and animals; and the North Carolina Maritime Museum, which houses a collection of memorabilia pertaining to the vast nautical history of Southport. The Fort Fisher Civil War Museum is on the site of an earthen fort that kept the port open to blockade runners delivering vital supplies to the Confederate armies until it was destroyed in 1865.

Southport has five local art galleries, and a large art colony is located in nearby Wilmington. Brunswick County has two community theater groups, a concert band, a community choral society, and an art guild. Silver Coast Winery offers tours and wine tastings. Annual Southport events include a North Carolina Fourth of July Festival, a Children's Crab Derby in September, a U.S. Open King Mackerel Tournament in October, and a Christmas by the Sea Festival in December.

A number of interesting sites are in Wilmington, including Orton Plantation Gardens, one of the most beautiful gardens on the East Coast, and the Battleship North Carolina Memorial, a famous World War II craft available for tours. Wilmington is a major center for the visual and performing arts. It has its own symphony orchestra, a vibrant chamber music series, a regular concert series, and dozens of ensemble groups. There are several theater companies. The Saint John's Museum of Art is one of the finest small art museums in the Southeast. Wilmington has captured a significant share of film and television production work and has had a working movie studio since 1985.

 MAIN STREET

Southport is a seafood lover's delight. The locally famous "calabash" style of cooking seafood, especially shrimp, originated in nearby Brunswick. At Fishy Fishy, where you have a good view of the old yacht basin, you can try one of their specialties—a steaming pot of fresh shellfish, new potatoes, corn, and sausage. Cape Fear Restaurant and lounge provides fine dining with a vista of the Cape Fear waterfront. Other popular seafood restaurants are Sandfiddlers, for family dining; 317 West Bay, for sunset views; and San Felipe, for Mexican fare. You can also find good seafood restaurants on Oak Island. Island Brew Coffee Shop and Café is a popular specialty coffee shop downtown.

Walking is the best way to tour the town's historic business district, which is filled with specialty and general gift shops as well as restaurants. Unusual gifts and home accessories are plentiful at Etcetera, Ricky Evans Gallery, and the Franklin Square Art Gallery, where local artisans exhibit paintings and pottery. Forty-eight antique dealers display their wares at two antique malls.

 HOUSING

Because of the vacation appeal of the Brunswick Islands, much of the housing market is designed to appeal to newcomers seeking beach and oceanfront living. Options in Southport and Oak Island include summer beach houses, patio homes, cottages on the rivers and marshes, traditional subdivisions, golf and gated communities, condominiums, and manufactured home communities. Prices range from the mid $100,000s for small ranch-style homes inland from the historic district to $2 million for houses in the private golf-course communities. Older homes in the historic district are in the $250,000 to $400,000 range. Several of the southern Brunswick Island residential golf communities include marinas for the residents. Arbor Creek is a rare, non-golf community with a clubhouse, tennis courts, a swimming pool, a community garden, and one-level homes; homesites are priced from $30,000 to $50,000 and homes from $299,000 to $469,000. The Village at Southport is a condominium complex close to the waterfront, offering one- and two-bedroom units for $200,000. Southport Crossing is a new planned community under construction, offering luxury condominiums and home sites. Prices will be in the mid three hundreds. Another residential community, St. James (due west of Southport), has incorporated as a town and has nearly one thousand residents. While there are no apartments in

Southport, Wilmington offers many choices.

 ECONOMICS

Number of employers with fifty or more employees—19

The local economy is driven by tourism and associated services. There are dozens of real estate companies and developers. The largest employers are the Brunswick County Board of Education, DAKAmericas (1,400 employees), and Progress Energy (700 employees). Employment opportunities are also available in the Wilmington area.

 EDUCATION

High schools—1; Middle schools—1; Elementary schools—2; Private schools—3

Brunswick Community College has a Southport campus and offers two-year programs for transfer to a four-year state university. Senior citizens may audit some classes without charge. Garner-Webb University offers classes on the Brunswick Community College campus. A Small Business Center is located at Brunswick Community College. The University of North Carolina at Wilmington (11,500 students) has undergraduate and graduate programs. Senior citizens can audit one class per term without charge. A special program of short courses of interest to seniors is offered.

 HEALTHCARE

Dosher Memorial Hospital—100 beds; Physicians—64; Dentists—7

Dosher Memorial Hospital offers a 24-hour emergency room, outpatient surgery, and extensive diagnostic imaging services. The Brunswick Community Hospital, located in the nearby town of Shallotte, is a sixty-bed facility with ninety-six attending physicians serving the Brunswick County area. More extensive medical and hospital facilities are located in Wilmington.

 SPIRITUAL LIFE

Twenty-two Christian denominations are represented. The closest synagogue is in Wilmington.

 STAYING CONNECTED

The *State Port Pilot* is an award-winning weekly newspaper serving Southport and the surrounding community, including Oak Island.

The daily *Wilmington Star News* is also delivered. Cable television is available and a number of radio stations cover the area. Several national internet services provide local access. There are two local bookstores.

 GETTING THERE

Southport is located south of Wilmington on the southeastern coast of North Carolina. The town lies sixteen miles east of US 17 and is on NC 211. NC 87 and NC 133 converge on the outskirts of town, intersecting with NC 211. Oak Island, the developed barrier island across the Intracoastal Waterway, is accessible via NC 133 and a bridge. The Brunswick County Airport handles private aircraft and has a 5,000-foot lighted and paved runway. The closest commercial airport is the Wilmington International Airport, with daily flights on US Airways (through Charlotte) and Delta. The Myrtle Beach Jet Port, a regional commercial airport, is located in South Carolina. Yachts, pleasure boats, and working fishing craft use the Intracoastal Waterway and several marinas close to downtown.

 RESOURCES

Southport–Oak Island
  Chamber of Commerce
4841 Long Beach Road S.E.
Southport, NC 28461.
(800) 457-6964
www.southport-oakisland.com

SOUTHPORT
VITAL STATISTICS

CLIMATE

Annual average rainfall	54 inches
Snowfall	0 inches
Elevation	6 feet

Temperatures (in degrees Fahrenheit)

	Jan	Apr	Jul	Oct
High	54	71	88	75
Low	32	49	70	51

OCCUPATIONS

	2006	Projected 2011
Blue collar	22.5%	22.2%
White collar	58.4%	59.4%
Services	19.1%	18.4%

ADULT EDUCATION

	2000
Less than High School	15.7%
High School	22.6%
Some College	27.2%
Associates Degree	8.0%
College Degree	18.1%
Graduate Degree	8.5%

POPULATION

2006	2,635
2000-2006 Population: Annual Compound Growth Rate	1.84%
2006-2011 Population: Annual Compound Growth Rate	3.32%

Population by age group

	2006	Projected 2011
0-4	3.5%	3.6%
5-9	4.0%	3.7%
10-14	4.8%	4.4%
15-19	5.1%	4.6%
20-24	4.8%	4.5%
25-29	4.1%	4.8%
30-34	3.2%	4.3%
35-39	4.6%	3.4%
40-44	6.5%	5.5%
45-49	7.2%	7.1%
50-54	9.0%	8.8%
55-59	10.3%	10.6%
60-64	7.0%	9.0%
65-69	7.5%	6.1%
70-74	6.3%	6.7%
75-79	4.3%	5.3%
80-84	3.9%	3.4%
85+	3.7%	4.2%

Sources for Vital Statistics listed above can be found in the Preface to this book.

SOUTH CAROLINA

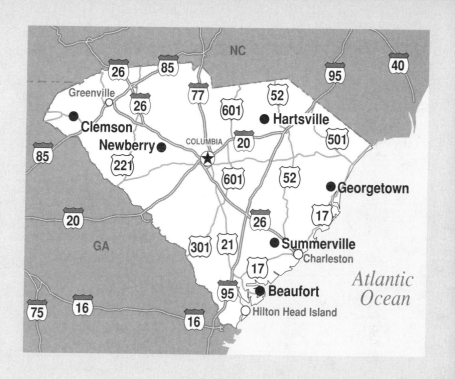

BEAUFORT

2006 POPULATION
14,035

NEAREST CITIES
Port Royal, SC (5 miles)
Hilton Head Island, SC (40 miles)
Savannah, GA (46 miles)
Charleston, SC (69 miles)

ESTIMATED 2006
MEDIAN HOUSEHOLD INCOME
$43,168

COST OF LIVING
Average 3-bdrm home—$343,317
Average rent, 2-bdrm apartment—
$700
Cost-of-living comparison—
102.3%

SALES TAX
5%

PROPERTY TAX
Average 3-bdrm home—$2,469

Listed as one of 2001's "Dozen Distinctive Destinations" by the National Trust for Historic Preservation, Beaufort exudes charm. The Beaufort Historic District is one of South Carolina's three National Historic Landmark Districts. The many historic homes, built in the late 1800s and early 1900s, enhance the town's colorful character. Beaufort's grand, white frame houses, wrapped with wide porches on multiple levels and adorned with widow's walks, gazebos, and wisteria-draped arbors in elegant gardens, stand side by side with multicolored bungalows. Live oak trees draped with Spanish moss grace the brick walkways and narrow streets; the town commands spectacular water views in three directions. No wonder several movies have been filmed in Beaufort.

Historians believe that Beaufort was originally inhabited by the Archaic tribe over four thousand years ago. The Spanish arrived in 1521, and from then on many different European powers battled to control the area. Formally established in the early 1700s, Beaufort Town was named after Henry Somerset, the Duke of Beaufort, and became the second permanent community in South Carolina. Cotton, rice ("Carolina Gold"), and indigo farming fed the local economy and were the main source of Beaufort's wealth and fame. Area plantation owners came to town in the summers to socialize and enjoy the cool breezes of the Beaufort River. Peace and prosperity ended temporarily with the Civil War, but the town's fate was secured when Beaufort became the headquarters for Union troops.

The setting is a natural for moviemakers. Some of the most famous movies made here include *The Big Chill, The Prince of Tides, Forrest Gump, GI Jane,* and *Forces of Nature.* The sight of enormous vans, large fans, and production staff bustling about getting ready for the next scene doesn't seem to faze the locals at all. It's all a part of living in this town.

While life in this small town can be heavenly, there are a few drawbacks. The summer humidity is intense and the "no-see-ums," tiny, mean, biting sand fleas, are a nuisance; however, the moderate year-round weather and the cool Atlantic Ocean breezes help to alleviate both of these discomforts. In spite of the growth this small town has seen in the last several years, real estate values are still reasonable. Beaufort is a desirable option for water lovers who prefer a relaxed and comfortable atmosphere. It is easy to see why Beaufort is referred to as the "Queen of the Sea Islands."

 RECREATION

Beaufort County has over thirty miles of white sandy beaches. The 5,000-acre Hunting Island State Park (16 miles) offers three miles of soft sand beaches edged with palm trees and backed by a subtropical forest. The park has wooded nature trails, a marsh walk, a fishing pier, camping facilities, and rental cabins. The boardwalk extends out over the edge of the Beaufort River and Battery Creek waterway. The park's lighthouse, built in 1873, stands 132 feet above the ground and offers incredible views of the ocean, beach, and marshland. A visit to the Low Country Estuarium helps to fill in the details about local marine life.

The Henry C. Chambers Waterfront Park along the Beaufort River has walkways, benches, a covered pavilion, and a playground. The park is a regular site for town events, festivals, picnics, and sunset strolls. Many of the town's best restaurants face the park and the river. Nearby Port Royal has a sand beach within a public park on Port Royal Sound.

Getting on the water quickly is no problem here. There are three marinas in Beaufort and five in the area, as well as seventeen public boat landings. Water activities include boating, sailing, swimming, crabbing, shrimping, waterskiing, jet skiing, and fishing. There are saltwater rivers, tidal creeks, and marsh creeks, as well as freshwater rivers, lakes, and ponds. The ACE Basin—named for its three rivers, the Ashepoo, Combahee, and the Edisto— is a salt-marsh ecosystem and wildlife wilderness area. Guided pontoon tours of the basin offer many opportunities to observe wildlife in their natural habitat. The Combahee River, a freshwater river that changes to saltwater near the county line, is home to red water pan fish, largemouth bass, catfish, and striped bass. At low tide, it is common to see boaters meet at a sandbar for group picnic rallies lasting only until the tide begins to go out.

Those who prefer solid ground can choose among the area's eight eighteen-hole championship golf courses, including some of the best-known courses in the world designed by Arnold Palmer, Tom Fazio, and Russell Breedon. There are also baseball fields, tennis courts, and a neighborhood recreation center with a gym and municipal pool.

 **CULTURAL SCENE**

Not too long ago, Beaufort residents drove to Savannah and Charleston for art, culture, and nightlife. Today, that is no longer necessary. The Hallelujah Singers and the Beaufort Chamber Orchestra perform regularly throughout the year. The University of South Carolina-Beaufort Performing Arts Center hosts community theater and performing arts groups, classical and experimental plays, and dance performances and concerts. Local and visiting artists can be seen all around town.

In 2004, The Beaufort Film Commission (part of the Tourism Committee of the Greater Beaufort Chamber of Commerce) was created to promote the region to filmmakers and to serve as a liaison with producers from the film, television, and photography industries. In February of 2007, Beaufort sponsored the Beaufort Film Festival.

The Beaufort Arsenal Museum, built in 1798, displays collections of early American artifacts, including plantation handicrafts and items from the Civil War. The Parris Island Museum at the U.S. Marine Corps Recruit Depot reveals the history of this famous Marine training ground, which dates from 1562. It is also the site of several statues and monuments dedicated to the commitment and sacrifice of Marines during both world wars. Penn Center, established in 1862, was the first school for former slaves and is now a museum preserving the Gullah culture of the Sea Islands. Four historic forts, several old churches, and ruins of other structures date back to pre-Revolutionary times.

Festivals are popular in Beaufort. The Art Walk is held in March and October at twelve downtown galleries. The Gullah Festival takes place in May and features arts and crafts exhibits, dance performances, plays, musicians, workshops, and international cuisine. In May, A Taste of Beaufort, sponsored by Main Street Beaufort USA, presents various culinary delights from almost twenty locally owned restaurants. In 2006 there were six bands playing blues, jazz, bluegrass, and funk on three stages; activities for children; and fabulous food tasting. July brings the Beaufort County Water Festival, one of the biggest events of the year, with parades, music, street dances, water shows, and sports events. Ten days of entertainment include concerts in the park, air shows, boat races, a river parade with decorated boats, and the traditional blessing of the fleet.

During the Shrimp Festival, local restaurants serve up scrumptious shrimp dishes. An arts and crafts show and dancing under the stars complete the celebration. Other local favorites are the Christmas parade and Main Street's Night on the Town, which brings out locals for holiday shopping, choir concerts, and a tree lighting. An Earth Day celebration, spring and fall Tours of Homes, the Asian-Pacific American Heritage Show, band concerts at Waterfront Park, the Mainstreet Winefest, Art Gallery Walks, and the Festival of Trees round out the calendar.

 MAIN STREET

Shrimp, crab, and fish—dietary staples for this community—are caught fresh daily and served at local restaurants. The Beaufort Inn received the prestigious four-diamond rating from AAA. Plum's offers casual dining on the waterfront. Firehouse Books and Espresso Bar has a great patio. Saltus River Grill overlooks Waterfront Park and specializes in contemporary grilled seafood, fine cuts of meat, and sushi. Luther's Rare and Well Done is a great place to eat lunch in a casual waterfront setting. Magnolia Bakery Café specializes in creative soups, salads, and sandwiches; wonderful Maryland style crab cakes; and espresso.

The Henry C. Chambers Waterfront Park is arguably the most popular hangout in Beaufort. Facing the river, the park is backed by a row of restaurants and businesses housed in restored Bay Street buildings. The downtown shopping district consists of tastefully renovated storefronts, including antiques shops, art galleries, elegant gift stores, and a variety of specialty shops. The Chocolate Tree can satisfy anyone's sweet tooth. Baystreet Outfitters, the local Orvis dealer, sells outdoor clothing and fishing equipment.

HOUSING

The Beaufort area housing options include older, historic homes in town as well as houses in newer, established neighborhoods in out-lying areas. Prices for prestigious historic district homes in this Sea Island town begin at around $395,000, and go to $764,000. Waterfront property, including tidal creek and riverfront proper-ties, can go as high as $2.2 million. Houses in subdivisions are more reasonable; they can start under $200,000 and many sell for around $300,000. Homes for under $200,000 sell very fast and can be harder to find. Nearby islands offer custom building options as well as gated communities with new construction prices averaging $500,000. Off-the-water condo-miniums range from $135,000 to $165,000 and waterfront units sell for around $300,000. Nearby Dataw Island and Fripp Island are among the top retirement com-munities in the country. Sun City, a 5,600-acre residential retirement community between Beaufort and Hilton Head, offers a variety of housing options. In spite of the rising real estate values in this area, it is still considered afford-able by some retirees and families seeking a spectacular waterfront town.

 ECONOMICS

Number of employers with fifty or more employees—34

A natural harbor and moderate cli-mate contributed to Beaufort's start as a commercial center. Port Royal developed a successful shipbuilding industry, complementing Beau-fort's plantation production and mercantile industry. In 1882, the Parris Island military training facil-ity opened; the military presence was expanded when the Marine Corps Air Station joined Parris Island in 1942. The Beaufort Naval Hospital opened in 1949 and cur-rently has 500 employees.

The primary industries include government, education, healthcare, military, and tourism. The latter, along with new businesses and res-idential development, has risen sig-nificantly in importance in recent years. The Beaufort County Board of Education (2,200 employees), is the largest employer. Beaufort County (955 employees) is second. The Marine Corps Recruit Depot employs over 450 workers, and the Marine Corps Air Station has 546 employees.

 EDUCATION

High schools—2; Middle schools—4; Elementary schools—10; Private schools—8

The Beaufort County School District includes three regions: Battery Creek, Beaufort, and Hilton Head. Higher education opportunities are available at the University of South Carolina at Beaufort, the newest four-year university in the state. There are now two campuses; the North Campus is in downtown Beaufort and the South Campus is located at the gateway to Hilton Head Island. The Learning Exchange Program, is part of USCB's continuing education program. The Technical College of the Lowcountry has a two-year program offering high-tech training and liberal arts courses. It is the home of the state-funded Special Schools Pre-Employment Program, which assists new and expanding businesses with start-up expenses related to training potential

workers. Nearby Park College at the Marine Corps Air Station offers bachelor's and associate's degrees. Webster University at the Naval Hospital offers two-year MA and MBA Programs. The Limestone College Block Program is a career education center.

 HEALTHCARE

Beaufort Memorial Hospital—197 beds; Beaufort Naval Hospital—350 beds; Physicians—88; Dentists—17

Beaufort Memorial Hospital, with a staff of 150 physicians, offers 24-hour emergency service and cancer screening and treatment, and provides access to a dock for dealing with water emergencies. Beaufort Naval Hospital treats active and retired military personnel in Beaufort County. There is also a nursing home and a mental-health facility located in the area.

 SPIRITUAL LIFE

Eleven Christian denominations and several nondenominational groups are represented. There is one synagogue located in Beaufort.

STAYING CONNECTED

There is one local daily newspaper, the *Beaufort Gazette*. The *Tri-Command Tribune* is published weekly and delivered to all local military units and housing areas. Daily newspapers from Hilton Head, Charleston, and Savannah are available. Beaufort has four local area radio stations. Cable television and internet service are available. There are ten local bookstores.

 GETTING THERE

Beaufort is situated in the coastal region of South Carolina between Charleston and Savannah and is surrounded by rivers, bays, and the Intracoastal Waterway. It is served by US 21 and has easy access to I-95 (22 miles). Air transportation is provided by the Charleston International Airport (75 miles); Savannah Municipal Airport (55 miles); Hilton Head Airport, with a 4,300-foot runway; and the Beaufort County Airport, with a 3,430-foot runway serving small aircraft. Port facilities are available in nearby Port Royal.

 RESOURCES

Beaufort Regional
  Chamber of Commerce
1106 Carteret Street
P.O. Box 910
Beaufort, SC 29901-0910
(800) 638-3525
www.beaufortsc.org

Additional area website:
www.beaufortusa.com

BEAUFORT
VITAL STATISTICS

TION

CLIMATE

Annual average rainfall		49.8 inches
Snowfall		1 inch
Elevation		21 feet

Temperatures (in degrees Fahrenheit)

	Jan	Apr	Jul	Oct
High	58	76	90	77
Low	38	54	72	57

OCCUPATIONS

	2006	Projected 2011
Blue collar	17.8%	15.9%
White collar	64.5%	65.1%
Services	17.7%	19.0%

ADULT EDUCATION

	2000
Less than High School	14.7%
High School	25.1%
Some College	25.2%
Associates Degree	6.3%
College Degree	16.4%
Graduate Degree	12.2%

POPULATION

2006	14,035
2000-2006 Population: Annual Compound Growth Rate	1.30%
2006-2011 Population: Annual Compound Growth Rate	2.39%

Population by age group

	2006	Projected 2011
0-4	6.7%	6.9%
5-9	5.6%	5.5%
10-14	5.2%	5.6%
15-19	6.6%	6.7%
20-24	15.7%	14.8%
25-29	9.5%	7.3%
30-34	7.4%	7.8%
35-39	6.6%	7.1%
40-44	5.8%	5.9%
45-49	5.5%	5.7%
50-54	5.4%	5.2%
55-59	4.6%	5.5%
60-64	3.4%	4.2%
65-69	2.9%	2.9%
70-74	2.8%	2.5%
75-79	2.3%	2.4%
80-84	2.1%	1.8%
85+	1.9%	2.1%

Sources for Vital Statistics listed above can be found in the Preface to this book.

CLEMSON

2006 POPULATION
12,802

NEAREST CITIES
Anderson, SC (18 miles)
Greenville, SC (30 miles)
Spartanburg, SC (62 miles)

ESTIMATED 2006 MEDIAN HOUSEHOLD INCOME
$34,035

COST OF LIVING
Average 3-bdrm home—$145,000
Average rent, 2-bdrm apartment—$600
Cost-of-living comparison—94.4%

SALES TAX
6%

PROPERTY TAX
Average 3-bdrm home—$1,000

The spirited college town of Clemson is located at the foot of the majestic Blue Ridge Mountains and on the edge of beautiful Lake Hartwell. Originally settled by the Cherokee, the area held appeal because of its rich soil and abundant natural resources. The land was eventually surrendered to the British, and cotton farms sprang up throughout the area. Years later, Clemson became a summer retreat for prosperous plantation owners and famous politicians like John C. Calhoun, former vice president of the United States.

Today Calhoun's plantation is the site of Clemson University, named for his son-in-law. The town, originally named Calhoun, has since changed its name to reflect the name of its university.

Established in 1889 as a land-grant institution for agriculture students, Clemson University is now a well-known center for architecture, engineering, and social research. The lovely tree-covered campus, built on John C. Calhoun's 1400-acre plantation, includes a number of historic buildings, an eighteen-hole golf course, and a state-of-the-art conference center. The university offers Clemson many benefits, including academic events, cultural activities, a diverse student population, and a nationally ranked football team that brings as many as eighty-five thousand fans to town on fall weekends. As a result, Clemson is known as "the biggest little town in South Carolina." The town attracts not only avid football fans, but also people who want to enjoy outdoor recreation in the area's many waterways, state parks, lakes, and the nearby Blue Ridge Mountains.

RECREATION

Clemson's town motto, "In season every season," refers to the many outdoor activities available regardless of the time of year. Three area reservoirs lie end-to-end: Lakes Hartwell, Jocassee, and Keowee. Lake Hartwell, the southernmost of the three, is a 56,000-acre man-made lake created by the construction of the Hartwell Dam. The lake area includes a 680-acre state park with fourteen miles of shoreline. Lake Keowee contains 18,500 acres and a 300-mile shoreline. Major golf communities and affluent subdivisions are located on its northern shores. Lake Jocassee consists of 7,565 acres of water for trout and bass fishing; it is also a terrific site to view the North Carolina mountains, birds, wild animals, and wildflowers. All three lakes are ideal for fishing, sailing, windsurfing, waterskiing, canoeing, jet skiing, inner tubing, boating, rafting, and kayaking.

The Cherokees called the Blue Ridge Mountains "the Blue Wall." Now the many Blue Ridge trails are filled with hikers and mountain bikers, and the outcrops provide opportunities for rock climbers. The scenic Chatooga River, known for wild white-water rapids (such as those seen in the movie *Deliverance),* winds through the mountain range. The area surrounding Clemson is a waterfall paradise; there are nearly fifty along the border between North and South Carolina. Deep gorges within the Blue Ridge Mountains add drama to many of the falls, som of which exceed 800 feet.

There are fifteen state parks and the 80,000-acre Sumter National Forest in the area. Oconee State Park is a 1,165-acre retreat with two pristine lakes in the Blue Ridge foothills; it was originally built in 1935 by the Civilian Conservation Corps as part of Roosevelt's New Deal. Natural materials were used to build cabins, a bathhouse, a waterwheel, an old stone "station" building (once used as an Indian Trading Post), and the stone wall on the hiking trail. Swimming, bass fishing, camping, and hiking are favorites here. The Foothills Trail, an eighty-five-mile trail connecting several state parks, attracts backpackers, and there are shorter trails for those seeking a less strenuous hike.

There are eleven area golf courses. The eighteen-hole Walker Golf Course, part of Clemson University, adjoins the South Carolina State Botanical Garden, Lake Hartwell, and the Blue Ridge Mountains. The Foothills Family YMCA offers many activities. Clemson has eleven town parks. The Littlejohn Community Center is built on the former site of the Littlejohn Grill, a popular venue during the '40s and '50s for such notable musicians as Fats Domino, Ray Charles, Harry Belafonte, James Brown, and Peabo Bryson. In the fall, football draws thousands for at-home games. The Clemson Tigers boast thirteen ACC Championships, have participated in twenty post-season bowl games, and won the 1981 National Championship. Soccer, basketball, baseball, and golf have also brought championship titles to Clemson University teams and players.

 CULTURAL SCENE

Good music is easy to come by in this university town. The Death Valley football stadium and Littlejohn Coliseum on the Clemson campus have hosted concerts by the Rolling Stones, U2, Elton John, the Eagles, Pink Floyd, and Billy Joel. The Robert Howell Brooks

Center for the Performing Arts on campus presents performances by famous orchestras, ballet and modern dance companies, and popular local entertainers, as well as theatrical productions. Local nightspots offer live music; options range from rock and alternative to country and jazz. The Astro Theater on College Avenue is a dollar movie house, within walking distance of many after-movie hangouts.

The Pendleton Playhouse and adjacent Cox Hall, both located in the nearby town of Pendleton, sponsor various performances, including productions by the Clemson Little Theater and the Clemson Area Youth Theater. The old movie house was renovated and is now a chic art deco–style theater. Other community theater groups are active in the nearby town of Seneca and city of Anderson.

The Old Calhoun Walking Tour begins near the Historic Depot (now the location for the Clemson Area Chamber of Commerce). Visitors to Clemson University can see Fort Hill, Calhoun's plantation home, and the 1716 Hanover House, a French Huguenot home relocated from the Lowcountry. The South Carolina State Botanical Garden, encompassing 270 acres adjacent to the university, has an extensive collection of conifers, camellias, azaleas, hostas, and wildflowers that attract butterflies and hummingbirds. The arboretum contains over one thousand trees and shrubs, and the outdoor garden serves as an education center for visitors. The Fran Hanson Discovery Center, opened in 2001 at the botanical garden. The Bob Campbell Natural History and Geology Museum, also on the garden grounds, houses the largest collection of gems and minerals in the Southeast, including a 50,000-carat star sapphire from Africa.

Fourteen festivals are scheduled throughout the year. Springtime brings the Daffodil Festival, Arts in April, and International Week. Clemsonfest takes place on the lake around the Fourth of July. Fall is the season for the Welcome Back Festival and the Festival of African-American Literature and Arts. The holidays are marked by the Clemson Christmas parade. There are six festivals in the historic town of Pendleton, including Holidays in the Village, during which the town is transformed into to a Victorian village.

One of the nice features of Clemson is its convenient access to other metropolitan areas. Since the town is only twelve miles from I-85 and near the borders of South Carolina, Georgia, and North Carolina, residents can easily reach Atlanta, Asheville, Greenville, and Charlotte.

 MAIN STREET

Over sixty restaurants in the Clemson area offer diverse cuisines. Calhoun Corners has multiple levels, a forty-foot Christmas tree at holiday time, and good food. Seasons by the Lake offers great views and an excellent lunch buffet. The Madren Center on the university campus serves Lowcountry southern cooking. Other popular gathering spots include Pixie and Bill's (upscale dining near a cozy fireplace); The Blue Heron (lunch specials); Sardi's Den (great barbecue and ribs in a relaxed atmosphere); and several local sandwich

and coffee shops. In Pendleton, The Lazy Islander serves terrific peel-and-eat shrimp and oysters, and Liberty Hall Inn offers wonderful menus for special nights out.

Clemson's downtown received a facelift in 2003; the streets and sidewalks were resurfaced and landscaped, and benches and decorative streetlights were installed. College Avenue, the main street and focal point of the town, is located directly across from the university campus. The city has recently completed the new Abernathy Waterfront Park—a network of scenic boardwalks, picnic shelters, and benches bordering on Lake Hartwell and adjacent to the restaurant area in town—which extends College Avenue to the edge of the lake.

 HOUSING

Ten- to fifteen-year-old houses in established neighborhoods range from $150,000 to $200,000 for approximately 1,800 square feet of living space. New housing subdivisions are popular in nearby Pendleton, approximately 4 miles south of Clemson. A new, large planned community, Pendleton Station, is under construction there. Detached single-family houses on very small lots (around 6,500 square feet) are less expensive. New houses on larger lots range from $250,000 to $350,000. Lakefront lots for custom-built homes start at $150,000 on Lake Hartwell and higher on Lake Keowee. Condominiums are increasingly popular in Clemson, and start as low as $125,000. They are mostly student occupied. Many apartments are available.

 ECONOMICS

Number of employers with fifty or more employees—10

The largest employer is Clemson University, with over eight thousand employees. The BASF Clemson Plant (carpet and yarn) employs 450 workers; and Ryobi Motor Products Corporation (hand tools) employs over 1,500 workers. The largest manufacturer of kayaks is located in Easley. Pickens County has lost textile jobs, but is finding economic growth through new industries and research at Clemson University. Today education, metalwork-

ing, industrial equipment, and construction of second homes on the lakes are the largest industries. Pickens County is one of the fastest growing counties in the state, and the recent establishment of several well-known manufacturers in the area, such as BMW near Greenville, has drawn attention to the Upstate Carolina region.

 EDUCATION

High schools—1; Middle schools—1; Elementary schools—2; Private schools—2

Higher education needs are met through Clemson University, serving 17,000 students and offering 70 fields of study and 110 graduate programs. Clemson was listed in *America's Best College Buys, 1999–2000,* and was ranked 28th among the nation's 162 public doctoral-granting universities by *U.S. News and World Report* in 2007. Southern Wesleyan University, ten minutes from Clemson, is a four-year, private liberal arts college founded in 1906 by the Wesleyan Church. Tri-County Technical College in Pendleton is a public, two-year, associate's degree college with an enrollment of approximately

4600 students. It's the largest technical college in the state. Other institutions of higher learning in the surrounding area include Furman University and Greenville Technical College in Greenville, Anderson University, and Wofford College in Spartanburg.

Clemson is a popular center for conferences, workshops, and corporate retreats. The Madren Conference Center and Inn on the Clemson University campus offers high-tech video-conferencing equipment and facilities. The Clemson University Outdoor Laboratory, which has a ropes course, is the site for many corporate retreats.

 HEALTHCARE

Clemson Health Center—135 beds; Physicians—32; Dentists—10
Clemson Health Center, developed by the two hospitals that serve this area—Oconee Memorial Hospital and AmMed Health of Anderson—offers urgent care and diagnostic services. Oconee Memorial in Seneca (8 miles) is a 160-bed facility and has women's, surgical, heart care, rehabilitation, emergency, and wellness centers. Anderson Area Medical in Anderson, a

587-bed facility, is the fifth-largest hospital in the state. This regional center offers a broad range of services.

 SPIRITUAL LIFE
Eight Christian denominations, a synagogue, and several nondenominational groups serve the Clemson area.

 STAYING CONNECTED
The *Daily Journal/Messenger* is published six days a week. The *Tiger*, the Clemson University newspaper, is published weekly. Daily newspapers from Greenville and Anderson are available, as are cable television, two radio stations, a college radio station, and internet service. There are three bookstores in Clemson in addition to the university bookstores.

 GETTING THERE
Clemson is located in the northwestern part of South Carolina in Pickens County on US 123 and US 76, connecting to I-85 (12 miles). Air transportation is available at the Greenville-Spartanburg Airport (30 miles). The Oconee County Airport has a

4,400-foot lighted runway. The Clemson Area Transit is a free town/campus public transportation system.

 RESOURCES

Clemson Area
 Chamber of Commerce
1105 Tiger Boulevard
Clemson, SC 29631
(864) 654-1200 or (800) 542-0746
www.clemsonchamber.org

Additional area website:
www.cityofclemson.org

CLEMSON
VITAL STATISTICS

CLIMATE

Annual average rainfall	48.8 inches
Snowfall	10.9 inches
Elevation	850 feet

Temperatures (in degrees Fahrenheit)

	Jan	Apr	Jul	Oct
High	50	72	88	73
Low	28	46	67	47

OCCUPATIONS

	2006	Projected 2011
Blue collar	10.9%	9.5%
White collar	67.2%	67.2%
Services	21.8%	23.3%

ADULT EDUCATION

	2000
Less than High School	8.6%
High School	12.8%
Some College	15.5%
Associates Degree	4.9%
College Degree	26.1%
Graduate Degree	32.1%

POPULATION

2006	12,802
2000-2006 Population: Annual Compound Growth Rate	1.12%
2006-2011 Population: Annual Compound Growth Rate	0.89%

Population by age group

	2006	Projected 2011
0-4	3.8%	3.9%
5-9	3.7%	3.6%
10-14	4.2%	4.0%
15-19	6.2%	5.8%
20-24	30.3%	30.3%
25-29	7.8%	7.0%
30-34	4.6%	4.9%
35-39	4.1%	4.0%
40-44	4.5%	4.3%
45-49	4.8%	4.6%
50-54	5.0%	4.8%
55-59	4.5%	5.0%
60-64	3.3%	4.0%
65-69	2.8%	2.9%
70-74	2.4%	2.3%
75-79	2.7%	2.6%
80-84	2.4%	2.4%
85+	3.0%	3.5%

Sources for Vital Statistics listed above can be found in the Preface to this book.

GEORGETOWN

2006 POPULATION
9,166

NEAREST CITIES
Myrtle Beach, SC (35 miles)
Charleston, SC (60 miles)

ESTIMATED 2006
MEDIAN HOUSEHOLD INCOME
$33,273

COST OF LIVING
Average 3-bdrm home—$275,000
Average rent, 2-bdrm apartment—$750
Cost-of-living comparison—92.4%

SALES TAX
5%

PROPERTY TAX
Average 3-bdrm home—$3,280

The historic seaport town of Georgetown lies near the point where five South Carolina rivers merge into Winyah Bay. As the sun rises, so does the activity level on Front Street, in the heart of the business district. The colorful pastel storefronts invite casual browsing in a variety of shops housing antiques, art, books, and more. The 1,500-foot Harborwalk along the Sampit River provides a picturesque setting for dining on Georgetown's fine Lowcountry cuisine. The Tidelands' distinctive beauty is evident in the surrounding swamp marshes, rice fields, nature preserves, and abundant wildlife.

This waterfront town, established in 1729, has a colorful history. Georgetown participated in the American Revolution and sent two representatives, Thomas Lynch

Sr. and Thomas Lynch Jr., to the signing of the Declaration of Independence. In the mid-1700s, Georgetown was known for its indigo crop, but by the 1840s, the town became a major producer of rice, called "Carolina Gold." The Civil War brought about social, economic, and political changes and, as rice production declined substantially, many of the old rice plantations became wildlife or hunting preserves. At the turn of the twentieth century, the economic focus shifted to the lumber industry, a trend that prevailed until the Great Depression. The main lumber company went bankrupt in the 1930s, throwing most of the townspeople out of work. Fortunately, a new mill was developed later in the decade by the Southern Kraft Division of the International Paper Company. Having learned the risks of being a single-industry town, Georgetown has since diversified and is now home to several other industries, including steel and tourism.

 RECREATION

Surrounded by five rivers, the Intracoastal Waterway, the swamps, and the Atlantic Ocean, Georgetown's residents can choose from countless water-related activities, including sailing, canoeing and kayaking, swimming and surfing, and fishing. Various canoe and boat tours provide access to many of the local waterways.

The Waccamaw Neck, a narrow peninsula between the Waccamaw River and the Atlantic Ocean, is home to Litchfield Beach, once a rice plantation, and Huntington Beach State Park in Murrell's Inlet (18 miles). The park has three miles of beautiful beach, short nature trails, boardwalks that stretch over salt marshes and lagoons, locations for surf fishing, and free coastal education programs. This is also the site of Atalaya, the historic castle and former home of Anna Hyatt Huntington, a famous American sculptress.

Sea oats accent the dunes of Pawley's Island beach (12 miles). This casual resort, the oldest in America, offers a laid-back lifestyle symbolized by their famous handcrafted rope hammocks. Hobcaw Barony, once home of American statesman and presidential advisor Bernard Baruch, is now a 17,500-acre wildlife refuge created from thirteen rice plantations. Reservations are required for the informative three-hour tours. The Benefield Nature Center, located in the refuge's visitors center, offers a variety of learning experiences.

Marshlands around Georgetown are ideal for hunting and bird watching. The Tom Yawkey Wildlife Center occupies 20,000 acres and three islands. The preserve is not open for self-guided tours, and weekly guided tours book up months in advance. The van tour almost guarantees sightings of wild turkeys, alligators, bald eagles, deer, and a wide variety of birds. The Santee-Delta Wildlife Management Area consists of 1,721 acres of wetlands. The area is open most of the year for wildlife and bird watching. Nearby is the Francis Marion National Forest with 250,000 acres of forests and miles of trails for hiking, biking, and horseback riding. The Sewee Visitor and Environmental Education Center, part of the national forest, is a 9,000-

square-foot facility highlighting the natural history of the Lowcountry. The Cape Romain National Wildlife Refuge, which runs along the coast for over twenty miles, incorporates 64,000 acres of barrier islands and salt marshes that provide homes for ring-necked ducks, loggerhead turtles, and migratory songbirds.

The Tidelands area has yearround indoor and outdoor tennis facilities and award-winning championship golf courses, some of which were designed by Gary Player and Jack Nicklaus. The Georgetown area has sixteen courses and Myrtle Beach over eighty. Organized sports are offered through the Georgetown Parks and Recreation Department.

 CULTURAL SCENE

Brookgreen Gardens, located in Murrell's Inlet, is a spectacular outdoor sculpture garden. Its 9,100 acres include over two thousand species of native plants, more than seven hundred extraordinary American sculptures, and a fifty-acre wildlife park.

The Rice Museum is housed in the 1842 Old Market Building

and features a clock tower, the symbol of Georgetown County. Rice has played an important role in Georgetown's history, and the museum exhibits tell the story of this crop. The Rice Museum is surrounded by Lafayette Park, which is maintained by a local garden club. The Kaminski House, built in 1769 on a prime spot overlooking Georgetown's Front Street and the Sampit River, contains a wonderful collection of American antiques. The Strand Theater is a 1936 art-deco theater featuring the original marquee. Today it is used by the Swamp Fox Players for community theater productions. The Georgetown Art Gallery, Inc. is a co-op exhibiting eighteen local artists.

Hampton Plantation, built in 1735 by the French Huguenots, is one of three rice plantations open for tours. This elegant, white-columned mansion, surrounded by mature trees and beautiful grounds, was the home of poet laureate Archibald Rutledge. Hopsewee Plantation, circa 1740, was the birthplace of Thomas Lynch Jr., who signed the Declaration of Independence. Mansfield Plantation is located on the Black River and is now a bed-and-breakfast. The Annual Tour of Plantations in the spring, provides an opportunity to visit many privately owned pre-Revolutionary and antebellum residences. The Hobcaw Barony, a 17,500-acre wildlife retreat on nearby Pawley's Island, offers tours of Bernard Baruch's 13,500-square-foot mansion, Bellefield Plantation, and Friendfield Village, the last remaining original slave street on the island.

The calendar of events for this area is too extensive to list. The Made in the Shade Concert Series presents local musicians and choral groups at a historic site throughout most of the year. Harborwalk Festival draws over 10,000 people every June. Artists come from as far away as New York and Florida to exhibit their creations, and the festivities include a fun run, powerboat races, and a street dance. Thousands attend the Georgetown Wooden Boat Exhibit, a popular boat-building competition, race, and exhibit. The owners, makers, and manufacturers are available to answer questions and describe the boat-making process.

Other popular festivals include the Festival of Wines, the Georgetown Watercolor Society Annual Exhibit, and the Festival of Trees. Treasures of the Tidelands is an amazing week-long festival in May, featuring dance performances, art exhibits, a variety of musical offerings, storytelling, Civil War reenactments, and much more.

Myrtle Beach offers many nightlife options, including dinner theaters, live music, and professional performances. Charleston is home to a sophisticated selection of performing arts, including the world-famous Spoleto Festival, symphony concerts, the ballet, and theater productions.

 MAIN STREET

There are many fine restaurants in Georgetown and surrounding towns. For fine dining overlooking Harborwalk, visit The Rice Paddy (spectacular lump crab cakes). You can eat inside or outdoors at Lands End Restaurant (juicy burgers, she-crab soup, and black-bottom pie). Some other favorites include The Dogwood Bar, overlooking the river and featuring Lowcountry cuisine; Thomas Café, a popular

breakfast spot for locals; and The Humidor, an upstairs coffee and wine bar with river views that has jazz on the weekends. Boaters can dock at the River Room Restaurant and enjoy great views of the Sampit River while dining on fresh grilled fish.

Georgetown is a fabulous walking town. A $4.5 million redevelopment plan implemented several years ago has resulted in a vibrant downtown in a historic setting with a variety of businesses, gift shops, restaurants, antique stores, and specialty shops.

 HOUSING

Georgetown housing accommodates diverse lifestyles; residents can choose among private gated communities, beachfront property, or in-town houses in the historic district. The historic area offers antebellum houses with about 3,000 square feet of living space from $450,000 to $650,000. Houses in attractive established neighborhoods outside of the historic district are priced at $180,000 to $250,000. Less expensive houses in Maryville, within five miles of the downtown district but still part of the city, range from $80,000 to $110,000. New home seekers will need to look to Pawley's Island and Litchfield, which cater to beach lovers, retiree, and golfers. Golf-community houses in Litchfield run from $250,000 to $400,000, and oceanfront properties usually sell for over $2 million. Waterfront housing is also possible on the Intracoastal Waterway, tidal estuaries, saltwater creeks, and the network of rivers. Large tracts of land, currently being developed, will offer a variety of price ranges and recreational opportunities.

 ECONOMICS

Number of companies with fifty or more employees—10

Because Georgetown has been an official port of entry since 1729, international as well as domestic markets have long been open to Georgetown. Today, industrial and manufacturing businesses (steel, timber, and textiles), agricultural and aqua-businesses, and tourism support the economy. Major employers include the Georgetown County School District, (1,850 employees); the International Paper Company (1,400 employees); Mittal

Steel Corporation (350 employees); and Georgetown Memorial Hospital (600 employees).

 EDUCATION

High schools—5; Middle schools—4; Elementary schools—9; Private schools—3

Locally, higher education needs are met through Coastal Carolina University and Horry-Georgetown Technical College, a part of South Carolina's sixteen-campus network of technical colleges that offer two-year programs for progressive technical training. Coastal Carolina University at Conway (40 miles) has approximately 4,500 students and offers four-year degree programs in thirty-eight areas of study, a master's degree program in education, and six cooperative programs with other state universities. There is a new branch at Litchfield. There are seven institutions for higher learning in the Charleston area, including Charleston Southern, The Citadel, University/College of Charleston, the Medical University of South Carolina, Johnson and Wales University, Webster University, and Trident Technical College.

HEALTHCARE

Georgetown Memorial Hospital—142 beds; Physicians—31; Dentists—10

Georgetown Memorial Hospital, an acute-care facility with all private rooms, offers cardiology, physical and occupational therapy, oncology/hematology, a Level III trauma center/emergency room, state-of-the-art diagnostic and imaging capabilities (including MRI and CAT scan services), and two satellite centers. The hospital has a medical staff of sixty-five physicians representing many specialties. A new hospital on the outskirts of Georgetown will be completed in 2008. Yawkey Cancer Center is a state-of-the-art facility. Other off-campus facilities include the Georgetown Outpatient Therapy Center, offering rehab services, and the Pain Therapy Center. HealthPoint, located on Pawley's Island, is a health and fitness center. An additional fifty-nine-bed hospital, planned for Murrell's Inlet within Georgetown County, will be a full-service, inpatient facility with emergency services and a nineteen-bed acute-care

rehab center. In addition, seven other hospitals, including the Medical University of South Carolina at Charleston, are within a forty-five-minute drive of Georgetown.

 SPIRITUAL LIFE

Twenty-seven Christian denominations are represented. There is one synagogue in Georgetown.

 STAYING CONNECTED

A local newspaper, *Georgetown Times,* published three times a week, and a northern county newspaper, the *Coastal Observer,* published once a week, serve the area. The *Sun News* is a daily paper based in Myrtle Beach with a satellite office in Georgetown. Local internet access and two radio stations are available. A twenty-six-mile fiber optic system offers high-speed, business-to-business data exchanges and teleconferencing. There are three bookstores in the area.

 GETTING THERE

Georgetown is located just off US 17 (Ocean Highway) at the intersection of US 521 and 701. US 521 connects to I-95 (66 miles).

US 17 runs north along the coast, connecting Georgetown to Myrtle Beach and to Charleston. I-26 links with US 17 in Charleston. The closest beach is twelve miles away at Pawley's Island. Myrtle Beach International Jetport is thirty-five miles away, and Charleston International Airport is sixty miles away. Both offer daily commercial flights to many major cities. The Georgetown County Airport has two 5,000-foot runways for private aircraft. The Seaboard Coast Line serves Georgetown County for railway services, and the Port of Georgetown is dedicated to cargo handling for South Carolina State Ports Authority.

 RESOURCES

Georgetown County
  Chamber of Commerce
531 Front Street
P.O. Box 1776
Georgetown, SC 29442-1776
(800) 777-7705
www.georgetownchamber.com

Additional area website
www.visitgeorgetowncountysc.
  com

GEORGETOWN
VITAL STATISTICS

CLIMATE

Annual average rainfall	49.9 inches
Snowfall	0 inches
Elevation	46.3 feet

Temperatures (in degrees Fahrenheit)

	Jan	Apr	Jul	Oct
High	58	76	90	77
Low	36	51	71	55

OCCUPATIONS

	2006	Projected 2011
Blue collar	30.0%	27.8%
White collar	46.6%	46.5%
Services	23.4%	25.6%

ADULT EDUCATION

	2000
Less than High School	30.8%
High School	29.6%
Some College	18.8%
Associates Degree	5.8%
College Degree	9.7%
Graduate Degree	5.3%

POPULATION

2006	9,166
2000-2006 Population: Annual Compound Growth Rate	0.38%
2006-2011 Population: Annual Compound Growth Rate	1.28%

Population by age group

	2006	Projected 2011
0-4	7.9%	8.1%
5-9	7.6%	7.2%
10-14	7.5%	7.7%
15-19	7.2%	7.0%
20-24	6.5%	6.5%
25-29	6.8%	6.0%
30-34	6.6%	6.4%
35-39	5.9%	6.0%
40-44	6.2%	6.2%
45-49	6.4%	6.3%
50-54	6.9%	5.9%
55-59	5.6%	6.8%
60-64	4.4%	5.3%
65-69	3.6%	3.8%
70-74	3.1%	3.1%
75-79	2.8%	2.5%
80-84	2.6%	2.3%
85+	2.4%	2.7%

Sources for Vital Statistics listed above can be found in the Preface to this book.

2006 POPULATION
  7,168

NEAREST CITIES
  Florence, SC (25 miles)
  Columbia, SC (70 miles)
  Myrtle Beach, SC (80 miles)
  Charlotte, NC (80 miles)

ESTIMATED 2006
MEDIAN HOUSEHOLD INCOME
  $33,687

COST OF LIVING
  Average 3-bdrm home—$125,000
  Average rent, 2-bdrm apartment—
$500
  Cost-of-living comparison—
94.8%

SALES TAX
  6%

PROPERTY TAX
  Average 3-bdrm home—$500

Named as an "All-America City" in 1996, Hartsville has lived up to the honor and continued its pattern of progressive development. The downtown area has an appealing streetscape with Victorian street lighting, brick walkways, a downtown park, and underground wires, a rare amenity for small, older towns. Situated within a few blocks of the heart of town, Coker College offers a variety of cultural arts to the community.

The first settler in this area was Thomas E. Hart, who purchased 8,000 acres along Black Creek and built a plantation known as Kalmia. Home Avenue was built to connect the area to Society Hill, where the main plantation house still stands today. Major Hart's vision for Hartsville included building a carriage factory, gristmill, powered sawmill, post office, store, school, and Baptist church. Eventually Hart sold the carriage factory to James Lide Coker, who moved to Hartsville in 1857, determined to apply his Harvard agricultural knowledge to the farmland. Coker's love of education was the force behind the establishment of the Welsh Neck High School in 1894. This later became Coker College, the first private women's college in this part of the state, and now a coeducational liberal arts college. Over the years, Major Coker and his sons started many companies, including Southern Novelty Company, a paper company that evolved into Sonoco Products Company (a Fortune 500 company). Sonoco's international headquarters is still located in Hartsville.

The historic district is within walking distance of the downtown area. A marked walking tour leads visitors past a number of ornate homes from the 1800s. Many of the beautiful old oak trees that line the streets of Hartsville were planted by Major Coker in the late nineteenth century. The other side of the downtown area is graced with lovely homes in established neighborhoods, some of which border on a lake. With a serene environment and an active community of residents and townspeople, Hartsville is an attractive place to spend a few days or a lifetime.

RECREATION

There are three state parks within thirty miles of Hartsville. The Civilian Conservation Corps originally built Cheraw State Park in the 1930s. Visitors to the park can enjoy Lake Juniper, a 360-acre lake for fishing and water sports, as well as an eighteen-hole championship golf course and pro shop. Rental cabins and lakefront campsites are available. Lee State Park, also built by the CCC, is the entrance to the beautiful Lynches River. Artesian springs and an extensive hardwood forest provide an enchanting environment for observing plant and animal life, especially sandhill cranes. An equestrian facility and hiking trails offer alternative means for exploring the park. The Carolina Sandhills National Wildlife Refuge includes 46,000 acres of land and water, including an eight-mile wildlife drive for automobile tours. Observation towers make it easy to spot white-tailed deer, fox squirrels, and wood ducks. The Sand Hills State Forest is adjacent to the wildlife refuge and offers trails for hiking, off-road biking, and horseback riding.

Delightful Kalmia Gardens, located less than three miles from Hartsville, is a thirty-acre garden maintained by Coker College. It was originally the site of Thomas Hart's 1820 plantation house, the oldest structure in the area. In the 1930s, Mrs. David Coker (known as "Miss May") built the garden on a sixty-foot drop that falls from a bluff to Black Creek. Today it includes walking trails, laurel thickets, a black-water swamp, a beech bluff, and pin oak and holly uplands. On the other side of Black Creek is the 796-acre Segars-McKinnon Preserve, which offers hiking trails.

Lake Robinson, approximately ten miles north of Hartsville, is the site of Progress Energy H. B. Robinson Nuclear Plant. The water temperature is strictly monitored for the fish and plant life. Fishing for bluegill, chain pickerel, and largemouth bass is good here. Boating, sailing, swimming, and other water sports are also popular. Black Creek connects Lake Robinson with Prestwood Lake. Canoe trips are available through Kalmia Gardens.

Fishing, boating, and jet skiing are allowed on Prestwood Lake, which wraps around a lovely established neighborhood. City-owned Lawton Park, adjoining Prestwood Lake, offers lighted tennis courts, a playground, and a recreation center. Hartsville Country Club features an eighteen-hole championship golf course, tennis courts, a pool, and a clubhouse. There are additional courses within thirty minutes of town. The local YMCA, which has a membership of over three thousand, recently underwent a $2.4 million renovation and expansion. It offers sports activities, classes, a fitness center, a gym, and an indoor pool. The Hartsville Recreation Department has an indoor gym. Byerly Park is a multi-use recreation complex that includes six soccer fields, an eight-lane track and field facility, two playgrounds, walking trails, and six tennis courts. The Patrick Sawyer Bike Path runs through the heart of Hartsville.

Darlington Raceway, in the nearby town of Darlington, hosts a variety of NASCAR races throughout the year. Myrtle Beach is about ninety minutes away.

 CULTURAL SCENE

Coker College's Elizabeth Boatwright Coker Performing Arts Center includes the 466-seat state-of-the-art Watson Theater, a black box theater (used as a television studio and performance space), two dance studios, a music recording and rehearsal studio, a gallery, and shops for costumes and scenery. The $6.5 million facility hosts the Coker College Performing Arts Series and houses the departments of dance, music, and theater. The dance department hosts fall and spring dance concerts. The New York–based International Film Circuit helps coordinate an international film series at the center. The Coker Singers, a student choral group, perform throughout the East Coast and with orchestras such as the South Carolina Philharmonic and the Charleston Symphony. Other musical options include the Coker College Performing Arts Series, visiting symphony orchestras, and the Hartsville Civic Chorale. The Hartsville Community Concert Association sponsors four concerts a year by well-known artists.

The Hartsville Community Players have presented thirty years of theater productions such as *Steel Magnolias* and children's performances such as *Alice in Wonderland*. Center Theater, an 867-seat theater on the National Register of Historic Places, hosts special art and business events. The Black Creek Arts Center offers art classes and programs and includes a 1,600-square foot gallery for art exhibits. The Charles W. and Joan S. Coker Library-Information Technology Center offers students access to collections and the latest information technology. The Black Creek Arts Council schedules many cultural events for the county.

There are two museums in Hartsville. The Jacob Kelley House Museum, built in 1820, presents monthly demonstrations of historic relevance. The Hartsville Museum, once the old post office, displays Native American artifacts and samples of silver handcrafted in Hartsville. The John Lide Hart Cottage, built around 1846, is the oldest building in town and is open for tours.

Hartsville is located on the South Carolina Cotton Trail, which extends from I-95 to I-20. Many towns along this trail have historic homes, museums, gardens, and even working cotton fields. Significant African-American historical sites are also highlighted along the trail.

RenoFest, a lively bluegrass festival held in March, celebrates the music of the late Don Reno, a famed musician. It was named the 2005 Event of the Year by the South Carolina Festival and Event Association. There are instrument competitions, lots of music, and even a hoedown. Christmas in April, sponsored by the National Civic League, brings the community together once a year to improve the homes of elderly, poor, and handicapped residents. Jazz! Carolina is a popular

late summer festival, featuring Dixieland and swing bands. Other popular occasions are the July Fourth Family Fireworks Festival; the Taste of Hartsville food festival held in the spring at Kalmia Gardens at Coker College; and the Hartsville holiday events, which include a traditional Christmas parade, a singing Christmas tree, and a downtown open house.

 MAIN STREET

Bizzell's Food and Spirits serves upscale Southern fare, including shrimp and grits, as well as spectacular chocolate cobbler. Mr. B's, just outside of town, is a popular place for traditional Southern food. Other must-visit eateries include Westwood BBQ (phenomenal barbecue); The Culinary Company (good lunches and coffee anytime); the Carolina Lunch (Southern-style breakfast with grits); Ruth's Drive-In, a Hartsville tradition; and The Midnight Rooster, a coffee shop.

The revitalization of downtown has received recognition by state and national associations, and Hartsville was chosen as an

All-America City in 1996. The All-state Foundation gives this award to only ten cities a year, saluting locales that display cooperation for the purpose of community improvement.

 HOUSING

Residential options in Hartsville include homes in the historic district, housing in established neighborhoods and new-home subdivisions, and upper-story apartments over commercial businesses. Housing costs are reasonable and property taxes are low. Property taxes on owner-occupied dwellings are reduced by contributions from a local option sales tax, and there is a statewide reduction program for owner-occupied residential properties.

Historic district homes range from $100,000 to $200,000. It is possible to find a few fixer-uppers in the Historic District for less than $100,000. Mature, established neighborhoods offer variety in home style and can cost from $125,000 for a home needing renovation to $350,000 for a large, remodeled home thirty-five to forty years old. There are many new home subdivisions to choose from; small houses begin at approximately $80,000 and go to $135,000. Houses on lots of one to four acres are priced at $225,000 to $350,000. Large new homes are $300,000 and up.

There are no condominiums in Hartsville, but there are apartments, some of which are urban-style living spaces above commercial properties in the downtown area. Full-time options for the elderly include two nursing homes that meet extended-care needs.

 ECONOMICS

Number of employers with fifty or more employees—19

The major industries in Hartsville include manufacturing, agriculture, and service. Some of the major crops are cotton, tobacco, and soybeans. Manufacturing makes up one-third of Hartsville's jobs. Sonoco Products Company, a Fortune 500 company employing about 1,600 people, is the largest employer in Hartsville. Others include Progress Energy (650 employees); A. O. Smith Water Products Company (700 employees); Talley Metals Technology

(230 employees); Roller Bearing Company of America (150 employees); and Stingray Boat Company (130 employees).

EDUCATION

High schools—1; Middle schools— 1; Elementary schools—6; Private schools—5

Hartsville is the site of the South Carolina Governor's School for Science and Mathematics, the state's magnet school for gifted high school juniors and seniors. Higher education in Hartsville is provided by Coker College, a private, four-year, coeducational liberal arts college. Founded in 1908, the school is known for its interactive roundtable learning approach and offers twenty-eight majors and eighteen minors. Coker offers night degree programs as well as nondegree opportunities.

Francis Marion University, a comprehensive, state-supported university located in Florence, offers graduate and undergraduate degree programs to more than 3,700 students. The main campus of Florence-Darlington Technical College is in Florence, but there is a satellite campus in Hartsville.

The college was established in 1963 and has over three thousand students. The central campus of The University of South Carolina is in Columbia; seven additional campuses are located throughout the state. Chartered in 1801, USC offers over three hundred programs for those pursuing bachelor's, master's, doctoral, and professional degrees at the Columbia campus.

HEALTHCARE

Carolina Pines Regional Medical Center—116 beds; Physicians—65; Dentists—12

The community is served by Carolina Pines Regional Medical Center, which offers specialties such as pediatrics, women's services, surgical services, urology, sports medicine rehabilitation, nephrology, industrial medicine, and others. In addition to the sixty-five physicians on staff, there are forty consulting and courtesy physicians. The 175,000-square foot medical campus opened in 1999 and serves four counties. Columbia is within an hour's drive and offers additional extensive healthcare services.

SPIRITUAL LIFE

Eighteen Christian denominations are represented. The closest synagogue is in Florence.

 STAYING CONNECTED

The local paper, the *Messenger,* is published twice a week. Metro area dailies from Columbia (the *State*) and from Charlotte (the *Charlotte Observer*) are available, as are local internet service and cable television. The town has one local bookstore, and there is a student bookstore on the Coker College campus.

 GETTING THERE

Hartsville is located on US 15 just north of the intersection with SC 151. US 15 intersects I-20 approximately sixteen miles south of Hartsville and twenty-six miles west of I-95. Air transportation is provided through the Columbia Airport and the Charlotte Airport. The Florence Regional Airport offers daily flights on two commercial airlines to Charlotte and Atlanta. The Hartsville Regional Airport, with its 5,005-foot runway, serves small aircraft.

 RESOURCES

Greater Hartsville
  Chamber of Commerce
214 N. Fifth Street
P.O. Box 578
Hartsville, SC 29551-0578
(843) 332-6401
www.hartsvillechamber.org

Additional area website:
www.hartsvillesc.com

HARTSVILLE
VITAL STATISTICS

CLIMATE

Annual average rainfall	45.2 inches
Snowfall	5 inches
Elevation	226 feet

Temperatures (in degrees Fahrenheit)

	Jan	Apr	Jul	Oct
High	55	77	91	77
Low	32	49	69	50

OCCUPATIONS

	2006	Projected 2011
Blue collar	24.0%	22.1%
White collar	57.9%	57.6%
Services	18.1%	20.3%

ADULT EDUCATION

	2000
Less than High School	27.3%
High School	25.3%
Some College	20.2%
Associates Degree	5.2%
College Degree	13.9%
Graduate Degree	8.1%

POPULATION

2006	7,168
2000-2006 Population: Annual Compound Growth Rate	-0.84%
2006-2011 Population: Annual Compound Growth Rate	-0.25%

Population by age group

	2006	Projected 2011
0-4	6.8%	6.6%
5-9	6.4%	6.2%
10-14	6.8%	6.4%
15-19	7.0%	7.5%
20-24	7.5%	7.1%
25-29	6.3%	5.6%
30-34	5.5%	5.9%
35-39	4.9%	5.2%
40-44	6.6%	5.4%
45-49	7.4%	6.8%
50-54	6.8%	7.0%
55-59	6.3%	7.1%
60-64	5.2%	6.0%
65-69	4.0%	4.6%
70-74	3.8%	3.5%
75-79	3.7%	3.3%
80-84	2.8%	2.9%
85+	2.3%	2.7%

Sources for Vital Statistics listed above can be found in the Preface to this book.

NEWBERRY

2006 Population
10,733

Nearest Cities
Columbia, SC (40 miles)
Greenville, SC (60 miles)
Spartanburg, SC (65 miles)

Estimated 2006 Median Household Income
$34,008

Cost of Living
Average 3-bdrm home—$120,000
Average rent, 2-bdrm apartment—$600
Cost-of-living comparison—94.8%

Sales Tax
6%

Property Tax
Average 3-bdrm home—$1,645

Founded in 1789, Newberry is a unique blend of college town traditions, a heartfelt interest in the arts, and a spirited dedication to an economic renaissance. Rolling hills, extensive woodlands, two large lakes, and four rivers provide an attractive setting. Elegant homes and lush gardens line the streets of the historic district. The town is home to a delightful Japanese garden, a rare orchid farm, and incredible antique rose beds. Living is easy in Newberry; residents are known not only for their friendliness and warm hospitality but also for an air of intellectual sophistication, an artistic flair, a sense of determination, and a willingness to make things happen.

Newberry was settled by Scotch-Irish, English, and German immigrants in the mid-1700s. The settlers made a living farming cotton, but the Cherokee War left the town economically depressed. Starting in the early 1800s, local humanitarian John Belton worked to improve conditions for slaves and also advocated diversification of crops and other soil conservation methods. By 1851, a railroad line was built, and the cotton industry brought prosperity to Newberry. The introduction of the cotton gin, which shifted industry from small farms to large plantations, affected the region both economically and socially.

Today, Newberry's downtown area is impressive; the buildings have been restored and renovated. The main thoroughfare has a European feel, with narrow, brick-paved streets and brown brick storefronts dating back to pre–Civil War times. The prime attraction is the restored opera house, a French Gothic structure in the heart of town. Built in 1882 and renovated in 1998, this cultural center hosts Broadway productions, dance troupes, and musical performances ranging from classical to jazz to country.

Newberry College offers a variety of cultural activities. The establishment of several foreign-based businesses has brought an international flavor to this small town. A commuter train is planned to connect the town with Columbia.

RECREATION

Newberry is surrounded by waterways and is ideal for fishing, boating, sailing, canoeing, kayaking, waterskiing, and swimming. It is located near four rivers (the Broad, Enoree, Tyger, and Saluda) as well as Lake Murray (50,000 acres) and Lake Greenwood (11,400 acres). Forty-one-mile-long Lake Murray provides hydroelectric power and recreational options for this part of the state. There are numerous boat landings and marinas. The lake is also home to 348-acre Dreher Island State Park, a recreational area made up of three islands linked by bridges and a causeway. There are twelve miles of shoreline, a marina, camping facilities, picnic areas, villa rentals, and a park store. Lake Greenwood State Park, developed by the Civilian Conservation Corps, is a 914-acre park with camping, nature trails, fishing, and boating.

Seventy percent of the county is wooded land. Sumter National Forest provides 56,595 acres for nature trails, hunting, horseback riding, and boating and fishing on the Enoree River. The 276-acre Lynches Woods features a 4.7-mile trail for hiking, biking, and horseback riding. Palmetto Trail–Sumter Passage is a fourteen-mile trail.

Newberry has two eighteen-hole golf courses at local country clubs, which also provide swimming and tennis facilities. There is one nine-hole course as well. Local recreation facilities include eleven parks with playgrounds and city-sponsored youth programs. The Newberry County YMCA offers after-school childcare, soccer, roller hockey, swimming, basketball, and gymnastics.

 CULTURAL SCENE

The Newberry Opera House is the cultural center of Newberry. The building was previously used as a combination firehouse, jail, office complex, and performance hall. In 1969, the Newberry Historical Society, along with individuals and other community groups, advocated the preservation of the opera house, which was placed on the National Register of Historic Places. Renovation was completed in 1998. This 426-seat facility has a state of the art sound and lighting system. The original tower clock is still in place.

The Newberry Community Players perform at the Ritz, a 1936 art-deco theater. The Newberry Ballet Guild and Newberry College's departments of music and theater also perform regularly. Newberry boasts a number of historic districts, including Main Street, Historic Boundary Street, Newberry Cotton Mills Historic District, and College Street Historic District. Many of the structures date from the 1870s to the 1920s, with the earliest, the Gauntee House, dating back to 1808.

The Ballentine Farm Museum is open by appointment and includes an extensive private collection of farm equipment. The Wells Japanese Garden features small ponds, pagoda, and a teahouse. Newberry is also home to Carter and Holmes Orchids, a rare orchid farm where visitors can tour eighteen green-houses.

Newberry College offers a wide range of classes, lectures, and special events on its wooded, sixty-acre campus. The Newberry County Agri-Fest is a popular event, and there are several other arts, crafts, and music festivals throughout the year.

 MAIN STREET

Locals and visitors frequent Steven W's Downtown Bistro for gourmet seafood and pasta in an inviting atmosphere. The Cabana Café is a popular lunch spot; downstairs in the Storm Cellar, diners enjoy local entertainment and generous portions of beef, seafood, and chicken. Other favorites are The Rose Garden Tea Room (lunch and afternoon tea); Grille on Main (casual lunch and dinner); Blue Moon Sports Bar (sandwiches, salads, wings, ribs and steaks); and, in nearby Prosperity, SC, The Back Porch (home-style cooking with fresh breads and desserts) and Hawg Heaven (you guessed it—barbecue). Bubba's Martin Street Beer Parlor is a favorite after-work hangout for locals.

There are eighteen antique shops, including two antique malls and several gift shops. The visitors center is housed in an 1852 Greek Revival building that was once the Old Court House. Atop the massive portico on the courthouse stands a unique sculpture depicting an eagle uprooting a palmetto tree. This allegorical figure symbolizes the injustice of the Reconstructionists as seen through the eyes of Southerners.

 HOUSING

Housing options are dominated by older and historic houses; only a small number of newly built custom houses are scattered around the area. There is a wide selection of homes that are one hundred years old or more, priced from $325,000 to $400,000 for approximately 4,000 square feet. Country-style or Victorian houses offering 3,000 square feet of renovated living space cost about $155,000. A fifty-year-old house with 2,400 square feet is priced around $100,000 and will probably need some renovation and updating. A fifteen- to twenty-year-old ranch-style house with 1,300 square feet costs around $95,000. There are no condominiums or town houses, but there are some apartments and duplexes.

 ECONOMICS

Number of employers with fifty or more employees—29

Agriculture, manufacturing industries (food processing, textiles, wood processing, and wood products), wholesale and retail trade, and government are the primary employers. Forest products top agricultural sales, followed by livestock, eggs, and dairy products. Major manufacturing companies include the Louis Rich Company (1,600 employees); American Fiber & Finishing (700 employees); and Shakespeare Company Composites & Electronics Division (400 employees).

 EDUCATION

High schools—1; Middle schools—2; Elementary schools—4; Private schools—2

Higher education needs are met through Newberry College, which has an enrollment of approximately seven hundred students. Newberry College, established in 1856 by the Lutheran Church, is a four-year liberal arts institution situated on a sixty-acre wooded campus. Bachelors degrees are offered in arts, music, music education, and science. Piedmont Technical College-Newberry County Branch is a two-year college serving a seven-county area. Other colleges within forty miles of Newberry include the University of South Carolina (main campus at Columbia), Columbia College, Allen University, Benedict College, Columbia Bible College, Presbyterian College, Lander University, and Midlands Technical College.

 HEALTHCARE

Newberry County Memorial Hospital—102 beds; Physicians—12; Dentists—5

The Newberry County Memorial Hospital is a community hospital offering a 24-hour emergency department, a cardiac rehabilitation program, a medical nursing unit, a surgical nursing unit, an industrial wellness program, pain and respiratory therapies, and other services.

SPIRITUAL LIFE

Twenty-four Christian denominations are represented. The closest synagogue is located in Columbia.

 STAYING CONNECTED

The *Newberry Observer* is published three times a week, and the *Whitmire News* is published weekly. There are two metro-area dailies from Greenville and Columbia. Local internet service, two radio stations, and cable television are available. Newberry has four bookstores.

 GETTING THERE

Newberry is located in Newberry County in the lower Piedmont area of South Carolina, near the geographic center of the state. It is situated just off of I-26, which connects Columbia with Asheville, North Carolina. Newberry is also served by US 76 and 176 and SC 121 and 34. Air transportation is available through Columbia Metropolitan Airport and Greenville-Spartanburg Jetport. The Newberry Municipal Airport has a 3,500-foot runway suitable for small private aircraft.

 RESOURCES

Newberry County
   Chamber of Commerce
P.O. Box 396
Newberry, SC 29108
(803) 276-4274
www.newberrycounty.org

Additional area websites:
www.cityofnewberry.com
www.newberry-sc.com
www.newberryoperahouse.com

NEWBERRY
VITAL STATISTICS

CLIMATE

Annual average rainfall	49.2 inches
Snowfall	3.5 inches
Elevation	502 feet

Temperatures (in degrees Fahrenheit)

	Jan	Apr	Jul	Oct
High	54	76	91	75
Low	31	48	68	49

OCCUPATIONS

	2006	Projected 2011
Blue collar	32.1%	29.8%
White collar	48.8%	48.5%
Services	19.1%	21.7%

ADULT EDUCATION

	2000
Less than High School	33.9%
High School	28.3%
Some College	13.6%
Associates Degree	3.9%
College Degree	13.4%
Graduate Degree	6.9%

POPULATION

2006	10,733
2000-2006 Population: Annual Compound Growth Rate	0.23%
2006-2011 Population: Annual Compound Growth Rate	0.52%

Population by age group

	2006	Projected 2011
0-4	7.1%	7.1%
5-9	6.4%	6.3%
10-14	5.9%	6.4%
15-19	8.5%	8.3%
20-24	9.1%	9.1%
25-29	7.5%	6.1%
30-34	7.0%	6.8%
35-39	5.6%	6.3%
40-44	6.3%	5.7%
45-49	6.3%	6.4%
50-54	6.3%	6.1%
55-59	5.4%	6.3%
60-64	4.2%	5.2%
65-69	3.1%	3.5%
70-74	3.0%	2.6%
75-79	2.8%	2.7%
80-84	2.5%	2.3%
85+	3.0%	3.1%

Sources for Vital Statistics listed above can be found in the Preface to this book.

SUMMERVILLE

2006 POPULATION
31,923

NEAREST CITIES
Charleston, SC (25 miles)
Beaufort, SC (78 miles)
Columbia, SC (95 miles)

ESTIMATED 2006
MEDIAN HOUSEHOLD INCOME
$53,336

COST OF LIVING
Average 3-bdrm home—$222,000
Average rent, 2-bdrm apartment—
$825
Cost-of-living comparison—98%

SALES TAX
5%

PROPERTY TAX
Average 3-bdrm home—$2,404

It's no surprise that the colorful community of Summerville is known as the "Flowertown in the Pines." Originally it was a summertime retreat for the plantation owners of "Charles Town" (now Charleston) looking for relief from swamp fever and mosquitoes. Later Summerville blossomed into a healing center; it was thought to be one of the healthiest places in the world for the treatment and cure of pulmonary disease because of turpentine released by the giant pine trees. In 1998, *Kiplinger's Personal Finance* magazine named Summerville one of the best retirement locations in America.

Seven hundred homes and buildings in the town center and surrounding neighborhood are listed on the National Register of

Historic Places. Raised plantation-style homes and elegant Victorians with inviting wraparound porches line the streets of this historic village. Nearby Azalea Park is an eight-acre piece of heaven with fountains, walking paths, gazebos, pines, and, of course, azaleas. The park, the site of the Flowertown Festival, draws 200,000 visitors each year. There is much to appreciate and experience in this "Pineland Village," and opportunities abound for outdoor recreation, cultural events, and fabulous dining.

 RECREATION

The Atlantic Ocean is only thirty minutes away and there are many beaches in the area, including Folly Beach, Edisto Island, Sullivan's Island, Isle of Palms, and Kiawah Island. The Audubon Center at Francis Beidler Forest is a 13,000-acre swamp forest with three hundred species of wildlife, a 1.75-mile boardwalk, and an amazing network of creeks. It contains the largest remaining stand of virgin bald cypress and tupelo gum swamp forest anywhere in the world. Canoe trips and naturalist guided walks are available. Nearby rivers have endless estuaries and inlets for canoe exploring or kayaking. Outside the town, you can ride at one of six stables or fish for large-mouthed bass, bream, or catfish at one of the many freshwater lakes.

There are forty golf courses within an hour's drive of Summerville, in addition to three private country clubs and three public courses in town. Tennis is available at public parks, private clubs, and the local YMCA, which also offers youth, adult, and senior programs, and a wellness center with an indoor pool, a sauna, and a steam room.

 CULTURAL SCENE

Art, music, and theater are all well-represented in this progressive community. The Flowertown Players offer five productions a year at the James F. Dean Community Theatre. The Summerville Community Orchestra performs classical music. Art Central is a historic district gallery owned and operated by local award-winning artists. The Flowertown Festival is an annual spring event that draws over 300,000 people—one of the largest events in the region. Sculpture in the South is held every May in Azalea Park. Thirty minutes away in Charleston, cultural opportunities include the renowned Spoleto Festival USA, featuring performers from all over the world, and the Piccolo Spoleto Festival, showcasing local and regional artists. The Charleston Symphony Orchestra, nine theater groups, two dance companies, an opera company, and a ballet company provide an extraordinary selection of activities within a short drive of Summerville.

MAIN STREET

For good Lowcountry cuisine, try Oscar's Place; if you're looking for a friendly after-hours gathering spot, O'Lacy's and McGuire's Irish Pub are the places to go. Locals and tourists also frequent Breck's (great steaks); Sticky Fingers (barbeque and ribs); Mustard Seed (fabulous seafood in a fun atmosphere); Eclectic Chef (a popular sandwich spot); CR's Bar & Grill; Club Whatever (a teen favorite); McNeill's Restaurant; and Charleston Crab House. Woodlands Resort and Inn, a AAA

Diamond Award winner, is known for its Old South charm and elegant dining.

The town square is the location for special celebrations on the Fourth of July, Halloween, and Christmas. The Red, White, and Blue On the Green is the annual Fourth of July celebration, which features a parade that includes everything from tricycles to marching bands. At the Christmas Tree Lighting, everyone joins in caroling and other festivities. Shops on the square sell original art, collectibles and antiques, handmade quilts, hand-smocked baby clothes, fanciful bed linens, and other intriguing goods.

HOUSING

There are abundant housing choices, including Victorian cottages and plantation style homes. In the historic district, prices range from $239,900 to $1.35 million. Old houses outside the historic district start at approximately $175,000. New housing construction is plentiful; condominiums and duplexes range from $125,000 to $196,000, and single-family houses from $110,000 to $175,000.

Practical prefabricated housing is also available. Golf and tennis communities, very popular in Summerville, offer houses priced from $134,000 to $800,000. Mini-farms may also appeal. There are nineteen apartment complexes in the area. Six special apartment projects are designed for low-income and handicapped elderly persons.

 ECONOMICS

Number of employers with fifty or more employees—10

Easy access to Port of Charleston and the railroad (the first commercial railroad in the United States) contribute to the growth of manufacturing businesses and industries from all over the world. Today there are twenty foreign-owned firms in the area. The largest employers in Dorchester County are the Robert Bosch Corporation (2,243 employees) in Charleston, and LINQ Industrial Fabrics (343 employees) in Summerville.

 EDUCATION

High schools—2; Middle schools—1; Elementary schools—8; Private schools—3

There are seven institutions of higher learning within twenty-five

miles of Summerville. Charleston Southern (12 miles) is a church-affiliated university offering thirty programs of study. The Citadel, located in Charleston, was established in 1842. This liberal arts college with a strong military influence is coeducational and has over 3,138 students. The urban College of Charleston is the largest four-year university in the area, with almost 15,000 students. The Medical University of South Carolina, also in Charleston, has six affiliated colleges. Trident Technical College, home to 12,000 students, is a two-year institution and part of the statewide system. It is also home to Charleston's new culinary institute, which features programs in culinary, baking, and pastry arts, as well as hospitality management. The newer Charleston campus of Johnson & Wales University features programs in culinary arts, baking and pastry arts, hospitality management, and travel tourism management. Webster University, a branch of the St. Louis school, provides programs in the arts and business administration.

HEALTHCARE

Summerville Medical Center— 94 beds; Trident Medical Center— 300 beds; Physicians—83; Dentists—53

Both medical centers are full-service hospitals offering 24-hour emergency service, critical care/cardiac services, cancer care, and many other special programs. In 1998, HCIA and William H. Mercer Inc. ranked Summerville Medical Center and Trident Medical Center among the top one hundred hospitals in the country. Care Alliance Health Services has three hospitals in the tri-county area, with a total of seven hundred beds, and provides outpatient services. There are also rehabilitation centers, nursing homes, assisted-living facilities, and nine home healthcare service providers in this area.

 SPIRITUAL LIFE

Thirty-one denominations are represented. The closest synagogue is in Charleston.

 STAYING CONNECTED

Two local newspapers are available, the weekly *Dorchester Eagle-Record* and the biweekly *Journal Scene.* Charleston's daily, the *Post and Courier,* is also delivered to Summerville. Cable television, two radio stations, and internet access are available. There are six bookstores in the area.

 GETTING THERE

Summerville is in Dorchester County northwest of Charleston, near the intersection of I-26 and SC 17A. Airports serving this area include Charleston International Airport (12 miles) and a general aviation airport in Summerville.

 RESOURCES

Greater Summerville/Dorchester
  County Chamber of Commerce
P.O. Box 670
402 North Main Street
Summerville, SC 29484
(843) 875-8535
www.greatersummerville.org
www.summerville.sc.us
www.visitsummerville.com

SUMMERVILLE VITAL STATISTICS

CLIMATE

Annual average rainfall	50 inches
Snowfall	1 inch
Elevation	72 feet

Temperatures (in degrees Fahrenheit)

	Jan	Apr	Jul	Oct
High	59	76	89	77
Low	38	55	71	57

OCCUPATIONS

	2006	Projected 2011
Blue collar	23.3%	22.0%
White collar	61.4%	62.1%
Services	15.3%	15.8%

ADULT EDUCATION

	2000
Less than High School	13.9%
High School	27.2%
Some College	25.2%
Associates Degree	7.0%
College Degree	17.9%
Graduate Degree	8.7%

POPULATION

2006	31,923
2000-2006 Population: Annual Compound Growth Rate	2.27%
2006-2011 Population: Annual Compound Growth Rate	3.08%

Population by age group

	2006	Projected 2011
0-4	6.5%	6.8%
5-9	6.1%	6.0%
10-14	7.5%	6.4%
15-19	8.2%	7.0%
20-24	7.4%	7.8%
25-29	5.7%	7.3%
30-34	6.1%	5.8%
35-39	6.7%	5.9%
40-44	7.9%	7.0%
45-49	8.0%	7.9%
50-54	7.4%	7.6%
55-59	6.8%	7.2%
60-64	4.7%	5.8%
65-69	3.2%	3.8%
70-74	2.7%	2.6%
75-79	1.8%	2.2%
80-84	1.7%	1.4%
85+	1.5%	1.7%

Sources for Vital Statistics listed above can be found in the Preface to this book.

TENNESSEE

2006 POPULATION
9,172

NEAREST CITIES
Knoxville, TN (75 miles)
Chattanooga, TN (74 miles)

ESTIMATED 2006
MEDIAN HOUSEHOLD INCOME
$31,419

COST OF LIVING
Average 3-bdrm home—$145,000
Average rent, 2-bdrm apartment—$500
Cost-of-living comparison—80.9%

SALES TAX
9.75%

PROPERTY TAX
Average 3-bdrm home—$730

Crossville is situated amid the abundant rolling valleys, towering forests, crystal clear lakes, and imposing peaks of the majestic Cumberland Mountains and Plateau. Cool temperatures prevail in the summer thanks to the 2,000-foot elevation, but winters are mild. The climate makes this area attractive to new residents moving from the north or the south.

Prior to 1805, all of Cumberland County was Native-American territory. In 1794, Francis Bailey, the son of an English banker, wrote of the area, "It is a fine, large plain, or natural meadow, containing many hundred acres and covered throughout its whole extent with a tall, rich grass surrounded on every side by the neighboring mountains and watered with several fine springs which flow from one end to the other." This early description captures the essence of the area, now home to numerous major resort communities that boast amenities like golf courses, tennis clubs, and lakes for fishing, swimming, and boating.

John W. Dodge, known to many as the "Johnny Appleseed of Cumberland County" because he planted 42,000 apple trees, settled in this area, then known as Pomona, in 1849. In 1856, Cumberland County was created. James Scott, proprietor of Scott's Tavern, deeded forty acres of property to the new county on the condition that Crossville be named the county seat. Crossville was incorporated as a town in 1901 and celebrated its centennial anniversary in 2001.

Many of the downtown structures, walkways, and patios are composed of a unique buff-colored stone. This hard sandstone, found exclusively on the Cumberland Plateau, is called Crab Orchard stone, named after the oldest community in Cumberland County. The stone was used in the construction not only of numerous local government and commercial buildings, but also of such national sites as the vice presidential residence in Washington, D.C., Rockefeller Center, and Elvis Presley's pool at Graceland.

 RECREATION

The nationally known Catoosa Wildlife Management Preserve, featuring 79,700 acres of state-owned woodlands, offers seasonal access for limited hunting of deer, turkey, boar, and other wildlife. Cumberland Mountain State Park, which covers 1,700 timbered acres, provides cabins, a large swimming pool, a small lake for fishing and boating, playgrounds, tennis courts, ball fields, a golf course, campsites, and a restaurant.

Crossville Centennial Park is a forty-acre outdoor park with multiple-use fields, tennis and volleyball courts, a picnic area, and a walking trail. Crossville's 300-acre Meadow Park Lake is one of the best fishing lakes in the state. The Cumberland County Community Complex is the site of a recreational park with a playground, a picnic area, walking trails, and ball fields. This complex is also the venue for the annual rodeo and county fair.

According to *Golf Digest,* three of the top ten places to play golf in Tennessee are located in Cumberland County. Stonehenge Golf Course at Fairfield Glade resort was rated the best course in Tennessee, and Bear Trace at Cumberland Mountain was named one of the top ten. There are six public eighteen-hole courses.

 **CULTURAL SCENE**

The Cumberland County Playhouse opened in 1965 after a successful community fundraising effort; it is now a major nonprofit professional performing arts resource in rural Tennessee. One of the ten largest professional theaters in rural America, it is also the top indoor tourist attraction in the Cumberland Mountains. The Playhouse draws more than 145,000 visitors annually for its young audience productions, dance program, concert series, and touring shows on two indoor and two outdoor stages. The theater regularly produces new works based on Tennessee and southeastern history and culture, and revives works with Appalachian themes, as well as Broadway productions such as *Oklahoma!* and *Cats.*

The Cumberland Homesteads Tower and Museum tells the story of a local community that was built during the 1930s as part of President Roosevelt's New Deal to combat the effects of the Great Depression. The picturesque stone cottages in manicured settings are reminiscent of dwellings in the English countryside.

A group of early settlers established the first vineyards near the historic colony at Rugby (35 miles); the wines they produced won a number of gold medals at wine-tasting competitions in the 1880s. Today, the Stonehaus Winery continues this venture, still creating award-winning wines from the same vineyards.

Popular annual events include Crossville Depot Days in June, with arts and crafts exhibits, entertainment, a street fair, parade, music, dancing, crafts, and a barbecue cook-off; Cumberland County Mule Show in May; Pioneer Days and the Apple Festival in September; Oktoberfest in October; Streetscape Christmas Parade in December; and a Chili Cook-off in the summer.

Residents of Crossville who are seeking city attractions are only a couple of hours from Chattanooga and Knoxville.

 MAIN STREET

Favorite local restaurants include the Bean Pot Restaurant, a good family eatery; Genesis Italian Grill; and Vegas Steakhouse. Halcyon Days serves yummy sweet potato fries, and Mitchell's Drug Store on Main Street in downtown is known for its tasty milkshakes.

The thriving downtown shopping district offers a small-town array of specialty shops and local department stores. Crossville's restored 1920s-style downtown train depot, where famed Sgt. Alvin York said his good-byes en route to his World War I exploits, now contains a gift shop featuring railroad memorabilia. The Palace Theater, otherwise known as the "Jewel of Main Street," was originally built in the 1930s and still hosts live performances, pageants, and classic movies. Mountain crafts associated with the Cumberland Mountains are readily available in local stores; you can find quilts, pottery, baskets, hand-carved wood items (birds,

toys, walking canes), soap, and candles. Forty outlet stores at Crossville Outlet Center sell brand merchandise at discount prices.

 HOUSING

Housing choices range from modest ranch styles priced from the mid $70,000s to sprawling estates selling for $1 million plus. Recent house building has been dominated by two categories: 1,200- to 1,600-square-foot ranches in the $130,000 to $150,000 range and 1,600- to 1,900-square-foot houses in the $150,000 to $180,000 range. Over 5,000 residents live in Fairfield, a large resort, built on 12,700 acres. Options include condominiums starting as low as $100,000. Prices average $160,000 for a modest three-bedroom, two-bath home; $230,000 for a 2,800-square-foot three-bedroom, two- bath home; and $270,000 for an exclusive three-bedroom, two-bath home on a lake with a boat dock.

 ECONOMICS

Number of employers with fifty or more employees—21

The major industry is manufacturing—apparel, automotive

equipment, baked goods, canned foods, ceramic tile, stone and wood products, charcoal, and rubber products. Large employers include Flower's Snacks of Tennessee (500 employees); MasterBrand (270 employees); CoLink (500 employees); and Manchester Tank (190 employees). The tourism and retirement industries are growing steadily as a result of the golf and lake resorts in the area and from the sales of second homes.

 EDUCATION

High schools—2; Elementary schools (K to 8)—8; Private schools—2

Roane State Community College offers continuing education classes and courses for transfer to the state university system. A local satellite campus of Roane State Community College serves more than 800 students in partnership with Tennessee Technological University; Crossville is thirty minutes from the main campus of 9,300 students in Cooksville, where students can obtain bachelor's or doctorate degrees in different fields of engineering.

 HEALTHCARE

Cumberland Medical Center—182 beds; Physicians—70; Dentists—19

Cumberland Medical Center, a not-for-profit regional facility, features a 24-hour physician-staffed emergency department, surgery, outpatient services, cardiac and pulmonary rehabilitation, and a regional cancer center. Three nursing homes and two assisted-living facilities are located in the county.

 SPIRITUAL LIFE

Twenty Christian denominations are represented. The nearest synagogues are located in Knoxville and Chattanooga.

 STAYING CONNECTED

The *Crossville Chronicle* is a local newspaper published triweekly. The *Glade Sun* (for Fairview Glade residents) and the *Glade Vista* are published weekly. The daily Knoxville and Chattanooga newspapers are delivered to the Crossville area. Several cable television operators and local AM and FM stations serve the area. Local internet service is available. Network affiliate television stations are located in Nashville and Knoxville. There are local bookstores, including three Christian bookstores.

 GETTING THERE

Crossville is located in the eastern part of central Tennessee, east of Nashville and west of Knoxville. It is two miles from I-40 at US 127. Daily commercial airline service is available at the Knoxville and Nashville airports. Airlines such as AirTran, Comair, US Airways, Delta, American, Northwest, and United serve Knoxville, while American, Delta, Southwest, Skywest, Frontier, Continental, and US Airways serve the Nashville International Airport. Crossville Memorial Airport, a general aviation airport with a 5,400-foot paved and lighted runway, provides full aircraft service and maintenance, aircraft rental, flight instruction, and charter flights.

 RESOURCES

Crossville Cumberland County
 Chamber of Commerce
34 South Main Street
Crossville, TN 38555
(888) 465-3961
www.crossville-chamber.com

CROSSVILLE VITAL STATISTICS

CLIMATE

Annual average rainfall	52 inches
Snowfall	12 inches
Elevation	1980 feet

Temperatures (in degrees Fahrenheit)

	Jan	Apr	Jul	Oct
High	42	66	83	67
Low	24	44	63	44

OCCUPATIONS

	2006	Projected 2011
Blue collar	28.5%	27.9%
White collar	50.6%	49.8%
Services	20.8%	22.3%

ADULT EDUCATION

	2000
Less than High School	32.3%
High School	33.5%
Some College	16.7%
Associates Degree	4.5%
College Degree	8.2%
Graduate Degree	4.7%

POPULATION

2006	9,172
2000-2006 Population: Annual Compound Growth Rate	0.34%
2006-2011 Population: Annual Compound Growth Rate	1.02%

Population by age group

	2006	Projected 2011
0-4	6.7%	6.6%
5-9	5.9%	5.8%
10-14	6.6%	5.9%
15-19	5.6%	6.3%
20-24	6.0%	5.8%
25-29	6.5%	5.7%
30-34	7.0%	6.1%
35-39	6.4%	6.5%
40-44	6.5%	6.6%
45-49	6.7%	6.6%
50-54	5.5%	6.6%
55-59	5.8%	5.8%
60-64	5.5%	5.6%
65-69	5.4%	4.9%
70-74	4.1%	4.6%
75-79	4.1%	3.8%
80-84	3.1%	3.4%
85+	2.9%	3.4%

Sources for Vital Statistics listed above can be found in the Preface to this book.

DYERSBURG

2006 POPULATION
  17,475

NEAREST CITIES
  Jackson, TN (48 miles)
  Memphis, TN (76 miles)

ESTIMATED 2006
MEDIAN HOUSEHOLD INCOME
  $35,151

COST OF LIVING
  Average 3-bdrm home—$150,000
  Average rent, 2-bdrm apart-
  ment—$535
  Cost-of-living comparison—
  87.5%

SALES TAX
  9.75%

PROPERTY TAX
  Average 3-bdrm home—$1,250

Wine-colored awnings protect sidewalk strollers from the sun's rays as they explore the quaint stores in this 1800s Tennessee town. The dark brick courthouse, surrounded by dogwoods, azaleas, and deep green hedges, is the focal point of the town square. Multi-storied Victorian homes on manicured lawns grace residential areas close to downtown. As a regional center in northwest Tennessee, Dyersburg draws people from ten surrounding counties in Tennessee, Missouri, and Arkansas. It offers retail, medical, employment, and educational services as well as several nearby recreational attractions. Newcomers are enticed by quality schools, a moderate climate, a low cost of living, and numerous activities.

Settlers from North Carolina, South Carolina, Virginia, and other eastern states discovered this rich, fertile land between the Tennessee and Mississippi Rivers. Dyersburg was carved from the wilderness on a sixty-acre tract donated by John McIver and Joel Dyer. The founders named the town and county after Colonel Robert H. Dyer, Joel Dyer's son and a veteran of the Indian wars and the War of 1812. Dyer County lies just south of Reelfoot Lake State Park, a 25,000-acre wildlife refuge known as the winter home of the American bald eagle. The lake was formed by a series of violent earthquakes during the winter of 1812. The old forest that stood at this site prior to the earthquakes still lies just beneath the surface and makes the lake one of the world's greatest natural fish hatcheries.

Dyersburg is within ninety minutes of a variety of nearby attractions, including the Casino Aztar in Caruthersville, Missouri, on the Mississippi River; Civil War battlefields; Memphis blues music, arts, and sports; and the north-central Tennessee lakes.

 RECREATION

Reelfoot Lake State Park is a sportsman's paradise, with 15,000 acres of water and wetlands. The primary game fish include bream, crappie, largemouth bass, and catfish. Reelfoot is a major stopping point for waterfowl migrating to and from Canada, and duck and goose hunting are popular. American eagle tours depart from the park lodge December through mid-March. A number of fishing camps and resorts are located around the lake, and a resort inn and restaurant are built out over the water on concrete pilings. Canoeing and cycling are popular pastimes. The park offers boat cruises and special programs about the lake's exceptional environment. It has its own 3,500-foot landing strip, making it accessible by plane.

The county has three golf courses, including the eighteen-hole Dyersburg Municipal Golf Course, ranked as one of the best municipal courses in the United States by *Golf Digest*. There are a total of five public parks, nine tennis courts, and three public pools.

Several organizations, including the YMCA and the Parks and Recreation Department, offer all-ages recreational activities, including team sports. The Dyersburg Neighborhood Community Center houses an Olympic-size swimming pool as well as a gymnasium, tennis courts, ball fields, a wooded picnic area, and facilities for senior citizens. A one-mile paved walking trail is located at Okeena Park, adjacent to Dyersburg State Community College.

 **CULTURAL SCENE**

Throughout the year the Dyersburg Area Community Concert Association brings to the community quality artists and various music, dance, and theater presentations, including the Memphis Symphony Orchestra's annual Dyersburg performance. The Choral Society, Community Orchestra, Community Concert Association, Dyersburg Arts Council, and Dyersburg Theatre Group also perform in town.

The Fine Arts Warehouse, a unique performing and visual arts organization, provides both group and private instruction in art, dance, drama, and music. The facility's twelve instructors offer classes such as voice, instrumental music, and piano to students of all ages. About twelve hundred students have already participated in the program.

The most popular event in Dyersburg is the annual Dogwood Festival, held in April at the Dyer County Fairgrounds. The festival draws big crowds and includes a chili cook-off, blues concert, fashion show, arts and crafts show, and car show. The Jimmy Dean Foods Barbecue Festival, a two-day event every July, features music, family fun, and four thousand pounds of pork barbecue. The Dyer County Fair is a weeklong event held in September at the county fairgrounds. The Dyersburg Christmas Parade occurs downtown the first Monday following Thanksgiving.

Nearby Memphis offers extensive cultural opportunities within reach of Dyersburg residents.

 MAIN STREET

Some residents say Abe's Rib Eye Barn serves the best steaks in town. Neil's Barbecue and Grill is known for Memphis-style barbecue. Numerous outlying shopping centers and a 190,000-square-foot mall supplement the attractive, centrally located town square. Since Dyersburg is a regional center, shopping choices are above average for a town of this size.

 HOUSING

Dyersburg offers a variety of housing prices and styles, including stately older homes and executive-style homes on large lots in new subdivisions. The median cost of housing, as compiled by the local chamber of commerce, is below the national average. In 2006, the estimated purchase price of a newly built 1,800-square-foot home in a middle-income subdivision on an 8,000-square-foot lot was approximately $140,000. Chickasaw Bluffs, an upscale community of homes with ample acreage, is on the high end of the housing market, with prices from $200,000 to $400,000. More than nine hundred apartment units offer rentals at rates well below the national average. Dyersburg also has condominiums and four assisted-living facilities.

 ECONOMICS

Number of employers with fifty or more employees—30

Since Dyersburg is within a day's drive of 76 percent of the country's major markets, it is attractive to companies needing a centralized distribution location. Forty percent of the local jobs are in manufacturing. Another significant employment source is the service sector; many residents work in government, healthcare, and education. The largest employer, Quebecor World, Inc., is a major commercial printing plant producing popular magazines and catalogs (1,100 employees). Another well-known local employer is Jimmy Dean Foods, a producer of sausage sold nationwide (900 employees).

 EDUCATION

High schools—1; Middle schools—1; Elementary schools—2; Private schools—1

Dyersburg High School was named a National School of Excellence in 2005. During the summer, Dyersburg State offers College for Kids, an enrichment program for children from prekindergarten through sixth grade. The Saturday Scholars Program features four weeks of classes during the school year for students in grades four through six who are academically and/or artistically gifted.

Dyersburg State Community College (2,000 students) offers a two-year program that transfers to any state university. The University of Memphis operates a satellite program at Dyersburg State Community College, and the University of Tennessee at Martin (forty-five minutes away) offers four-year college degrees in a variety of areas.

 HEALTHCARE

Methodist Health Care–Dyersburg Hospital—225 beds; Physicians—70; Dentists—15

Methodist Health Care–Dyersburg Hospital is a regional medical center for the surrounding ten counties. The hospital offers a variety of services, including surgical acute care, obstetrics and gynecology, outpatient surgery, radiology, CAT scans, MRI, radiation, oncology, cardiac rehabilitation, 24-hour emergency care, and a sleep disorders clinic. Eighteen medical

specialties are represented in the community. Additional medical services in Memphis are within a ninety-minute drive.

 SPIRITUAL LIFE

Twenty-five Christian denominations are represented. The nearest synagogue is in Jackson, Tennessee.

 STAYING CONNECTED

Several daily and weekly newspapers serve the community. The *State Gazette* has daily and weekly editions. The *Dyersburg News* is published weekly. The *Commercial Appeal*, Memphis's daily newspaper, is also delivered in the county. Cable television brings in network affiliates located in Memphis and Jackson, and local internet access is available. Four bookstores are located in the community.

 GETTING THERE

Dyersburg is located in the northwest corner of Tennessee, north of Memphis. US 412 connects the town with I-155, to the west over the Mississippi River (13 miles), and I-40 to the south. US 51 leads directly to Memphis from Dyersburg. Memphis International Airport is served by a dozen regional and major airlines. The Dyersburg Municipal Airport provides general aviation service and has a lighted, 5,000-foot concrete runway. The nearest port on the Mississippi River is twenty-two miles away in Caruthersville, Missouri.

 RESOURCES

Dyersburg–Dyer County
  Chamber of Commerce
2000 Commerce Avenue
Dyersburg, TN 38024
(731) 285-3433
www.dyerchamber.com

DYERSBURG
VITAL STATISTICS

CLIMATE

Annual average rainfall	52 inches
Snowfall	6.6 inches
Elevation	334 feet

Temperatures (in degrees Fahrenheit)

	Jan	Apr	Jul	Oct
High	44	71	90	72
Low	28	51	70	50

OCCUPATIONS

	2006	Projected 2011
Blue collar	30.4%	30.2%
White collar	50.9%	49.5%
Services	18.7%	20.2%

ADULT EDUCATION

	2000
Less than High School	35.2%
High School	29.2%
Some College	16.7%
Associates Degree	3.9%
College Degree	10.0%
Graduate Degree	5.1%

POPULATION

2006	17,475
2000-2006 Population: Annual Compound Growth Rate	0.02%
2006-2011 Population: Annual Compound Growth Rate	0.28%

Population by age group

	2006	Projected 2011
0-4	7.3%	7.4%
5-9	6.7%	6.7%
10-14	7.8%	6.6%
15-19	6.1%	7.2%
20-24	6.7%	6.5%
25-29	7.3%	6.3%
30-34	6.6%	6.8%
35-39	6.2%	6.1%
40-44	7.3%	6.5%
45-49	6.7%	7.2%
50-54	6.2%	6.3%
55-59	6.1%	6.2%
60-64	4.5%	5.6%
65-69	3.8%	3.8%
70-74	3.1%	3.1%
75-79	2.6%	2.7%
80-84	2.5%	2.2%
85+	2.6%	2.9%

Sources for Vital Statistics listed above can be found in the Preface to this book.

2006 POPULATION
15,507

NEAREST CITIES
Johnson City, TN (30 miles)
Knoxville, TN (70 miles)
Asheville, NC (70 miles)

ESTIMATED 2006
MEDIAN HOUSEHOLD INCOME
$31,008

COST OF LIVING
Average 3-bdrm home—$130,000
Average rent, 2-bdrm apartment—
$575
Cost-of-living comparison—
87.8%

SALES TAX
9.75%

PROPERTY TAX
Average 3-bdrm home—$750

Nestled in the shadows of the Smoky Mountains, Greeneville is Tennessee's second oldest town, founded in 1783. Greeneville has been listed in such books as *The 100 Best Small Towns in America* and *America's Most Charming Towns and Villages,* and was named one of only ten All-American Cities in 1999 by the National League Of Cities.

Named for Revolutionary War hero General Nathanael Greene, Greeneville is rich with history. Several churches have been in continual use since their construction in the 1780s and 1800s. Greeneville was the capital of the "Lost State of Franklin," the smallest and most short-lived state in the history of the United States, which existed only from 1785 to 1788. This Tennessee town was the birthplace of frontiersman Davy

Crockett, one of the heroes of the battle at the Alamo.

At the time of the Civil War, Tennessee voted to secede from the Union; East Tennessee, however, was an island of predominately Union sentiment. Captain John Morgan, known as the "Thunderbolt of the Confederacy," was killed in Greeneville by a surprise attack. After the Civil War, the town built memorials on the courthouse square to both Confederate and Union soldiers.

Often referred to as "a presidential town," Greeneville was once the home of Andrew Johnson, our seventeenth president; the Andrew Johnson National Historic Site is located here. The town is also the home of Tusculum College, founded in 1794. It is America's oldest Presbyterian college, the oldest college west of the Allegheny Mountains, and the oldest college in Tennessee.

Greeneville is the smallest non-state capital in U.S. history to have a naval vessel named after it, the submarine U.S.S. *Greeneville.*

The western slopes of the Smoky Mountains provide a beautiful backdrop for the town. With four distinct but mild seasons, residents can engage in year-round recreational activities ranging from golf to skiing. Arts and cultural offerings are excellent for a town the size of Greeneville, and housing costs are very attractive. Additional shopping, culture, and medical services are available in Johnson City and Knoxville.

RECREATION

Kinser Park, located on the Nolichuckey River, has over one hundred recreational vehicle sites, a swimming pool, a picnic area, a playground, a water slide, a golf course and driving range, tennis courts, facilities for go-carts and putt-putt golf, fishing areas, and a boat ramp for Greeneville residents. Clear mountain streams provide some of the best fly-fishing in the East. Tennessee Valley Authority (TVA) lakes are within an hour's drive, and the Appalachian Trail is an hour to the east. Snow skiing at North Carolina ski resorts is also within an hour's drive.

Greeneville is home to two eighteen-hole public courses and three nine-hole public courses.

Nine golf courses lie in the scenic valley of the Appalachian Mountain range. Two courses are located in nearby Chuckey: Graysburg Hills Golf Course, which has twenty-seven holes over three courses, and Twin Creeks Golf Course, an eighteen-hole public course.

The local YMCA has a complete family recreation center, and the city operates parks and recreational facilities, including swimming pools, tennis courts, and bicycle paths. Tusculum College offers fourteen varsity sports teams, and Greeneville residents can also attend college football games and other spectator events in Knoxville, home of the University of Tennessee.

CULTURAL SCENE

Many of the historic sites downtown are open to the public. The Andrew Johnson National Historic Site includes his home, a tailor shop, and his burial place, as well as a visitors center. The Doak House Museum is in the home of Samual Doak, the frontier Presbyterian minister and educator who founded Tusculum College. The Nathanael Greene Museum features exhibits on local history.

A self-guided walking tour through the downtown historic district includes thirty-one buildings, several churches, a number of houses, a graveyard, and a spring; some sites date back to the late 1700s. Another walking tour lists an additional twenty-eight historic houses close to downtown; the accompanying guidebook provides a glimpse into the lives of the people and the lifestyle of the pre–Civil War era. The Dickson-Williams Mansion, one of the historic houses featured on the tour, is surrounded by a formal garden covering an entire city block. The mansion was known throughout the region as a place of lavish hospitality in the early 1800s. Tusculum College Historic District has its own walking tour, showcasing eight buildings that date from 1841 through 1928. Andrew Johnson's personal library and papers are kept at a museum and library at the college.

The General Morgan Inn and Conference Center, a downtown

landmark, was created from four interconnected "railroad hotels" dating from the late 1800s. Constructed from rich red brick, the building is decorated with an ornate white molding and a white facade on the street level.

The arts are important in Greeneville. An active community theater, a YMCA symphony, community concerts, a new state-of-the-art performing arts center, and various programs at Tusculum College enrich the town's cultural life. Storytelling events are also popular. Additional cultural offerings are available in Johnson City, home of Eastern Tennessee State University.

Major festivals include the Iris Festival, a May weekend downtown event that includes local and regional artists, food, and entertainment; the annual Fall Fest Chillin and Grillin; the Fourth of July celebration; and Christmas in Olde Greene, which features a parade and other holiday activities.

 MAIN STREET

Favorite local restaurants include Donielle's for gourmet dining;

Stan's Bar-B-Q; The Tannery, a downtown soup and sandwich restaurant; and Brumley's, a dining room at the General Morgan Inn.

Greeneville is a member of the Main Street Redevelopment Program, and its appearance reflects the program's emphasis on attractive landscaping, downtown festivals, and a strong retail base of shops and restaurants. Main Street is enhanced with wide red brick and concrete sidewalks, period light fixtures, and shade trees. Among the downtown shops are A Gathering of Friends Craft Mall, with over one hundred vendors offering craft and gift items, and the Greeneville Antique Market, housing over sixty quality dealers.

 HOUSING

Charming, well-cared-for houses in the historic district sell for under $200,000. While the average price for a new house is $130,000, some three-bedroom frame homes are available at prices starting at $75,000. A new subdivision with lots priced at $37,500 and up is being developed inside the city limits adjacent to Tusculum College. Elegant golf-course community homes with 4,500 square feet, four bedrooms, and three bathrooms are under $400,000. Homes in rural areas with several acres and mountain views offer appealing options; prices are very reasonable at $5,000 to $8,000 per acre. Manufactured homes in rural parts of the county provide housing at low prices; owners usually purchase multi-acre sites. Several single-story condominium developments are available; prices range from $120,000 to $175,000. Apartments and an assisted-living facility are also available.

 ECONOMICS

Number of employers with fifty or more employees—35

The Five Rivers Electronic Innovations, LLC is the largest employer (1,700 employees). Another large business, Plus Mark, Inc., manufactures cards and wrapping paper (900 employees). Several manufacturers are suppliers to the automobile assembly business, a growth industry for the state. For those willing to commute, additional employment opportunities are available in Johnson City, where a major university and hospitals are among the large employers.

 EDUCATION

High schools—1; Middle schools—1; Elementary schools—4; Private schools—4

The city school system has a nearly 96 percent graduation rate; 75 percent of its graduates go on to higher education. The Greene County School System serves the county outside the city limits.

The Greeneville/Greene County Center for Technology provides courses in business and industrial skills to nearly five thousand adults and high school students yearly. Tusculum College offers a bachelor of arts degree in more than twenty areas and a master's degree in two programs. The Greeneville Center of Walters State Community College has two-year academic programs that can be transferred to the University of Tennessee system. A Small Business Development Center associated with Walters State features small business consulting and services. Other Tennessee colleges and universities within a one-hour drive are East Tennessee State University in Johnson City, Carson-Newman College in Jefferson City, Bristol University and King College in Bristol, and the University of Tennessee in Knoxville.

 HEALTHCARE

Laughlin Memorial Hospital—140 beds; Takoma Adventist Hospital— 115 beds; Physicians—75; Dentists—20

Laughlin Memorial Hospital has 109 physicians on staff. Medical services include 24-hour emergency care, oncology, neurology, intensive/coronary care, obstetrics, outpatient surgery, radiation, CAT scans, nuclear medicine, and a women's diagnostic center. Takoma Adventist Hospital is staffed by seventy-five staff physicians and offers 24-hour full-service emergency care, MRI, CAT scans, and same-day surgery. Occupational medicine is a major focus at the hospital, which also has a twenty-bed skilled nursing unit and a senior care program. A Veteran's Administration hospital and medical center is located in Johnson City. The University of Tennessee Medical Hospital is in Knoxville.

 SPIRITUAL LIFE

Eighteen Christian denominations are represented. The nearest synagogue is located in Knoxville.

 STAYING CONNECTED

The *Greeneville Sun* is published six days a week. Daily newspapers published in both Johnson City and Knoxville are delivered to Greeneville. There are three local radio stations. Major network television affiliates are in Johnson City and Knoxville, and cable television is available throughout Greeneville. Local and national internet service is available. There are two local bookstores, and national chain bookstores are located in both Johnson City and Knoxville.

 GETTING THERE

Greeneville is located in northeast Tennessee on US 321. Tennessee Highways 34, 70, and 93 also offer access to Greeneville, and it is eleven miles from I-81. The Tri-City Regional Airport is forty miles from Greeneville and is served by seven regional or major airlines connecting to major cities in the South, the East, and the Midwest.

The McGhee Tyson Airport in Knoxville has one hundred flights daily by eight feeder and major airlines to twelve major hubs. The Greeneville/Greene County Municipal Airport is a very active general aviation airport with a 6,300-foot lighted, asphalt runway.

 RESOURCES

Greene County Partnership
115 Academy Street
Greeneville, TN 37743
(423) 638-4111
www.greeneville.com
www.greene.xtn.net

GREENEVILLE
VITAL STATISTICS

CLIMATE

Annual average rainfall	44 inches
Snowfall	14 inches
Elevation	1,320 feet

Temperatures (in degrees Fahrenheit)

	Jan	Apr	Jul	Oct
High	45	68	86	70
Low	22	41	63	42

OCCUPATIONS

	2006	Projected 2011
Blue collar	28.7%	28.4%
White collar	52.3%	51.0%
Services	19.0%	20.6%

ADULT EDUCATION

	2000
Less than High School	27.1%
High School	32.7%
Some College	15.8%
Associates Degree	4.0%
College Degree	12.2%
Graduate Degree	8.2%

POPULATION

2006	15,507
2000-2006 Population: Annual Compound Growth Rate	0.32%
2006-2011 Population: Annual Compound Growth Rate	0.58%

Population by age group

	2006	Projected 2011
0-4	5.7%	5.8%
5-9	5.2%	4.9%
10-14	5.9%	5.6%
15-19	5.7%	5.9%
20-24	5.1%	5.5%
25-29	6.0%	4.8%
30-34	6.5%	5.7%
35-39	6.5%	6.4%
40-44	7.2%	6.8%
45-49	6.8%	7.5%
50-54	6.8%	6.7%
55-59	6.4%	7.2%
60-64	5.4%	6.2%
65-69	5.1%	4.7%
70-74	4.5%	4.6%
75-79	4.5%	4.2%
80-84	3.1%	3.7%
85+	3.5%	3.9%

Sources for Vital Statistics listed above can be found in the Preface to this book.

LAWRENCEBURG

2006 POPULATION
  10,819

NEAREST CITIES
  Columbia, TN (33 miles)
  Florence, AL (40 miles)
  Huntsville, AL (55 miles)
  Nashville, TN (65 miles)

ESTIMATED 2006
MEDIAN HOUSEHOLD INCOME
  $31,585

COST OF LIVING
  Average 3-bdrm home—$110,000
  Average rent, 2-bdrm apartment—
  $450
  Cost-of-living comparison—
  93.7%

SALES TAX
  9.75%

PROPERTY TAX
  Average 3-bdrm home—$550

Lawrenceburg was named after Captain James Lawrence, the naval hero of the War of 1812, known for his words "Don't give up the ship." The history of Lawrenceburg, however, is most clearly identified with David Crockett, the famous frontiersman, soldier, legislator, statesman, and hero of the Alamo. In 1817, after the Chickasaw Indians ceded their land to the United States, Crockett, one of the city's first five commissioners, helped incorporate the town. He also served as a justice of the peace and a state representative. He built a gristmill and distillery along the banks of Shoal Creek in what is now the David Crockett State Park. After a flood in 1821 washed away the buildings, he moved to west Tennessee, where he was elected to Congress. He died at the Alamo in 1836.

The Lawrenceburg Public Square is clean and has a more spacious appearance than most other Southern town squares. Thanks in part to the Main Street Redevelopment Program, the storefronts are largely occupied with antique stores, gift shops, professional offices, and banks. There's even an old-fashioned pharmacy with wood floors and a soda fountain. A large gazebo, crowned with a four-sided clock, sits in the center of the square and is the site of annual festivals. A bronze, life-size statue of David Crockett stands on the south side of the square, and a monument to the Lawrenceburg citizens who fought in the Mexican War is on the north side. There are several historic attractions within walking distance of the square, including the Old Jail Museum, which is on the National Register of Historic Buildings.

Lawrenceburg, known as the birthplace of Southern gospel music, is home to the Vaughan Gospel Music Museum, also located on the square. James Vaughn's gospel music enterprise included music publishing, songwriting, and radio; his school of music, which attracted students from all over the South, operated from 1911 until the early 1930s. A mural on a nearby music shop depicts one of Vaughan's quartets out on the road selling the company's popular songbooks.

RECREATION

The Tennessee Valley Authority (TVA) plays a major role in this area, not only providing low-cost, reliable electric power and promoting economic development, but also supporting a mammoth recreational system. Fishing, boating, and waterskiing are popular on nearby TVA lakes and waterways in northern Alabama, particularly around the Muscle Shoals area.

The 1,000-acre David Crockett State Park lies within one mile of the city limits and offers a forty-acre lake for fishing and boating, a large camp facility for recreational vehicles, an Olympic-size pool, a paved bicycle trail, hiking trails, tennis courts, ball fields, and a 240-seat restaurant open year round. Shoal Creek, which borders the park, and Buffalo River are scenic natural waterways suitable for canoeing. Laurel Hill Lake, located fourteen miles from Lawrenceburg, is a 325-acre fishing facility run by the state.

The local Rotary Club operates a twenty-eight-acre recreation park in town that includes tennis courts, softball fields, and indoor recreational facilities. Walking and racking horse riding (popular forms of show horseback riding) and competition can be enjoyed in the park and the nearby town of St. Joseph. The Lawrenceburg Golf and Country Club welcomes out-of-county players for a daily fee. The Clax Branch course in Loretto and Dixie Oaks near Summertown are also nearby.

 **CULTURAL SCENE**

The Marguerite Rose Burton Gallery in the Crockett Arts Center hosts art exhibits. Adjacent to the Center is the historic Crockett Theater, an acoustically perfect venue seating 1,200. Shows have included the Nashville Symphony, an annual Christmas Pops concert, and the James Vaughan Festival, which features some of the nation's best gospel quartets during the last weekend in July.

Lawrenceburg Community Theater also performs several shows during the year. The Crockett Museum, located in the David Crockett State Park, offers milling demonstrations and exhibits that portray life in Crockett's time.

Lawrenceburg's calendar of events is full most of the year. Some of the popular events include Tennessee Valley Jamboree's version of "Grand Ole Opry," held in early February at the Crockett Theater; the state championship Barbecue Cook-off in June; a heritage festival at the downtown public square, also in June; the South's biggest Antique Tractor and Engine Show in August; the annual award-winning Middle Tennessee District Fair in early October; Christmas in the Country, an annual show with over 150 exhibitors and entertainment in mid-November at Rotary Park; and the Lawrence County Christmas Parade in December.

There are some interesting historical attractions in several of the nearby towns. Pulaski, Tennessee, has one of the most beautiful old courthouses in the South. In 1944, an Amish community was started in nearby Ethridge, Tennessee, and today visitors can purchase wonderful handcrafted Amish furniture, quilts, baskets, breads, produce, and preserves. The cultural attractions of Huntsville, Alabama, and Nashville, Tennessee, are approximately one hour away.

MAIN STREET

Local favorite restaurants include the Brass Lantern (American fare); The Chaparral (good steaks); Rick's BBQ; and Big John's BBQ; and several restaurants that offer Chinese and Mexican cuisine. The restaurant at the David Crockett Park, a favorite meeting place, offers catering and private dining rooms.

The convenient downtown square and several small strip shopping centers are home to a variety of stores. Columbia, Florence, and other major towns within an hour's drive provide an abundance of shopping options.

HOUSING

Lawrenceburg enjoys a low cost of living as a result of TVA-provided electric power, low property taxes, and low housing prices. Housing options include traditional houses in town or ranch and two-story houses on large lots in nearby subdivisions. Houses in the rural area immediately outside town often include acreage and perhaps a small barn. Brick, three-bedroom, two-bath homes from 1,600 to 2,000 square feet in nice subdivisions or in town are available for $150,000 or less. A brick, four-bedroom, three-bath, 2,400-square-foot home with a pool in the Country Club Estates subdivision is listed in the low $170,000s. An attractive area called Woodland Estates has 2,300-square-foot, three-bedroom, two-bath homes in the $170,000 to $190,000 price range. A "gentleman's farm" with a 3,700-square-foot home on twenty-five-acres with a horse barn and ponds is approximately $250,000. Lawrenceburg has a good supply of apartments and one assisted-living facility. The community has recently enjoyed a surge in transplants from areas such as Florida and California where overcrowding and high cost-of-living have folks—especially retirees—seeking out the area's slower pace of life and ever-changing but moderate climate.

 ECONOMICS

Number of employers with fifty or more employees—20

Murray Ohio Manufacturing Company, the county's largest employer for almost fifty years, recently closed, but new business has already begun to move into the company's 2.5 million square feet of space. Among the other large manufacturers are Dura Automotive (700 employees); Graphic Packaging (350 employees); and Modine Manufacturing Co. (230 employees). There is also a nationwide distribution center for Jones Apparel Group that employs about 500. The county is also known for high-tech industrial support industries, the casket industry, and companies that produce transportation equipment.

The Lawrence County Chamber of Commerce, a partnership of local government and the private sector, markets Lawrence County to prospective new businesses and industries, conducts a retention and expansion program, and conducts a wide range of community development projects, many aimed at improving the community's education levels. Some of the county residents commute to Huntsville, Alabama, for employment.

 EDUCATION

High schools—3; Middle schools—1; Elementary schools (most include middle schools)—9; Private schools—4

Columbia State Community College (4,400 students) is located in adjoining Maury County and has a branch in Lawrenceburg. It offers two-year and some four-year programs, with credits transferable to state universities, and certificate programs in technical fields. Tennessee Technology Center is a statewide technical training institution with a major campus in nearby Pulaski and a branch in Lawrenceburg. A Community Learning Network housed at the local branch of Columbia State Community College provides video conferencing and computer-based training. State universities in the area include Tennessee State University in Nashville and Middle Tennessee State University in Murfreesboro. The University of

North Alabama is 40 miles away in Florence, Alabama. Adult enrichment classes are available at Columbia State Community College.

 HEALTHCARE

Crockett Hospital—107 beds; Physicians—27; Dentists—12
Crockett Hospital is an acute-care facility providing 24-hour emergency services, a LifeFlight helicopter, surgery, women's healthcare with full obstetrical and delivery services, nuclear medicine, physical therapy, and both CAT scan and MRI equipment. Major medical services and facilities are available in Nashville.

 SPIRITUAL LIFE

Nineteen Christian denominations are represented. The nearest synagogue is located in Huntsville.

 STAYING CONNECTED

There are two biweekly local newspapers, the *Democrat-Union* and the *Lawrence County Advocate*. A daily newspaper from Nashville is delivered locally. Several radio stations serve the community, and cable television is available. High-speed fiber optic internet service is available. National chain bookstores are located in Columbia, Murfreesboro, and Florence, Alabama.

 GETTING THERE

Lawrenceburg is in the south central part of Tennessee, at the intersection of US Highways 43 and 64. Highway 64 is currently undergoing new construction for an upgrade to four lanes. Two commercial airports are within ninety minutes of the county. The Nashville International Airport is served by fourteen airlines. The Huntsville International Airport is about seventy-five minutes from Lawrenceburg and has daily nonstop flights to Atlanta, Chicago, Washington, D.C., and other major cities. The Lawrenceburg–Lawrence County Airport has won several awards from state and national agencies. It has a 5,000-foot paved and lighted runway for general aviation. The Tennessee-Tombigbee Waterway connects the Tennessee River, west of Lawrence County, with the Warrior-Tombigbee Waterway and the Gulf of Mexico at Mobile, Alabama. The Port of

Florence is forty miles away and is connected to Lawrenceburg and the CSX railroad system.

 RESOURCES

Lawrence County
  Chamber of Commerce
P.O. Box 86
Lawrenceburg, TN 38464
(931) 762-4911
www.chamberofcommerce.
lawrence.tn.us

LAWRENCEBURG VITAL STATISTICS

CLIMATE

Annual average rainfall	43 inches	
Snowfall	5 inches	
Elevation	836 feet	

Temperatures (in degrees Fahrenheit)

	Jan	Apr	Jul	Oct
High	46	70	87	71
Low	25	44	64	44

OCCUPATIONS

	2006	Projected 2011
Blue collar	36.8%	36.6%
White collar	46.9%	46.7%
Services	16.2%	16.7%

ADULT EDUCATION

	2000
Less than	
High School	35.9%
High School	32.7%
Some College	7.7%
Associates Degree	3.0%
College Degree	5.7%
Graduate Degree	5.0%

POPULATION

2006	10,189
2000-2006 Population: Annual	
Compound Growth Rate	0.03%
2006-2011 Population: Annual	
Compound Growth Rate	0.24%

Population by age group

	2006	Projected 2011
0-4	6.1%	6.1%
5-9	5.5%	5.4%
10-14	6.5%	5.6%
15-19	5.7%	6.4%
20-24	5.9%	5.4%
25-29	6.6%	5.7%
30-34	6.2%	6.1%
35-39	6.6%	5.9%
40-44	7.0%	7.2%
45-49	6.8%	7.3%
50-54	6.4%	6.8%
55-59	6.4%	6.9%
60-64	5.9%	6.4%
65-69	4.6%	5.0%
70-74	3.8%	3.7%
75-79	3.7%	3.5%
80-84	2.9%	3.4%
85+	3.2%	3.2%

Sources for Vital Statistics listed above can be found in the Preface to this book.

McMINNVILLE

2006 POPULATION
13,158

NEAREST CITIES
Murfreesboro, TN (45 miles)
Cookeville, TN (45 miles)
Chattanooga, TN (69 miles)

ESTIMATED 2006
MEDIAN HOUSEHOLD INCOME
$31,131

COST OF LIVING
Average 3-bdrm home—$135,000
Average rent, 2-bdrm apartment—$600
Cost-of-living comparison—91.6%

SALES TAX
9.75%

PROPERTY TAX
Average 3-bdrm home—$500

Nestled in a broad, lush green valley with rolling hills to the north and west and the Cumberland Mountains to the southeast, McMinnville offers a pleasant retreat from city traffic and asphalt roads. Known as the "Nursery Capital of the World," the McMinnville area has more native plant species than any other region of the United States and is home to 450 registered nurseries. The combination of abundant rainfall, an extended growing season, and a wide range of elevations has produced this exceptional botanical variety. Hardwood forests and carpets of green pastures, highlighted by hundreds of acres of flowering shrubs and trees, enhance the landscape.

The oldest homes and structures date back to 1825. Like many other eastern Tennessee towns,

McMinnville was occupied by both Union and Confederate armies, and it changed hands seven times during the Civil War. The town square, which includes a red brick courthouse, has been completely revitalized. There is a beautiful landscaped park and the sidewalks are lined with historic markers, memorial bricks, and historically replicated street lamps. Tall steeples rise among the thriving business establishments on Main Street.

 RECREATION

Four state parks in the McMinnville area offer a wide variety of opportunities for outdoor recreation. Fall Creek Falls State Park, located in the mountains on the eastern edge of the county, is considered the "crown jewel" of Tennessee state parks and hosts a million visitors each year. At 256 feet, the majestic falls are the highest east of the Rockies. In addition to a public golf course, the park has paddleboats, hiking trails, bicycle paths, and facilities for horseback riding, swimming, and fishing. Rock Island State Park, situated near the Great Falls Dam on the Collins River, has become a popular training site for kayakers. There is also camping, picnicking, swimming, and cabins. Center Hill Lake is a haven for houseboaters, a playground for water-skiers, and a favorite spot for anglers. Edger Evins State Park on the shore of Center Hill Lake provides places for picnicking and swimming, a marina, a boat ramp, and nature trails. Cumberland Caverns, Tennessee's largest cave system, is only a few minutes' drive from McMinnville.

In addition to the golf course at Fall Creek Falls State Resort Park, there is another public course at Willowbrook Golf Club. The McMinnville Civic Center offers many indoor recreation activities, such as aerobics, tennis, basketball, volleyball, and weight training. The Parks and Recreations Department oversees seven ball fields, four tennis courts, and several organized youth team sports. The Civic Center is home to the Gilley Pool, an Olympic-size swimming pool and water park with multiple slides and diving boards, and to the Jungle Jym, a playground area for kids of all ages.

⏏ CULTURAL SCENE

McMinnville is home to the Lively Museum, the Southern Museum and Galleries, Chole's Art Gallery and Studio, and The Station— Pure Art. The Park Theatre underwent a complete revitalization. Main Street McMinnville offers "Main Street Live," live performances of a variety of music including bluegrass, country, and gospel on Friday nights during the summer. The Arts Center of Cannon County (adjoining Warren County) provides workshops, sponsors community theater productions, and houses local historical artifacts and exhibits.

The Appalachian Center for Crafts near Center Hill Lake, operated by Tennessee Technological University, is a professional crafts center teaching and exhibiting fine Appalachian and contemporary crafts, with an emphasis on wood, metal, fiber, glass, and clay. Over 250 craft vendors from all over the Southeast display their wares on the last weekend in August at the Beersheba Springs Craft Fair, on the grounds of a mountaintop mineral-springs resort whose popularity predates the Civil War.

The Historic Falcon Manor, a 10,000-square-foot Victorian mansion built in 1896 by wealthy entrepreneur Clay Faulkner, has been restored to its original splendor. It is open for small group tours. A bed and-breakfast is open on the grounds, and meals are served in the Victorian Tea Room and shop.

McMinnville hosts many festivals and events. The Black House May Day Celebration, which takes place in the spring, is named for the town's oldest brick house. The Highland Rim Cycling Classic, during the second weekend in May, draws hundreds of cyclists from around the country. Summer events include the Fourth of July celebration and the gospel music concert in August. In September, the Warren County Fair offers carnival rides, craft vendors, concerts, and main stage events. Located at the fairgrounds, Fairfield Village is a re-creation of a pioneer village, including a schoolhouse, church, bank, hardware store, and funeral home. The Autumn Street Fair takes place in downtown the third weekend in

October. The Warren County Arts and Crafts Fair is held in November. The Christmas season kicks off with a parade on the first Saturday in December; Christmas in the Village is on the first Tuesday in December at the Pioneer Village at the Fairgrounds.

Residents can also drive to Nashville, Chattanooga, and Cookeville (home of Tennessee Technology University) for a wider selection of cultural attractions.

 MAIN STREET

Local popular restaurants include Charley's Bar-B-Que, Capalano's Coffee House & Café, New York Grill, Willie Lee Lee's Bar-B-Que, Wilma Jean's, the Falcon Rest Victorian Tea Room, and the Inn at Harvest Farms. The town participates in the Main Street Program, and the downtown district is filled with stores selling antiques and country crafts.

 HOUSING

Mountain retreats, lakeside homes, condominiums, and apartments are all available in McMinnville and Warren County. There are plenty of in-town houses with three bedrooms, two bathrooms, and 2,000 square feet or more in the $120,000 to $150,000 range. All-brick cluster houses and condominiums are priced from $150,000 to $170,000. Local builders have constructed executive-size houses for a fraction of what they would cost in a large metropolitan area. Five- to ten-acre tracts of land with both wooded and cleared areas are available for mini-farms. Prices for lake lots and riverfront parcels for custom building range from $5,000 to $8,000 per acre. Housing prices, property taxes, and TVA power are considerably less expensive than in metro areas like Chattanooga, Nashville, and Knoxville.

 ECONOMICS

Number of employers with fifty or more employees—22

The nursery industry is extensive: 450 small companies employ a total of 3,500 workers. Other major employers include Bridgestone/Firestone (1,000 employees); Yorozu Automotive of Tennessee (900 employees); Oster Professional Products (600 employees); and Morrison Tool & Fab (150 employees). The county economy is diverse; local companies produce truck parts, electric motors, valves, tires, hardwood flooring, and nursery-related products. Tourism continues to expand.

 EDUCATION

High schools—1; Middle schools—1; Elementary schools—8; Private schools—2

Motlow State Community College, a two-year institution, offers career-oriented classes and a curriculum leading to an associate's degree for transfer to four-year colleges. Motlow also offers a program through Tennessee Technological University in which students in the school of education can achieve a bachelor's degree on the McMinnville campus. The Tennessee Technology Center in McMinnville provides vocational specialties for upgrading job skills and for job placement. Universities and four-year colleges (also offering adult continuing education classes) within commuting distance include Tennessee Technological University in Cookeville, Middle Tennessee State University in Murfreesboro,

and the University of the South in Sewanee (45 miles).

 HEALTHCARE

River Park Hospital—127 beds; Physicians—55; Dentists—14

River Park Hospital, owned by Capella Corporation, provides 24-hour emergency room service; cardiology services, diabetes, family birth, and rehabilitation centers; occupational medicine; physical and respiratory therapy; and oncology, radiology, nephrology, neurology, and gastroenterology services. Clients needing more extensive medical services can be referred to the university hospital and specialists in Nashville.

 SPIRITUAL LIFE

Twenty Christian denominations are represented. The nearest synagogue is located in Chattanooga.

 STAYING CONNECTED

The local newspaper, the *Southern Standard*, is published three times per week. Daily newspapers from Knoxville, Chattanooga, and Nashville are delivered locally. Five local radio stations cover the county, and cable television is available,

with network affiliates in Knoxville, Chattanooga, and Nashville.
Internet service is available. There
are two local bookstores.

 GETTING THERE

Located in the eastern part of
middle Tennessee, McMinnville is
on US 70-S and Tennessee Highways 8, 30, 55, 56, and 108. I-24
is twenty-three miles southwest,
while I-40 is thirty-three miles
north. The nearest commercial
airports are the Nashville International Airport (75 miles), an
American Airlines hub and home
to fourteen other airlines, and the
Chattanooga Metropolitan Airport, with several major airlines.
General aviation needs are met by
the Warren County Memorial Airport, which has a 5,300-foot
asphalt and lighted runway.

 RESOURCES

McMinnville–Warren County
 Chamber of Commerce
110 Court Square
McMinnville, TN 37111
(931) 473-6611
www.warrentn.com

MCMINNVILLE
VITAL STATISTICS

CLIMATE

Annual average rainfall	52 inches
Snowfall	6 inches
Elevation	950 feet

Temperatures (in degrees Fahrenheit)

	Jan	**Apr**	**Jul**	**Oct**
High	47	71	88	71
Low	27	46	65	46

OCCUPATIONS

	2006	**Projected 2011**
Blue collar	38.5%	38.7%
White collar	44.7%	43.0%
Services	16.8%	18.3%

ADULT EDUCATION

	2000
Less than High School	34.9%
High School	35.4%
Some College	16.9%
Associates Degree	1.9%
College Degree	7.1%
Graduate Degree	0.9%

POPULATION

2006	13,158

2000-2006 Population: Annual Compound Growth Rate 0.51%

2006-2011 Population: Annual Compound Growth Rate 0.55%

Population by age group

	2006	**Projected 2011**
0-4	7.3%	7.4%
5-9	6.5%	6.2%
10-14	5.7%	6.4%
15-19	5.9%	5.7%
20-24	6.7%	6.9%
25-29	7.4%	5.8%
30-34	7.2%	6.9%
35-39	6.5%	6.5%
40-44	7.0%	6.7%
45-49	6.7%	6.8%
50-54	5.9%	6.5%
55-59	5.7%	6.3%
60-64	4.6%	5.4%
65-69	4.2%	3.9%
70-74	3.6%	3.7%
75-79	3.1%	3.0%
80-84	3.0%	2.8%
85+	2.8%	3.3%

Sources for Vital Statistics listed above can be found in the Preface to this book.

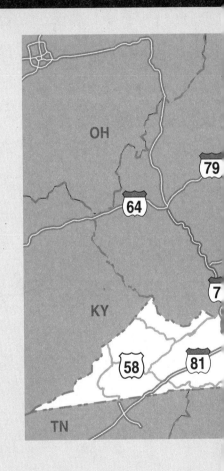

VIRGINIA

BLACKSBURG

2006 POPULATION
40,596

NEAREST CITIES
Roanoke, VA (40 miles)
Greensboro, NC (130 miles)

ESTIMATED 2006
MEDIAN HOUSEHOLD INCOME
$28,938

COST OF LIVING
Average 3-bdrm home—$186,000
Average rent, 2-bdrm apartment—
$600
Cost-of-living comparison—
91.1%

SALES TAX
4.5%

PROPERTY TAX
Average 3-bdrm home—$1,637

The scenic Virginia town of Blacksburg is situated on a gentle plateau between the Allegheny Mountains and the majestic Blue Ridge Mountains. Stately highlands provide the backdrop for this high-tech town where energy and innovation are the way of life.

While leading an expedition party in 1748, Thomas Walker discovered the area now known as Blacksburg. Impressed by the incredible beauty of the New River Valley and encouraged by a wealth of natural resources, the group felt compelled to stay. In 1755, their plans were disrupted when Shawnee Indians captured and killed most of the settlers in the Draper's Meadow Massacre. Mary Draper Ingles, one of those captured, traveled over 850 miles to escape. Her journey is portrayed in the outdoor historical drama

The Long Way Home, performed annually during the summer months in Radford (13 miles). After a donation of thirty-eight acres by William Black, the Town of Blacksburg was incorporated in 1798 and initially formed a grid of "sixteen squares."

Blacksburg is home to Virginia Polytechnic Institute and State University, known as Virginia Tech. The largest university in the state, Virginia Tech is a research-oriented university supporting an international community with an academic focus on business, agriculture, forestry, architecture, and veterinary medicine.

The distinctive charm of yesteryear is evident in the downtown historic buildings dating back to the mid-1700s, many of which are located in the sixteen-block square of the original town. Renovated historic buildings house distinctive boutiques, shops, and restaurants serving everything from international cuisine to down-home country cooking.

 RECREATION

Blacksburg is a paradise for outdoor enthusiasts. The Jefferson National Forest's 690,000 acres includes eleven wilderness areas for camping, hunting, caving, and fishing and 950 miles of trails for hiking and backpacking. The Nature Conservancy's 655-acre Falls Ridge Preserve, designated a rare ecosystem, has a spectacular thirty-meter travertine waterfall. Claytor Lake State Park covers 472 acres and has a 4,500-acre lake. The Wilderness Conservancy at Mountain Lake is a terrific place to spot red-tailed hawks, wild turkeys, eastern box turtles, black bears, and bobcats. (The film *Dirty Dancing* was filmed at Mountain Lake.) The Cascades recreation area features a sixty-eight-foot waterfall; its trails are well suited for mountain biking and easy hiking.

The New River has Class II and III rapids for tubing, kayaking, and canoeing. The annual Wilderness Road Bicycle Ride offers twenty-, fifty- and seventy-five-mile rides along the original "Wilderness Road" explored by Daniel Boone. In winter, skiing is available at Snowshoe, West Virginia, a two-hour drive away.

For less strenuous outdoor enjoyment, Blacksburg residents can easily reach the Blue Ridge

Parkway. This 355-mile scenic highway through the Appalachian Mountains connects Shenandoah National Park with Great Smoky Mountains National Park; it offers walking paths, hiking trails, and fishing locations. Pandapas Pond is a lovely eight-acre manmade lake; a one-mile loop trail circles the pond and numerous additional trails spike out from the loop.

Taking the back roads from Blacksburg to Roanoke via Route 785 is a treat. This road, designated as a Virginia Byway, runs through scenic Catawba Valley past quaint farmhouses, historic sites, fields of grazing cattle and horses, and restaurants specializing in country cooking.

Golfers can enjoy Virginia Tech's eighteen-hole public course or two nearby private country clubs. Blacksburg has a 28,000-square-foot community center, a six-lane aquatic center, a municipal golf course, tennis courts, athletic programs for adults and children, and many local parks. Hand-in-Hand Playground is a two-acre recreational area built by the community. The Blacksburg Bikeway and Walkway is practical for commuters going to downtown Blacksburg. College sports fans will see plenty of action at Virginia Tech and Radford College. The Virginia Tech Hokies have a high-ranking football team.

CULTURAL SCENE

Blacksburg offers extraordinary options for cultural activities. The Blacksburg Regional Art Association, the New River Arts Council, and the Blacksburg Regional Art Association all actively promote the arts in the New River Valley. There are five local art galleries within the town and thirteen more in the area.

The Silverman Fine Arts Center in Radford is a 500-seat theater and art gallery. The 1500-seat Preston Hall hosts student exhibits and performances as well as appearances by visiting groups such as the Martha Graham Dance Ensemble and the New York City Opera National Company. The Lyric Theater in Blacksburg, a five-hundred-seat 1929 theater restored in 1998, offers classic movies, theatrical performances, concerts, and other special events. Playmakers and Company mounts live theater productions for the Blacksburg/ Christiansburg area. The Virginia Tech Union of Lively Arts presents Broadway shows, concerts, ballets, and other productions. Virginia Tech and Radford University offer a range of plays, dance, art exhibits, concerts, and lectures. The Squire's Student Center and Buruss Auditorium host performances by the University Symphony and the New Virginians musical group, as well as touring Broadway shows.

There are also professional theater groups in Roanoke, student theater groups in Radford, and local community theaters in surrounding towns. A variety of dance troupes in the area, such as the Roanoke Ballet, offer ballet, modern dance, folk dancing, jazz, and clogging performances.

Summer concerts as well as opera, chorale, and brass ensemble performances are offered at Virginia Tech, Radford, and Roanoke area colleges. The New River Valley Symphony in Blacksburg and the Roanoke Symphony perform year-round. Traditional folk and country music with Appalachian roots is also performed locally. The annual Old Fiddlers' Convention in Galax is a gathering of bluegrass musicians. The Black Dog Jazz Concert at the Chateau Morrisette Winery on the Blue Ridge Parkway at Meadows of Dan is another popular event.

The Smithfield Plantation House in Blacksburg, built in 1773, is a Virginia landmark. This Tidewater plantation-style home adjoining the Virginia Tech campus is open for tours. Other sites of interest are the Virginia Tech Museum of Geological Sciences and the Virginia Tech Museum of Natural History.

The Downtown Merchants of Blacksburg sponsor the International Street Fair, held one week in April to promote cultural awareness among students and the community. Art Along the Fence is a one-day affair at which area artists display their work along the iron fence on College Avenue while dance, drama, music, and poetry readings keep the crowd entertained. Spring and summer bring outdoor lawn concerts and a local Saturday farmer's market. Steppin' Out in August is a weekend arts and crafts festival. The Wilderness Trail Festival, sponsored by the Montgomery County Chamber of Commerce, is an annual tribute to the site where Daniel Boone crossed the Continental Divide and entered the wilderness. This thirty-three year tradition is held in downtown Christiansburg and showcases music, food, and crafts that evoke the culture and heritage of the area. Late October brings an afternoon of music at the Jazzburg Music Festival. Holidays at Smithfield and other special events in December add to the annual festivities.

 MAIN STREET

Many of the popular Blacksburg eateries cater to the college crowd. P. K.'s is a student hangout known for Octoberfest and Shrimpfest, and the Ton-80 Club attracts customers with games and a good selection of beers. Bogen's, located close to campus, offers a variety of specials. Other local haunts are Mike's Grill (huge, tasty burgers); Gilli's (vegetarian fare); Souvlaki Ltd. (Greek sandwiches); Boudreaux's Restaurant (authentic Cajun food); and the Mill Mountain Tea and Coffee Shop (sinful

desserts). Baylee's is a bar and restaurant with live music. Top of the Stairs (TOTS) claims the best BBQ in the New River Valley and also offers live entertainment. Bollo's is a popular coffee shop, Our Daily Bread is a favorite stop for baked goods, and Carol Lee's is the choice for donuts. Brazilian, Italian, Japanese, Mexican, Indian, and German restaurants spice up dining alternatives.

Downtown Blacksburg is just plain fun to walk around. Since it is adjacent to the Virginia Tech campus, there is activity day or night on the streets or in the coffeehouses. Unique shops selling items like Venezuelan sweaters or one-of-a-kind art keep the browsing stimulating. As in most college towns, there are excellent music shops, as well as new and used bookstores.

 HOUSING

Real estate prices have gone up as a result of Blacksburg's popularity, the presence of Virginia Tech, and the steady growth of businesses. Houses dating back to the 1920s and 1930s are in high demand and sell for $230,000 and more. Those

in other established neighborhoods start as low as $135,000 but
can still exceed $200,000. There
are many new subdivisions, some
with houses in the $160,000 to
$200,000 range. Prices in other
subdivisions with new houses,
twenty- to thirty-year-old large
homes, or custom-built houses on
two wooded acres can go as high
as $500,000. Two-acre lots cost
$60,000 to $70,000. Other housing
options include town homes ranging from $90,000 to $220,000 and
condominiums ranging from
$50,000 to $100,000. Apartments
are plentiful; many are rented by
Virginia Tech students. There is
one large assisted-living facility in
the area.

 ECONOMICS

**Number of employers with fifty or
more employees—15**
Among the thousand businesses in
the Blacksburg area, the primary
employers are Virginia Tech (8,273
employees); Montgomery County
Schools (1,500 employees); Alliant
Techsystems (1,250 employees);
Federal-Mogul Corporation (899
employees); Poly-Scientific Litton,
Inc. (600 employees); Hubbell

Lighting, Inc. (556 employees);
Columbia Montgomery Regional
Hospital (531 employees); and
Electro-Tec Corporation (299
employees). There are a number of
engineering and engineering consulting firms in the Blacksburg
area, and there are internet and
biotech companies in the Virginia
Tech Corporate Research Park.

 EDUCATION

**High schools—1; Middle schools—
1; Elementary schools—5; Private
schools—4**
Virginia Tech University (25,754
students) ranks among the top
fifty research institutions in the
country. The school has 8 colleges
and graduate schools, 70 bachelor's
degree programs, and 150 master's
and doctoral degree programs.
Adjacent to the 2,600-acre campus
is a corporate research center.
Other higher education options
include Radford University (8,034
students), which has 112 program
options for undergraduate and
graduate students, and New River
Community College in Christiansburg (10 miles), a two-year comprehensive community college with
forty academic programs. In

Roanoke are Roanoke College (1,700 students), offering bachelor's of arts, bachelor's of science, and bachelor's of business administration programs; Hollins University (1,000 students), a four-year independent liberal arts university offering twenty-nine majors and five master's programs; and Virginia Western Community College (8,200 students), a two-year community college offering thirty-four majors.

 HEALTHCARE

Columbia Montgomery Regional Hospital—146 beds; Carilion New River Valley Medical Center (Radford)—175 beds; Physicians—100; Dentists—27

The medical staff at Columbia Montgomery consists of more than eighty physicians representing many specialties, including neurology, ophthalmology, and urology. This facility provides surgery, extended care, diagnostic imaging, intensive care, coronary care, and 24-hour emergency service. Carilion New River Valley Medical Center, a full-service hospital with a medical staff of seventy-eight physicians representing over twenty specialties, provides

24-hour emergency care facilities (Level III trauma center), surgical services, radiology, and a comprehensive heart center.

 SPIRITUAL LIFE

There are twenty Christian denominations, a Jewish community center, a Buddhist center, a Friends meeting group, an Islamic center, and several nonsectarian groups.

 STAYING CONNECTED

One local newspaper, the *News Messenger,* is published twice a week. The *Roanoke Times,* the Roanoke daily newspaper, is also available in Blacksburg. The *Collegiate Times* is the Virginia Tech student-published newspaper. The Blacksburg area has three television stations, sixteen radio stations, and two cable television companies. The Blacksburg Electronic Village offers internet service to the university and some municipal offices; most local civic groups and individual citizens are served by local providers. There are three bookstores owned by the university, two that are privately owned, and one that sells used books.

 **GETTING THERE**

Blacksburg is located off I-81 in the southwestern region of Virginia. It is served by US 460 and US 114 and South Carolina Highways 11, 100, and 8. Home Ride of Virginia, is a weekend shuttle bus service from Blacksburg and Radford to northern Virginia, Harrisonburg, Charlottesville, Richmond, and the Tidewater area. The Two Town Trolley runs hourly service between Blacksburg and Christiansburg, and the Blacksburg Transit offers local service, including door-to-door accessible van service for those who need it. Roanoke Regional Airport provides air transportation to many major cities. The Virginia Tech Airport, owned and operated by the Virginia Tech University, is a public-use facility with a 4,500-foot runway serving private and corporate small aircraft.

 RESOURCES

Montgomery County
  Chamber of Commerce
103 Professional Park Drive
Blacksburg, VA 24060
(540) 552-2636
www.montgomerycc.org

Additional area websites:
www.bev.net
www.downtownblacksburg.com

BLACKSBURG
VITAL STATISTICS

CLIMATE

Annual average rainfall	39.9 inches
Snowfall	22 inches
Elevation	2,000 feet

Temperatures (in degrees Fahrenheit)

	Jan	Apr	Jul	Oct
High	41	65	82	66
Low	20	38	58	39

OCCUPATIONS

	2006	Projected 2011
Blue collar	7.7%	6.9%
White collar	74.8%	77.7%
Services	17.6%	15.4%

ADULT EDUCATION

	2000
Less than High School	7.1%
High School	10.7%
Some College	13.3%
Associates Degree	4.8%
College Degree	25.3%
Graduate Degree	38.9%

POPULATION

2006	40,956
2000-2006 Population: Annual Compound Growth Rate	0.41%
2006-2011 Population: Annual Compound Growth Rate	0.53%

Population by age group

	2006	Projected 2011
0-4	2.7%	2.6%
5-9	2.3%	2.1%
10-14	2.5%	2.4%
15-19	20.1%	19.3%
20-24	39.1%	40.8%
25-29	7.3%	6.8%
30-34	4.0%	3.7%
35-39	2.9%	2.6%
40-44	3.0%	2.8%
45-49	3.2%	3.2%
50-54	2.9%	2.9%
55-59	2.7%	2.8%
60-64	2.0%	2.4%
65-69	1.6%	1.6%
70-74	1.3%	1.3%
75-79	0.9%	1.0%
80-84	0.9%	0.8%
85+	0.7%	0.8%

Sources for Vital Statistics listed above can be found in the Preface to this book.

KILMARNOCK

2006 POPULATION
1,331

NEAREST CITIES
Williamsburg, VA (60 miles)
Fredericksburg, VA (60 miles)
Richmond, VA (70 miles)

ESTIMATED 2006
MEDIAN HOUSEHOLD INCOME
$44,897

COST OF LIVING
Average 3-bdrm home—$200,000
Average rent, 2-bdrm apartment—$650
Cost-of-living comparison—106.3%

SALES TAX
4.5%

PROPERTY TAX
Average 3-bdrm home—$1,080

Kilmarnock is sheltered among the inland waterways of the Chesapeake Bay Region. The area has four distinct seasons, but the Chesapeake Bay softens the typical Virginia winter and extends the fall and spring a few extra weeks. The setting is so peaceful you can feel your heart rate slow down and your breathing get deeper. Many visitors who come for a weekend decide to stay for a lifetime.

Captain John Smith, the principal founder of Jamestown, Virginia, and the first visitor to this area in the early 1600s, noted the fertile soil, the mild climate, and the bountiful resources of the many waterways. Lancaster County was created in 1651 and named for the city in England. Planters prospered in the 1700s, primarily by growing tobacco. During the Civil War, Union soldiers raided the county, leaving the farms in ruins. Eventually, the steamboat industry helped rebuild the county. The nearby town of Irvington, a charming waterfront village, was a stop for the Chesapeake Bay steamboats between Baltimore and Norfolk. Farm produce and seafood were shipped from Lancaster County to Baltimore until the 1950s, when automobiles became the primary mode of transportation for local farmers and businesses.

Many of the town's nineteenth-century buildings house interesting specialty shops. Hope and Glory Inn is a beautifully restored 1890s schoolhouse with a hopelessly romantic ambience. The proximity of Kilmarnock to the Washington, D.C., area (135 miles), together with the appeal of a more relaxed lifestyle and an idyllic setting, has contributed to an influx of telecommuters and at-home business entrepreneurs. Richmond, Williamsburg, and Fredericksburg—all within seventy-five minutes—are close enough for dinner, theater, concerts, lectures, or gallery hopping.

 RECREATION

Kilmarnock is located near the Chesapeake Bay with easy access to the Rappahannock, Potomac, and Corrotoman Rivers and many smaller waterways. The town is a water lover's paradise; boating, sailing, waterskiing, swimming, fishing, and crabbing are all popular. The Chesapeake Bay, the largest estuary in North America, extends for two hundred miles and has over two thousand forms of marine life. Natural beauty and wildlife are abundant in this bay region; American bald eagles, turkeys, deer, otters, beavers, herons, and other wildlife can be observed in their natural habitat.

Seven-hundred-acre Belle Isle State Park, located near the town of Lively in Lancaster County, has seven miles of waterfront on the Rappahannock River. The Corrotoman River Nature Trail leads hikers on three marked trails along the western branch of the river; Hickory Hollow Trail is a two-mile marked hiking path. Breezewood Farms offers horseback riding trails. Hughlett's Point Nature Preserve has a sandy beach on the bay and on Dividing Creek. Cruise tours are available to explore the Corrotoman River, Tangier Island, and Smith Island. There are many opportunities for charter fishing trips; those who don't want to venture out on a boat can catch fresh crabs directly from most docks.

There are plenty of opportunities for organized sports in the area. The Youth Club of Lancaster County has a twenty-team baseball organization with 400 participants. An active YMCA offers a variety of classes, sports activities, and teams, as well as a summer camp program. A local health spa has a twenty-five-yard indoor heated pool.

There are three eighteen-hole golf courses and one nine-hole course in the area. *Golf Digest* rates the Golden Eagle championship golf course at The Tides Inn as one of the top ten in Virginia and one of the top one hundred in the United States. The inn also offers meeting facilities, a spa, swimming pools, and a marina.

Another option is Tartan Course, once a part of The Tides Inn, now a privately owned club open to the public. The course was designed by Sir Guy Campbell, the designer of the St. Andrews Course in Scotland. The King Carter Golf Course is an 18-hole, championship sculpted golf course located in Hills Quarter, a golf course community in scenic Irvington, Virginia.

 CULTURAL SCENE

The lifestyle in this coastal community may seem laid-back, but its citizens are active in culture and the arts. The Center for the Arts hosts theatrical, dance, and musical productions, while the Rappahannock Foundation for the Arts promotes the arts and sponsors programs throughout the year, including art exhibits at its gallery and a juried art show in September. The Lancaster Players Playhouse is a dinner theater in nearby White Stone.

Historic landmarks dot the countryside in and around

Kilmarnock. Three miles south of town is Christ Church, built in 1732 by Robert "King" Carter, a wealthy planter. This colonial-era church is on the National Register of Historic Places and has high-back pews and a three-level pulpit, features distinctive to that period. The main building of the Mary Ball Washington Museum and Library was built originally as an 1830s club or tavern and now houses many historic collections. Other buildings in the complex include the Old Jail, the Old Clerk's Office, and the Old Post Office. St. Mary's White Chapel, built in 1669, is a state landmark open for tours. Stratford Hall Plantation, built in the 1730s, was the birthplace of Robert E. Lee; the 1,600-acre working farm is open for tours. The Kilmarnock Museum tells the history of the town through exhibits on business and commerce. The Merry Point Ferry is one of the last cable ferries; it will take you across the Corrotoman River. Visitors can also tour the Ingleside Plantation Vineyards and taste their wines or visit the Potomac River Brewing

Company, the area microbrewery.

Multiple events are held throughout the year. The county Chamber of Commerce sponsors the Spring Festival held at Belle Isle State Park. Other popular events include the Spring Barrel Tastings and Blendings at Ingleside Plantation Vineyards, Garden Week festivities in April, the Bay Seafood Festival in September, Scottish Days in October, and the annual Christmas parade. The calendar is also filled with fishing derbies, Native American pow-wows, arts and crafts festivals, and seafood festivals.

There are six wineries located between Irvington and the King George area. White Fences Vineyard & Winery in Irvington; Vault Field Vineyards in Kinsale; and Buena Vista Farm in Hague are growing vineyards. Belle Mount Vineyards; Ingleside Vineyards; and Oak Crest Vineyard & Winery are producing vineyards.

 MAIN STREET

Lee's Restaurant on Main Street is a favorite meeting place. Carried Away Cuisine, located on Main

Street, has great homemade daily specials, salads, pastas, and desserts. Diners at Landscape Landing enjoy a nice view of the river, and on Fridays they are treated to entertainment. Other popular eateries include Rose's Crab House, The Break Pad, Dixie Deli, and Willaby's Restaurant, a good place for lunch specials and order-ahead homemade pies and desserts.

Downtown Kilmarnock is an interesting mix: unique shops, galleries, and cafés stand alongside furniture stores, repair shops, banks, and other basic businesses. Part of the charm of Kilmarnock is the amazing number of specialties catering to a wide range of needs. There are home décor shops, art galleries, antique shops, bookstores, a chocolate shop, gift shops, dance studios, massage therapists, publishers, and, of course, wholesale seafood businesses.

 HOUSING

Property taxes are low in Lancaster County, reducing the overall cost of living and attracting retirees. Housing options include waterfront property on rivers, creeks, and the bay; historic homes; and new houses in subdivisions. Waterfront property starts at $500,000 for cottages and goes over $2 million for estates or historic plantations. In-town prices are considerably lower. Houses, including some from the seventeenth and eighteenth centuries, in established neighborhoods in Kilmarnock and surrounding towns range from $250,000 to $500,000. Houses with water access also range from $250,000 to $500,000, and rural property can be found for as low as $150,000 or up into the millions, depending on the size of the home and the amount of acreage. Waterfront condominiums in this area sell for $350,000 to $950,000. There are very few apartments. A full-service continuing care facility and retirement home with an assisted-living option serves the community.

 ECONOMICS

Number of employers with fifty or more employees—11

The primary local industries include agriculture, aquaculture (fish farming), and service-based industries, including hospitals, financial institutions, resort facilities (including The Tides Inn), retail shops, the public school system, and the government. The arrival of a biotechnology firm and a telecommunications company added diversity to the local business scene. A large number of professionals and skilled workers have migrated here from nearby larger metropolitan areas, seeking a slower paced lifestyle in a beautiful setting. Among the large employers are Rappahannock General Hospital (425 employees); Lancaster County School System (258 employees); and Rappahannock Westminster-Canterbury (150 employees). The town of Kilmarnock works with the Kilmarnock Technology Park and the Kilmarnock Downtown Revitalization Project to realize the town's goals.

EDUCATION

High schools—1; Middle schools—1; Elementary schools—1; Private schools—3

Higher education needs are met in Lancaster County through the north and south campuses of Rappahannock Community College (both within 30 miles). Four-year colleges and universities in Richmond, Hampton Roads, Williamsburg, and Fredericksburg are within commuting distance.

HEALTHCARE

Rappahannock General Hospital—77 beds; Physicians—35; Dentists—7

Rappahannock General, located within the town limits, provides full-service healthcare to the Northern Neck and Middle Peninsula of the state. All medical specialties are represented, including 24-hour emergency care, satellite accessibility, an oncology center, an MRI unit, and a CAT scan unit. Helicopter service is available for transport to top heart and trauma hospitals in Richmond. Thirteen clinics in the area offer a variety of treatment services. There is a full-service continuing care facility.

SPIRITUAL LIFE

Eight Christian denominations are represented. The nearest synagogue is in Richmond.

 **STAYING CONNECTED**

The *Rappahannock Record* is the local weekly newspaper. Daily newspapers are available from Richmond *(Richmond Times-Dispatch)* and Newport News *(Newport News Daily Press)*. Local internet service is available. Satellite television is offered in addition to cable television. There is one local radio station and one in nearby Warsaw. There are three bookstores in the area.

 **GETTING THERE**

Kilmarnock is located in the Northern Neck of Virginia, facing the Chesapeake Bay, on scenic and historic Routes 3 and 200. These state roads lead to primary VA 360 and 17, which connect Kilmarnock with northern Virginia, Washington, D.C., and Hampton Roads, an international port. The Rappahannock River is a short distance to the west of town. Richmond International Airport and Norfolk International Airport provide air transportation to major cities. There is a municipal airport at Hummel Field in Middlesex

County (just across the Rappahannock River) for small, private aircraft.

 RESOURCES

Kilmarnock
  Chamber of Commerce
P.O. Box 1357
Kilmarnock, VA 22482
(804) 435-2273
www.kilmarnockchamber.org

Lancaster County
  Chamber of Commerce
506 North Main Street
P.O. Box 1868
Chesapeake Commons
Kilmarnock, VA 22482
(804) 435-6092
www.lancasterva.com

Town of Kilmarnock
514 Main Street
PO Box 1357
Kilmarnock, VA 22482
(804) 435-1552
www.townofkilmarnockva.com

Northern Neck Tourism Council
P.O. Box 1707
Warsaw, VA 22572
(800) 393-6180
www.northernneck.org

Additional area website:
www.lancova.com

KILMARNOCK
VITAL STATISTICS

CLIMATE

Annual average rainfall	41.7 inches
Snowfall	13.9 inches
Elevation	Sea Level

Temperatures (in degrees Fahrenheit)

	Jan	**Apr**	**Jul**	**Oct**
High	46	67	86	70
Low	28	45	68	50

OCCUPATIONS

	2006	**Projected 2011**
Blue collar	21.0%	19.9%
White collar	55.8%	57.5%
Services	23.3%	22.4%

ADULT EDUCATION

	2000
Less than High School	26.4%
High School	29.0%
Some College	15.3%
Associates Degree	5.8%
College Degree	15.5%
Graduate Degree	8.0%

POPULATION

2006	1,331
2000-2006 Population: Annual Compound Growth Rate	1.09%
2006-2011 Population: Annual Compound Growth Rate	-0.17%

Population by age group

	2006	**Projected 2011**
0-4	4.2%	4.1%
5-9	3.5%	3.6%
10-14	4.7%	3.9%
15-19	4.2%	4.4%
20-24	4.4%	3.6%
25-29	3.2%	4.2%
30-34	3.0%	2.8%
35-39	3.3%	3.3%
40-44	4.9%	3.6%
45-49	6.6%	5.8%
50-54	6.8%	8.2%
55-59	6.2%	7.4%
60-64	8.0%	7.4%
65-69	7.0%	8.6%
70-74	7.7%	7.1%
75-79	5.7%	6.1%
80-84	7.1%	6.2%
85+	9.2%	9.6%

Sources for Vital Statistics listed above can be found in the Preface to this book.

LEXINGTON

2006 POPULATION
6,895

NEAREST CITIES
Roanoke, VA (50 miles)
Charlottesville, VA (55 miles)
Richmond, VA (115 miles)

ESTIMATED 2006
MEDIAN HOUSEHOLD INCOME
$35,143

COST OF LIVING
Average 3-bdrm home—$215,000
Average rent, 2-bdrm apartment—$300
Cost-of-living comparison—97.3%

SALES TAX
4.5%

PROPERTY TAX
Average 3-bdrm home—$1,200

Situated in the southern Shenandoah Valley, Lexington is framed on the west by the Allegheny Mountains and on the east by the colorful Blue Ridge Mountains. Once inhabited by the Cherokee and Monacan Indians and later settled by Europeans in the 1730s, Lexington has evolved into a charismatic Virginia college town. The serene setting features rolling green hills neatly fenced for horses and cattle, old tin-roofed farmhouses, and beautiful mountain views.

This charming Virginia town tucked in the valley between mountain ranges is rich with historic homes and landmarks and tales of unforgettable heroes. Lexington was home to the famous Confederate generals Thomas J. "Stonewall" Jackson and Robert E. Lee, as well as to General George C.

Marshall, Harry S. Truman's secretary of state and secretary of defense, originator of the Marshall Plan and recipient of the Nobel Peace Prize. Robert E. Lee headed Washington College, renamed Washington and Lee University after the Civil War, and Jackson taught at Virginia Military Institute after the Mexican War. A statue of Jackson stands proudly on the VMI campus, surrounded by cannons.

Much of Lexington's late eighteenth- and nineteenth-century architecture has been preserved and restored; the town has been a Virginia Main Street community since 1987. The architecturally significant campuses of Virginia Military Institute and of Washington and Lee University sit side by side on a hilltop at the edge of town. The stark stone gothic architecture of VMI enhances the strong presence of this military college steeped in classic tradition. The Washington and Lee campus features large red brick buildings, fronted with huge white columns overlooking neatly manicured lawns stretching down the hill to town.

Lexington is strategically located near two major interstates: I-81

and I-64. In less than one hour, residents can reach the larger cities of Roanoke, Charlottesville, and Harrisonburg (35 miles) for shopping, healthcare, and a variety of other services and activities.

RECREATION

Lying between two mountain ranges, Lexington is surrounded by rolling hills, rivers, and lakes. The Blue Ridge Parkway is fifteen minutes away. Lake Robertson, perched on the slopes of the Allegheny Mountains, offers a wide range of outdoor activities on its 581 acres. The Maury and James Rivers attract visitors for canoeing and kayaking, as well as for swimming, fishing, and whitewater rafting.

The Chessie Nature Trail follows the abandoned C & O Railroad bed between Lexington and Buena Vista for six miles. The walking is easy and the views spectacular. More serious hikers can take to the Appalachian Trail on the eastern side of Rockbridge County. The George Washington and the Jefferson National Forests and the Goshen Pass offer other options for hiking. Goshen Pass cuts through the Allegheny Mountains twelve miles north of Lexington, creating a deep gorge ideal for kayaking, tubing, and swimming. One of the seven natural wonders of the world is only twelve miles from Lexington. Natural Bridge, a twenty-three-story natural bridge that crosses Cedar Creek, draws thousands of curious visitors each year.

Horse enthusiasts from all over the country converge on Lexington for horse shows, rodeos, training programs, concerts, and other special events. The Virginia Horse Center attracts state, national, and international horse competitions to the four-thousand-seat coliseum.

The Rockbridge Area Recreation Organization offers programs for all ages, including football, soccer, basketball, T-ball, baseball, softball, wrestling, tennis, and field and track. Stock car and drag racing and shooting ranges can also be found in the area. Tennis and golf are available at the Lexington Golf and Country Club. Less than two hours away are two of the most elegant resorts in the Southeast, The Homestead in Hot Springs, Virginia, and The Green-

brier Hotel and Spa in White Sulphur Springs, West Virginia; each offers three golf courses.

 CULTURAL SCENE

The Lime Kiln Theater was an old limestone quarry and kiln, the former workplace of master stonemasons; now the stone ruins are an open-air stage, situated on twelve acres. Professional outdoor performances are presented from Memorial Day through Labor Day. *Stonewall Country,* based on the life and times of Stonewall Jackson, is one of the regular productions. Past concerts here featured music from a variety of genres, including blues, Cajun, zydeco, country rock, and bluegrass.

"Friday's Alive" presents music from jazz to rock and roll. Washington and Lee University and the Virginia Military Institute offer lectures, concerts, dance performances, and athletic events. The Rockbridge Choral Society and the Ballet and Modern Dance Ensemble also perform in town.

Local organizations such as the Rockbridge Arts Guild and the Rockbridge Chapter of the Virginia Museum of Fine Arts provide and promote a wide variety of special exhibits and events. Seven art galleries participate in a gallery walk through Historic Lexington.

Lexington also offers over one hundred historic sites, battlegrounds, and cemeteries. The VMI Museum houses Jackson's personal belongings as well as artifacts that date back to the Revolutionary War. The Lee Chapel and Museum displays Edward Valentine's statue of General Lee and Charles Wilson Peale's portrait of George Washington. The George C. Marshall Library and Museum is home to Marshall's papers and artifacts. Other interesting sites north of Lexington include the Buffalo Springs Herb Garden, Wade Mill (a water-powered gristmill), and the Rockbridge Vineyard. The former home of Cyrus McCormick, the inventor of the grain reaper, is also located north of Lexington. His company ultimately became International Harvester.

Year-round events in Lexington include festivals, fairs, artists markets, garden tours, and parades. The Rockbridge Mountain Music and Dance Festival and the Maury River Fiddler's Convention in nearby Buena Vista enliven the local entertainment scene. The Rockville Regional Fair is held at the Virginia Horse Center, a couple of miles north of Lexington. The Fourth of July Balloon Rally takes place on the VMI parade grounds; a colorful bike parade goes through town and culminates with a lawn party on Hopkins Green. In December, festivities include a weekend of caroling, theatrical performances, a parade, and the tree-lighting ceremony.

 MAIN STREET

For quality dining in a historic atmosphere, locals frequent the Sheridan's Livery Inn, a converted 1800s livery stable. The Palms, popular with the college crowd, features a diverse menu, and the Southern Inn offers a relaxed bar atmosphere, entertainment, and Sunday brunch. Café Michel, a restaurant in Clifton Forge, serves superb French food, but be sure to make a reservation.

This town draws the tourist trade with walking tours of the historic district and specialty shops guaranteed to attract attention.

Shoppers will find it hard to pass up the Irish and Scottish delights of Celtic Connection, the Virginia-made products at Virginia Born and Bred, and the specialty items and gourmet foods at Shenandoah Attic. The Lexington Coffee Shop is strategically placed for a caffeine boost to aid weary shoppers.

HOUSING

A variety of housing options are available in this desirable community. The historic district offers large houses, many with 3,000 to 4,500 square feet, ranging in price from $300,000 to $800,000. The average price for an in-town home outside the historic district is approximately $215,000; homes in new subdivisions are available for $150,000 to $295,000. Large farms with 20 to 250 acres can start as low as $150,000 and go to $1 million. A country subdivision offers two to ten acres of land at an average price of $188,000. There are few townhouses and apartments in the area. Most rentals are single-family homes starting at about $800 per month. One retirement home serves the area. There are no gated communities.

ECONOMICS

Number of employers with fifty or more employees—20

Historically, agriculture has been the primary mainstay for the local economy. Today, the beef and cattle industry continues to be strong, and farmers are expanding production to include nontraditional crops such as garlic, grapes for wine, poultry, and Christmas trees. While agriculture is still the largest industry in the county, the town of Lexington draws significant revenue from tourism and manufacturing. Major employers include Mohawk Industries (1,000 employees); Des Champs Laboratories (265 employees); the universities; and the hospital system.

The Lexington Downtown Development Association was formed in 1985 to retain the character of the historic district while encouraging business development. As a member of the National Main Street program, Lexington is eligible for assistance to maintain and promote the downtown area.

 EDUCATION

High schools—1 (City/County Consolidated); Middle schools (city)—1; Middle schools (county)—2; Elementary schools (city)—1; Private schools—6

Lexington is served by a city and a county school system. Washington and Lee University, founded in 1749, is a private coeducational University with undergraduate programs and a law school. Virginia Military Institute, founded in 1839, is the nation's oldest state-supported military college. It is coeducational and offers four-year degree programs in liberal arts, science, and engineering. Dabney S. Lancaster Community College, whose main campus is thirty miles away in Clifton Forge, and the Rockbridge Regional Center offer technical and continuing education programs with twenty-seven associate's degrees and certificate programs. Southern Virginia College in Buena Vista is a four-year coeducational college. The college's majestic Main Hall was once an 1890s grand hotel.

 HEALTHCARE

Stonewall Jackson Hospital—80 beds; Physicians—35; Dentists—15

The Stonewall Jackson Hospital is a primary care hospital with a fifty-bed extended care facility adjoining the hospital. The hospital provides 24-hour emergency care, laboratory and drug testing, physical therapy, outpatient surgery, general and medical surgical care, cardiac rehabilitation, ambulance and wheelchair transportation, and community health education programs.

 SPIRITUAL LIFE

Nine Christian denominations are represented. There is one Buddhist Center in Lexington. One synagogue is located in Roanoke and one in Staunton (35 miles).

 STAYING CONNECTED

There are three local newspapers in Lexington: the weekly *News-Gazette,* the *Rockbridge Weekly,* and the monthly *Advocate.* The *Roanoke Times,* the *New York Times,* the *Richmond Times Dispatch,* and the *Washington Post* are

available daily. WMRA is the local
public radio station. Cable television and internet service are
available. There are five local
bookstores, including one selling
out-of-print books and one college store.

 GETTING THERE

Lexington is located in Rockbridge
County in the southwestern part of
Virginia between Roanoke and
Staunton, near the intersection of
I-81 and I-64. The Roanoke Muni-
cipal Airport provides commercial
flights to many major cities.

 RESOURCES

Lexington-Rockbridge County
  Chamber of Commerce
100 East Washington Street
Lexington, VA 24450
(540) 463-5375
www.lexrockchamber.com

Lexington Visitors Center
106 East Washington Street
Lexington, VA 24450
(540) 463-3777
www.lexingtonvirginia.com

LEXINGTON
VITAL STATISTICS

CLIMATE

Annual average rainfall	38 inches
Snowfall	21.4 inches
Elevation	1,100 feet

Temperatures (in degrees Fahrenheit)

	Jan	Apr	Jul	Oct
High	44	69	87	69
Low	22	40	62	43

OCCUPATIONS

	2006	Projected 2011
Blue collar	13.9%	13.1%
White collar	69.0%	71.6%
Services	17.1%	15.3%

ADULT EDUCATION

	2000
Less than High School	22.9%
High School	17.3%
Some College	11.8%
Associates Degree	5.5%
College Degree	21.1%
Graduate Degree	21.6%

POPULATION

2006	6,895
2000-2006 Population: Annual Compound Growth Rate	0.07%
2006-2011 Population: Annual Compound Growth Rate	-0.14%

Population by age group

	2006	Projected 2011
0-4	2.7%	2.9%
5-9	2.5%	2.2%
10-14	2.8%	2.8%
15-19	20.3%	20.1%
20-24	24.3%	25.3%
25-29	4.3%	3.4%
30-34	3.4%	3.1%
35-39	2.6%	3.0%
40-44	3.3%	3.0%
45-49	3.8%	4.0%
50-54	4.5%	3.6%
55-59	4.5%	5.0%
60-64	4.3%	4.7%
65-69	3.8%	4.2%
70-74	3.5%	3.2%
75-79	3.4%	3.2%
80-84	3.1%	2.9%
85+	3.0%	3.3%

Sources for Vital Statistics listed above can be found in the Preface to this book.

ORANGE

2006 POPULATION
4,611

NEAREST CITIES
Culpeper, VA (18 miles)
Charlottesville, VA (27 miles)
Fredericksburg, VA (35 miles)
Richmond, VA (70 miles)
Washington, D.C. (75 miles)

ESTIMATED 2006
MEDIAN HOUSEHOLD INCOME
$40,660

COST OF LIVING
Average 3-bdrm home—$250,000
Average rent, 2-bdrm apartment—
$800
Cost-of-living comparison—
107.7%

SALES TAX
5%

PROPERTY TAX
Average 3-bdrm home—$2,175

The vibrant, historic town of Orange lies in the Piedmont region of Virginia. Driving into town, you'll pass gently rolling hills and lush green pastures set against the majestic backdrop of the Blue Ridge Mountains. Orange fits nicely into this setting, with attractively restored historic buildings, distinguished nineteenth-century homes, and a train depot in the heart of town. While the architecture is historic, the town is also home to an art gallery and an art center, a spa, and an herb shop, and colorful murals are painted on the walls of some businesses in town.

The town was settled in 1722 by James Taylor II, who built his plantation, Bloomsbury, nearby. Two of his grandsons later became presidents of the United States: James Madison, also known as the

"Father of the Constitution," and Zachary Taylor. The town, named in honor of William IV, Prince of Orange, was incorporated in 1872. During the Civil War, Orange was a stopping point for trains transporting troops and supplies and a drop-off point for wounded soldiers in need of medical care. Two famous battles were fought in this area: the Battle at the Wilderness between Lee and Grant, and the 1864 Campaign.

In 1999, Orange was named a national and state historic district. This distinction has spurred the ongoing restoration of sixty-one architecturally significant downtown buildings. Orange is strategically located within an easy drive of four large metro areas, making it accessible to a wide range of performing arts venues, educational institutions, diverse museums, and top-rated restaurants.

 RECREATION

The Shenandoah National Park covers over 195,000 acres in the Blue Ridge Mountains. Wildflowers and waterfalls are abundant, creating an awesome environment for hiking, biking, backpacking, camping, mountain climbing, and picnicking. The Appalachian Trail runs for one hundred miles through the Shenandoah National Park. The Shenandoah River is at the base of the park and is perfect for canoeing, kayaking, and fishing. More than thirty trout streams are found in the area; some of the biggest brook trout can be found in the Rose River, one of the larger streams in the park. The Skyline Drive offers a gentle alternative to these rigorous activities. This two-lane, one-hundred-mile road stretches the entire length of the Shenandoah National Park. The Blue Ridge Mountains and the George Washington and Jefferson National Forests, covering over one million acres, are also hot spots for hiking, biking, skydiving, camping, and nature walks. The Rapidan River is popular for trout fishing, rafting, tubing, and canoeing. Lake Anna is a well-stocked 13,000-acre lake, noted for its largemouth bass. Lake Orange, a 125-acre lake with a full marina, is fifteen miles from town. Both lakes offer fishing, boating, and swimming.

The terrain is ideal for horse-back riding. The Montpelier Hunt Races is one of the many annual events. Hot air ballooning, cross-country skiing, skydiving, and hunting are but a few other outdoor adventure possibilities.

Golf is available at the Meadows Farm Golf Course, which boasts the longest hole in the United States and a forty-five-foot-high waterfall. Somerset Golf Club has an eighteen-hole course. The Shenandoah Crossing Resort and Country Club, located in nearby Gordonsville, has an eighteen-hole championship golf course. The Orange County Department of Recreation offers residents of all ages a wide variety of recreation programs.

 CULTURAL SCENE

Downtown Orange has been designated as a national and a state historic district. Historic sites include the county courthouse, dating back to 1858, and St. Thomas Episcopal Church, built in 1833 to 1834 and featuring a Tiffany stained-glass window. The town has sixty-one architecturally significant buildings.

Tours of Montpelier, the historic home of James and Dolly Madison, are available. This beautiful 2,700-acre majestic property, just four miles from Orange, has restored nineteenth-century gardens and a full restoration of the mansion is scheduled to be completed in 2008. The James Madison Museum in Orange also tells the story of James and Dolly Madison and displays some of their personal belongings; a Hall of Architecture shows farm implements from the last two centuries. Monticello, the home of Thomas Jefferson, is an elegant plantation thirty-five miles from Orange. In nearby Gordonsville, you can find Civil War trails and the Exchange Hotel Civil War Museum (a former Civil War hospital). The Wilderness Battlefield is near Lake of the Woods.

There are 150 antebellum homes in the towns and countryside of Orange County. Tours of historic homes, battlefields, vineyards and orchards add to the choices in this area. A local Civil War expert offers tours of the area battlefields and historic sites. Barboursville Vineyards and Horton

Vineyards are open for tours and tastings.

The Four County Players offers theatrical productions in a nearby village playhouse. Every August, the Four County Players present Shakespeare at the Ruins in an open-air theater at the historic Barboursville Ruins. In downtown Orange, art classes and exhibits are offered at the Art Center, a self-supporting nonprofit organization, and a number of art studios and galleries can be found in Orange and nearby towns. The Orange School of Performing Arts also offers classes. The restored train station in the heart of town serves as the visitors bureau, a community activity space, and a transportation center.

This upbeat town offers engaging activities throughout the year. On Fridays from June to September, the Orange Downtown Alliance sponsors "Arts Alive in Orange." Free musical performances, including jazz, folk, Irish, and pop, plus classic movie screenings, are held at Taylor Park. Other special occasions include Somerset Steam & Gas Festival, the award winning

Orange County Country Fair, trick or treating at downtown merchants, and the annual Orange Street Festival in September. The local Harley-Davidson Owners Group is active in the community and sponsors several events throughout the year, including the annual HOG Toys for Tots Kick-Off in November. In December, there's a traditional holiday parade and pictures with Santa at the Train Station; local businesses offer holiday specials during the season.

 MAIN STREET

The Silk Mill Grill is a sports bar and restaurant in an authentic mill adorned with old farm implements. Willow Grove Inn is a 1778 plantation where patrons can relax in the quaint pub or dine in elegant surroundings. Elmwood at Sparks features gourmet lunches and super sandwiches, quiche, and soups. Other favorite local restaurants include Not the Same Old Grind (specialty coffees, quiche, and soups); Dave's Café and Deli (a great spot on the railroad tracks); Cape Porpoise Lobster House (fresh Maine seafood); El

Vaquero Mexican Restaurant (a popular spot with a large menu); Mario's Italian Restaurant (tasty, consistent Italian food); Dairy Korner Restaurant (down-home country cookin'); Jean's Café (an excellent country breakfast); the Happy Gardens Chinese Restaurant; and The Great Wall.

Getting around Orange is easy with the help of the local Town of Orange Transportation (TOOT), which makes seventeen stops throughout the town Monday through Friday. Three shopping centers in the area offer grocery chains, hardware stores, and other shops. In downtown, you'll find antique stores, art galleries, gift shops, and an interesting assortment of specialty businesses— including a Harley-Davidson dealer and museum, a day spa, dance supplies, and a florist. A farmer's market is held on Wednesdays and Saturdays from May to October in Taylor Park and offers certified organic products and handmade crafts. The farmer's market continues through the winter on Saturdays in the Train Station.

HOUSING

In-town living is an attractive option in Orange. Gracious historic houses in need of restoration cost from $230,000 to $250,000. If restoration has been completed, prices range from $275,000 to $350,000. There are some new subdivisions in this area and plans for more; available houses cost from $350,000 to $450,000. For horse lovers interested in acreage and a barn, a nice house on ten acres or more will cost $450,000 and up. There are plenty of opportunities to custom build, starting at $350,000 for a large home on three or more acres. For those willing to go twenty-five miles outside of town, Lake of the Woods, a new gated community, includes 2,600 acres, three lakes, and an eighteen-hole PGA golf course. Prices range from $150,000 to $500,000. There are a few duplexes and town homes selling for approximately $150,000, but most of these are used as investment properties. Apartments are available, and a renovated schoolhouse provides apartment living for the elderly. There are two nursing homes and assisted living facilities in Orange County.

 ECONOMICS

Number of employers with fifty or more employees—21

The primary industries in Orange are agribusiness, manufacturing, commercial/retail services, and tourism. Some leading employers include Von Holtzbrinck Publishing Services (305 employees); PBM Products; ABG American Woodmark Corporation (265 employees); and American Press, Inc. (210 employees). Orange County is one of Virginia's top grape producers; Barboursville Vineyards and Horton Cellars/Montdomaine Winery are the major contributors.

Orange is a participant in the official Virginia Main Street Program, which provides technical training and assistance in downtown revitalization techniques. The Orange Downtown Alliance is a local organization committed to economic development and historic restoration. As of 1996, Orange was designated as an Enterprise Zone by the Virginia General Assembly, encouraging new business development and existing business expansion through the allocation of local and state incentives. The County actively works with many regional, state, and federal partners to provide services to the business sector.

 EDUCATION

High schools—1; Middle schools— 1; Elementary schools—5; Private schools—2

Woodberry Forest School, four miles from town, is a private boys' prep school founded in 1889. Grymes Memorial School is an independent, K – 8 day school opened in 1947. Higher education needs are met through Germanna Community College, a two-year institution under the Virginia Community College System, which has two full-service campuses (Locust Grove and Fredericksburg); Piedmont Virginia Community College; the University of Virginia (Charlottesville); James Madison University (Harrisonburg, 60 miles); the University of Richmond; and University of Mary Washington (Fredericksburg).

HEALTHCARE

Culpeper Regional Hospital—70 beds; Martha Jefferson Hospital (Charlottesville)—200 beds; University of Virginia Hospital (Charlottesville)—565 beds; Physicians—85; Dentists—7

Culpeper Regional Hospital is an acute-care, not-for profit healthcare organization with a medical staff of eighty-five physicians. Some of the services include a 24-hour, physician staffed emergency room, a family birth center, family care home health & hospice, surgical services, cancer center, cardiovascular center, and intensive care unit. Martha Jefferson Hospital has a medical staff of 350 physicians. The University of Virginia Hospital has a full-time faculty of 692 physicians and 705 residents and fellows.

 SPIRITUAL LIFE

Eleven Christian denominations and several non-Christian organizations are represented. A synagogue is located in Charlottesville.

 STAYING CONNECTED

Orange has one local weekly newspaper, the *Orange County Review*.

Also available in the area are the *Culpeper Star-Exponent*, the *Free Lance-Star* (Fredericksburg), the *Richmond Times-Dispatch*, the *Daily Progress* (Charlottesville), and the *Washington Post*. Local high-speed internet service and cable television are available in Orange. Many television and radio stations are located within fifty miles. There is a bookstore in downtown Orange.

 GETTING THERE

Orange is located in the north central part of Virginia, midway between Charlottesville and Fredericksburg in the Piedmont Region. It is served by US 15 and 20. Interstates 95, 66, 64, and 81 are all within forty miles of Orange County. Air transportation is provided through the Charlottesville Airport (20 miles), Dulles International Airport (70 miles), Richmond International Airport (70 miles), and Reagan International Airport (83 miles). The Orange County Airport has a 3,200-foot runway, and the Gordonville Airport (9 miles) has a 2,300-foot runway. Both are suitable for private aircraft.

RESOURCES

Orange County
  Chamber of Commerce
P.O. Box 146
103 Perry Plaza
Orange, VA 22960
(540) 672-5216
www.orangevachamber.com

Orange County Department
  of Tourism and Visitors Bureau
122 E. Main Street
Orange, VA 22960
(877) 222-8072

Orange Downtown Alliance
PO Box 283
130 W. Main Street
Orange, VA 22960
(540) 672-2540
www.orangedowntownalliance.org

ORANGE
VITAL STATISTICS

CLIMATE

Annual average rainfall	40.5 inches
Snowfall	18.1 inches
Elevation	600 feet

Temperatures (in degrees Fahrenheit)

	Jan	Apr	Jul	Oct
High	42	66	86	68
Low	22	42	65	44

OCCUPATIONS

	2006	Projected 2011
Blue collar	22.7%	21.1%
White collar	59.6%	62.4%
Services	17.7%	16.5%

ADULT EDUCATION

	2000
Less than High School	29.2%
High School	31.0%
Some College	14.1%
Associates Degree	4.8%
College Degree	11.1%
Graduate Degree	9.9%

POPULATION

2006	4,611
2000-2006 Population: Annual Compound Growth Rate	1.81%
2006-2011 Population: Annual Compound Growth Rate	2.50%

Population by age group

	2006	Projected 2011
0-4	6.5%	6.5%
5-9	6.4%	5.9%
10-14	6.0%	6.7%
15-19	5.6%	5.7%
20-24	6.1%	5.4%
25-29	5.9%	6.0%
30-34	5.7%	5.8%
35-39	7.0%	5.5%
40-44	7.2%	7.2%
45-49	6.9%	7.3%
50-54	6.8%	6.7%
55-59	5.7%	7.0%
60-64	4.3%	5.4%
65-69	4.5%	3.7%
70-74	4.0%	4.0%
75-79	3.9%	3.5%
80-84	3.6%	3.6%
85+	4.1%	4.1%

Sources for Vital Statistics listed above can be found in the Preface to this book.

SMITHFIELD

2006 POPULATION
7,173

NEAREST CITIES
Newport News (17 miles)
Hampton (20 miles)
Norfolk, VA (28 miles)
Virginia Beach, VA (38 miles)
Williamsburg, VA (42 miles)

**ESTIMATED 2006
MEDIAN HOUSEHOLD INCOME**
$53,699

COST OF LIVING
Average 3-bdrm home—$247,000
Average rent, 2-bdrm apartment—
$650
Cost-of-living comparison—
101.1%

SALES TAX
4.5%

PROPERTY TAX
Average 3-bdrm home—$2,200

Located on the Pagan River, Smithfield is a picturesque traditional seaport that exudes colonial-era character. The Pagan flows into the nearby James River, providing access to the port of Hampton Roads. This river town was settled in 1752 by Arthur Smith IV; because of its riverfront location, it soon became a stopping point for shippers and merchants. As trade and commerce developed, so did Smithfield's industry. Four plants in the area are involved in the process of curing Smithfield ham, the town's claim to fame and now a Virginia tradition.

In 1989, Historic Downtown Smithfield, Inc. was created and the Main Street Beautification Project began. The project was completed in 1999, and today the town is a unique mixture of eighteenth-century brick homes, nineteenth-century Federal homes, and ornate Victorian homes. The National Register of Historic Places district and the local historic district cover a total of 295-acres and include sixty notable homes.

Unique shops, brick sidewalks, and period streetlights and signs blend nicely, inviting pedestrians to explore the heart of this quaint Virginia village. The location is excellent and offers all the conveniences of a modernized small town within thirty miles of metropolitan areas such as Newport News, Chesapeake, Portsmouth, Norfolk, and Virginia Beach.

 RECREATION

Because Smithfield is located on the Pagan River and near the Atlantic coastal plain of Tidewater, Virginia, residents have easy access to many recreation areas within this network of waterways. Mogarts Beach on the James River is seven miles from town; the Atlantic Ocean is only an hour away. Whale- or dolphin-watching cruises are available, as are surfing, sea kayaking, wind surfing, jet skiing, or scuba diving. Sailing and boating are popular pastimes, and Smithfield's two marinas are always busy. Fishing is fabulous in the area's many creeks, streams, and rivers.

Several parks in the Smithfield area offer playing fields, tennis courts, a senior center, biking and hiking trails, basketball courts, playgrounds, and a nearly five-acre fishing pond. The Robert S. Clontz Memorial Park is great for walking, picnicking, pier fishing, or just relaxing in the gazebo. The nearby Chippokes Plantation State Park includes a plantation with historical and recreational features and hosts the annual Pork, Peanut, and Pine Festival in July. Excellent golf is available at the Cypress Creek Golf Club, an eighteen-hole championship golf course, and the Smithfield Downs Golf Course. The YMCA and the Isle of Wight Recreation Department offer many activities and sports for the enjoyment of residents.

 **CULTURAL SCENE**

If ham is Smithfield's claim to fame, history is its foundation. The old courthouse dates back to 1750 and was modeled after the capitol building in colonial Williamsburg. Today it is home to the Association for the Preservation of American Antiquities (APVA). St. Luke's Shrine, built around 1632, is the only remaining brick Gothic church in America and the oldest existing American church of English origin. This "Old Brick Church" witnessed historic events that span four centuries and is one of the most revered buildings in America. The Isle of Wight Museum tells the history of Smithfield ham and how it is cured. The museum also houses exhibits of Civil War and Native American artifacts. The Old Towne Walking Tour—a self-guided tour that includes sixty Federal, Georgian, and Victorian period houses and buildings—captures the diversity of the town's architectural styles. Visitors can tour Bacon's Castle, a plantation home with beautiful gardens. The castle, built in 1665, is in the form of a Greek cross. Fort Boykin Historic Park overlooks the James River; the fort, shaped like a seven-point star, was once used to fend off hostile Indians and Spaniards.

Housed in a magnificent Main Street Victorian, the Isle of Wight Arts League exhibits local and regional art and offers art classes. The Outdoor Concert Series, a Friday night summer event, hosts a variety of musical groups and entertainers performing on the green in town. The Smithfield Little Theater is a local theater group offering performances throughout the year.

Smithfield is convenient to the cities of the Hampton Roads area. Residents have easy access to events of all types, including ballet, opera, drama, concerts and symphonies, and art exhibits. Some of the many area attractions include historic Williamsburg and Jamestown; the Virginia Air and Space Center in Hampton (20 miles); the Mariner's Museum, the Peninsula Fine Arts Center, and the Ferguson Center for the Arts, all in Newport News; the Children's Museum of Virginia in Portsmouth (24 miles); the Virginia Marine Science Museum in Virginia Beach; and Yorktown National Battlefields.

The Smithfield calendar

provides a variety of festivals and events. At the Chocolate Lovers' Evening in February, chefs and locals compete to create the most delicious and decadent chocolate dessert. Patriot's Day is a multi-faceted springtime event that includes heritage crafters, Colonial dancers, and interactive conversations with past residents of Virginia. The Isle of Wight County Old-Fashioned Fair includes livestock events, local artisans and crafters, and regional and national entertainment. Christmas in Smithfield is a month-long festivity that includes a parade, historic home tours, special antique shows and sales, light-decorated boats on the Pagan River, and holiday concerts.

 MAIN STREET

Smithfield Inn and Tavern, housed in an elegant 1752 building, offers excellent seafood and great ham biscuits. Smithfield Station Restaurant is a popular waterfront establishment featuring seafood dishes and Sunday brunch. Smithfield Confectionary and Ice Cream Parlor has an old-fashioned lunch counter with swivel stools. Miss Bessie's Best Cookies and Candies is an old-fashioned vintage candy store. Other local favorites are the Battery Park Grill; Smithfield Gourmet Bakery and Café (great sandwiches, homemade soup, and scrumptious desserts); and Twin's Ole Towne Inn (outstanding barbecue, biscuits, and homemade pies).

Main Street browsing makes a fun afternoon; the itinerary could include stops at the ice cream parlor, several antique and gift shops, the ham shop, and The Christmas Store. The Olde Towne Curb Market, a farmer's market, runs through the summer months. The Smithfield Center, a state-of-the-art conference/community center on the Pagan River, is home base for several unusual events.

 HOUSING

Prices for houses range from $150,000 to $800,000; the average price is $247,000. Starter homes in established, comfortable neighborhoods begin at $150,000. New houses on the golf course at Cypress Creek, houses overlooking the marina at Gatling Point, or custom-built homes on or accessible to the water range from $450,000 to $1 million. Houses in new subdivisions can cost $350,000 and up, depending on location and house size. Rural houses average $234,000. Condominiums and town houses average $198,000. Some apartments are also available.

 ECONOMICS

Number of employers with fifty or more employees—10

Smithfield is nationally known for its ham products produced by Gwaltney of Smithfield and the Smithfield Packing Company, both subsidiaries of Smithfield Foods Inc., a Fortune 500 company. Combined employment for both companies is 5,200 workers. Other major employers include International Paper (1,300 employees); Union Camp Corporation, Fine Paper Division (1,800 employees); Carroll's Farms Inc. (435 employees); and Franklin Equipment Company (300 employees). The primary industries in Smithfield are meatpacking, communications, government, and computer technology. Major tourism is a steadily increasing industry, as over 2.3 million people live within one hour of Smithfield. This business-friendly community offers a wealth of natural resources and encourages growth with effective planning.

 EDUCATION

High schools—1; Middle schools—1; Elementary schools—1

Higher education needs are met through Paul D. Camp Community College and eight colleges and universities in Newport News, Hampton, Chesapeake, Hampton Roads, Norfolk, and Williamsburg (all within forty-five minutes). The list includes Christopher Newport University, Thomas Nelson Community College, Hampton University, Norfolk State University, Old Dominion University, the College of William and Mary, Regent University, and Tidewater Community College, which has four campuses in Hampton Roads.

HEALTHCARE

Riverside Regional Hospital (Newport News)—576 beds; Sentara Obici Hospital (Suffolk)—222 beds; Southampton Memorial Hospital (Franklin)—90 beds; Physicians—13; Dentists—4

Three hospitals are located near Smithfield, and two private medical centers with urgent-care facilities are located in town. The Isle of Wight Health Department has a large health facility in downtown Smithfield.

 SPIRITUAL LIFE

Six Christian denominations are represented. The closest synagogue is twenty miles away in Newport News.

 STAYING CONNECTED

The *Smithfield Times* is the local weekly newspaper. Two metro area daily newspapers—Norfolk's the *Virginian-Pilot* and the *Newport News Daily Press*—are delivered locally. Internet service and cable television are available. There is one bookstore in Smithfield, and numerous bookstores are in nearby Hampton Roads.

 GETTING THERE

Smithfield is located in Isle of Wight County in southeastern Virginia just off US 17 with connections to Interstates 664/64. US 258 in Smithfield connects to US 460 and I-95. Air transportation is provided through the Williamsburg–Newport News International Airport (45 minutes) and Norfolk International and Richmond International (both 75 minutes). Franklin Municipal Airport in Isle of Wight County has a 5,200-foot lighted runway for private aircraft. The James River provides direct access to major port facilities in the Hampton Roads cities.

 RESOURCES

Isle of Wight/Smithfield/Windsor
  Chamber of Commerce
100 Main Street
P.O. Box 38
Smithfield, VA 23431.
(757) 357-3502
www.theisle.org

Isle of Wight Convention
 and Visitors Bureau
130 Main Street
P.O. Box 37
Smithfield, VA 23431-0037
(800) 365-9339
www.smithfield-virginia.com

Additional area websites:
www.co.smithfield.va.us
www.co.isle-of-wightva.us

SMITHFIELD VITAL STATISTICS

CLIMATE

Annual average rainfall	43 inches
Snowfall	11.7 inches
Elevation	70 feet

Temperatures (in degrees Fahrenheit)

	Jan	Apr	Jul	Oct
High	47	69	87	70
Low	28	46	68	49

OCCUPATIONS

	2006	Projected 2011
Blue collar	24.8%	23.3%
White collar	65.3%	67.8%
Services	9.9%	8.9%

ADULT EDUCATION

	2000
Less than High School	24.1%
High School	22.5%
Some College	25.7%
Associates Degree	8.3%
College Degree	13.5%
Graduate Degree	5.8%

POPULATION

2006	7,173
2000-2006 Population: Annual Compound Growth Rate	2.04%
2006-2011 Population: Annual Compound Growth Rate	2.12%

Population by age group

	2006	Projected 2011
0-4	6.6%	6.5%
5-9	7.1%	6.7%
10-14	7.2%	7.7%
15-19	6.6%	6.6%
20-24	4.6%	4.8%
25-29	4.5%	4.0%
30-34	5.2%	5.0%
35-39	6.3%	5.5%
40-44	9.0%	7.2%
45-49	9.0%	9.5%
50-54	7.4%	8.7%
55-59	7.0%	7.4%
60-64	4.6%	6.1%
65-69	4.1%	3.8%
70-74	3.6%	3.2%
75-79	2.8%	2.9%
80-84	2.0%	2.2%
85+	2.4%	2.3%

Sources for Vital Statistics listed above can be found in the Preface to this book.

STRASBURG

2006 POPULATION
   5,130

NEAREST CITIES
   Front Royal, VA (15 miles)
   Woodstock, VA (17 miles)
   Winchester, VA (20 miles)
   Harrisonburg, VA (54 miles)
   Washington, D.C. (84 miles)

ESTIMATED 2006
MEDIAN HOUSEHOLD INCOME
   $42,367

COST OF LIVING
   Average 3-bdrm home—$199,000
   Average rent, 2-bdrm apartment—
$600
   Cost-of-living comparison—
104.3%

SALES TAX
   4.5%

PROPERTY TAX
   Average 3-bdrm home—$1,500

Strasburg is an enchanting valley town situated between the Massanutten and Blue Ridge mountains. In the early 1700s, the town was laid out in lots and streets by Peter Stover and named by German settlers who were possibly from Strasburg. The town was formally established by the Virginia General Assembly in 1761. It was originally referred to as "Pot Town" for the quality pottery produced here. A visiting monk, who was a master potter, introduced the trade to locals.

In the early years of the Civil War, Strasburg became a strategic town for rail traffic when General Thomas "Stonewall" Jackson captured train engines from the Union in Martinsburg, West Virginia, and pulled them by horsepower back to Strasburg, where they were sent south for use in the war. Strasburg was the site of much of Jackson's Valley Campaign of 1862 and Federal General Philip Sheridan's Shenandoah Valley Campaign of 1864. Two important battlefields lie on either side of Strasburg: Cedar Creek Battlefield on the north and Fisher's Hill Battlefield on the south. Every October thousands of reenactors from across the United States relive the Battle of Cedar Creek; this is one of a handful of Civil War reenactments that take place on the actual battle site. The area has been protected from development by the 2003 creation of The Cedar Creek and Belle Grove National Historical Park.

Majestic mountains surround the famous Shenandoah Valley. US 11 south of Winchester meanders through breathtaking countryside, connecting charming small towns; the highway has been called the "String of Pearls" because of the "gems" found along the way. Also known as the Antique Capital of Virginia, Strasburg attracts many tourists and antique hunters to the numerous shops in and near town. A lovely historic district, Civil War battlefields, and talented local artists and craftspeople make Strasburg a "small town with surprises," as the local chamber of commerce puts it.

In the past five years, Strasburg has experienced significant growth, resulting in a 32 percent increase in population, a massive housing boom, and a general spur to the already prosperous local economy. More than 42 percent of households moving to Strasburg in the past five years come from the Washington, D.C., area. Nevertheless, Strasburg retains its traditional warmth and neighborliness. When surveyed recently, 90 percent of the local residents who participated cited the town's "small-town atmosphere" and "scenic beauty" as reasons they chose to live in Strasburg. A demographic survey and study, authorized by the Town Council, was released in the spring of 2006 and is being used as a planning guide in many spheres of activity.

RECREATION

Outdoor fun centers on three places: the scenic Shenandoah River, which offers canoeing, rafting, fishing, scuba diving, and tubing; the George Washington National Forest, which has over a million picturesque acres for hiking; and the 195,000-acre Shenandoah National Park, which is perfect for camping, hiking, and biking. Located within minutes of town, Half-Moon Beach has five acres of white sand bordering a sixteen-acre lake. Sky Meadows State Park serves as an access point to the Appalachian Trail and has a bridle path for horseback riders. Elizabeth Furnace is a recreational area for hiking and camping with easy access to the hiking trails of the Massanutten Mountain Range. This area was originally the site of several nineteenth-century iron furnaces where iron was purified into "pig iron" and transported to Winchester for further processing.

Skyline Drive, a spectacular 105-mile route along the Blue Ridge Mountains, provides superb scenery that's best in the fall but worthwhile any time of year. Snow skiing is available at Massanutten Resort near Harrisonburg; Bryce Mountain Resort in Basye; The Homestead in Hot Springs; and Wintergreen Resort in Wintergreen. Other activities include cavern exploring at Crystal Caverns at Hupp's Hill (.5 mile) and at Luray Caverns (25 miles) and bass and trout fishing on nearby lakes.

Strasburg and Shenandoah County provide twenty-two tennis courts, fifteen ball fields, five swimming pools, two golf courses, six public parks, and numerous other recreational activities for all ages throughout the year. Golf, tennis, skating, hunting, and fishing are all available in or near this magical valley town. The Parks and Recreation Department also organizes bus trips to Washington Nationals baseball games and to cultural events.

 CULTURAL SCENE

A self-guided walking tour of Strasburg's historic district features buildings dating back to the mid-1700s and a wide range of architectural styles. The Victorian

Hotel Strasburg, originally built in 1890 as a hospital, offers romantic dining and lodging. The Great Strasburg Emporium, Virginia's largest antique collection, houses over one hundred antique and art dealers.

The Strasburg Museum exhibits local Native American artifacts, relics from the Civil War, pottery displays, and other items reflecting the history of the area. The Museum of American Presidents is home to the personal collection of Leo M. Bernstein. History buffs also will appreciate touring Cedar Creek Battlefield, Fisher's Hill Battlefield, and Hupp's Hill Battlefield Museum. Belle Grove Plantation, a 1797 historic manor house in nearby Middletown and the home of President James Madison's sister, is open for tours.

Strasburg Theater offers food, drink, and live music and other performances. Numerous festivals throughout the year include Mayfest, Oktoberfest, and the Antique and Classic Car Show. The Shenandoah University Conservatory in Winchester presents over four hundred performances a year, including music and theater. Also in Winchester are a ballet academy, concert series, art leagues, lectures, exhibits, and a state arboretum. Performing arts are presented at the Wayside Theater in Middletown, five miles from Strasburg.

The Shenandoah Music Festival is a beloved 44-year tradition in the area. This event in nearby Ortney Springs features the nation's best known musicians performing in every musical genre.

 MAIN STREET

The Old Mill Restaurant, housed in an authentic old mill, offers traditional home-cooked meals and an acclaimed Sunday buffet. Historic Hotel Strasburg features excellent menus for lunch and dinner. The Depot Lounge, located at the Hotel Strasburg, is a popular spot where locals congregate before and after athletic events and town council meetings. Hi Neighbor (great country cooking and "pudding meat") is also a favorite. The Great Strasburg Emporium, ByGones, Sullivan's Country House, and Vilnis's are among many fine antique shops in Strasburg.

Housing

Housing options include charming, historic homes in town and homes in new and established neighborhoods. Most houses in town range from $175,000 to $350,000 regardless of age. Those in new subdivisions range from $250,000 to $450,000. Rural properties range from $150,000 to $450,000, depending on location and acreage. Riverfront cabins and houses range from $170,000 to $500,000. Mini-farms are also popular for those who want acreage and the option to keep horses. These can range from $300,000 to $600,000 for approximately five acres of land.

Economics

Number of employers with fifty or more employees—11

The local economy is primarily supported through Perry-Judd's Inc. (500 employees); Lear Corporation (500 employees); and Shenandoah County School System (800 employees). Other major industries that contribute to the local economy include agriculture, manufacturing (including food processing, plastics, and printing), distribution, and tourism. Unemployment is less than 2 percent.

Education

High schools—1; Middle schools—1; Elementary schools—1; Private schools—4

Higher education needs are served by Christendom College in Front Royal (15 miles); Shenandoah University in Winchester; Lord Fairfax Community College in Middletown; James Madison University and Eastern Mennonite College in Harrisonburg; Bridgewater College in Bridgewater (45 miles); the University of Virginia in Charlottesville (98 miles); and Virginia Tech in Blacksburg (103 miles).

Healthcare

Shenandoah Memorial Hospital (Woodstock)—133 beds; Winchester Medical Center—405 beds; Warren Memorial Hospital (Front Royal)—111 beds; Physicians—3; Dentists—2

There are thirty-nine physicians and fourteen dentists throughout the county. Shenandoah Memorial Hospital offers general medical facilities, intensive care, surgery, a

CAT scan unit, ultrasound, nuclear medicine, rehabilitation, long-term care, and other services. The Winchester Medical Center is an acute-care facility with an attending medical staff of more than 225 physicians representing all specialties. Facilities include a 24-hour emergency room and helipad, an outpatient diagnostic center, and an urgent care center. In nearby Front Royal, the Warren Memorial Hospital has a staff of forty physicians. Some of the finest medical facilities in the country are located in the Washington, D.C., area.

 SPIRITUAL LIFE

Eight Christian denominations are represented. The closest synagogue is in Winchester.

 STAYING CONNECTED

Local newspapers include the *Northern Virginia Daily*, published in Strasburg, and the *Winchester Star*. The *Washington Post* also offers home delivery. The *Shenandoah Valley Herald* and the *Free Press* are weekly publications. A monthly literary newspaper, the *Bryce Mountain Courier*, enjoys a growing circulation. Cable television and internet service are available.

 GETTING THERE

Strasburg is located in Shenandoah County in the northwestern part of Virginia on the north fork of the Shenandoah River and at the base of the Massanutten Mountains. It is conveniently positioned at the junction of I-66 and I-81 on US 11 and SC 55. The stretch on I-81 between Winchester and Roanoke, Virginia, has been called one of the ten most scenic highways in the United States.

Air transportation is provided by Washington-Dulles International Airport (70 miles) and Reagan National Airport (90 miles). The Winchester Regional Airport is a general aviation facility with a 5,500-foot runway that can accommodate the largest corporate jet aircraft.

RESOURCES

Strasburg Chamber of Commerce
368 East King Street
P.O. Box 42
Strasburg, VA 22657
(540) 465-3187
www.strasburgchamber.com

Shenandoah County
Tourism Office
600 North Main Street
Suite 101
Woodstock, VA 22664
(888) 367-3966
www.co.shenandoah.va.us

Additional area website:
www.strasburgva.com

STRASBURG
VITAL STATISTICS

CLIMATE

Annual average rainfall	41.7 inches
Snowfall	43.6 inches
Elevation	578 feet

Temperatures (in degrees Fahrenheit)

	Jan	Apr	Jul	Oct
High	43	68	87	69
Low	21	40	61	42

OCCUPATIONS

	2006	Projected 2011
Blue collar	40.2%	38.4%
White collar	42.7%	45.6%
Services	17.1%	16.0%

ADULT EDUCATION

	2000
Less than High School	29.4%
High School	40.9%
Some College	16.4%
Associates Degree	4.6%
College Degree	5.7%
Graduate Degree	3.0%

POPULATION

2006	5,130
2000-2006 Population: Annual Compound Growth Rate	3.99%
2006-2011 Population: Annual Compound Growth Rate	3.05%

Population by age group

	2006	Projected 2011
0-4	6.4%	6.5%
5-9	5.6%	5.8%
10-14	7.3%	5.7%
15-19	6.7%	6.9%
20-24	6.4%	6.9%
25-29	4.5%	6.3%
30-34	7.3%	4.4%
35-39	7.3%	6.9%
40-44	9.0%	7.7%
45-49	8.1%	9.1%
50-54	6.1%	7.8%
55-59	6.0%	6.2%
60-64	4.8%	5.4%
65-69	4.2%	3.9%
70-74	3.5%	3.4%
75-79	3.2%	2.9%
80-84	1.9%	2.4%
85+	1.7%	1.8%

Sources for Vital Statistics listed above can be found in the Preface to this book.

COLLEGE TOWNS

The allure of college towns is growing for American retirees, young educated families, and internet savvy entrepreneurs. The pairing of a college environment with a small town provides the community with an expanded array of cultural and entertainment offerings. Nearly all the fifty towns selected for this book have at least a two-year technical school or community college. Others are located near colleges within easy commuting distances. The following towns, listed alphabetically by state, have four-year colleges located within the town itself.

Florida
DeLand (Stetson University)

Georgia
Carrollton (West Georgia College;
University of Georgia at Carrollton)
Dahlonega (North Georgia College;
University of Georgia at Dahlonega)

Kentucky
Berea (Berea College)
Danville (Centre College)

Mississippi
Holly Springs (Rust College)
Oxford (University of Mississippi)

North Carolina
Boone (Appalachian State University;
University of North Carolina
at Boone)

South Carolina
Beaufort (University of South Carolina
at Beaufort; Park College)
Clemson (Clemson University)
Hartsville (Coker College)
Newberry (Newberry College)

Tennessee
Greeneville (Tusculum College)

Virginia
Blacksburg (Virginia Polytechnic
Institute & State University)
Lexington (Virginia Military Institute;
Washington and Lee University)

GEOGRAPHICAL SETTING

MOUNTAIN TOWNS

Alabama
Fort Payne

Georgia
Dahlonega

Kentucky
Berea

North Carolina
Boone
Hendersonville
Morganton
Mount Airy

Tennessee
Crossville
Greeneville
McMinnville

Virginia
Blacksburg
Lexington
Strasburg

COASTAL TOWNS

Alabama
Fairhope

Florida
Apalachicola
New Smyrna Beach
Stuart

Georgia
St. Marys
St. Simons Island

Mississippi
Ocean Springs

North Carolina
Southport

South Carolina
Beaufort

Virginia
Kilmarnock

TOWNS NEAR LAKES OR RIVERS

Alabama
Albertville

Florida
DeLand
Mount Dora

Kentucky
Versailles

Mississippi
Madison
Oxford
West Point

South Carolina
Clemson
Georgetown
Newberry

Virginia
Smithfield

ROLLING PLAINS

Alabama
Cullman
Hartselle

Florida
DeFuniak Springs

Georgia
Carrollton
Covington
Perry

Kentucky
Bardstown
Danville
Franklin

Mississippi
Holly Springs

North Carolina
Lincolnton

South Carolina
Hartsville
Summerville

Tennessee
Dyersburg
Lawrenceburg

Virginia
Orange

APPENDIX C

POPULATION

1,000–5,000

Florida
Apalachicola   2,566
Georgia
Dahlonega   4,703
North Carolina
Southport   2,635
Virginia
Kilmarnock   1,331
Orange   4,611

5,001–10,000

Florida
DeFuniak Springs   5,661
Kentucky
Franklin   8,155
Versailles   7,997
Mississippi
Holly Springs   8,140
North Carolina
Mount Airy   8,043
South Carolina
Georgetown   9,166
Hartsville   7,168
Tennessee
Crossville   9,172
Virginia
Lexington   6,895
Smithfield   7,173
Strasburg   5,130

10,001–15,000

Alabama
Cullman   13,938
Fairhope   14,219
Fort Payne   13,251
Hartselle   12,926
Florida
Mount Dora   10,423
Georgia
Perry   10,083
St. Simons   14,140
Kentucky
Berea   10,671
Bardstown   11,326
Mississippi
Oxford   12,862
West Point   11,704
North Carolina
Boone   13,518
Hendersonville   10,809
Lincolnton   10,422
South Carolina
Beaufort   14,035
Clemson   12,802
Newberry   10,733
Tennessee
Lawrenceburg   10,819
McMinnville   13,158

15,001–25,000

Alabama
Albertville   18,424
Florida
DeLand   22,777
New Smyrna Beach   21,592
Stuart   16,369
Georgia
Carrollton   23,314
Covington   15,962
St. Marys   16,458
Kentucky
Danville   15,780
Mississippi
Madison   17,369
Ocean Springs   17,982
North Carolina
Morganton   17,310
Tennessee
Dyersburg   17,475
Greeneville   15,507

OVER 25,000

South Carolina
Summerville   31,923
Virginia
Blacksburg   40,596

CLIMATE

YEAR-ROUND WARM TO HOT WITH HUMIDITY

Florida
  Apalachicola
  DeFuniak Springs
  DeLand
  Mount Dora
  New Smyrna Beach
  Stuart
Georgia
  St. Marys
  St. Simons Island
Mississippi
  Ocean Springs

YEAR-ROUND MILD WITH HUMID SUMMERS

Alabama
  Fairhope
Georgia
  Carrollton
  Covington
  Perry
Mississippi
  Madison
South Carolina
  Beaufort
  Summerville

MILD TO WARM WITH SEASONAL CHANGES AND POSSIBLE SNOW

Alabama
  Albertville
  Cullman
  Fort Payne
  Hartselle
Mississippi
  Holly Springs
  Oxford
  West Point
North Carolina
  Lincolnton
  Southport
South Carolina
  Clemson
  Georgetown
  Hartsville
  Newberry
Tennessee
  Dyersburg
  Lawrenceville
  McMinnville

MODERATE TO COOL WITH SEASONAL CHANGES AND SNOW

Georgia
  Dahlonega
Kentucky
  Bardstown
  Berea
  Danville
  Franklin
  Versailles
North Carolina
  Boone
  Hendersonville
  Morganton
  Mount Airy
Tennessee
  Crossville
  Greeneville
Virginia
  Blacksburg
  Kilmarnock
  Lexington
  Orange
  Smithfield
  Strasburg

APPENDIX E

Cost of Living Index

COST OF LIVING		URBAN AREA
80%–90%		
Alabama		
Albertville	88.4%	Albertville, AL
Cullman	89.1%	Decatur-Hartselle, AL
Fairhope	89.8%	Mobile, AL
Hartselle	89.1%	Decatur-Hartselle, AL
Mississippi		
Madison	87.2%	Jackson, MS
Oxford	86.6%	Tupelo, MS
West Point	86.6%	Tupelo, MS
North Carolina		
Boone	89.9%	North Wilkesboro, NC
Morganton	80.0%	Morganton, NC
Tennessee		
Crossville	80.9%	Knoxville, TN
Dyersburg	87.5%	Dyersburg, TN
Greenville	87.8%	Kingsport-Bristol, TN

90.1%–95%		
Alabama		
Fort Payne	92.7%	Anniston, AL
Georgia		
Perry	92.4%	Warner Robbins, GA
St. Marys	93%	Jacksonville, FL
St. Simons	93%	Jacksonville, FL
Kentucky		
Bardstown	94.7%	Louisville, KY
Franklin	93.9%	Bowling Green, KY
Mississippi		
Holly Springs	91.5%	Memphis, TN
Ocean Springs	93.5%	Gulfport, MS
North Carolina		
Lincolnton	92.8%	Charlotte, NC
Mount Airy	90.1%	Winston-Salem, NC
South Carolina		
Clemson	94.4%	Anderson, SC
Georgetown	92.4%	Myrtle Beach, SC
Hartsville	94.8%	Columbia, SC
Newberry	94.8%	Columbia, SC
Tennessee		
Lawrenceburg	93.7%	Nashville, TN
McMinnville	91.6%	Cleveland, TN

Virginia		
Blacksburg	91.1%	Roanoke, VA
95.1%–99.9%		
Florida		
Apalachicola	97.7%	Panama City, FL
DeFuniak Springs	98.7%	Fort Walton Beach, Destin, FL
Deland	98.4%	Palm Coast, FL
Mount Dora	97.2%	Leesburg FL
New Smyrna Beach	98.4%	Palm Coast, FL
Georgia		
Carrollton	98.4%	Douglasville, GA
Covington	97.1%	Atlanta, GA
Dahlonega	97.1%	Atlanta, GA
Kentucky		
Berea	95.6%	Lexington, KY
Danville	95.6%	Lexington, KY
Versailles	95.6%	Lexington, KY
North Carolina		
Southport	96.1%	Wilmington, NC
South Carolina		
Summerville	98%	Charleston, SC
Virginia		
Lexington	97.3%	Non-Metro Lexington, Buena Vista

100%–108%		
Florida		
Stuart	102%	Vero Beach, FL
North Carolina		
Hendersonville	100%	Asheville, NC
South Carolina		
Beaufort	102.3%	Hilton Head, SC
Virginia		
Kilmarnock	106.3%	Richmond, VA
Orange	107.7%	Charlottesville, VA
Smithfield	101.1%	Virginia Beach, Norfolk, VA
Strasburg	104.3%	Harrisburg, VA

ADDITIONAL SMALL SOUTHERN TOWNS OF INTEREST

Alabama
Athens
Silacauga
Ozark

Florida
Inverness
Monticello
Winter Garden

Georgia
Cartersville
Sandersville
Thomasville

Kentucky
Midway
Murphy
Nicholasville

Mississippi
Aberdeen
Brookhaven
Corinth
Laurel

North Carolina
Black Mountain
Edenton
Oxford
Southern Pines

South Carolina
Camden
Conway
Greer
Lexington
Seneca

Tennessee
Dayton
Fayetteville
Lebanon

Virginia
Abingdon
Bedford
Front Royal
Radford
Staunton

REFERENCES

ACCRA. Cost of Living Data. Arlington, VA: ACCRA, 2007. Available at www.coli.org

"America's 50 Hottest Little Boomtowns." *Money* (April, 1996).

"Americans Fleeing Nation's Big Cities." *Associated Press* (April 20, 2006).

Brandon, Emily. "Ten Bargain Retirement Spots." *U.S. News & World Report* (June 3, 2007).

Dart, Bob. "Americans Are Moving South." *Atlanta Journal-Constitution* (July 23, 1998).

Dent, Harry S. Jr. THE ROARING 2000'S: BUILDING THE WEALTH AND LIFESTYLE YOU DESIRE IN THE GREATEST BOOM IN HISTORY. New York: Simon and Schuster, 1998.

ESRI (www.esri.com).

Frey, William H., and Russ C. DeVol. AMERICA'S DEMOGRAPHY IN THE NEW CENTURY: AGING BABY BOOMERS AND NEW IMMIGRANTS AS MAJOR PLAYERS. Santa Monica, CA: The Milken Institute, March, 2000.

"How Tax Friendly Is Your State?" CNN-Money.com (July 2, 2006).

"Metro Home Prices Begin to Cool but Appreciation Remains Strong" A press release prepared by the National Association of Realtors. (May 15, 2006). Available at www.realtor.org.

Nasser, Haya El and Paul Overberg. "Growth Stretches Areas of the Sun Belt." *USA Today* (June 21, 2006).

Nasser, Haya El and Paul Overberg. "Metro Area 'Fringes' Are Booming." *USA Today* (March 16, 2006).

Retirement Living Information Center (www.retirementliving.com)

Southern Business and Development Magazine (Spring 2006) www.sb-d.com.

U.S. Department of Commerce, U.S. Bureau of the Census. "Phoenix and San Antonio Lead Largest Cities in Growth; Small Cities Grow Fastest." A press release prepared by the U.S. Bureau of the Census (June 30, 1999). Available at www.census.gov.

U.S. Department of Commerce, U.S. Bureau of the Census. "Domestic Net Migration in the United States: 2000 to 2004" (April 2006). Available at www.census.gov.

The Weather Channel. Climatology Data. Atlanta, GA: The Weather Channel, 2001-2005. Available at www.weatherchannel.com.

ABOUT THE AUTHORS

Gerald W. Sweitzer is a graduate of the University of Florida. He holds an MBA from Georgia State University and also attended Dartmouth University and the Candler School of Theology at Emory University. In 2005, he moved from Atlanta to Easley, South Carolina, a town about 12 miles west of Greenville. Jerry is semi-retired and consults with non-profit organizations. He maintains a website *(www.ruralburbia.com)* and can be contacted there.

Kathy M. Fields is a Licensed Professional Counselor in private practice in Atlanta. She grew up in Roanoke, Virginia, and currently resides in Decatur, Georgia. Kathy has a BA from Mount St. Agnes College and a MEd and an EdS from Georgia State University. Kathy now owns two coastal properties: a condominium in St. Simons, Georgia, and a home in Mount Pleasant, South Carolina (near Charleston). Kathy plans to retire in Mount Pleasant.